A World of Three Cultures

A World of Three Cultures

HONOR, ACHIEVEMENT AND JOY

Miguel E. Basáñez
with
Foreword by Ronald F. Inglehart

OXFORD
UNIVERSITY PRESS

OXFORD
UNIVERSITY PRESS

Oxford University Press is a department of the University of
Oxford. It furthers the University's objective of excellence in research,
scholarship, and education by publishing worldwide.

Oxford   New York
Auckland   Cape Town   Dar es Salaam   Hong Kong   Karachi
Kuala Lumpur   Madrid   Melbourne   Mexico City   Nairobi
New Delhi   Shanghai   Taipei   Toronto

With offices in
Argentina   Austria   Brazil   Chile   Czech Republic   France   Greece
Guatemala   Hungary   Italy   Japan   Poland   Portugal   Singapore
South Korea   Switzerland   Thailand   Turkey   Ukraine   Vietnam

Oxford is a registered trademark of Oxford University Press
in the UK and certain other countries.

Published in the United States of America by
Oxford University Press
198 Madison Avenue, New York, NY 10016

Library of Congress Cataloging-in-Publication Data
Basáñez, Miguel, author.
A world of three cultures : honor, achievement and joy / Miguel E. Basáñez;
with foreword by Ronald F. Inglehart.
pages cm
Includes bibliographical references and index.
ISBN 978–0–19–027036–0 (hardcover : alk. paper) — ISBN 978–0–19–027037–7 (pbk. : alk.
paper)   1. Social values.   2. Culture.   3. Social evolution.   4. Cultural geography.   I. Title.
HM681.B377 2016
303.3'72—dc23
2015023133

9 8 7 6 5 4 3 2
Printed in the United States of America on acid-free paper
Printed by Edwards Brothers

To Tatiana

CONTENTS

FOREWORD

A quarter century ago, when I was launching the 1990 wave of the World Values Survey, I asked Peter Smith, a leading expert on Latin American politics, to recommend the most competent person he knew to carry out the Mexican component of the survey. He recommended Miguel Basáñez, whom I contacted immediately. Miguel accepted my invitation enthusiastically, and within a few weeks visited me in person, along with his colleague Enrique Alduncin. Miguel proceeded to conduct the survey, with the support of Carlos Slim, and this was the start of a close friendship and fruitful collaboration that continues today. As soon as the data were available, Miguel and I, together with our Canadian colleague Neil Nevitte, wrote *Convergencia en Norteamerica: Comercio, Politica y Cultura* (Mexico City: Siglo XXI, 1994), which was also published as *The North American Trajectory: Social Institutions and Social Change*. Since then, we have published three sourcebooks based on successive waves of the World Values Survey, and at this writing we are in the process of preparing a fourth.

My collaboration with Miguel opened the way to train young Mexican social scientists in public opinion survey design and analysis through the ICPSR summer program at the University of Michigan. Alejandro Moreno, current vice president of the World Values Survey Association and outgoing president of the World Association for Public Opinion Research, was one of our first students. After doing his undergraduate work with Miguel at ITAM, he worked with me, earning his Ph.D. at the University of Michigan. It has been a great pleasure to work with Alejandro and many other talented young Mexican social scientists.

The hypotheses that Miguel began investigating in the 1986 article, cited in his introduction to this book, found their first empirical support in the data from the subsequent waves of the World Values Survey, leading him to develop a map of trust and autonomy (Figure 0.1), which showed the impact of religion on the locations of countries (Figure 0.2). The map was presented at the conference convened by Peter Smith in Quito, Ecuador, in the summer of 1993, and at a conference in El Paular, Spain, a few weeks later, where we met colleagues from the WVS network. Subsequently, Huntington published his article "Clash of Civilizations," and the first version of my global cultural map (Figure 2.4) appeared in an article co-authored with Marita Carballo, "Does Latin America Exist?" laying the groundwork for a series of global cultural maps demonstrating that the cultural clusters underlying this map were remarkably robust features of cross-national cultural variation.

Basáñez divides the current work into three main sections: values, cultures, and development. In the first, he examines the basis of values research in theoretical discussions, paradigms and data from the World Values Survey, but also delves into the work of Hofstede and Schwartz, demonstrating striking similarities between their findings and our own work on the WVS data (Chapter 2). This review results in his own proposal for an *axiological cube* (Chapter 3) formed by the three key axes that he proposed in 1986 (trust–distrust, work as prize or punishment, and autonomy–obedience), which helped him discover the evolution and chronology of the three hypercultures.

In the second part of the book, the author proceeds to illustrate the existence of three cultures with geographical cases (Chapter 4), and in Chapters 5 and 6 he elaborates on the theme, using empirical data from the World Values Surveys. He first addresses cultures of honor, tradition, and respect, where, he argues, all countries began—from the nomadic tribes of hunter-gatherers and then the first agricultural societies, culminating in the civilizations of antiquity and the great agrarian empires. He then argues that achievement cultures—with their emphasis on punctuality, efficiency, and end results—were triggered by the industrial revolution, especially in Protestant Europe and particularly the British Empire and its colonies, like banners of modernity. Finally, humanity began to strive toward cultures of joy, family, and friendship after World War II, with the emergence of the postmaterial, postindustrial society—a topic that I have also studied for several decades. In Chapters 7, 8, and 9, the author emphasizes that culture is not destiny, since all cultures are in a permanent process of change. He analyzes six agents of change—family, school, religion, media, leadership, and the law—and highlights some successful historical processes of cultural change, showing his concern for leveraging theoretical knowledge to provide practical solutions to current problems.

The final part of the book is devoted to reflection on, measurement of, and challenges to the concept of development. Chapter 10 responds to the invitation of the Sarkozy committee by developing an Objective Development Index (ODI), a new measurement based on objective indicators. In addition to income, education, and health indicators already included in the Human Development Index, it incorporates civil liberties and political rights, gender equality, and income distribution. Judging by the resulting ranking, Sarkozy's intuition was not wrong: France rises to 11th place (from 20th in HDI), while the United States falls to 41st (from 3rd in HDI).

Also in Chapter 10, the author translates the cultural map derived from the World Values Survey into a linear measurement called the Subjective Development Index (SDI), which Matteo Marini used to quantify the contribution of culture in development (Table 12.3). After reviewing the material and cultural factors that Marx and Weber respectively proposed as drivers of development (Chapters 11 and 12), he concludes by suggesting that there is a third factor—the interaction between the two, which is embodied in innovation, both technological and institutional.

This book takes the reader on a fascinating theoretical, historical, and empirical tour through history that demonstrates the existence of a dialectic and cyclical process incorporating both virtuous and vicious spirals. Basáñez argues that a civilization's very success can lead to pride that degenerates into arrogance, which can bring decline. But decline is not inevitable: it depends on human decisions that shape the values and institutions influencing our future.

Ronald F. Inglehart
University of Michigan

ACKNOWLEDGMENTS

Acknowledgments generally end with a brief mention of the support and tolerance of the author's spouse, but in this case it would be unfair not to give my wife the credit she merits. In 45 years of undeservedly happy matrimony with Tatiana, we have experienced the cultural shocks of life in new countries, we have grown intellectually together, we have fully shared our respective graduate studies, we have debated almost every paragraph of this book, and of course, she did not escape the torture of reading, rereading, and discussing the latest three versions of the manuscript. So my deepest gratitude is to Tatiana, the fiercest and most beautiful of my critics.

In addition, Jerry Kagan, Pedro Ángel Palou, Miguel de la Torre, Armando Ortiz Rocha, Kate Taylor, and Nancy Doherty made close readings of the manuscript, and their valuable observations, suggestions, and comments were enormously useful. Matteo Marini, Enrique Alduncin, Luis Grané, Alejandro Moreno, and Pablo Parás gave me important comments on some portions of the work, as did my colleagues in Tepoztlán Group during a discussion we had in September 2013. I am also grateful to my editor extraordinaire at Oxford University Press, Angela Chnapko, for her support and encouragement, as well as her keen and insightful editorial touch.

My gratitude also goes to the founder of the Cultural Change Institute (CCI), Larry Harrison, for inviting me to take over after his retirement, which precipitated my move to the Boston area. I would also like to thank the Fletcher School of Tufts University, which has housed me since 2008, and has provided me with the brightest and most intellectually stimulating students any professor could wish for. Also, thanks to my colleagues and friends in the CCI for their very valuable insights: Jerry Kagan, Peter Berger, Fernando Reimers, Reese Schonfeld, Richard Lamm, James Fox, Robert Kleinbaum, and Octavio Sánchez. For their valuable work in collecting, reviewing, and processing data, I owe much gratitude to my research assistants over the past several years: my daughter Tatiana Basáñez, Nina Skagerlind, Juan Balderas, Roger Aleph Méndez, Roberto Foa, Christopher Ellison, Ignacio del Busto, Aleksey Dolinskiy, Maria Snegovaya, Ilya Lozovsky, and Kevin O'Brien.

For their academic and intellectual stimulation, I thank the excellent students in the ten courses I've had the pleasure of teaching at The Fletcher School (listed below), whose ideas, concerns, and questions are very much present in my thoughts. Likewise, I thank IDEAS (Advanced Studies Institute for Development Economics) from Japan, the University of Calabria, and Naples Parthenope University for inviting me to discuss the progress of the book with their faculty and students (listed below). The probing questions, curiosity, challenges, and lively discussions that took place in both the classroom and at social events with students and colleagues from around 50 countries in the last seven years helped make this manuscript more entertaining, engaging, and relatable. Finally, I thank Dolores de los Ríos and Lupita Ervin for their diligent and efficient help in typing and formatting the manuscript.

Fletcher students—Spring 2009: Zara Aleksanyan (Armenia); Evelyn A. Brensinger; Philip K. Buchanan; Aleksey V. Dolinskiy (Russia); Jong Woong Jeon (South Korea); Carolina Martine (Brazil); Tara A. Medeiros (Portugal); Elen Zargaryan (Armenia) / **Spring 2010**: Ariel Heifetz (Israel); Hector Brown; Juan Carlos Estrada (Mexico); Justin Chinyanta (Zambia); Kathleen McLaughlin; Khartini Abdul Khalid (Singapore); Manal Quota; Marc Frankel; Miki Matsura (Japan); Patrick Karuretwa (Rwanda); Richard Wright; Shailaja Bista; Sogdiana Azhibenova; Tara Leung / **Spring 2011**: Loren Austin; Colin A. Canham; Mary Dulatre (Philippines); Stewart K. Kelly (Ireland); Kimberley Liao; Ilya Lozovsky; Omar Mahmood; Frederick Meyer; J. R. Siegel; Nicholas Strutt; Daiji Tateishi (Japan) / **Spring 2012**: Ralph V. Abarquez; Annatina Aerne (Switzerland); Samuel Chapple-Sokol; Mariana Benitez (Mexico); Lisa J. De Bode; Emilie Falguieres; Kathryn L. Genereux; Alejandra Hernandez (Mexico); Sasha G. Kapadia (Afganhistan); Bonnie S. Kovatch; Victoria-Alicia Lopez; Elizabeth M. Mengesha; Hannah Schiff; Leila Seradj / **Fall 2012**: Madeeha Ansari (Pakistan); Jane M. Church (Canada); Mariana Diaz Kraus (Colombia); Katherine E. Dutko; Christina C. Failma (Philippines); Matthew H. Foerster; Hana Frankova; Catherine A. Gartland; Mohammed Harba (Iraq); Michael C. Jones; Tuck Choy Lim (Malaysia); Lorena Macias (Mexico); Mallory Minter; Jacqueline M. Mulders; David Mulet (Guatemala); Chris Paci; Julia P. Radice; Samara Y. Sabin (Mexico); Nina A. Skagerlind (Sweden); Sarah J. Willis; Sachiyo Yanahi (Japan) / **Spring 2013**: Maliheh Birjandi Feriz (Iran); Ana de Alba Gonzalez (Mexico); Manon Garin (France); Pablo A. Jimenez Meza (Mexico); Dinar D. Kharisma (Indonesia); Beatriz Navarro (Mexico); Sybil Ottenstein (Israel); Maive Rute (Estonia) / **Fall 2013**: Carolina Aguirre (Colombia); Sofi Alexander (Finland); Jennifer Ambrose; Deborshi Barat (India); Ignacio del Busto (Spain); Rahul Dwivedi (India); Lale Eray; Samantha Hackney; Kenichi Kitamura (Japan); Li Li (China); Akane Okade (Japan); John Paxton; David Powers; Javin Smith; Gabrielle Soltys; Roberta Sotomaior (Brazil) / **Spring 2014**: Natalia Arruda (Brazil); Ryan Leary; Julia Livick; Anna McCallie; Siddarth Nagaraj; Diego Ortiz (Mexico); Jacqueline Page; Marie Principe; Lisa Setrakian (Lebanon); Shams Tabrez (India); Symeon Tegos (Greece); Elsa Tung; Namsai Wongsaeree (Thailand); Anna Valeria Zuccolotto(Mexico) / **Fall 2014**: Jack Berger; Maria Rita Borba (Brazil); Bill Dangel; Xue Jia (China); Samantha Karlin; Ji Yean Lee (South Korea); Marisa Lloyd; Gizelle Lopez; Zdenka Mislikova (Czech Republic); Rajiv Nair (India); Felipe Navarro (Colombia); Phebe Philips (Nigeria); Gaspar Rodriguez (Chile); Hitomi Teraoka (Japan); Ahsen Utku (Turkey); Eliza Waterman / **Spring 2015**: Barry Ang; Jung Woo Chun (South Korea); Patricia de Jesus (Puerto Rico); Dara Fisher; Abigail Fried; David Gilmore (Colombia); Terrell Levine; Saeko Hashimoto (Japan); Magdolna Pongor (Hungary); Sirinrat Satondee (Thailand);

Kelsey Smithwood; Bradley Toney; Alicia Tozur; Tran, Ngoc Bao (VietNam); and Rubén Useche (Colombia).

IDEAS students in Japan—November 2014: Zakir Abdullaev (Uzbekistan); Zubeir Abubakar (Nigeria); Nangamso Marcus Baliso (South Africa); Viriya Chanthaphasouk (Lao Pdr); Synan Chhounni (Cambodia); Abdoulaye Coulibaly (Côte d'Ivoire); Pabitra Dangol (Nepal); Sonam Dorji (Bhutan); Reagan Chandra Dey (Bangladesh); Inoka Gunasekara (Sri Lanka); Masami Hamaoka; Natsuko Hatano; Nurul Istiqomah (Indonesia); Shoko Matsuoka; Takashi Miyahara; Tsubasa Mizuguchi; Ayasgalan Molor (Mongolia); Idrees Muhammad (Pakistan); Misuzu Nakamura; Yen Thi Hai Nguyen (Vietnam); Vivian Rutaihwa (Tanzania); Takahisa Shimbo; Rei Shirakawa; Helmie Thein (Myanmar); Benson Waweru (Kenya); and Sota Yoshie.

The cover art, "Rock, Paper, Scissors," was created by Luis Grané. I am in the artist's debt for creating an image that so perfectly captures the theme of this book.

A World of Three Cultures

Introduction

You don't realize how many cultural differences exist around the world until you travel. A few weeks after my arrival in England in 1973, I needed to get my driver's license. The first thing I anticipated were the obstacles the Warwick office of the government licensing agency was sure to put before me, as was customary in my home country. So I prepared a battery of *arguments* ranging from the comic to the tragic. When the woman at the window asked whether I had a valid license in Mexico and I answered "yes," she told me that it was enough, and I could use it to drive. I asked whether I needed to bring a letter from my embassy. Her expression made me immediately take it back, and offer to at least show her my license. She looked at me again peculiarly and asked why. "*Your word is enough.*" I was out of there in three minutes, overwhelmed. It was the first time in my life I had ever heard someone's word given such weight!

This is a book for globalized decision-makers about cultural values and development around the world from a historical, empirical, and philosophical perspective. *Values* are the building blocks of culture. *Culture* in turn is an important factor that either speeds up or slows down *development*. But values and cultures are not static. They change slowly by generational replacement—or sometimes rapidly, as a reaction to catastrophic or highly impactful historical events.

Researchers have not been able to agree on a commonly accepted definition of development, nor on which countries should be considered most highly developed. According to one list, for instance, the United States is at the top of the rankings; on a second it is 8th; on a third it is 37th.[1] Also, researchers and policymakers have long argued over what causes development: changes in material conditions or the power of ideas? If the former, development policy needs to focus on climate, geography, demographics, economics, politics, and sociological factors, among the obvious items. If the latter, it needs to focus on philosophy, religion, law, traditions, and the evolution of thought—namely, on culture. Or, could it be that a country's development is the result of the combined effect of both the material and cultural as they interact through society and bring about technological and institutional innovations?

In the discussion that follows, culture is meant not in its sense of the fine arts, but rather how people feel, think, and behave. This book examines social, economic, and political development and the links between development and values systems. It describes three hyper clusters of culture in the world, as they appeared chronologically: *honor, achievement,* and *joy*.[2] These three cultural clusters emerge from the analysis of the largest bodies of empirical data in the social sciences, gathered in the last quarter of the 20th century from over 100 countries, by Geert Hofstede, Shalom Schwartz, and Ronald Inglehart. The three hyper clusters mirror the agrarian, industrial, and service societies (pre-industrial, industrial, and postindustrial) described by Daniel Bell (1976, chapter 4).

Empirical research shows that cultures are dynamic, not static, because they inevitably change over time. Countries' cultural foundations leave a long-lasting imprint—coded in the laws and rooted in religions—but cultures evolve together with societies. That is why it is impossible to properly understand the present without the aid of history.

The study of cultures necessarily draws on many fields: politics, law, sociology, economics, social psychology, philosophy, demography, anthropology, geography, history, cognitive science, pedagogy, management, health, communication, literature, music, and linguistics, among the most relevant. This makes many scholars uncomfortable, but I don't see an easy way to avoid such a multidisciplinary range.

How I Became Drawn to the Topic

My fascination with cultural contrasts began in 1973. It grew from a succession of cultural shocks that I experienced as a young Mexican graduate student during two stays in England in the 1970s and from a trip to Japan in 1984. I began a process of reducing cognitive dissonance through building hypotheses, but the empirical testing had to wait a full 20 years until 1993, when the second wave of the World Values Survey (WVS) was made available.[3]

During the 1974 oil crisis in England, the government rationed gasoline coupons alphabetically by last name. I found this out two weeks after my turn had come up. I was sure that this time they would require—at the very least—that I plead my case all the way up to the prime minister! With my Latin American mindset, I prepared a whole story that, likewise, never had to see the light of day. Just as soon as I said at the window, "I didn't find out in time," the clerk wrote down my name and handed over the coupons in an exchange lasting no more than a single minute. I was again astonished by the credibility that my word held.

On another occasion, I forgot my tennis shoes, spray, and lotion in the university's gym locker room. Two days later I returned, never expecting to find everything just as I had left it—but no one had so much as touched anything. This scrupulous honesty was unknown to me. I found it so strange. It seemed as if in England the belief was "what is not mine, is someone else's." This implies that one shouldn't take an object even if it looks like it has been lost or thrown away.

In my culture, the more typical attitude was "what isn't in someone else's possession is mine. Therefore I am free to appropriate whatever is not obviously under someone's custody, or near someone who could stop me."

Back in Mexico in 1975, I worked in the Ministry of Agriculture and I had to go on a trip to the northern state of Chihuahua. I had the opportunity to visit a very prosperous Mennonite community, and I was deeply impressed by what I saw. I was used to associating cart horses and unpaved roads with poverty. Here, although there were no cars or other mechanization, the town was highly industrious and successful. Such memories became sharper year by year as I encountered and accumulated new ones.

As a contrast, consider the following: I used to vacation with my wife and children on the Pacific Coast beaches of Puerto Vallarta, where we would set up a sun tent over our four chairs. Invariably, as soon as we stepped away to swim or stroll over the sand, the beach-soccer players, ignoring the obvious evidence that the chairs and tent were occupied, would proceed to take them over for a few minutes, with no concern for having violated any social norm whatsoever.

The last anecdote I share comes from my first doctoral seminar in London in 1978. As soon as I finished my presentation, a classmate on my left said that he disagreed with what I had said. My blood started boiling—I stopped listening and began thinking about how to drag the guy out of the classroom and challenge him to a fight. However, since nobody else showed any reaction, I stayed calm. On my right, another classmate said that she did agree with me, and thought the first comment was slightly out of focus. Of course, I liked her. Then a third participant took a bit of each of the first two and elaborated further. At that point I started cooling down, and began listening again. To my surprise, that open exchange of frank opinions—totally unknown in my Mexican culture and to me—was valuable and constructive. By the seminar's end, I had a better idea of the topic and felt enriched by the discussion.

I became convinced. There had to be an explanation for the many differences I'd encountered after three years in England. Patterns had emerged; hence there ought to be explanations. Some find foreign that which for others is familiar.

In the spring of 1983, I had lunch in Mexico City with my best friend Roderic Camp, a top US expert on Mexican politics. I complained about the extreme schedule of my job in the Mexican government, which forced me to stay at my office so late that not only was I unable to spend time with my family, friends, and books, but also I was teetering on the verge of exhaustion. This was in obvious contrast to Camp's academic life in that peculiar Dutch oasis of eight thousand people in the Iowa countryside, Pella.

We spoke of a book unknown in Mexico, *The Public Man*, by Dealy, published in 1977. In Camp's opinion, Dealy made a very suggestive interpretation of the contrasts between Protestantism and Catholicism, along the lines of Max Weber's arguments, as the reasons behind the Latin attitude toward *power*. I tried unsuccessfully to buy it in the local specialty bookstores for English books. Camp failed to find it in the United States, but at last he sent me a photocopy.

I read it with enthusiasm and approached one of Mexico's best academic publishers, suggesting that they publish it. To my surprise, reviewers rejected it on the grounds that it was derogatory and offensive to Mexican culture! I just could not believe it. Reviewers had had the same reaction 20 years earlier to a highly influential anthropological study, *The Children of Sánchez* (Lewis, 1961). That event prompted me to continue searching for an explanation for the cultural extremes I had encountered firsthand.

My search was further stimulated by a trip to Japan in 1984. I was lucky enough to visit that country with a governmental delegation led by a Mexican-Japanese colleague, Carlos Kasuga, raised in Mexico, who offered me suggestive interpretations of many Japanese customs and behaviors that were to me very distant. In our first conversations, we addressed the obligatory questions of why the Japanese showed such a vigorous work ethic, why they took such meticulous care in the quality of their products, why their strikes were carried out by speeding up—rather than stopping—their work, why they paid so much attention to flowers, trees and gardens, and so on.

In answer, Kasuga touched on an insight that has held my attention ever since: the influence religious belief has on economic culture and, through it, on social and political cultures. He reminded me of Weber and Dealy. He piqued my curiosity when he furthered his interpretation, explaining what he had achieved in Mexico by involving and motivating the workers of a little workshop, which over time had become an important factory.

He spoke of thousands of Shinto *gods* of life, combined with Buddhism for death; of the symbolism of trees as *generational chains* with one's ancestors; of strikes as actions that should not interfere with the *great chain* of production; of the possibility of transcending death and achieving afterlife through manual labor and quality in workmanship.

He discussed the concept of family dignity and continued communication with their gods through close, known interlocutors: parents, grandparents, and deceased ancestors, who are watching the living and will be made proud or ashamed by their actions. In his belief system, a sin could not be expiated by confession before a priest, as in Catholicism, but rather by means of positive acts that compensate for the damage done. He also explained why, when someone commits an unforgivable offense, the only honorable exit would be expiation by death (*hara-kiri*).

These insights into such a different set of behaviors highlighted for me how humankind's concern for life after death seems to have structured the two great explanations offered to individuals as hope for overcoming their mortality. For the Japanese culture, the way to *eternal life* was through an active, aggressive, transforming attitude—individual *action* relative to one's environment. For the culture I was used to, the way was paradoxically through passivity, submission, suffering, resignation, pain, abnegation, acceptance—*inaction* in relation with one's circumstances. In this way, *hard work* had become central: a *reward* in the Japanese tradition and a *punishment* in my culture.

In Shintoism, the individual achieves access to *eternal life* through the perfection of the product of one's hands (manual labor), which brings satisfaction to the recipient and adds to the account of its maker. In Judaism and Protestantism, eternal life is achieved through triumph in earthly life, which is seen as proof of being chosen. It is a product of personal discipline accomplished through work, frugality, and saving. In *cultures of honor*, however, access is obtained through the accumulation of merits through pain, suffering, resignation, abnegation, and submission—without hard work or study playing any role.

The Three *Value-Axes* Model: Trust, Hard Work, and Autonomy

My search for answers to the cultural contrasts I had observed in England and Japan became my focus of attention. The hypothesis-building process I began was more in line with the *participant-observation* techniques typical of qualitative research, based on personal observations and experiences, than anything else. On my return from London, I got a high-level job at the president of Mexico's office, where I worked from 1980 to 1982, an enviable position from which to gain a panoramic view of the country. Additionally, I began conducting public opinion polling, although at that time I didn't really have a systematic or theoretically oriented process or a truly specific quantitative empirical experimental model to test.

I built the hypothesis upon the assumption of three **key dimensions** of culture (social, economic, and political), following the ideas of Marx, Weber, and Gramsci. My concern was discovering the **key values** that drove those dimensions. The answer to my question began revealing itself as *trust, hard work*, and *autonomy*, assisted by thinking of the differences between Catholics and Protestants (Basáñez, 1986). Back then, I didn't see the connection between the three key dimensions (social, economic, and political) and Weber's rationale of social action (goals, norms, emotion, and tradition). Finding the connection helped me to understand that when an individual, a corporation, or a country is making decisions, only one of the three dimensions will prevail, while the other two will subordinate. I couldn't help thinking about a triangle, in which only one of the three components can be at the top corner and the other two at the base corners. Some years later, I came to depict these values in the form of three *axes* with two opposing polarities: trust–distrust; work as prize or as punishment; and autonomy–obedience (Basáñez, 1993).

It may perhaps seem difficult to believe that just three values (trust, hard work, and autonomy–obedience) explain not only the three primary cultural clusters (honor, achievement, and joy), but also such an enormous number of micro cultures (7,000, based on number of languages). However, if you consider that only three basic colors (red, blue, and yellow) can produce the entire color spectrum, the argument becomes more understandable. As will be explored in Chapter 2, three empirical analysts of values and cultures (Hofstede, Inglehart, and Schwartz), using separate databases, different methodologies, and distinctive terminologies, nevertheless arrive at conclusions very similar to my own.

My point of departure was thinking about Mexican Catholics (*Catholics* is a category that is applicable throughout Latin America); when referring to contrasts with Protestants, I had WASP[4] Americans mostly in mind. Additionally, it is important to consider that all cultural processes are very slowly *simmered*. That is, they take place throughout decades. The Protestant values of the United States, despite the historic diversity of migrants and cultural influences (Woodward, 2011), come from the colonial era and were crystallized in the laws and institutions of the new nation, as was the case in Latin America with its Catholic values. However, as the decades passed, the original values and cultures that the two regions adopted began slowly changing. The stereotypes I had in mind when writing the original article in 1986 mostly corresponded to the historical image of each region, rather than the cutting edge and rapidly changing profiles of today.

The contrasts between Latin- and Anglo-Americans are useful in view of each region's quite distinct process of colonization. First, Latin America was extremely densely populated by highly complex indigenous societies numbering many millions, while historians tend to agree that the indigenous population of what is now the United States and Canada was smaller, and relatively more diffuse and decentralized (Jacobs, 1974). Second, the arriving Spaniards and Portuguese were not hard-working families, but young bachelors seeking money, sex, and power. Third, the colonizers were not fleeing persecution, but rather were sent by the crown and frequently with reluctance. Fourth, the Europeans in Latin America did not engage in developing egalitarian laws. On the contrary, they brought from Europe an array of extractive institutions designed to dominate the indigenous population and take as much gold, silver, and sugar cane for the benefit of Spain or Portugal as possible (Sokoloff and Engerman, 2000). Finally, the Spanish and Portuguese crowns seized the leadership, the land, and the full dominion of their territories, completely the opposite of the North American case. These were the differing environments in which the values and institutions of each region evolved.

The reason I find it relevant to include the *three key values* (trust, hard work, and autonomy) in my analysis is because, while on my part they were the outcome of a deeply considered intuition, they have since been empirically confirmed. As will be shown in Part I, the three empirical authors I have been following, Hofstede, Inglehart and Schwartz, arrived at quite similar notions after painstaking statistical analysis. The following updates some selected excerpts from my original 1986 article.

AXIS 1—THE ECONOMIC DIMENSION: *HARD WORK AS PRIZE OR PUNISHMENT* (THE MARKET)

One contrast between *Protestants* and *Catholics* that caught my attention powerfully was the work ethic, profoundly explored by Max Weber (1905). I found very intriguing the difference between work as a *reward* and work as a *punishment* from the 16th to 19th centuries.

The concept of hard work discussed in Weber's *Protestant Ethic* has traditionally been the highest value in *cultures of achievement* (McClelland, 1961), whereas it has been relatively absent in both the *cultures of honor* and *of joy*. However, it is important to observe that Europe in the Middle Ages had a troubled relationship with *hard work*—above all, the idea of manual labor. This conflict has roots as far back as the age of imperial Rome, when nobles and patricians were not responsible for manual tasks, which were the province of servants and slaves.

The Roman contempt for manual work continued through the centuries into the age of European feudalism—and later to the magnificent *Serenissima* Republic of Venice, and to Florence, Spain, and Portugal—with no impact on economic success, due to the abundance of servants and slaves, as well as the expansion by conquest of foreign territories. After the Protestant Reformation, however, the Netherlands, England, and the Nordic and other European countries began to benefit economically from the Protestant concept of *hard work* and the institutions it produced. The aftermath of the Black Death, too, took its toll in producing labor scarcity.

The impact of the Protestant ethic did not stop there. The diametrically opposed worldviews of Reformation and Counter-Reformation Europe were disseminated through the colonization process until they reached the Americas (Anglo and Latin), where today they are exceptional examples of each worldview.

Contempt for manual labor in Portugal and Spain before the 16th century did not cause a problem, because these countries had funneled manual labor (trade, medicine, finance, agriculture, etc.) onto the Jews and Muslims, who ultimately achieved tremendous success in every industry they entered. However, after the establishment of the Spanish Inquisition in 1480 and the expulsion of the Jews and Muslims in 1492, the problem of manual labor became extreme (Cantera, 2008).

Making the Spanish situation more pitiful, the nobles' insistence on easy income from taxing sheep led them to promote livestock but not agriculture, discouraging food production and domestic industry. As the years went by, Spain exported wool to Europe and purchased manufactured fabric and food from its neighbors.

Matters grew even worse as the Spanish became obsessed with *blood purity*, which effectively put a stop to many trades. Spaniards did not want to risk being accused of Jewish heritage by performing work commonly associated with members of that faith. From an economic standpoint, the consequences were devastating, because Spain started importing all consumer goods from Holland, France, and England, which they barely paid for with the extraction of precious metals from Latin America.

Contempt for manual labor quickly set in among the elites of Latin America, who found in the New World an abundance of potential servants and slaves. In the Spanish and Portuguese American colonies, Jews or Muslim migrants from time to time caused micro-economies to flourish. However, as soon as their prosperity became apparent, it was destroyed—just as it had been in Spain—by the Inquisition, which crippled the existing webs of commerce and finance, as well as entire industries that might pose a threat to royal monopolies.

The New Spain nobility and clergy were the beneficiaries of privileges gained from a highly complicated system of taxation that ravaged the common and native segments of the population. The elite members were already installed in the culture of *joy*, totally removed from the values prized by cultures of *achievement*. For the common people, the situation was the opposite, for it was their hard work and sacrifices that guaranteed the well-being of the nobility and clergy.

One passage of the Judaic/Christian Bible supports the concept of *punishment* that, after the Reformation, would apply in a totally different light to Catholics and Protestants. Upon expulsion from Eden, Adam was condemned to "earn your bread by the sweat of your brow." This was the original reasoning that has spawned numerous adages in colonial Catholic countries such as "work is so bad they actually pay you for it," or "there's no work in Heaven." Seen in this light, hard work is clearly contemptible and should be left to less favored members of the social pyramid.

Daily work thus was not regarded as a *prize* in itself, as leading to *eternal salvation*; the Protestant meaning of *hard work* was absent in Latin America. Instead, it was a necessary evil. However, as a way to counterbalance such a harsh punishment, the Catholic missionaries began extensively teaching the biblical parable of the *Camel and the Needle* (it is easier for a camel to pass through the eye of a needle than for a rich man to enter the kingdom of God). Whereas the parable is highly popular in the colonial Catholic world to justify poverty, along with a consequential aversion to savings, it is relatively unknown in Catholic Europe and does not compel the Protestant to avoid savings. *Salvation* for colonial Catholics was reached through selfless and resigned suffering, rather than by hard work and success.

If the idea of *hard work* in Spain and Latin America was viewed with suspicion and disdain, that of *leisure* carried with it a certain aura of respect, whether among the nobles or beggars. In fact, in the 17th century great debates were conducted and passionate treatises were written in Spain as the society sought to determine whether begging was something that should be promoted or curtailed (Cantera, 2008). Meanwhile, there was no limit to vain pageantry and prodigious waste.

As *hard work* was and is a punishment for the Latin American, so *leisure* was and is a prize, in direct contradiction to the Protestant ethic. Citizens of Protestant countries would find it difficult to think of leisure as a virtue, because all their lives they've been taught about the virtue of activity. They occupy their free time (vacations, sabbaticals, even retirement) in productive activities: mowing the lawn, painting the house, building a boat, taking courses, or reading.

A revealing illustration of the idea of *work as punishment* can be found in a song that rapidly became a top hit throughout Latin America, after being recorded in 1954. The song presents a narrative of life in the sugar towns (*bateys*) of the Dominican Republic in those days, reflecting the prevailing cultural attitudes. It was the most famous *merengue* song of the second half of the 20th century: "The Batey's Little Blacky" ("El Negrito del Batey"):

"EL NEGRITO DEL BATEY"	"THE BATEY'S LITTLE BLACKY"
A mí me llaman el negrito del batey,	They call me the *batey*'s little blacky,
porque *el trabajo para mí es un enemigo,*	as *working is for me just an enemy*;
el trabajar yo se lo dejo todo al buey,	working, I leave it all to losers,
porque el trabajo lo hizo Dios *como un castigo* [. . .].	as God has rigged *working as a punishment* [. . .].
Y dime si no es verdad,	And tell me if it ain't so,
el merengue es mucho mejor,	that merengue is so much better,
porque eso de trabajar	as all that working
a mí me causa dolor. . . .	causes me pain. . . .

It is not difficult to imagine the result of diligent hard work and frugality: save, accumulate, and capitalize. When multiplied through a society, such individual discipline builds a flourishing, prosperous economic system. In Protestant America, *entrepreneurs* have been the engines of the economy and government bureaucrats the followers, while in *Catholic* Latin America, at least during the 20th century, the opposite has been the case. The question that jumps out from the contrast is whether we are actually in the presence of comparable economic and political systems in the two cultural traditions.

However, this is a concept that is very difficult to measure directly today. Attitudes to *hard work* reflect on one side the scarcity or abundance of jobs in each nation; but also and probably more problematically, it is a value that originated in a pre-capitalist Europe of the 16th century, as opposed to the current late capitalist 21st century.

Working hard is highly valued in agricultural and industrial societies, where muscular strength and effort are needed to increase production. As an economy transitions toward a postindustrial or service stage, the need for muscular strength diminishes, the contribution of women rises, and the concept of *hard work* starts declining in favor of *smart work*, a way of producing the same output—but more efficiently and with less effort. That's why the concept of *hard work* is different in 16th- versus 21st-century Europe or in rural versus metropolitan areas.

The most important consequence of this perception of work is the profound impact on the economy. Highly productive economic systems would appear to be constructed on two basic notions of Protestant WASPs: *hard work* (as a prize) and *savings*, both of which are absent from colonial Catholic countries.

Scorn for manual labor in the 16th century extended also into *contempt for study*, given that education was an invitation to be persecuted by the Spanish Inquisition. Unless an individual could provide irrefutable proof of his lineage and *blood purity*, association with the world of sciences, arts, and letters was considered highly suspect: it implied *impurity*,[5] which could mean terrible consequences not only for the accused, but for his entire family. The persecutions of the Inquisition had other effects as well: they eroded compassion, and brought about an extreme distrust in others.

AXIS 2—THE SOCIAL DIMENSION: *TRUST AND DISTRUST* (THE FAMILY)

Another transcendent expression of colonial Catholics materializes in the concept of whom you can *trust*, that is, the *radius* of trust, a topic extensively analyzed by Fukuyama (1995) and Putnam (2000). The extent of the impact of the radius of trust becomes evident when comparing cultures. At one extreme lies the Protestant attitude with the broadest radius; at the other end, the colonial Catholic concept, restricting trust to the family and intimate persons in a very closed circle and regarding everyone else as essentially *strangers*.

To deal with that situation requires a double set of standards, a *double code*, for treating different people: very *ethically* with family and close friends, while very *unethically* with the rest, which is termed *amoral familism* (Banfield, 1958). To colonial Catholics, outside the *family and close friends*, the code for the inner circles does not apply. They therefore practice a series of rules applicable to outsiders, strangers, unknown, adversaries, or enemies. It is understood that it is *fair* to delay, cheat, and dominate. In this sense, to colonial Catholics the *stranger* is anyone outside a closed circle of relatives and close friends. It is not a question of conflict or competition, rather simply of the prevailing status.

Such conduct makes no sense to WASP Americans, because they cannot restrict their radius of trust to just their *inner circle*, cutting off the rest of society. They are historically, if unconsciously, conditioned to apply the same code of conduct to every person (at least, to every fellow WASP citizen). Thus to Latin Americans anyone outside the family and close friends is essentially a stranger, but to WASP Americans this is not so.

Latin Americans tend to form tight social circles and close them. The same psychological pattern for behavior is expressed in social, architectural, labor, and academic dimensions. The concept of the *stranger* is as deeply ingrained and real as are the walls that surround and separate the colonial house from the undesirable open streets of the *strangers*. Observe also how desks in traditional government offices in small towns were placed in circles, against the wall, so no one has their back to someone else.

In contrast, observe that the typical American home is located in the middle of a garden surrounded by grass with just a small fence. There is no need to separate it from the undesirable streets full of *strangers*. Observe the long rows of desks in many American offices where everybody sees the back of his or her neighbor.

There are two further expressions of Latin American double standards or *double code* worth pointing out. One is *unpunctuality*; the other is the reaction provoked when *success* is perceived in a *stranger*. Tardiness is a display of superiority, the ability to show *higher rank*, which also expresses contempt. Reacting to another's *success* with jealousy reveals a zero-sum game view: "What someone else has is at the cost of what I potentially lose; so all others losing equals my potential gain." The corrosive consequences that this reasoning has on incentives to accomplishment and success by individual members of a society would not seem too difficult to discover.

AXIS 3—THE POLITICAL DIMENSION: *AUTONOMY VERSUS OBEDIENCE* (THE STATE)

The *third axis* I developed is *autonomy-obedience,* expressed through attitudes toward *dissent*, which are tightly linked to dogmatism and are of great consequence in the configuration of political culture and democracy. Among colonial Catholics, one unintended consequence of believing in original sin—the legacy of Adam and Eve's expulsion from the Garden of Eden by eating from the *tree of knowledge*—is that they associate learning, studying, dissenting, and debating with evil. Hence, acceptance, resignation, obedience, and consensus are considered better.

To some extent, the negative attitude toward autonomy and dissent is also linked to the rejection of *hard work*. The Protestant view of manual labor as dignifying—not shared in the colonial Catholic tradition—implicitly refers to the human capacity to *master* nature. This process requires the individual to establish direct contact with the physical world, which grows into an exercise of coupling the mind with that physical world, as well as a search for facts. This focus prevents speculative abstraction and theory divorced from practice.

Factual reality demands coupling between the transforming agent and the transformed object, an exercise in congruence that implies a necessary search for the understanding of that reality. That is, discipline is required to search for honest knowledge—truth. That difficult individual task may be facilitated through teamwork (as illustrated in the Hindu story of *the Blind Men and the Elephant*), exchange of individual findings, and adversarial debate—another set of values antithetical to the colonial Catholic tradition. Dialogue and debate would be the methodology for its achievement, realized by the exchange of ideas and mutual constructive criticism, until better understanding of the truth is gained. *Autonomic dissent* has a clear utility value that enriches the common aim.

The colonial Catholic tradition lacks a positive and useful concept of autonomy and dissent. This is another reason for the lack of appreciation and social recognition for research and technology. The upshot of this feature, when combined with the importance given to rank and hierarchy, is that an explanation given by someone with *authority* may acquire the status of formal truth regardless of its link to reality. This starts a process of dogmatic knowledge and practice.

Such behavior and attitudes are transmitted imperceptibly from generation to generation without any obvious challenge, through family, school, and peers. When in traditional Latin American families do mother, father, and children gather over a meal to decide where to go for an outing? The norm, rather, is a vision as monarchical and hierarchical as any organizational diagram: father at the apex of the pyramid, with mother directly underneath and all the children together on a third level, unless the firstborn enjoys some privilege over the siblings.

The father is the authority in this family structure, and his word is law. The mother could hardly call him out, at least in front of the children. Any sign of hesitation or indecision on his part may demote him quickly relative to the others. As a result, family decisions are not even brought up for discussion, they are simply announced. The lessons children learn are non-dialogue, non-debate, non-discussion, non-dissent, non-autonomy, and reinforcement of the facets of hierarchy, dogmatism, submission, acceptance, and resignation, but above all *obedience*.

Empirical Exploration

The cognitive dissonance that began in 1973 during my years as a student in England was still unresolved in my mind 20 years later. It was an intellectual struggle brought about by a variety of cultural clashes that I attributed to my Mexican origin and to the differences between Catholicism and Protestantism. In 1993, while spending the summer at the University of Michigan at the invitation of Ronald Inglehart, my colleague at the Institute for Social Research (ISR), I became inspired to research these issues further. I was able to do so in large part because of data gathered through the WVS.

With access to the most recent WVS data, I began to look for the characteristics that separated Catholics and Protestants the most.[6] Two variables became readily self-evident: *trust in others* and *respect for parents*, which I interpreted on a scale ranging from obedience to autonomy/dissent. My original chart contrasted only Catholics and Protestants. It revealed citizens in Protestant nations to be *trusting* and *autonomous, dissenting-prone*, while those in Catholic countries appeared *distrustful* and *obedient*.

The updated chart, Figure 0.1, now includes all the principal religions highlighted by the WVS. In the upper-right quadrant (trust and autonomy) we see the proximity of Protestantism, Confucianism, Judaism, and non-religious, in contrast to the close grouping of Islamic, Catholic, and Orthodox religions in the lower-left quadrant (distrust and obedience). The proximity of Hinduism and Buddhism, as well as their location near the center of the upper-left quadrant (trust and obedience) had not been anticipated in 1993.

These findings suggest something about the effects that the Protestant ethos might have on democracy and capitalism, as metaphorical *children* of dissenting and trustful people. On the other hand, obedient and distrustful people, as in the Catholic ethos, lack the foundational and supportive values to nourish democracy and capitalism.

Until this way of analysis emerged, it was considered extremely politically incorrect to attribute any positive or negative effect to any culture or religion. Furthermore, that same year an influential and highly controversial article, *Clash of Civilizations* (Huntington, 1993), appeared, putting the issue of cultures

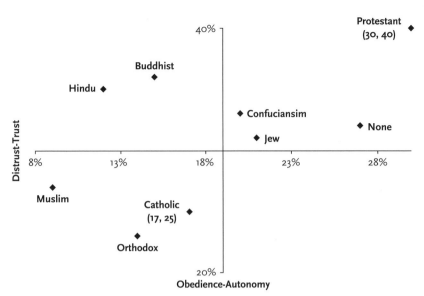

FIGURE 0.1 A trust and autonomy map

Data from World Values Survey

and religions squarely on the discussion table. I initially linked cultures to religious roots, but I eventually began also to see a connection to the three current legal systems of the world: common law (Anglo Saxon), civil law (Roman, either Germanic or French), and Islamic law.[7]

Figure 0.1 not only drew attention to the functionality or dysfunctionality of values systems with democracy and capitalism, but also pointed to the existence of two cultural hyper clusters, parallel but of opposing polarity, shown in Figure 0.2: **achievement** (upper-right quadrant) and **honor** (lower-left quadrant), which I had originally labeled as *combative* and *contemplative* (Basáñez, 1986). Several countries that show up in the middle of the figure (US, Canada, Japan, Australia, Switzerland, UK, etc.) made the exploration intriguing and piqued my curiosity to continue exploring the topic. If they are clearly *achieving cultures*, why do they fall in the middle?

For some, one possible explanation is their blend of Protestantism and Catholicism; in the case of Japan, the influence of Confucianism pulls it closer to China.

The trip to Japan made evident to me the existence of at least two contrasting belief systems that markedly influence the social, economic, and political behavior of individuals. One of these turned out to be what I now refer to as *cultures of achievement*, motivated by hard work and study, which find deep roots in Confucianism, Judaism, and Protestantism and are coded in the Anglo Saxon legal system. The other belief system is represented by *cultures of honor*, which are motivated by respect for traditions, hierarchies, and authority, find deep roots in Islam and Russian Orthodoxy, and are also coded in the Islamic legal system.

FIGURE 0.2 Countries in the *trust* and *autonomy* map

Data from World Values Survey

My current research shows that a more balanced culture, avoiding the excesses of the antithetical cultures of honor and achievement, does indeed exist. This third culture has its fullest expression among Catholic European countries (as Italy, Spain, Portugal, etc.). It also exists to some extent (1) as an aspiration in the mature, peaceful, and developed societies of the Nordic countries; (2) as a goal of Buddhism; and (3) as an unintended outcome in former colonial Catholic countries. In summary, between the cultures of achievement and cultures of honor lie the cultures of joy, motivated by social interactions and leisurely life, rooted in Catholicism, Buddhism, and coded in the Roman legal system.

What is Culture?

Values are the building blocks of cultures. Culture is a *context* phenomenon, **a shared system of meanings**.[8] Once a culture is formed, it is transmitted from generation to generation through six agents: family, school, religion, media, leadership, and the law. Hence, culture is not simply a *psychological* variable, because it is not just located within the individual's mind. Culture exists as more than a sum of individuals' values.

The first term, **shared**, reveals culture as the product of human action and social interaction; culture is collective in nature, and therefore it requires an *identity* (family, group, ethnic, or national) and a means of communication (*language*). **System** implies that culture is not a static and incoherent sum of unrelated

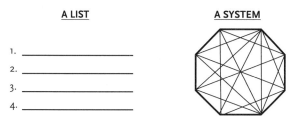

FIGURE 0.3 Difference between a *list* (static) and a *system* (dynamic)

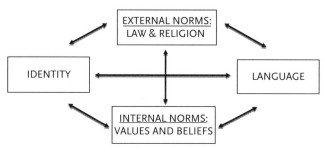

FIGURE 0.4 Essential elements of culture

parts; it is not just a *list* of values.[9] On the contrary, it is an integrated, interconnected whole, whose parts are in constant exchange. In a *system,* the essential elements are not the *parts* (units, items, or individuals), but the set of interactions among those parts (see Figure 0.3).

Therefore the phrase *shared system* emphasizes that the locus of culture is not the individual, but the *interaction* between individuals. Culture occurs *outside* the individual's mind and then becomes internalized. **Meanings** point to values and beliefs. **Values** highlight the intuition, feelings, emotions, and subjective judgments that confer esteem and preferences. And **beliefs** underscore cognition, reflection, objectivity, or analysis, which culminates in an idea. In the language of Daniel Kahneman (2011), these are the product of *system 1,* intuition (values), and *system 2,* reasoning (beliefs). In the musical analogy, values are the *notes* while cultures are the *symphonies.* In optics, values are the *primary colors* red, yellow, and blue, while cultures are the *chromatic gamut.*[10]

This concept yields four essential elements of culture: (1) the **identity** of a social group that carries the culture; (2) the common **language** the group uses to transmit and transform their culture; (3) the **external norms** (legal, religious or social) that govern the group's behavior; and (4) the **internal norms** (the system of values and beliefs) that synthesize the three former elements (identity, language, and external norms). These four elements, represented in Figure 0.4, comprise a *shared system of meanings.*

I am not using the term *culture* in its high-end meaning of *fine arts* (opera, ballet, classical music, etc.), nor in its generic meaning,[11] such as *Southern* culture, *corporate* culture, and the like, because these usages produce a myriad of

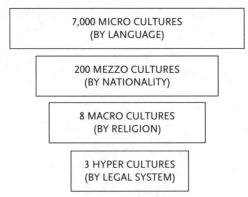

FIGURE 0.5 Number of cultures

cultures. By this definition, each city in the world would have its own *culture*. In fact, the same could be said of each village and neighborhood or of each family, making *culture* an unmanageable category. I am trying to define culture at a higher level of abstraction, to produce a meaning that is useful and consequential. This does not mean, however, that there is such a thing as a monolithic, monothematic, and coherent national culture. Countries are full of regional, historical, ethnic, and socio-demographic cultural differences and contradictions. Much less are there are multinational or continental cultures. However, despite all that internal variation, it is possible to identify commonalities. Hence, while it is far from being deterministic, a search for probabilistic propensities is possible.

The idea behind the search for commonalities in cultures, namely the pursuit of key values, is the same principle behind improving human health. All individuals on the planet are unique, but it is the human commonalities that have allowed medical science to develop; otherwise medicine as we know it could not exist. Cultures may be as many millions as the number of families, or neighborhoods, or towns on the globe, but it is their commonalities that allow categorization, as the next paragraph explains.

By using the four elements of Figure 0.4, one may define a maximum and minimum number of cultures in the world, as shown in Figure 0.5: from as many as 7,000 hypothetical *micro* **cultures** (roughly the number of current *languages* in the world) it could collapse into about 200 *mezzo* **cultures** (the approximate number of nations or *identities*); and can be further narrowed into the eight *macro* **cultures** based on the largest *global* philosophical and religious systems. These are finally grouped into as few as three *hyper* **cultural clusters** based on the opposing legal systems of Islamic and Anglo-Saxon (or common) law, with the Roman law tradition between the two. There are *three* legal systems and *three* cultural hyper clusters that respond to the political, economic, and social rationalities, respectively: namely, cultures of *honor, achievement,* and *joy.*

A country's legal and religious systems have a deep impact on its development, for they preserve the rules of the game. The more rigid and dogmatic the

FIGURE 0.6 Cultures of honor, achievement, and joy

legal and religious structure, the less business-friendly and more difficult it is for economic growth and development to occur. On the other hand, flexibility and pragmatism facilitate business and development.

As previously mentioned, there are three legal systems in the world today. The most rigid is the **Islamic**, where the Koran is the law; and the most flexible is the **Anglo-Saxon** or common law, in which judges, aided by precedents, effectively create laws through their rulings and written opinions. In between exist two variants of the **Roman** legal system or civil law: the German version, widely used in continental Europe and Asia, is more flexible; while the French version, commonly found in the former European colonies (except the British ones), is more dogmatic (La Porta, 2008).

Among societies around the globe there are eight principal systems of established beliefs. **Hinduism**, **Christian Orthodoxy**, and **Islam** focus on respect, tradition, and patriarchy (father, husband, boss, leader, chief) and emphasize obedience, acceptance, passivity, and sacrifice. They are functional to a *political rationality*. **Judaism**, **Confucianism**, and **Protestantism** convey a high sense of *agency*, giving the individual a clear sense of empowerment. Each of these offers individuals significant transformative opportunities, whether through emphasis on *study* and *learning* (Confucianism) or *hard work* (Protestantism). Judaism emphasizes both. They are functional to an *economic rationality*. **Buddhism** and **Catholicism** focus on human interactions, particularly family and friendship. They are functional to a *social rationality*.

The combination of law and religion produces a parallel arrangement of cultural *hyper cultures* with opposing polarity: one, the cultures of *achievement, productivity, and punctuality* linked to the Anglo Saxon law tradition; the other, the cultures of *honor, respect, and tradition* attuned to the Islamic law tradition. In between the two, the *cultures of joy and human interactions* appear at the intersection of the Roman legal system and Catholicism or Buddhism, tilting between both polarities, as Figure 0.6 suggests.

Cultures of honor favor tradition, hierarchy, loyalty, discipline, and obedience; they are oriented toward political interaction, a flexible time schedule, putting family duties over job duties, and de-emphasizing savings because the future seems so uncertain. *Cultures of achievement* are oriented toward productivity and achieving goals; they emphasize hard work and punctuality, a job well done *and* on time, savings and frugality, deferred gratification, putting job duties before family duties, an early-to-bed, early-to-rise routine—in other words, *economic life. Cultures of joy* embrace values somewhere between the two, being oriented toward social interaction, emphasizing family and friends and staying late in bed to enjoy the moment when possible—in other words, *social life*. All three types of cultures are *ideal types* in the Weberian sense; that is, they are abstract constructions that do not correspond exactly to any real country, but are hypothetical approximations that try to capture the essence displayed by real countries.

Much like the Anglo-Saxon (or common law) legal system, Judaism, Confucianism, and Protestantism are functional systems within *cultures of achievement*, while Islam (both a religious and a legal system), Hinduism, and Christian Orthodoxy are functional systems within *cultures of honor*. Catholicism, Buddhism, and the Roman legal system fall somewhere between the two as *cultures of joy*. However, although countries overall can be culturally defined by their historically predominant legal and religious systems, specific regions or pockets of population may fall into a different cultural zone. For instance, while the United States—founded as a Protestant, common law country—has a *culture of achievement* overall, population segments in the Deep South lean toward a *culture of honor*, while the West and East Coasts lean toward a *culture of joy*, because of their historical roots, the origins of their settlers, or their current conditions.

Carrying roots in one culture or another has implications for development, however defined. Hence, *honor* societies generally show higher levels of conformity to authority; *achieving* societies, higher levels of economic performance; and *joy* societies, higher levels of happiness. What is considered development is explored in Parts V and VI of this book.

HOW DID CULTURES BEGIN?

Humans evolved by giving priority to dominance (De Waal, 1982; Wilkinson, 2010, p. 203). War and conquest formed the primary framework for both common men and leaders (Pinker, 2011). The human race lived under the power of *political drivers*, in which dominance came first and wealth followed. I propose naming these **honor-oriented cultures**. This *mood* remained valid from the time of primitive isolated tribes to the rise of the great Ancient Empires (Egypt, Hindus Valley, Persian, Assyrian, Babylonian, China, Greece, Rome, and Arab) made possible by the technological revolution of agriculture.

After a long historical winter (the European Middle Ages), the Renaissance, Reformation, and Enlightenment triggered the industrial revolution. The world began giving priority to wealth. Hence, efficiency, competition, and markets became the primary framework of both common men and leaders. The human race began living under the power of *economic drivers*, in which wealth came first and dominance followed. I propose naming these **achievement-oriented cultures**. That was the *mood* that began developing in the modern empires from Venice to the United States, passing through Spain, Portugal, Holland, and France until reaching its apex in England and finally the United States.

After World War II, in a few countries that had achieved peace as well as political order and wealth, a new awakening began. Material needs had been met in the postindustrial world, hence postmaterialism emerged, with an emphasis on human relations, environmental sustainability, and the expansion of rights. People slowly began sensing the relevance of *social drivers*, in which a balance between the extremes of the previous two cultures prevails, and wealth without dominance follows. I propose naming these **joy-oriented cultures**. That is the *mood* of the Catholic European countries. Many of those joy-oriented elements are present (unintentionally) in the Catholic colonial countries, as well as in the social philosophy of Buddhism (intentionally). Paradoxically, such a mood is also taking root among postmaterialists in Europe, particularly the Nordic countries, due to their developmental path.

This transition from honor to achievement and to joy cultures brings the reflection back to the three-dimensions triangle, where only one of the three can be on the top corner of the triangle, with the other two subordinate at the bottom two corners. Thus, in *honor* cultures the political dimension prevails and the other two (economic and social dimensions) subordinate; in *achievement* cultures the economic dimension crowns at the top; in *joy* cultures, the social dimension is at the top. However, some trade-offs are to be paid. *Honor* cultures may live a more *honorable* life at the expense of material comfort; *achievement* cultures may live more materially plentiful and comfortable lives, but *honorable* living is not a priority. *Joy* cultures share a bit of the former two advantages and disadvantages.

SHAPING CULTURE

How do individuals internalize a shared system of meanings? Chapter 7 is devoted to discussing how, as part of people's natural maturation, they begin the process of absorption and transmission from **parents and families** from around 18–24 months to 4–6 years of age (Kagan, 1962). This is the most formative stage of an individual's axiological infrastructure, built upon the power of observation as well as reward and punishment mechanisms. During this stage, family and gender identity are formed, both of which remain central throughout one's life in normal development. Another important factor in development is whether the child has siblings and where he or she is in the birth order (Kagan, 2010b).

The second formative agent is **education and schools**. This relationship may be *formal*, such as between teachers and students in a school, or *informal*, such as the relationship between a tutor and pupil or the leader and followers in a gang. In either case, *peer pressure* increases these effects and is determinant until around 11–13 years of age. School systems provide many benefits, beginning with literacy. However, in authoritarian societies teaching typically reproduces authoritarian dynamics: obedience, discipline, and rote memorization are emphasized, while questioning and critical thinking are effectively restricted.

The third agent, the **media**, enters soon after school influence weakens, as adolescence starts. Teenagers default to the media through TV, music, and sports. The early beginnings of the power of the media can be traced back to the invention of writing, followed by the invention of the press, radio, TV, and the Internet. Examples of big social changes prompted by the media are the European Lutheran and Calvinist Reformation in the 16th century and the French Enlightenment in the 18th century. Unfortunately, in the battle for wider audiences today, media often exploit the peculiarities, superstitions, and fears of the people they seek to attract.

The fourth agent, **religion,** gains weight as the individual begins to wake up to what it means to live in society, and forms new identities based on his or her religious group, ethnicity, or country. The full effect of religion on the individual appears with the onset of adolescence. Religion is powerful because it acts not just directly on the individual, but also indirectly, as the institutional root and background as well as axiological frame for the other five agents of cultural transmission.

The fifth agent, **leadership** (political, business, intellectual, or social) is also powerful. If we fast-forward another 8 or 10 years and think about starting one's first job or going to college, we begin to recognize patterns of influence similar to those that operate within the family or circle of friends. For young adults, starting around 15–17 years of age, institutional life begins to make itself felt through the conduct of people and leaders in their lives who, little by little, set a course influenced by decisions, policies, norms, and institutions. Once again, that which leaders value and believe powerfully influences the ways in which the individual, the group, and the community behave. Local, state, and national politics, as the highest level of collective action, take place in a manner very similar to that described here. A leader of a group, a city, a region, an industry, or a country has the ability to introduce or impose change in his or her environment. However, those changes are typically ephemeral and only exceptionally do they extend beyond the leader's term in office or outside his or her geography. Lasting legacies are scarce, although there are some: Lincoln in the United States, the Meiji restoration in Japan, Ataturk in Turkey, Gandhi in India, Lee Kuan Yew in Singapore, and Mandela in South Africa are among the most important.

Finally the sixth agent of change, the **law**, is also very powerful. As one digs deeper into the differences between legal systems, one comes to understand the three main systems used in the world today: Anglo-Saxon common law, Roman civil law, and Islamic law. Each of these traditions has a different impact on the development of the countries that adopt them. The more rigid and dogmatic the legal system, the more difficult it is for a country to develop; the more flexible and pragmatic, the easier.

It is through all these mechanisms of incentives and disincentives, punishment and reward, pride and shame that values and beliefs are formed, consolidated, changed, and used to construct identities.

If we set individual development aside and shift the discussion to the collective level, other factors appear. In the formation of a group's *shared system* in primary school, one's neighborhood, or one's peer group, peer pressure plays a huge role as to whether or not one fits in, enjoys support, or is subjected to harassment from others. At the same time, collective group behavior is profoundly influenced by what people collectively value and believe, and the position that each person holds in the group: is he or she on top, at the bottom, or in between? If we keep our focus at the collective level, we see primary school, the neighborhood, and town or city as a whole.

In sum, a group is not a list of individuals, a town or city is not a list of groups, and a country is not a list of cities. Groups, towns, and countries are *systems* of individuals, groups, and cities that influence and interact with each other, creating *cultures* and *subcultures*.

What Is Development and How Is It Measured?

A simple concept of improvement may be expressed by means of very **basic dichotomies**: health is preferable to sickness—as is life to death, prosperity to poverty, liberty to submission (Inglehart, 2004, p. 2). Of course the list may be extended to include, at the very least, the notion that eating is preferable to hunger, justice to injustice, education to ignorance. However, the concepts of *progress* and *development* have evolved in a much more complex way.

For thousands of years, societies were essentially static, lacking any idea of *progress*. It took 150,000 years for the population of the world to increase from a few dozen people to 250 million, and the global population stayed at that level until the 11th century AD (Maddison, 2006, p. 30).

Throughout most of history, the improvement of life's material conditions was very slow—almost imperceptible—and a civilization's *progress* was measured by its access to food. Ample food was critical to the formation of civilizations, as it produced a **demographic explosion**, followed by military and political expansion. This metric was as true for ancient empires as it was for the people of distant islands and remote jungles.

The concept of growth and progress is actually relatively new: it originated with the processes of discovery and expansion in the 16th century, expanded with increasingly international movements of capital and commerce, and became entrenched with the explosion of technological and institutional innovations of the nineteenth century. In fact, up until the 18th century, people generally expected to remain in the same social positions and professional activities as their parents, and they believed that their own children would do likewise. For thousands of years, the level of wealth in all countries was basically the same: $444 (1990 international US dollars) per capita in the year 0 and $435 in AD 1000, with the richest and poorest countries varying only by about 10% (Maddison, 2006, p. 30). Beginning in the 19th century, however, everything changed.

The idea of **progress** started to take on its modern character during the Enlightenment of the 18th century—the age of Adam Smith (1723–1790)—and was further developed by the classical liberals in the 19th century. John Stuart Mill (1806–1873) and Herbert Spencer (1820–1903) believed that scientific progress would spur a rapid modernization of both society and the economy, and that this modernization would lead to a general improvement of material conditions. In the 20th century, however, the two great wars prompted intellectuals to reconsider the notion that progress was linear—after all, new technology was proving to be devastatingly destructive—and to further investigate the complementary concept of decline.

Before the outset of the Great Depression, in 1929 and 1930, the measurement of a country's gross domestic product (GDP) had never been employed in economic analysis. It was not until Simon Kuznets's report to the US Congress in 1934 that the measurement of a country's total annual production became a staple of global financial inquiry. It proved a great advance in world economics.

But researchers quickly realized that the size of the economy represented by the GDP reflected above all the size of the population: in general, the larger the population, the higher the GDP. Introducing *per capita* GDP solved this problem. It is now clear that even GDP per capita does not tell the whole story. While oil-producing countries in the Middle East are ranked very high in terms of per capita GDP, wealth alone does not spark development.

The idea that *progress* was a more or less direct result of economic growth finally began to change after the end of World War II, when the concept of a more balanced economic and political *development* gained favor among social scientists. At the time, much emphasis was given to the idea of the market economy, as well as to the idea of democracy, as a result of sustained and coordinated action on the part of governments and international agencies.

Passage of the **Universal Declaration of Human Rights** helped signal the idea of *development*. The new global economic order emerging from the 1944 Bretton Woods Agreements, as well as the creation shortly thereafter of the United Nations and the International Bank of Reconstruction and Development (predecessor of the current World Bank and the International Monetary Fund), helped establish the atmosphere for human rights, although its *universality* is still challenged today in some countries.

In its 30 articles, the Declaration establishes eight groups of essential rights for all people: (1) life, liberty, and security of person; (2) equality under the law; (3) freedom of thought, association, opinion, conscience, and belief; (4) form part of the government and to elect leaders; (5) work, unionization, equal pay, and rest; (6) a dignified life; (7) medical assistance and social services; and (8) free primary education.

As basic as these rights may seem, the process of negotiation and approval was not without difficulties. The UN General Assembly of December 10, 1948, approved the Declaration with the vote of 48 countries and eight abstentions (Soviet Union, Ukrainian, Byelorussian, Yugoslavia, Poland,

South Africa, Czechoslovakia, and Saudi Arabia).[12] The American Association of Anthropology impugned the very idea of the Declaration from the outset, including accusations of ethnocentrism. The full *universality* of the Declaration is still questioned today in some countries.[13]

Indian economist and Nobel laureate Amartya Sen has greatly refined the measurement of development. His ideas emphasize the three essential dimensions (economics, politics, and society) that show development as a constant process of creating new conditions through the combined effects of population growth and the innovation and dissemination of technology. Population growth instigates new problems and new values that affect parties of political opposition, who in turn introduce new demands within the political sphere (Sen, 1996, p. 156). One of the influential expressions of Sen's ideas today is the UN Human Development Index (HDI), which combines income, education, and health measures. The absence of health and education, Sen argues, curtails freedom.

WHY WERE PROGRESS AND CULTURE DISCREDITED IN THE UNITED STATES?

In academic and political circles in the United States during the last five decades, the discussion of *culture* became toxic—a live grenade. This was in part due to the following:

> The reticence was a legacy of the ugly battles that erupted after Daniel Patrick Moynihan, then an assistant labor secretary in the Johnson administration, introduced the idea of a "culture of poverty" to the public in a startling 1965 report. Although Moynihan didn't coin the phrase (that distinction belongs to the anthropologist Oscar Lewis), his description of the urban black family as caught in an inescapable "tangle of pathology" of unmarried mothers and welfare dependency was seen as attributing self-perpetuating moral deficiencies to black people, as if blaming them for their own misfortune. (Cohen, 2010)

Nonetheless, today the discussion is back on the table. In fact, the journal *Annals of the American Academy of Political and Social Science* dedicated a special issue to the subject, in which it expressly stated that

> [t]he emerging generation of culture scholars is often at pains to distance itself from the earlier one, and for good reason. The earlier scholars were repeatedly accused of *blaming the victims* for their problems, because they seemed to imply that people might cease to be poor if they changed their culture [. . .] Contemporary researchers rarely claim that culture will perpetuate itself for multiple generations regardless of structural changes, and they practically never use the term *pathology*. But the new generation of scholars also conceives of culture in substantially different ways. (Small et al, 2010)

In the 1960s the United States undertook a greater effort to help Latin American countries as an overall regional effort after the Cuban revolution. The Alliance for Progress was inspired by the European success story of the Marshall Plan and was propelled by the worry that the Cuban Revolution might spread throughout the Americas. The hope was that by the 1970s the region would be much further ahead along the road to democratic stability and sustained economic growth. This did not come to pass. Why not?

The idea of *progress* arose out of the French Enlightenment, when illustrious European and American thinkers became enthusiastic concerning the scientific advances of the 16th and 17th centuries. They could glimpse a rapid modernization of the economy and society that would necessarily bring with it an overall improvement. Critical thinkers including Thomas Malthus, Friedrich Nietzsche, Oswald Spengler, Pitrim Sorokin, Karl Popper, and, above all, the two world wars of the 20th century, placed a big question mark at the end of this linear ideal, due to the destructive power of new technologies. The idea of *progress* as a direct result of economic growth began to lose strength and to change into a more comprehensive concept that would take social issues into account: *development*.

Structure of the Book

This book helps to show that Acemoglu and Robinson (2012) are wrong in their book *Why Nations Fail* to discard the importance of both geography and culture, but are brilliantly right in their exposition of extractive and inclusive institutions. This book also demonstrates that the world is not divided into only two cultures, as current academic convention states: individualist and collectivist (Fiske, 1991), or materialist and postmaterialist (Inglehart, 1977), which makes categorization incomplete; nor is the world divided into about 200 cultures (the number of nation-states), which would make the field unmanageable for practical purposes in business, governmental relations, military operations, or international NGO initiatives. Not even dividing the world into eight or nine cultures (according to the number of world religions and philosophies) would make the field more manageable. The book puts forward the idea that the world is divided into three cultures: *honor, achievement,* and *joy,* following the three basic dimensions (political, economic, and social, also mirrored in Bell's ideas) that speed up or slow down development and improve the understanding of cultural differences and help the effectiveness and success of real life operations. It also shows that countries are not culturally monolithic; nor are individuals. Reality is complex, and cultures blend and interweave. Nevertheless, dominant trends as well as regional profiles are identifiable by legal and religious roots. The book reveals that development is not lineal and endless (on the contrary, it is cyclical and full of material limits), and that *progress* and *achievement* are not the universal goals that all societies are pursuing or ought to (Harrison, 2006). This book also discusses the difficult but important need for countries on the international scene to achieve a healthy balance between the lack of self-confidence among some and the overabundance of arrogance among others.

Part I explores values as the building blocks of culture and presents a literature review from a *descriptive* perspective, without entering in the *normative* side of values. It begins with the historical approach and contributions of Tocqueville (1835), Weber (1905), and Dealy (1977). These three authors discuss the contributions of values from different perspectives: Alexis de Tocqueville, after a nine-month trip to the United States in 1831; Max Weber, after studying the differences between German Catholics and Protestants followed by a two-month trip to the United States; and Glen Dealy, after a trip through the United States with a group of graduate Latin American students.

Chapter 2 focuses on Geert Hofstede (1980), Shalom Schwartz (1987), and Ronald Inglehart (1997), the major players in the last quarter century of empirical research on the importance of culture. These three authors began discussing values from different angles and disciplines: the Dutch Hofstede, as an IBM consultant in the mid-1960s from management sciences; Schwartz, an Israeli social psychologist from the Hebrew University of Jerusalem; and Ronald Inglehart, an American political scientist at the University of Michigan and leader since 1990 of the World Values Survey group.

Part II begins by exploring the benefit of building a spatial representation of the three key dimensions (economic, political, and social) on three axes, following Schwartz's theoretical contributions, rather than forcing them into a two-axes chart as the conventional cultural maps are currently represented. The second section of Part II reviews the way in which cultures disseminated around the world, through those laws and religions brought about by the age of colonization, into the three cultural geographies of *honor* (Africa, Islam, and Orthodox countries), *achievement* (Confucian, Jews, and Protestant countries), and *joy* (colonial Catholics). This section illustrates the three cultural clusters with a case-by-case approach through groups of countries: African, Islamic, Orthodox, Confucian, Western, and Catholic. It begins by following the path of the continental migrations and historical forces as they crystallized into the economic, social, political, legal, and religious environment that helps explain how and why countries ended up where they are today. Two polar cultures start emerging from this review: *honor* and *achievement*. Meanwhile, the values of the cultures of *joy* remain somewhere in between the two, as illustrated in the *axiological cube* proposed in this section.

Part III is devoted to the **three key cultures** of honor, achievement, and joy. The chapter reviews the strengths and weaknesses of the key cultures. Strengths among the *cultures of achievement* clearly are punctuality, productivity, use of time, trust, innovation, dissent, autonomy, independence, agency, strong learners, work as a prize, study oriented; but these cultures also show some weaknesses: time obsessed, fast living, guilt obsessed, family distant, enjoyment and socially impaired. Strengths among the *cultures of honor* are time relaxed, relaxed living, family close, enjoyment virtuosi, socially oriented; but they also show some weaknesses: no sense of timing, unpunctual, unproductive, distrustful, no innovation, dependent, no agency, learning adverse, obedient, work as punishment, study adverse. *Cultures of joy* share the strengths and weaknesses of both, but at the same time become social environments of enjoyment.

Selected tables from the 2010 WVS are presented to illustrate the diversity of opinions among countries, as well as among population segments (gender, age, income, education). The main conclusion of that review is that the three cultures (honor, achievement, and joy) pursue different goals (respect for tradition, material success, and enjoyment of human interaction) and obey different rationalities (political, economic, and social). However, a further complexity arises within the cultures of *joy*: the existence of at least three different meanings of joy. The first—the *work hard, play hard* type—is more common among cultures of achievement. Another, *contemplative joy*, is more common among cultures of honor. Finally, prevalent among cultures of joy is a *carefree* type of joy, which remains difficult to understand for cultures of both achievement and honor. In order for mutual understanding to happen, either in business or diplomacy, as well as among individuals in this increasingly globalized world, culture and values need to be brought into the picture.

Part IV is dedicated to the agents and processes of **cultural change**, as well as a way to diagnose axiology. Chapter 7 focuses on six agents of preservation and change: parents and families, teachers and schools, churches and religion, the media, leadership, and law. It discusses the last of these—the law—at some length, since the World Bank study, *Where Is the Wealth of Nations*, argues convincingly that a disproportionately high contribution to wealth comes from the quality of the legal system. In addition, the positive consequences for *business* associated with the flexibility of the Anglo-Saxon law, as opposed to the rigidity of the Roman law of the French branch (different from the Germanic branch), needs to be taken into consideration. The rigidity of the Islamic law, with its detrimental effect on business, is even more pronounced.

Chapter 8 examines how all cultures change along with the changes of the physical and social environments. The change can happen slowly as countries modernize, or sometimes leaders may try to speed it up. Some successful cases of cultural change by political leaders are briefly discussed (the Meiji restoration, Turkey under Ataturk, Singapore under Lee Kuan Yew). The section briefly reviews the slow process of modernization as experienced in Ireland, Spain, and Mexico, as well as one recent attempt to promote an accelerated culture change in Bogotá. Chapter 9 presents an application of the methodology developed at the Cultural Change Institute (CCI) of the Fletcher School, Tufts University, the *Axiological Diagnosis*, to measure the value system of any country, based on the CCI's 25-factor typology and applied to the case of Mexico. It first identifies the values profile of a country, followed by a domestic debate as to what, how, where, and when to act upon strengths and weaknesses (internally defined) in order to arrive at some selected goals (which must also be internally established).

Part V is devoted to **measuring development**. It provides an overview of the evolution of the basic concepts and metrics for ranking countries' progress. This book proposes to move one step forward by adding democracy, gender equality, and income distribution into the equation of *objective* development indicators (ODI). Some Americans will certainly object, as the United States falls from #1 in GDP to #41 in ODI. I also propose creating and using a *subjective* index (SDI), made from *soft* data (i.e., public opinion polling) as a contrast with *objective* indicators made from hard data, in order to gain an additional perspective and a more accurate view of how to help countries move forward.

Part VI deals with the three **drivers of development**: structures, culture, and interaction. It begins with a review of the rationalists' debate. Then it continues with an examination of the *forces of nature* (climate, geography, and demography) and of *human action* (economics, politics, society), including the expansion of empires and colonialism. Next, it discusses the drivers of *culture and ideas*. Finally, it covers the *interaction* of both these sets of drivers in the form of *institutional and technological innovations*.

In sum, development turns out to be a dependent variable of three main forces: material structures, intangible ideas, and their interaction. The impact of values and beliefs—that is, culture—on economic, political, and social structures is of great consequence in the speeding up or slowing down of nations' development.

PART I

Values as the Building Blocks of Culture

LITERATURE REVIEW

Among animals, man is uniquely *dominated by culture*, by influences learned and handed down. Some would say that culture is so important that genes, whether selfish or not, are virtually irrelevant to the understanding of human nature. Others would disagree.

—RICHARD DAWKINS, *THE SELFISH GENE*, P. 3 (MY EMPHASIS)

1

Historical Analysis

Values are the building blocks of cultures. They can be studied from a normative or descriptive perspective. Ethical and philosophical discussions of values as *norms* have been going on since ancient times. Religions and philosophers have produced many normative lists of values that have guided the moral conduct of many civilizations. But this study is not about *normative* values.

The *descriptive approach* to values as incentives is more recent. Analysis linking values to social conduct and its outcomes are clear in the works of Tocqueville (1835), Weber (1905), and Dealy (1977), among others.[1] A deeper *empirical* understanding of values through survey research began in the last quarter of the 20th century with the works of Hofstede (1980), Schwartz (1987) and Inglehart (1997).[2]

Historical Analysis: Alexis de Tocqueville, Max Weber, and Glen Dealy

ALEXIS DE TOCQUEVILLE (1805–1859)

Tocqueville was a very young Frenchman when he traveled to the United States as an official envoy with a colleague and close friend to examine prisons and penitentiaries. They traveled widely,[3] and he took extensive notes about his observations and reflections. At that time the United States was in the process of building its new institutions, barely 50 years after independence. Despite Tocqueville's youth (25 years old), his insights were very sharp, in great part due to the significant cultural contrasts he observed as an aristocrat in the highly egalitarian new nation, and as a Catholic in a country deeply influenced by the Protestant ethic.

Tocqueville's outlook was framed by the very unstable political events surrounding his family and personal life. France had gone through the 1789 Enlightenment-inspired revolution against the absolute monarchy of the *ancien régime*. However, the 10-month terror of 1793–1794 during the First Republic nearly killed Tocqueville's parents (his father, an officer of King Louis XVI's guard, was spared the death penalty only by the fall of Robespierre in 1794) and was followed by 15 years of Napoleon's rule (1800–1815), which left a lasting impression on his family, who left France for exile in England. The Bourbon restoration of 1815–1830 as a hereditary constitutional monarchy brought back by the European powers was followed by the July Revolution (1830) handing power to the House of Orléans as a liberal (based on popular vote) constitutional monarchy—all of which highlighted the political hesitations of France.

It was within this historical context that Tocqueville began his political career in 1830. But because he was unhappy with the July Revolution, he sought the trip to the United States. Tocqueville was an avid traveler and prolific writer. He wrote *Democracy in America* framed by the contradiction of his aristocratic background and his democratic political outlook. On his return, he continued as an active politician while he published his book.

The world in 1830 was at the apex of the industrial revolution led by England, and Europe held center stage in world power, due to the fact that Spain and Portugal had lost most of their colonies. Europe continued under the rule of diverse monarchies engaged in constant warfare. Hence, the American experiment, which transferred the origin of legitimate political power from God or a royal lineage to the common people, a revival of the Hellenic ideal, was a worthy subject for an ambitious politician to observe on a trip. After all, the Americans had borrowed those ideas from the European Enlightenment.

The American and the French revolutions had taken place almost simultaneously (13 years apart), historically speaking. However, by 1830 the United States had elected seven presidents in 11 free elections, while France had not been able to advance its path toward *freedom*. Tocqueville understood the difficulties of changing a political, economic, and social order that had been developing in Europe for 13 centuries, since the collapse of the Roman Empire. But he thought it would be just a matter of patience, and the United States could show what to expect from the future.

He observed that the American colonies had been relatively empty lands populated by hard-working families fleeing from religious persecution in Europe. The people shared very similar material conditions; hence they were very egalitarian. They sought an opportunity to get a piece of land to sustain their families and prosper. Bound together by the strong beliefs of a powerful axiology based in a variety of Protestant denominations, they were forced to accept their diversity and keep religion out of government. It was just natural for Americans to develop traditions and laws that could help them achieve their dreams. Thus Tocqueville stated

> I have come to the conclusion that all the causes tending to maintain a democratic republic in the United States fall into three categories: The first is the peculiar and accidental situation in which Providence has placed the Americans. Their laws are the second. Their habits and *mores* are the third [my emphasis]. (Tocqueville, 1835 [1988], p. 277)

By *mores*,[4] he was referring to the values upon which American culture had been built. Tocqueville also understood that South America belonged to a very different category and would develop radically opposite *mores* (p. 280). Just a few years after the democratic experiment began in the United States, the newly independent countries of Latin America adopted it at the beginning of the 19th century. This was an important step forward for democracy and the presidential federal systems.

Tocqueville wrote *Democracy in America* not only as a foreigner, which already gave his account a feeling of neutrality and detachment, but also as a Frenchman—with all the aura associated with being a son of the French Revolution and a successor of great thinkers of the *Enlightenment.*

Following along the same thread of values, a trip to Algeria in 1837 led him to read the Koran as a way to understand the Algeria–France conflict. Tocqueville reached the conclusion that values (*mores*) were the most important of the three elements he had observed in America, as is confirmed when he stated that

> I am convinced that the luckiest of geographical circumstances and the best of laws cannot maintain a constitution in despite of *mores*, whereas the latter can turn even the most unfavorable circumstances and the worst laws to advantage. The importance of *mores* is a universal truth to which study and experience continually bring us back. I find it occupies the central position in my thoughts; all my ideas come back to it in the end. [my emphasis] (Tocqueville, 1835 [1988], p. 308).

Tocqueville's contribution to democracy was crucial, because it strongly reinforced and disseminated the American model among many countries. Today there are roughly as many American-inspired presidential systems in the world as there are UK-inspired parliamentary systems, as Table 1.1 shows.

However, Tocqueville clearly warned against exporting the American model to other nations:

> Those who, after having read this book, should imagine that my intention in writing it was to propose the laws and customs of the Anglo-Americans for the imitation of all democratic communities would make a great mistake; they must have paid more attention to the form than to the substance of my

TABLE 1.1
Parliamentary and Presidential Systems*

	Parliamentary	Presidential	Other**
Europe	35	8	4
Americas and the Caribbean	12	22	1
Asia	11	14	7
Pacific	11	1	2
Africa	9	40	6
Middle East	4	4	8
Total	81	89	29

* Data are from http://en.wikipedia.org/wiki/List_of_countries_by_system_of_government, accessed February 26, 2015.

** "Other" includes active and absolute monarchies, theocracies, transitional governments, military juntas, and single-political movement states.

thought. My aim has been to show, by the example of America, that laws, and especially customs, may allow a democratic people to remain free. But I am very far from thinking that we ought to follow the example of the American democracy and copy the means that it has employed to attain this end; for I am well aware of the influence which the nature of a country and its political antecedents exercise upon its political constitution. (Tocqueville, 1835 [1988], p. 315)

And Tocqueville was right. The historical, physical, demographic, and cultural conditions upon which democracy had developed in the United States were not practically replicable anywhere in the world, with the possible exceptions of the main largest British colonies: Canada, Australia, and New Zealand. This is particularly true of the individualistic autonomy and deep Protestantism of the 17th- and 18th-century *frontier* Americans (Foa, 2013, p. 5)—that is, their *mores*. Hence, the world today is waiting for one *non-individualistic* country[5] to successfully develop an open, participatory, inclusive political system that finds a way to encourage and excite its population into a better and fairer system than the ones currently available.

MAX WEBER (1864–1920)

Karl Emil Maximilian (Max) Weber was the most important social scientist of the 20th century, according to the *Stanford Encyclopedia of Philosophy*. From a prosperous Protestant family, he was a bright German student with very rigorous schooling who developed a strong love for learning. He thus landed a full professorship at the very young age of 30 and was promoted two years later to a chair in economics at the prestigious University of Heidelberg. However, in 1897, after three years of a successful career, he suffered a severe nervous breakdown that forced him to withdraw from teaching in 1903.

The text for which he is best known today is *The Protestant Ethic and the Spirit of Capitalism*, about the influence of religious values on human action. He wrote it in three periods: the first, during the summer of 1903 as he began to recover his health; the second, after a two-month trip to the United States in the autumn of 1904 that deeply affected his outlook; and the third, a deep revision of the essay in 1919. Since its first publication in 1905 the book has provoked strong controversy and criticism, and has influenced many scholars.

Although *The Protestant Ethic* (PE) is the widest read of Weber's works, his *magnum opus* is *Economy and Society* (1922), published by his widow. There we find his many contributions to social, economic, and political thinking, which are essential for a better understanding of the PE. Particularly relevant are his propositions on the three rationales of social action (tradition/norms, goals, and emotion);[6] the concept of *ideal types* (a hypothetical or abstract prototype used to describe the key features of a phenomenon); the sources of legitimacy (charisma, tradition, law); bureaucracy as an institution that encapsulates culture; the meta-theory on the ascendance of the West; and the anti-Marxist explanation of capitalism. In addition to *Economy and Society*, four other books are essential to properly understand the PE: his *Sociology of Religion* (1922 [1993]), *Ancient Judaism* (1917 [1952]), *The Religion of India* (1917 [1958]), and *The Religion of China* (1917 [1968]).

Weber began analyzing occupational statistics for the state of Baden in 1897, and in the PE he noted a phenomenon that saw lively debate among Catholics: "Business leaders and owners of capital, as well as the skilled higher strata of the labor force, and specially the higher technical or commercially trained staff of modern enterprises tend to be predominantly *Protestant*" (Weber, 1905 [2002], p. 1).

He referred to some aspects of both Catholics (*punishing heretics, but treating sinners gently*) and Protestants (*the very opposite of the enjoyment of life*) that they used to criticize each other. He then began to define the concept of the *spirit of capitalism*, quoting Benjamin Franklin's moral precepts extensively.[7]

The first part of the PE is full of Weber's criticisms of Marx's central concepts. He accused him of a "naïve historical materialism" and rejected the notion that *ideas* come about as a *reflection* or *superstructure* of an economic base (p. 14). He says that "[a] person does not *by nature* want to make more and more money, but simply to live—to live in the manner in which he is accustomed to live, and to earn as much as is necessary for this" (p. 16). Furthermore, he adds: "To speak of [capitalism as] a reflection of the material conditions in the superstructure of ideas would be *sheer nonsense*" [my emphasis] (p. 26).

Weber began developing his idea of capitalism as a process of *rationalization*.[8] He then closes the first part of the PE with Luther's concept of *calling* that inspired the original capitalist—the idea that God has appointed each individual a task in daily life, be it professional, vocational, or voluntary. However, he recognizes that while Protestantism served to *jump-start* capitalism, the original Protestant inspiration had already been lost.

After returning from the US trip, he finished the second part of *The Protestant Ethic*, which is made up of two sections: one, about the religious foundations of inner world asceticism that he found in Calvinism, Pietism, Methodism, and the Baptist movement; and the second, developing further the link between asceticism and capitalism, where he really digs deep into his core ideas, making extensive use of quotes from an outstanding literary representative of the Puritan ethic, Richard Baxter.

Weber quotes Baxter's asceticism and the behaviors Baxter emphasizes as *reprehensible* to highlight the Protestant nuances of the connection between values and capitalism:

> What is really reprehensible is *resting* on one's possessions, *enjoyment* of wealth with its consequence of idleness and the lust of the flesh, and particularly of distraction from striving for a 'holy' life. [. . .] *Wasting time* is therefore the first and most serious of all sins. The span of life is infinitely short and precious, and must be used to secure one's own calling. Loss of time through socializing, idle talk, luxurious living, even more sleep than is required for

health—six to eight hours at the most—is morally absolutely reprehensible. (p. 106)

Weber insists that the rejection of idleness and enjoyment among Puritans is really strong. He relates how "Asceticism turns all its force [...] against one thing in particular: the *uninhibited enjoyment* of life and of the pleasures it has to offer" (p. 112). He also mentions that "Puritans—even the Quakers—were by no means opposed to sports in principle. It did, however, have to serve the *rational* purpose of providing sufficient recreation to maintain physical fitness. [...] *Instinctual* enjoyment of life [...] was quite simply the enemy of rational asceticism" (p. 113).

The bottom line of his analysis is summarized as follows:

[As] Protestant asceticism works with all its force against [...] *enjoyment* of possessions; it discourages *consumption*, especially the consumption of luxuries. Conversely, it has the effect of liberating the *acquisition of wealth* from the inhibitions of traditionalist ethics; it breaks the fetters of striving for gain by not only legalizing it, but [...] seeing it as directly willed by God. (p. 115)

The implication of this kind of hard-working behavior, combined with an asceticism that inhibits consumption, should not be difficult to guess: it is conducive to investment and consequently to enrichment. However, in the original Protestant ethic, enrichment is not the goal, but an unintended consequence.

Given the centrality of Weber's research and ideas to the field of values and culture, it is also important to review some relevant criticisms. One comes from Henryk Grossman (1934 [2006]), who argues that it was legislation that physically forced people from serfdom into wage labor. So capitalism came about largely by force and not by any vocational training. While that was true, it does not explain why the same did not happen in Catholic countries. Rather, it is possible that it was precisely the Protestant ethic that legitimized those actions.

In an empirical analysis, Blum and Dudley (2001) reviewed evidence of falling wages in Catholic cities and rising wages in Protestant cities between 1500 and 1750, during the spread of literacy. These results were inconsistent with most theoretical models of economic growth. Hence, they aimed to test Weber's alternative explanation based on culture. They conclude that

[t]he great leap forward of northwestern Europe does not seem to be explained by the economic behavior of individual adherents to the new Protestant denominations: all other things being equal, urban economic growth seems to have been no more rapid in the north than in the south. However, other things were not equal. There is strong support for an interpretation of Weber's hypothesis in terms of information networks. Protestant cities, but not Catholic cities, with direct access to the Atlantic were able to take advantage of advances in transportation technology that reduced the cost of ocean shipping. Protestant printing centers experienced high growth rates while heavily restricted Catholic printing centers stagnated. Above all, there emerged a hierarchy of specialization among Protestant cities based roughly on distance from London that had no equivalent in Catholic Europe.

Generalized literacy along with a high propensity of Protestants to honor contracts with people they did not know personally seem to have provided the random links that converted regional economies with tenuous ties into a "small world" network. (Blum and Dudley, 2001, p. 27)

On the other hand, Davide Cantoni (2009), using population and economic growth by city size, got opposite results. One observation is that he does not use relative real wage growth, which was Weber's main dependent variable. Cantoni's abstract reads:

Using population figures in a dataset comprising 276 cities in the years 1300–1900, I find no effects of Protestantism on economic growth. The finding is robust to the inclusion of a variety of controls, and does not appear to depend on data selection or small sample size. In addition, Protestantism has no effect when interacted with other likely determinants of economic development. (Cantoni, 2009, abstract)

GLEN DEALY

Although not at the same level of influence and depth as the previous two authors, Glen Dealy looks into the topic in a contemporary setting. He wrote his book, *The Public Man* (1977), as a result of a journey through the United States with his Latin American graduate students. He starts off with this anecdote:

I suffered stress every morning over what could only be termed a clash of cultures. My problem stemmed from the fact that we were traveling by motor coach, and each evening the driver had to be informed as to the appropriate time to pick us up at the motel on the following morning. Departure time varied depending upon the day's schedule. From the first day of the trip we had trouble with this arrangement. Invariably, few students would have appeared by the announced time of departure.

Various remedies were tried such as group discussions of what we would miss if we did not leave at such-and-such time, canceling of some early morning appointments, and my telling the group we needed to depart the motel earlier than we in fact had to leave. All schemes met with extremely relative success. One morning late in the tour and forty-five minutes behind the day's schedule, I asked the roommate of the yet-to-appear and perennial tardy student, "Why can't your friend ---- get up in the morning?" The ensuing conversation went somewhat as follows:

"Oh, he doesn't have any trouble getting up in the morning!" / "Then why isn't he down here?" / "He *wants* to be late." / "You must be kidding me." / "No, as a matter of fact, he gets up earlier than most people. He has been up for over two hours now. He's just waiting." / "Just waiting?" / "Sure. Every morning on this trip he has gotten up before I did. He always gets dressed and then just waits." / "What is he waiting for?" / "For everyone else to come down to the bus. He wants to be last." / "But why would he want to be last?

Doesn't he know everyone else will be waiting for him?" / "Sure he knows. *That is why he comes down late*! The president never enters until his cabinet is assembled." (Dealy, 1977, p. 1)

This behavior, so familiar to any Latin American, was a watershed for the Anglo-Saxon professor. It made him forget his prejudice that *traditional societies* have a *primitive indifference* to the division of the day into hours, minutes, and seconds. In the behavior of the *student-president* he found nothing erratic or random, but rather a carefully calculated understanding of time and space. He observed that the young student invariably arrived one or two minutes after the next to last member of the group.

As a social scientist, he was captivated to find not only the repetition of this behavior, but also a theory that lent congruence and consistency to such behavior. That is what gave rise to his quest for the rationale behind Latin American unpunctuality; *The Public Man* was his answer. What began as an explanation for delay was expanded to cover the Latin American concept of democracy and of capitalism, as well as the difficulty some Anglo Americans have in understanding Latin Americans' worldview.

A personal experience during my stay in London helped me understand that anecdote. For 40 weeks, every time I returned from dropping off my children at school I invariably saw my Mexican best friend, who lived a few blocks from my home, leaving his children at the same school. He was just about always two or three minutes late! I don't know if this has ever happened to the reader, but it shows that in Latin American cultures—as the student tried to explain to Dealy—this kind of behavior is perfectly rational.

One of *The Public Man*'s most important contributions is its search for a causal explanation of a unique Latin American lifestyle that simply does not fit into the Western idea of *backward* in the capitalist continuum.

Dealy questions whether capitalism and democracy are unique modes of existence tied to economic rationality. Instead, he proposes another *lifestyle* that could be labeled a *culture of dignity* (he labels it *Caudillaje*), indigenous to societies that arose in Spain and oriented toward values of status, public power, and display.

Starting from this hypothesis, the essay dives into the torrent of thought initiated by Weber's *Protestant Ethic*, directing itself to analyzing the Catholic ethic. He finds that the Catholic motivation is based on public life, outward, as much as the Protestant's is motivated by private life, inward. This drives the Catholic to seek accumulation of power—not necessarily and strictly political power, but power to be publicly recognized. The Protestant, on the other hand, seeks to accumulate wealth.

Latin American people take great pride in their free time, extroversion, and pleasure, while the Anglo American is proud of work, reinvestment, and frugality. The former desires to have an impact on others and influence them; the latter desires to build his own business. This is why the old adage holds that *prestige is to power what credit is to money*. From this viewpoint, although friends are less tangible than numbers in a bank statement, the *culture of dignity* should be understood in similar terms to capitalism, because friends can be added, accumulated, saved, and spent in much the same way as money.

Although Dealy makes no generic correlation between Catholic, Latin American, and culture of dignity on one side of the ledger and Protestant, Anglo American, and capitalist on the other, it is nonetheless patent in his breakdown. The contrast is of even greater consequence when five values are taken into account, values that are more aspiration than reality. For *cultures of dignity*, the five *public virtues* are leisure, grandeur, generosity, dignity, and manliness—a world apart from those that move the Anglo American of industriousness, humility, frugality, spirit of service, and honesty.

He points out that for citizens of a Protestant-ethic country, it is perhaps difficult to think of **leisure** as a virtue, because all their lives they have been taught the virtue of *activity*. They occupy their free time (vacations, sabbaticals, even retirement) in *productive* activities: mowing the lawn, painting the house, building a boat, taking courses, or reading. In a *culture of dignity*, citizens employ free time for the advancement of their goal of public power: making friends and *aggregating* persons through conversation, partying, or enjoying life. This is why the concept of time has such a distinct connotation in each culture. A *culture of dignity* believes that

> . . . [l]eisure to be useful must be observed by others. The man of public power obviously is a person that cannot be bothered by trifles such as the clock. Therefore, like kings of old, he arrives when he arrives. [. . .] When a person of power makes his grand entrance, his retainers should be waiting and events may only then proceed. (1977, pp. 34–35).

This is why the custom of going to bed late in *culture of dignity* societies is so clear and justifiable—one is spending time with friends—just as in Protestant societies going to bed early means being more productive the next morning. The former has a proclivity toward enjoyment of the here and now, *time is joy*; the latter toward producing here and now, *time is gold*. This rationalization taps into the long-standing belief in colonial Catholic culture that joy ennobles and labor—especially manual labor—degrades.

The second virtue according to Dealy, **grandeur**, may well be best expressed through oratory, that sophisticated form of art cultivated in *cultures of dignity* that has little to do with demonstrating facts or empirical reality, because its purpose is to win others over to the speaker's point of view. Rhetoric elevates the importance of the manner of presentation of ideas above the topic of debate; verbal style takes precedence over content. Dealy comments on an experience he had when he began to give classes in a Latin American country. In the first session he asked his graduate students whether Bolivar's concept of *faction* was clear.

> There was only the slightest of pauses before a young man's hand went up. I recognized him. Whereupon he stood, cleared his throat, squared his shoulders, buttoned his coat, and began a twenty-five minute discourse of

the glories of Bolivar: the profundities of his thought, the factions against which he had fought so gloriously, etc., etc. While it was quite obvious—to me—that he had no idea at all of Bolivar's specific writings, speeches, or ideas on politics, this orator did know what a faction was, he did know who Bolivar was, he did know about the Godos, creoles, and the war with Spain. He therefore put them all together and gave a moving, impassioned call for a return to the ideals of the *Libertador* building up to a *crescendo* with a plea for the freedom of his own *patria* from the demagogues who were ruining it. Students wildly applauded when he finished. Grandeur again triumphed over facts. (p. 44)

I could hardly hold back my laughter when reading this passage, recalling my first day at a 1978 seminar of the London School of Economics' Institute for Latin American Studies in Tavistock Square. If I had not been there, if someone had told it to me, I would be sure that it was the same story, barring the final applause.

It is frequent to find in so many Latin Americans this aversion to admitting ignorance on a subject.

[...] explicit and often wrong answers have become part of the landscape of caudillaje culture. The grandeur of a public man, whether giving directions to a place he's never heard of or discussing international events about which he is largely uninformed, depends upon his providing definite, incontrovertible information. Of course, those who live in caudillaje society are quite aware that much of what is said contains error, bombast, and fiction. Rarely, however, do they challenge such authority directly. To do so, would open a state of war and question the integrity of the speaker. And toward what end? One probably did not listen to him in the first place for information but because of his place and station within the society, or due to the possibility of including the speaker in one's circle of friends. (p. 48)

Culture of dignity's third virtue of **generosity** exists insofar as it is public and serves to accrue the *capital* of friends. When generosity is private, it loses meaning and acquires a religious-like connotation of piety and charity, useless in a climb toward power. This establishes a particularly Latin American outlook on taxation and savings.

Protestants easily confound generosity with waste or squander, because to them it implies the risk of diminishing economic capital, save those gifts or donations that are tax deductible. It also takes on an aspect of fomenting *vices* of sloth and disorder in one's relative or close friend.

A Latin American feels no compunction to abstain from private gratification in order to improve the chances that some John Doe may be better fed, have medical services, or be housed. Paying taxes falls into this category. It is a private matter, imposed by the government, and serves no family or religious purpose. It leads to no public display of generosity, and no one would ever know whether our *hero* honestly pays his or her taxes. Therefore paying them seems senseless.

Savings, so key to the Protestant ethic, operate in a particularly curious fashion in the Catholic ethos. "Save money in private to flash it in public," goes the old maxim. How many families live in miserable homes but drive ostentatious cars? There would appear to be no positive economic motivation toward saving among colonial Catholics; on the contrary, saving appears as a distasteful synonym for selfishness—contradicting the proviso that "the Lord provides." It is widely understood that "if you have money, they ask you for it. If you don't lend, they get mad. If you do, they don't repay and you get mad. And if not, you get sick and spend it all. And if not, they steal it. You're better off without it." Manuel and Paula's scene in the book *Children of Sánchez* is illustrative.

> Once I decided to try to save and I said to Paula, "Sweety, put away this money so that some day we have a little pile." When we had ninety pesos laid away, pum! My father got sick and I have to give all to him for doctors and medicines. It was the only time I had helped him, the only time I had tried to save. I said to Paula, "There you are! Why should we save if someone gets sick and we have to spend it all!" *Sometimes I even think that saving brings on illness.* (Lewis, 1982, p. 171)

Dignity is the fourth quality that Dealy explores, finding it associated with the notion of *rank* so crucial to *cultures of dignity*. He equates it to the Protestant's accumulated capital; hence, loss of dignity is to him what bankruptcy is to the capitalist. No Spanish speaker can overlook the importance that tradition invests in the formal address (*you* and *thou*), titles, politeness, courtesies, and the observance of formalities as expressions of *dignity*.

I have a vivid recollection of having felt my *dignity* insulted a couple of decades ago. I had been conducting the initial political opinion polls in Mexico, and was in talks about donating my databank to an American university. The original cost of those surveys may well have been around a million dollars. I would have felt honored to make the donation—without any financial remuneration—but when the university offered to pay $100 for each of the 40 or 50 surveys, I felt insulted and the process ended.

The fifth and final virtue that encompasses all the others is **manliness**. Manliness provides the framework for the leader–follower, dominator–dominated relationship in which both sides may take comfort in their respective roles. Dealy argues that this is why *cultures of dignity* tend toward physical activities that involve personal skill *visible to others*—team sports among Spanish gentlemen are thus uninteresting.

The Public Man does take note of the change in attitude in recent generations. The modern *cultures of dignity* more and more often turn to appearances to reach the goal of power and demonstrate excellence. Thus grandeur degenerates into *ostentation*, dignity into *posturing* and rigid formalisms, generosity into *mercantilism*, and manliness into *machismo*.

Dealy arrives at his principal conclusion: the Latin American double set of standards, a *double code* of conduct. One is valid for the *intimate* circle of family and close friends, the other applicable to *outside* life.

A fundamental and profound difference established here is between the Anglo American and the Latin American. To the former, ethical values are the same in public and private life; to the latter, they are distinct. We find the extreme case that without a doubt illustrates the Latin American double set of standards, the *double code* of the Mafia. They are accused of great *immorality*, without taking into account that their private life is

> [. . .] generally spotless. They are good fathers, good husbands, good sons; their word is sacred; they fastidiously refrain from having anything to do with spying, prostitution, drugs, or dishonest swindles. They never betray a friend. They are always devoted churchmen, who give large sums to the local parish or to the deserving poor. Many have sisters in convents and brothers in holy orders. (Dealy, p. 72)

The division of public and private extends among Latin Americans into architecture. Home is the internal, safe, reliable, private refuge. The street is falsehood, insecurity, danger, and adventure. Typical colonial houses face the central patio or garden, protected from the view of *strangers* by massive walls. An American house, on the contrary, is constructed in the middle of its land, surrounded by gardens and has very low border fencing, if any, because there is no reason to separate it from the street.

The origin of the Latin American double standard, the *double code,* would appear to lie in the historic process that gave rise to Christianity, which in its early days divided humanity into two groups: public men and sinners on one side, and Christians on the other. Saint Augustine (354–430 AD), the Christian bishop of what is today Algeria, reinforced this vision with his concept of two cities: God's and Man's. With the conversion of Emperor Constantine, Christianity's anti-political ethic took a sharp turn, but the feature of dualism did not subside. Those who wish to enter political life should prepare themselves to adopt the methods, styles, and ends of the City of Man (public morals), while the morality of the City of God (private morals) prevails in the Christian home and church.

This dualism had an additional consequence: unlike the original Protestants, Latin Americans feel no compunction to *Christianize* life outside the home, because they find no incongruence in the existence of two worlds or in the maintenance of two codes. The Protestant ethic demands of the individual a single construct of values for public and private spheres, while the Catholic ethic does not. This is why Anglo Americans engage in public life by putting into practice the same values used in private life, while Latin Americans use a distinct system of values for public life.

Catholicism put into practice a formula that resolved the *sins* that reigned in the City of Man. Because *good works* were insufficient to gain entry into the City of God, indulgences and absolution came in, at first through the recitation of prayer, later by donations to the church. Thereby the central problem of *salvation* for medieval Catholics was mediated and became routine through the Church as an institution. Christianity as a system of values was relegated to second place.

But this is not how it happened in the Protestant Anglo American culture. Splitting humanity into *damned* and *saved* meant that each person had to struggle for *personal salvation* through the daily accumulation of correct actions such as tolerance, humility, frugality, hard work, commitment, spirit of service, and honesty. Proof of salvation was obtained in material success; therefore all efforts were channeled into achieving it. From these diametrically opposite ideals of work are derived the key concepts of dissent and trust.

2

Empirical Analysis

Geert Hofstede, Ronald Inglehart, and Shalom Schwartz are the main contributors to the empirical analysis of values through survey research. They began discussing the field from different angles and disciplines. Geert Hofstede, as a Dutch IBM consultant in the mid-1960s, looked at values from the perspective of management sciences. This led him to publish his influential *Culture's Consequences* in 1980. Shalom Schwartz is an Israeli social psychologist from the Hebrew University of Jerusalem who has published over 200 articles and book chapters of great value. Finally, Ronald Inglehart is an American political science professor at the University of Michigan and leader of the World Values Survey group, who has contributed the *World Cultural Map* and the theoretical and empirical foundations behind it.

In Hofstede's view, culture exists *inside* people, as what he called *software of the mind*. For Schwartz, conversely, culture exists *outside* one's mental space and is measurable through its manifestations: children's stories, proverbs, film, literature, customs, and the like. While Hofstede proposes that the values of individuals might be aligned and analyzed along four separate axes or dimensions (which he later increased to six), Inglehart proposes two axes, and Schwartz proposes three.

And yet despite these separate outlooks—not to mention different languages, methods, and approaches—the works of all have refined and advanced the field. Even more so, as one follows the unfolding of these three authors' thinking, one can trace the mutual influence of their ideas on each other's work. A common thread among them is the intensive use of worldwide survey research to build their empirical findings. All agree that the world can be viewed in terms of distinct and broadly defined cultural constructs. They also all have in common a search for the key *dimensions* or *value axes* around which cultures spin. They are thus the founders of *cultural axiology*.[1]

Geert Hofstede: Four Axes

In the mid-1960s, IBM was the world's leading company, with offices in nearly every country and some 200,000 employees. Its leaders emphasized standardized training for all personnel, and they expected that such training would result in standardized behaviors and performances.

IBM enlisted the services of Geert Hofstede to investigate whether standard behavior was actually the case. Hofstede analyzed 88,000 interviews that IBM had collected with their staffers in 72 countries between 1967 and 1973. He found that despite receiving exactly the same training, the professional behavior of employees in different countries was far from uniform, and that these differences were ultimately explained by *culture*. His findings were published in his 1980 book, *Culture's Consequences*—perhaps the most influential book in the field of organizational culture. A second and completely revised edition was published in 2001, incorporating Schwartz's and Inglehart's valuable contributions.

Through a statistical analysis of the IBM data, Hofstede originally identified *four axes* along which cultures of different countries—and therefore behavioral differences—might be classified: power distance, uncertainty avoidance, individualism–collectivism, and masculinity–femininity. (Later research from Hofstede's colleagues and followers added two additional axes: *long-term orientation* (LTO) from Michael Bond's Chinese study in 1991, and *indulgence versus restraint* from Michael Minkov's study in 2010. (I briefly refer below to the four original axes only.)

Hofstede speaks of the *software of the mind*, a concept he developed from his empirical research in values. He believes that *values are not universally constant*, but rather are mediated by a nation's cultural unity; they are the sum of history, language, law, religion, and other factors expressed in the structure of institutions. If cultures are symphonies, values are the musical notes. In other words, it is his view that natural and human forces generate social norms, which in turn create external influences that affect the structure and functionality of familial, educational, social, political, economic, and religious institutions. These institutions bring about new standards and reinforce existing norms in a cycle of permanent interaction (Hofstede, 2001, p. 12).

AXIS ONE: POWER DISTANCE

The first axis (or dimension, in his terminology) derived from the IBM study is that of power distance, which is linked to the human domination impulse (2001, p. 79). This is an impulse whose implications are enormous. For example, in hierarchical countries—those characterized by a significant power distance—families emphasize obedience, hard work, loving and respecting one's parents, and supporting those parents in old age. In egalitarian countries, however—those with a relatively small power distance—families accentuate the opposite behaviors. Such differences are effectively repeated in schools, in work, in politics, in religion—indeed, everywhere (pp. 107, 116).

By analyzing a sample of 53 countries and ordering them from greatest to least power distance, Hofstede found that Malaysia had the greatest, with a power distance of 104. Next were Guatemala and Panama (95), the Philippines (94), and Mexico and Venezuela (81). On the opposite side of the spectrum, Austria with

TABLE 2.1

Power Distance Index (PDI)

Rank	Country	Score	Rank	Country	Score
1	Malaysia	104	29/30	Iran	58
2/3	Guatemala	95	29/30	Taiwan	58
2/3	Panama	95	31	Spain	57
4	Philippines	94	32	Pakistan	55
5/6	Mexico	81	33	Japan	54
5/6	Venezuela	81	34	Italy	50
7	Arab countries	80	35/36	Argentina	49
8/9	Ecuador	78	35/36	South Africa	49
8/9	Indonesia	78	37	Jamaica	45
10/11	India	77	38	United States	40
10/11	West Africa	77	39	Canada	39
12	Yugoslavia	76	40	Netherlands	38
13	Singapore	74	41	Australia	36
14	Brazil	69	42/44	Costa Rica	35
15/16	France	68	42/44	Germany (F.R.)	35
15/16	Hong Kong	68	42/44	Great Britain	35
17	Colombia	67	45	Switzerland	34
18/19	El Salvador	66	46	Finland	33
18/19	Turkey	66	47/48	Norway	31
20	Belgium	65	47/48	Sweden	31
21/23	East Africa	64	49	Ireland	28
21/23	Peru	64	50	New Zealand	22
21/23	Thailand	64	51	Denmark	18
24/25	Chile	63	52	Israel	13
24/25	Portugal	63	53	Austria	11
26	Uruguay	61			
27/28	Greece	60	Mean		57
27/28	South Korea	60	Standard deviation		22

Source: Hofstede (2001), p. 87.

11 points had the smallest power distance, followed by Israel (13), Denmark (18), New Zealand (22), and Ireland (28). The average power distance of these countries was 57, as shown in Table 2.1.

AXIS TWO: UNCERTAINTY AVOIDANCE

This axis is concerned with how societies manage anxiety about the future, and the resulting index measures the relative tolerance for ambiguity. Hofstede describes it as follows:

> A basic fact of life is that time goes only one-way. We are caught in a present that is just an infinitesimal borderline between the past and the future. We

have to live with a future that moves away as fast as we try to approach it, but onto which we project our present hopes and fears. In other words, we are living with an uncertainty of which we are conscious. (pp. 145–146).

He refers to Eric Fromm (1965), suggesting that societies with a low tolerance for the anxieties that freedom creates gave rise to fascism and Nazism due to the need to *escape from freedom*. Totalitarian ideologies try to avoid uncertainty.

Table 2.2 shows the same 53 countries as before, this time ordered from the most *intolerant* of uncertainty (Greece, with a score of 112) to the most *tolerant* of uncertainty (Singapore, with 8).

TABLE 2.2
Uncertainity Avoidance Index (UAI)

Rank	Country	Score	Rank	Country	Score
1	Greece	112	29	Germany (F.R.)	65
2	Portugal	104	30	Thailand	64
3	Guatemala	101	31/32	Iran	59
4	Uruguay	100	31/32	Finland	59
5/6	Belgium	94	33	Switzerland	58
5/6	El Salvador	94	34	West Africa	54
7	Japan	92	35	Netherlands	53
8	Yugoslavia	88	36	East Africa	52
9	Peru	87	37	Australia	51
10/15	Spain	86	38	Norway	50
10/15	Argentina	86	39/40	South Africa	49
10/15	Panama	86	39/40	New Zealand	49
10/15	France	86	41/42	Indonesia	48
10/15	Chile	86	41/42	Canada	48
10/15	Costa Rica	86	43	United States	46
16/17	Turkey	85	44	Philippines	44
16/17	South Korea	85	45	India	40
18	Mexico	82	46	Malaysia	36
19	Israel	81	47/48	Great Britain	35
20	Colombia	80	47/48	Ireland	35
21/22	Venezuela	76	49/50	Hong Kong	29
21/22	Brazil	76	49/50	Sweden	29
23	Italy	75	51	Denmark	23
24/25	Pakistan	70	52	Jamaica	13
24/25	Austria	70	53	Singapore	8
26	Taiwan	69			
27	Arab countries	68	Mean of 53		65
28	Ecuador	67	Standard deviation of 53		24

Source: Hofstede (2001), p. 151.

AXIS THREE: INDIVIDUALISM VERSUS COLLECTIVISM

The third axis, individualism and collectivism, describes the relationship between the individual and the community—a relationship that is linked to the gregarious impulse (p. 209). This impulse largely defines identity and our sense of trust or distrust. Moreover, it profoundly affects a wide variety of human behavior. For example, in individualist cultures, families are typically nuclear, children are independent, and family ties are relatively weak and rare. In collectivist cultures, however, families tend to be extended, children are much less independent, and ties are strong and frequent. In terms of personality characteristics, the individualist cultures emphasize individuality, extroversion, independence, confrontation, leadership, shared expressions of happiness, and rapid action, while collectivist cultures promote group exchanges, introversion, membership, harmony, cooperation, shared expressions of sadness, and deliberate action (Hofstede, 2001, p. 236).

In the individualism index, which ranks the same 53 countries in order from greatest amount of individualism to the least, the United States holds first place with a score of 91 points. Australia (90), Great Britain (89), Canada (80), and the Netherlands (80) are the next highest, while at the other end of the spectrum are the collectivist countries: Guatemala, Ecuador, Panama, Venezuela, and Colombia, whose scores range from 6 points to 13. As noted in Table 2.3, the average score in this study is 43 points.

It is worth noting that collectivist nations are typically those with greater power distance scores, which is to say that they are culturally authoritarian. Individualist countries, on the other hand, tend to be those with small power distance scores, suggestive of a more culturally egalitarian nature.

AXIS FOUR: MASCULINITY VERSUS FEMININITY

Hofstede's fourth axis ranges between notions of masculinity and femininity. We might also think of this scale as extending from the proactive to the reactive, or from domination to harmony. Additionally, this axis shows key differences in home, school, work, and public life, and emphasizes stereotypical gender differences.

In masculine cultures, fathers are responsible for facts and mothers for feelings; fathers decide the size of the family; children are discouraged from crying; and horseplay is solely the province of boys, who receive more attention than girls. In feminine cultures, none of these conditions exists (Hofstede, 2001, p. 306). In masculine cultures, one lives to work; in feminine cultures, one works to live. In masculine cultures, a boss gives orders and must be determined, aggressive, and resolute; in feminine cultures, a manager is an employee of equal stature and must be intuitive, emotional, and eager for consensus. Masculine cultures believe men to be better managers, while feminine cultures consider members of either sex equally capable of effective management (p. 318). In politics, masculine countries resolve international conflicts with the use of force, economic growth

TABLE 2.3
Individualism versus Collectivism Index (IDV)

Rank	Country	Score	Rank	Country	Score
1	United States	91	29	Uruguay	36
2	Australia	90	30	Greece	35
3	Great Britain	89	31	Philippines	32
4/5	Canada	80	32	Mexico	30
4/5	Netherlands	80	33/35	Yugoslavia	27
6	New Zealand	79	33/35	Portugal	27
7	Italy	76	33/35	East Africa	27
8	Belgium	75	36	Malaysia	26
9	Denmark	74	37	Hong Kong	25
10/11	Sweden	71	38	Chile	23
10/11	France	71	39/41	Singapore	20
12	Ireland	70	39/41	Thailand	20
13	Norway	69	39/41	West Africa	20
14	Switzerland	68	42	El Salvador	19
15	Germany (F.R.)	67	43	South Korea	18
16	South Africa	65	44	Taiwan	17
17	Finland	63	45	Peru	16
18	Austria	55	46	Costa Rica	15
19	Israel	54	47/48	Pakistan	14
20	Spain	51	47/48	Indonesia	14
21	India	48	49	Colombia	13
22/23	Japan	46	50	Venezuela	12
22/23	Argentina	46	51	Panama	11
24	Iran	41	52	Ecuador	8
25	Jamaica	39	53	Guatemala	6
26/27	Brazil	38			
26/27	Arab countries	38	Mean		43
28	Turkey	37	Standard deviation		25

Source: Hofstede (2001), p. 215.

takes priority over almost anything else, and few women are elected to office. In feminine countries, the reverse is true: negotiation and compromise resolve conflicts, preserving the environment takes priority, and men and women are elected in more equal numbers (p. 323).

By arranging the 53 surveyed countries in order from greatest to least in terms of masculinity, we see that Japan now has the top spot (95 points) followed by Austria (79), Venezuela (73), Italy (70), and Switzerland (70). On the opposite end of the spectrum are feminine Sweden (5 points), Norway (8), the Netherlands (14), Denmark (16), and Costa Rica (21). The average score among the surveyed countries is 49 points, as illustrated in Table 2.4.

TABLE 2.4
Masculinity versus Feminity Index (MAS)

Rank	Country	Score	Rank	Country	Score
1	Japan	95	29	Israel	47
2	Austria	79	30/31	Indonesia	46
3	Venezuela	73	30/31	West Africa	46
4/5	Italy	70	32/33	Turkey	45
4/5	Switzerland	70	32/33	Taiwan	45
6	Mexico	69	34	Panama	44
7/8	Ireland	68	35/36	Iran	43
7/8	Jamaica	68	35/36	France	43
9/10	Great Britain	66	37/38	Spain	42
9/10	Germany	66	37/38	Peru	42
11/12	Philippines	64	39	East Africa	41
11/12	Colombia	64	40	El Salvador	40
13/14	South Africa	66	41	South Korea	39
13/14	Ecuador	63	42	Uruguay	38
15	United States	62	43	Guatemala	37
16	Australia	61	44	Thailand	34
17	New Zealand	58	45	Portugal	31
18/19	Greece	57	46	Chile	28
18/19	Hong Kong	57	47	Finland	26
20/21	Argentina	56	48/49	Yugoslavia	21
20/21	India	56	48/49	Costa Rica	21
22	Belgium	54	50	Denmark	16
23	Arab countries	53	51	Netherlands	14
24	Canada	52	52	Norway	8
25/26	Malaysia	50	53	Sweden	5
25/26	Pakistan	50			
27	Brazil	49	Mean		49
28	Singapore	48	Standard deviation		18

Source: Hofstede (2001), p. 286.

Ronald Inglehart: Two Axes

In the early 1970s, Ronald Inglehart began to study the change in human values through public opinion surveys from the Eurobarometer.[2] Of special importance to this discussion are the theories relating to materialistic and post-materialistic values that he developed, as well as the connection he discovered between these values and a country's economic situation (Inglehart, 1971).

As Figures 2.1 and 2.2 show, being a member of a particular generation has serious consequences. The economic situation of the years in which one is born dictates whether one will be more or less materialistic in later life: if the personal or family economy is weak during a person's preadolescent period, his or

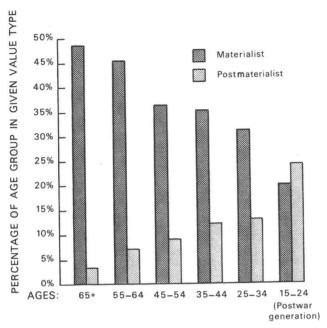

FIGURE 2.1 Materialism–postmaterialism in Europe by age

Republished with permission of Princeton University Press, from *Culture Shift in Advanced Industrial Society,* Ronald Inglehart, 1990, p. 76; permission conveyed through Copyright Clearance Center, Inc.

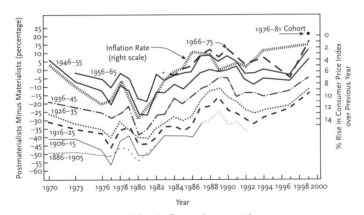

FIGURE 2.2 Materialism–postmaterialism in Europe by generation

Reprinted from *Modernization, Cultural Change, and Democracy,* Ronald Inglehart and Christian Welzel, 2005, p. 101. Reprinted with the permission of Cambridge University Press.

her daily preoccupations are likely to center on material things; however, if the economic situation is robust during that time, a person is more likely to be preoccupied by postmaterial concerns.

The binomial concept of materialism–postmaterialism based on Maslow's hierarchy of needs is revealed as powerful.

The shift from materialist to postmaterialist priorities [is] a shift from giving top priorities to economic and physical security, to self-expression and the quality of life [. . .] Postmaterialists are economically more secure than materialists, but much more sensitive to environmental risks. Individual security increases empathy, making people more aware of long-term risks. (Inglehart and Welzel, 2005, p. 33)

The interaction between the state of the economy (a structural feature) and the states of mind of individuals (a feature belonging to the world of ideas) is expressed in a variation of the materialist–postmaterialist attitude. Inglehart theorized, following Daniel Bell, that the explanation of changes in a country's public values might be the normal result of the transition from an agrarian society to an industrial (and, eventually, postindustrial) society. If the dominant material conditions are altered, that alteration will cause people to modify, however subconsciously, their own materialistic and postmaterialistic values.

According to Inglehart, two factors explain these changes:

1. *A scarcity hypothesis* [. . .] under conditions of scarcity, people give top priority to materialistic goals, whereas under conditions of prosperity, they become more likely to emphasize postmaterialistic goals;

2. *A socialization hypothesis* [. . .] one's basic values reflect the conditions that prevailed during one's preadult years [. . .] the cultural heritage is not easily dispelled, but if is inconsistent with one's firsthand experience, it can gradually erode. (Inglehart and Welzel, 2005, pp. 97–98)

In other words, there is clearly a translation or transmission that happens in the materialism–postmaterialism dimension: there is a connection between what happens in economic life and the interpretations and ideas that develop in the minds of individuals. As Figure 2.2 shows, Inglehart found that the values of European societies were oscillating between those two extremes.

This postmaterialistic effect of postindustrial society verified one of the hypotheses that were previously put forward by Daniel Bell (1973[1999], pp. xiv–xvii), but more important is the demonstration that a person's materialistic–postmaterialistic attitude fluctuates in accordance with the behavior of his or her country's economy, measured by its rate of inflation.

In Figure 2.2 we also see that as the rate of inflation decreases (inverted scale of the thick line in the graph), the postmaterial concerns of *all* generations increase. Therefore, it is not merely that young people skew to the postmaterialist side because they are inherently *romantic*, or that increasing age makes someone more of a *realist* and thus more likely to favor materialist concerns; it is that *all* generations become increasingly postmaterialist.

The materialist–postmaterialist dimension allowed the social sciences to navigate by a one-dimensional bipolar scale; it made it possible to observe how individuals and nations alike changed in response not only to economic shifts, but generational shifts as well.

Inglehart's first book, *The Silent Revolution* (1977), included a major contribution to the field: the analysis of that first materialist–postmaterialist dimension. When he published his second book, *Culture Shift in Advanced Industrial Society*, in 1990, Inglehart had advanced to more expansive and profound explorations of that same materialist–postmaterialist dimension: specifically, he analyzed how different generations have been affected (a pursuit known as *cohort analysis*) and how specific decades have been shaped (known as *periodization analysis*). This work expanded the discussion to include the impact of materialist and postmaterialist values on distinct regions and on subjects including religion, politics, trust, well-being, gender, democracy, security, and the environment.

After 1993, Inglehart began to deepen the exploratory bi-dimensional line of inquiry that I mentioned earlier. This bi-dimensional approach led him to formulate two more complex and robust factorial axes whose significant explanatory power stemmed from statistical analyses of data accumulated in the World Values Surveys of 1980, 1990, and 1995, as shown in Figure 2.3.

The vertical axis—which ranges from traditional values to secular-rational values—represents a *sociopolitical* continuum that may be profoundly affected by a country's religious and legal roots. In contrast, the horizontal, or economic, axis spans from values of survival to well-being or self-expression. The scores each value gets along those two axes are plotted as shown in Figure 2.3.

Thanks to these axes, we saw for the first time nine clusters of countries grouped according to religious origin. Inglehart's map also confirmed the cultural zones that Samuel Huntington proposed in 1993. These two axes allowed him to plot countries and values on a cartographic plane defined by one vertical *sociopolitical* axis and one horizontal *economic* axis. This map was first published in 1997 (Inglehart and Carballo, 1997, p. 43) and has since become known as the *World Cultural Map*, shown as Figure 2.4 (2008 update). A country's location on the *World Cultural Map* derives from the score it receives along the same two axes formed by the cultural values, as shown in Figure 2.3.

Various aspects stand out on these maps. First, countries are grouped in clusters according to their legal, religious and historical roots: (1) European Protestantism; (2) English Protestantism; (3) European Catholicism; (4) colonial Catholicism (Latin America and the Philippines); (5) Africa; (6) Islamic; (7) South Asia; (8) Orthodox ex-communists; and (9) Confucian Asia.

Second, at the highest level of economic development (the upper-right quadrant) there is the greatest presence of secular-rational values. However, with the exception of Ireland, the United States stands as the most traditional country ("traditional" in this case indicating a strong weight placed on religious beliefs in society) among those of high economic development. China (including Taiwan and Hong Kong), on the other hand, holds the opposite location to the United States on the map: less economic development, but less traditional.

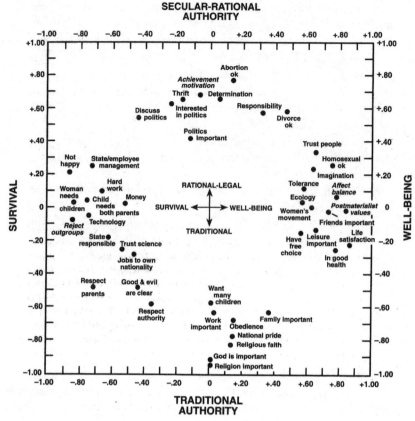

FIGURE 2.3 World Cultural Map, 2000, values

Republished with permission of Princeton University Press, from *Modernization and Postmodernization: Cultural, Economic, and Political Change in 43 Societies,* Ronald Inglehart, 1997, p. 82; permission conveyed through Copyright Clearance Center, Inc.

Third, the proximity of East and West Germans (shown on Figure 2.5) in the upper-right quadrant, even after four decades of separation by communism, testifies to the immense sweep and profound endurance of cultural values. Similarly, we will see in the next section the large *cultural distance* Schwartz found between Israeli Jews and Israeli Arabs and between French-speaking and English-speaking Canadians.

Since 1993 and the advent of my early *trust-autonomy* map (see Figure 0.1)— and even more since Inglehart's advances of 1997—the *cultural map* has been a useful and innovative tool in the social sciences, enabling researchers to see graphically the clustering of countries with common traits and patterns. What began as a mere sketch has turned into a dynamic, multidimensional photograph, a film in perpetual motion. It has become possible not only to verify that cultures do indeed change, but also to confirm empirically the direction of that change.

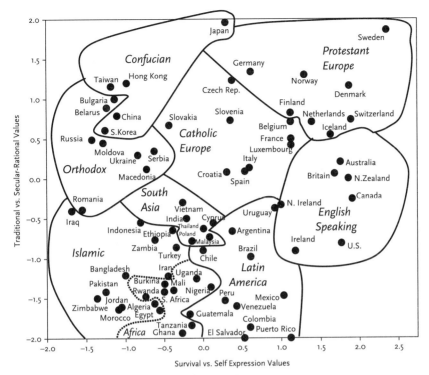

FIGURE 2.4 *World Cultural Map*, 2005–2008, countries

Inglehart, Basáñez, et al. (2010), p. 10.

The analysis of the dynamic expressed by Figure 2.5 is fascinating. In pausing to consider it for a moment, we can clearly see that the movement of the world in these dimensions is dictated by *secularization* and economic achievement—an assertion confirmed by the general shift toward the upper-right corner of the chart, where the Scandinavian countries now appear.

The same shift can be verified, as shown in Figure 2.6, by separating the data of different countries by age, education level, wealth, or materialist–postmaterialist orientation. A pattern appears: the youngest, most educated, wealthiest, most postmaterialist are nearer to that upper-right corner, while the older, less educated, poorer, more materialist are situated near the lower-left section. This pattern reveals the direction countries will be moving in the future as the newer generations replace the older, and as education increases, wealth accumulates, and the postindustrial stage advances.[3]

Shalom Schwartz: Three Axes

The theoretical path taken by Shalom Schwartz has been the opposite of that taken by the two previous authors. Hofstede and Inglehart began by observing and analyzing

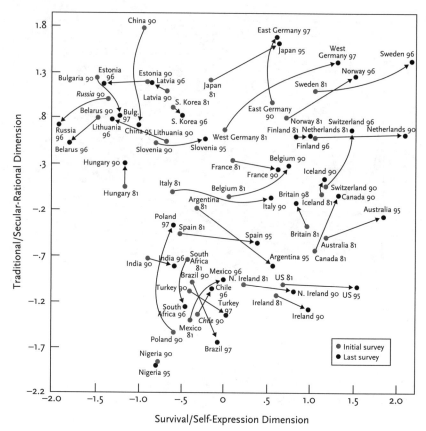

FIGURE 2.5 *World Cultural Map*, 1980–2000, dynamics

Inglehart and Baker (2000), p. 40.

data, which led to a theorization. Schwartz began with a theoretical search for *individual-level* values, which led him to construct a questionnaire to test his theory. As his data and statistical methods yielded insight, he dug further and expanded, slowly moving from the individual to the national level—that is, from values to cultures. Despite the extent of his own work, Hofstede asserts that it is Schwartz who has made the most extensive study of values to date (Hofstede, 2001, p. 8).

In 1987, Schwartz and Wolfgang Bilsky proposed a *universal psychological structure* of human values, derived from three types of *universal human requirements*: biologically based needs of the organism, social interactional requirements for interpersonal coordination, and social institutional demands for group welfare and survival (Schwartz and Bilsky, 1987, p. 551).

To test their hypothesis, they developed a survey questionnaire based on the 18 terminal and 18 instrumental values from the Rokeach Value Survey (Rokeach, 1973) and applied it to a sample of Israeli teachers and German students. They found seven individual-level *motivational domains*: enjoyment, achievement, self-direction, maturity, security, pro-social, and restrictive-conformity, with

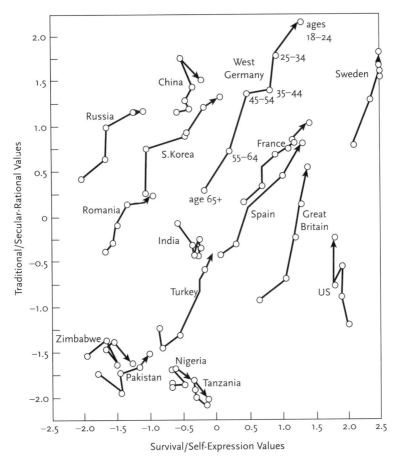

FIGURE 2.6 *World Cultural Map,* 2000, by age

Reprinted from *Modernization, Cultural Change, and Democracy,* Ronald Inglehart and Christian Welzel, 2005, p. 112. Reprinted with the permission of Cambridge University Press.

the possible addition of social power (Schwartz and Bilsky, 1987, p. 553). They adopted the statistical *smallest space analysis* (SSA) method to test and confirm their hypothesis of structural relations among value domains, implying meaningful proximity and distance along a circular continuum, as shown in Figure 2.7.

In 1990, Schwartz and Bilsky expanded their sample to add Australia, the United States, Hong Kong, Spain, and Finland, and warned that their theory was "not merely a typology; rather it develops rationales for dynamic relations among value priorities" (Schwartz and Bilsky, 1990, p. 878). They were encouraged by their findings and concluded that "this research tested the universality of elements of a theory of the content and structure of human values. Universality can be established definitively only by studying all cultures" (p. 888).

In 1992, Schwartz expanded his research to 20 countries and was encouraged once again by his confirmatory findings. He also expanded and refined his

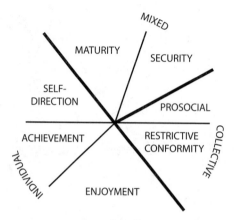

FIGURE 2.7 Structural relations among *individual-level* value domains (1987)

Shalom Schwartz and W. Bilsky, "Toward a Universal Psychological Structure of Human Values," *Journal of Personality and Social Psychology, 53*, 1987, p. 554. Reprinted with permission of the American Psychological Association.

scheme of structural relations among value domains from seven to 10 (Schwartz, 1992, p. 14). That year he made another important breakthrough when he found that the 10 value types could form groups along *two axes* that he called higher-order value types, as shown in Figure 2.8.

The 10 key value-types of individuals were summarized as follows:

1. **Power**: Social status and prestige; control or dominance over people and resources.
2. **Achievement**: Personal success through demonstrating competence according to society.
3. **Hedonism**: Wanting to focus on enjoying life; preoccupation with the idea of having a good time.
4. **Stimulation**: Excitement, novelty, challenges.
5. **Self-direction**: Independent thought and action-choosing; creation; exploration.
6. **Universalism**: Understanding, appreciation, tolerance, and protection of the welfare of everyone; believing in justice for all.
7. **Benevolence**: Preservation and enhancement of the welfare of all people.
8. **Tradition**: Respect for, commitment to, and acceptance of the customs and ideas provided by traditional culture, family, or religion.
9. **Conformity**: Restraint of actions, inclinations, and impulses; belief that people should do what they're told and follow rules at all times, even when no one is watching.
10. **Security**: Safety, harmony, and stability of society, of relationships, and of self.

Schwartz argued that there were

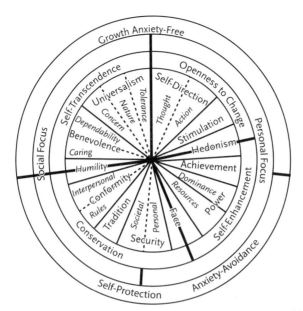

FIGURE 2.8 Schwartz's *Structure of 10 Value Types and Two Sets of Underlying Dimensions*

Shalom Schwartz et al., "Refining the Theory of Basic Individual Values," *Journal of Personality and Social Psychology*, *103*, 2012, p. 669. Reprinted with permission of the American Psychological Association.

[. . .] *two basic, bipolar, conceptual dimensions*. **The first basic dimension** places a higher order type combining stimulation and self-direction values in opposition to one combining security, conformity, and tradition values. We call this dimension **openness to change versus conservation**. It arrays values in terms of the extent to which they motivate people to follow their own intellectual and emotional interests in unpredictable and uncertain directions versus to preserve the status quo and the certainty it provides in relationships with close others, institutions, and traditions. [. . .]

The second basic dimension places a higher order type combining power, achievement, and hedonism values in opposition to one combining universalism and benevolence values (including a spiritual life). We call this dimension **self-enhancement versus self-transcendence**. It arrays values in terms of the extent to which they motivate people to enhance their own personal interests (even at the expense of others) versus the extent to which they motivate people to transcend selfish concerns and promote the welfare of others, close and distant, and of nature. [my emphasis] (1992, p. 43)

At this point, contrary to what he had first assumed, he began suspecting that the same dimensions would not apply equally to countries, *cultures*, and individuals. Schwartz's initial focus on the individual-level basic values and how they affect behavior yielded a reinforcement of a theory highly cherished by market researchers, because it helped them to promote sales by targeting consumers according to eight specific and diverse types and to encourage consumption.

It is worth noting that the two *basic bipolar dimensions* Schwartz found in 1992 correspond to the two Inglehart proposed in 1997. Schwartz's openness to change versus conservation can be associated with Inglehart's secular-rational versus traditional and Schwartz's self-enhancement versus self-transcendence with Inglehart's survival versus self-expression. However, as Schwartz continued researching the transference from the individual to the country level, he found that two axes were not enough to capture the full axiological phenomenon, and he began developing his third axis.

In 1994, Schwartz expanded his research to 41 cultural groups from 38 countries and moved fully from the individual to the country or *cultural* level. He described the *new* cultural dimensions and their links to the individual level dimensions as follows:

> In sum, two culture-level dimensions, consisting of opposing value types, are hypothesized: 1. **Autonomy versus Conservatism** (parallel to individual-level Openness to Change versus Conservation, and closest to the core idea of I/C [individualism/collectivism]; 2. **Hierarchy and Mastery versus Egalitarian Commitment and Harmony with Nature** (parallel to individual-level Self-Enhancement versus Self-Transcendence [my emphasis]. (Schwartz, 1994a, p. 98)

As Schwartz broadened the scope of his research and conducted surveys in more countries, he began to move away from the individual level and increasingly focused on the national level (i.e., countries). Schwartz moved away from values as a psychological variable and expressed his view of culture as

> [. . .] a latent, hypothetical variable that we can measure only through its manifestations. [. . .] In this view, culture is not located in the mind and actions of individual people. Rather, it is outside the individual. It refers to the press to which individuals are exposed by virtue of living in particular social systems. (Schwartz, 2008 p. 4)

He proposed that all such manifestations are really only partial and limited aspects of culture that express *axiological* emphases—so why not study those emphases directly?

> In order to measure cultural orientations as latent variables, we could analyze the themes of the popular children's stories in a society, proverbs, movies, literature, socialization practices, legal systems, or the ways economic exchange is organized. [. . .] When researchers try to identify culture by studying these type of manifestations, what they seek, implicitly or explicitly, are underlying value emphases. Hence, studying *value emphases* directly is

an especially efficient way to capture and characterize cultures. [my emphasis] (2008, p. 6).

That is what Schwartz eventually set out to do, and he began by examining possible social responses to three basic problems. The first problem dealt with the nature of relationships and boundaries between the individual and the group; the second concerned promoting responsible behavior in order to preserve the existing social fabric; and the third involved regulating how people treat human and natural resources (2008).

In response to the first problem, Schwartz created an axis whose poles he labeled *autonomy* and *embeddedness*, with autonomy being subdivided into intellectual and emotional fields. The second problem yielded an axis that extended from *egalitarianism* to *hierarchy*, and the third problem an axis ranging from *harmony* to *mastery*. Schwartz describes the axes as follows.

AUTONOMY-EMBEDDEDNESS (SOCIAL DIMENSION)

> In **autonomy cultures**, people are viewed as autonomous, bounded entities. They are encouraged to cultivate and express their own preferences, feelings, ideas, and abilities, and find meaning in their own uniqueness. There are two types of autonomy: *Intellectual autonomy* encourages individuals to pursue their own ideas and intellectual directions independently. Examples of important values in such cultures include broadmindedness, curiosity, and creativity. *Affective autonomy* encourages individuals to pursue affectively positive experience for themselves. Important values include pleasure, exciting life, and varied life. [. . .] In cultures with an emphasis on **embeddedness**, people are viewed as entities embedded in the collectivity. Meaning in life is expected to come largely through social relationships, through identifying with the group, participating in its shared way of life, and striving toward its shared goals. Embedded cultures emphasize maintaining the status quo and restraining actions that might disrupt in-group solidarity or the traditional order. Important values in such cultures are social order, respect for tradition, security, obedience, and wisdom. (2008, p. 7)

EGALITARIANISM VERSUS HIERARCHY (POLITICAL DIMENSION)

> The polar solution labeled **cultural egalitarianism** seeks to induce people to recognize one another as moral equals who share basic interests as human beings. People are socialized to internalize a commitment to cooperate and to feel concern for everyone's welfare. They are expected to act for the benefit of others as a matter of choice. Important values in such cultures include equality, social justice, responsibility, help, and honesty. [. . .] The polar alternative labeled **cultural hierarchy** relies on hierarchical systems of ascribed roles to insure responsible, productive behavior. It defines the

unequal distribution of power, roles, and resources as legitimate and even desirable. People are socialized to take the hierarchical distribution of roles for granted, to comply with the obligations and rules attached to their roles, to show deference to superiors and expect deference from subordinates. Values of social power, authority, humility, and wealth are highly important in hierarchical cultures. (2008, p. 8)

HARMONY VERSUS MASTERY (ECONOMIC DIMENSION)

Harmony emphasizes fitting into the social and natural world, trying to appreciate and accept rather than to change, direct, or exploit. Important values in harmony cultures include world at peace, unity with nature, protecting the environment, and accepting one's portion. **Mastery** is the polar cultural response to this problem. It encourages active self-assertion in order to master, direct, and change the natural and social environment to attain group or personal goals. Values such as ambition, success, daring, self-sufficiency, and competence are especially important in mastery cultures. (2008, p. 8)

Figure 2.9 illustrates the values associated with seven positions aligned around three axes, which I will discuss in more detail in the next section.

Schwartz identifies eight cultural clusters to which countries conform, basically the same ones Inglehart also identified, as shown in Figure 2.10.

It is very suggestive that Inglehart (Figure 2.4) and Schwartz (Figure 2.10) arrive basically at the same cultural zones by means of two relatively distinct empirical methods. I concur with Schwartz that there are *three* key axes (not four as Hofstede argues, nor two as Inglehart does) to explain reality. However, trying to force Schwartz's three axes into a bi-dimensional representation poses some problems, which are even more apparent in Figure 2.11, in which the 77 countries studied by Schwartz are shown in relation to his seven-value system.

Summary

On the theoretical side, Tocqueville made a powerful argument for the importance of values in the building of America and modern democracy. It was a highly influential descriptive narrative. Weber made one of the most important theoretical contributions to the study of values and culture in the social sciences by linking capitalism to Protestantism. Dealy built upon these two, and applied their contributions to a cultural comparison of Latin Americans and Anglo Americans, highlighting some of the contrasts in specific values and how values shape cultures.

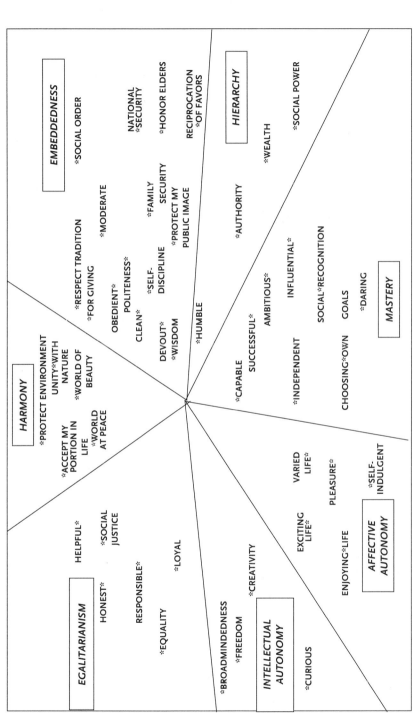

FIGURE 2.9 **Schwartz's values and axes (national level)**

Shalom Schwartz, "Cultural Value Orientations: Nature and Implications of National Differences." *Psychology Journal of the Higher School of Economics*, 5(2), 2008, p. 44. Reprinted with permission of the Higher School of Economics.

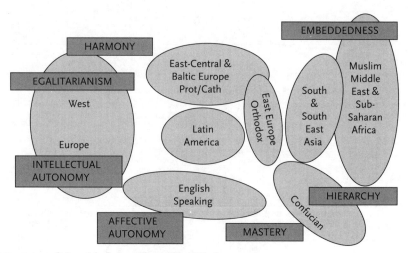

FIGURE 2.10 Schwartz's *Culture Map of World Regions*

Shalom Schwartz, "Cultural Value Orientations: Nature and Implications of National Differences." *Psychology Journal of the Higher School of Economics,* 5(2), 2008, p. 50. Reprinted with permission of the Higher School of Economics.

Also on the theoretical side, Hofstede contributed his notion of culture as the *software of the mind* as well as his identification of four key axes; Inglehart gave us his notion and measurement of materialism–postmaterialism, as well as his two axes and their interaction; and Schwartz presented his method-ological path to search for the axes from theoretical hypothesis to be tested by empirical data, the exact opposite of the approach taken by the other two authors.

On the empirical side, Hofstede made six *maps* combining his four original axes (Hofstede, 2001, pp. 152, 217, 249, 294, 299, and 334). But it is difficult to grasp which one or what combination of those six maps is a better or a more integral representation, or at least a simpler one, of the countries included. Inglehart's *World Cultural Map* has the simultaneous power and limitation of being based on *only* two axes—powerful for its clarity and simplicity, but limited because it cannot reflect the *three* essential dimensions of economic, political, and social life. The limitation comes from the selection of questions included in the factor analysis that yields only two axes and simply cannot yield a third meaningful axis. Certainly the World Values Survey questionnaire has enough questions to yield a third axis, but for that, further research still must be done.

Schwartz overcame the problem of too many or too few axes by first looking into the most complete available theories of human behavior and then build-ing and testing a questionnaire. By doing so, he was able to *fine-tune* the ques-tions to yield the three essential dimensions, except that his representation in a two-dimensional chart, as stated earlier, is problematic.

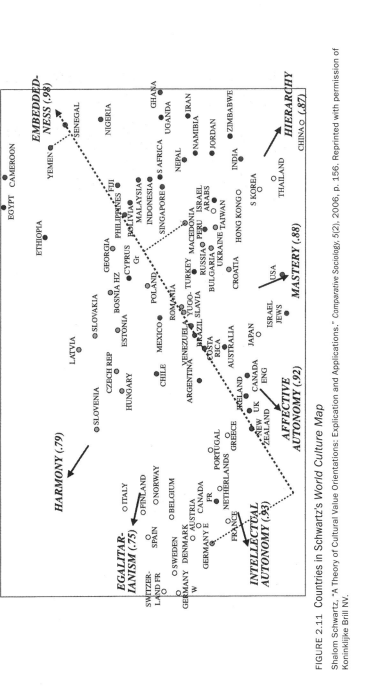

FIGURE 2.11 Countries in Schwartz's *World Culture Map*

To try to solve the problematic representation of the three axes, I propose as a guide for future research a three-dimensional representation, the *axiological cube*, which helps in visualizing the existence of the three key dimensions (social, political, and economic) and their associated values: trust-distrust, work as prize or punishment, and autonomy-obedience. Chapter 3 explores this idea.

PART II

Value Axes and the Geography of Cultures

[. . .] the shaping forces of society [. . .] are in three realms: *values*, the legitimating elements of the society; *culture*, the repository of expressive symbolism and sensibility; and *social structure* [. . .] concerned with the distribution of persons in occupations and in the polity [. . .]

—DANIEL BELL, *THE CULTURAL CONTRADICTIONS OF CAPITALISM*, P. 191

3

The Axiological Cube

Table 3.1 compares the main dimensions of Hofstede, Schwartz, Inglehart, and Basáñez in a simple way that may not do justice to their rich contributions. It may look more like a shoehorn than a natural fit, but it helps explain the proposition described in this section.

I propose a three-dimensional model representing the three axes that offers a better conceptualization and visualization of the field than previous models.

Inglehart and Schwartz's *cultural maps* suffice to outline the three key cultures that result from the interaction of history, religions, and legal systems: *honor*, *achievement*, and *joy*. Hence, I need not go over the empirical details that they have exhaustively covered. On Inglehart's cultural map (Figure 2.4 in Chapter 2) the top, right, and upper-right corners show *cultures of achievement* around the Protestant and Confucian clusters; the bottom, left, and bottom-left corner show *cultures of honor* comprising the Orthodox, South Asian, and Islamic clusters; and more or less in the middle ground are the *cultures of joy* around the Catholic (European and Latin American) cluster.

However, as useful as Inglehart's map is, such a two-dimensional representation forces the social and political dimensions into a single vertical axis (traditional-secular/rational). With only two axes, countries may appear misleadingly close together, as do, for example, Romania and Iraq, or Taiwan and Bulgaria, on Inglehart's map in Figure 2.4. The third axis of my axiological cube (presented later in this chapter in Figure 3.2) provides depth, making the actual position of each country much clearer. Schwartz's triple-axis formulation also solves that problem, except that his representation in a two-dimensional chart is problematic.

This chapter explores a potential development to solve the problematic representation of the three axes that Schwartz and I propose (rather than Hofstede's four or Inglehart's two), because they reflect precisely the three essential economic, political, and social dimensions that define human interactions: for the production of goods and services, for power relations, and for human relations, respectively. I borrow Schwartz's *axes labels* (rather than using my own) due to the preexisting, deep body of academic work based on his findings.

TABLE 3.1

Comparing Hofstede, Basáñez, Inglehart, and Schwartz

Dimensions	Economic	Political	Social
Hofstede 1980	Masculinity vs. Femininity	Power Distance	Individualism vs. Collectivism
	Uncertainty / Avoidance		
Basáñez 1986	Hard work: Prize vs. Punishment	Autonomy vs. Obedience	Trust vs. Distrust
Schwartz 1994	Harmony vs. Mastery	Egalitarianism vs. Hierarchy	Autonomy vs. Embeddedness
Inglehart 1997	Survival vs. Self-Expression	Secular-traditional	Survival vs. Self-Expression

Subsequent research will help to illuminate the seeming paradoxes of Schwartz's two-dimensional map shown in Figure 2.11 in Chapter 2, as in the case of Spain, France, and Italy, which appear far away in the left corner, against the more central position they would occupy in my axiological cube (presented in Figure 3.4 later in this chapter).

Figure 3.1 represents the three essential dimensions (economic, political, and social) in a spatial figure by simply using three axes (*x*, *y*, and *z*) intersecting in the center.

The three axes, in turn, form the core of a cube, as shown in Figure 3.2, in which six walls help to represent six polar dimensions. Borrowing Schwartz's terminology as well as his proximity and distance analysis, the top wall of the cube represents *egalitarianism*, and the bottom wall, *hierarchy*; the right wall, *mastery*, and the left wall, *harmony*; finally, the front wall represents *embeddedness*, and the back wall, *autonomy* (both intellectual and affective autonomy).

The location of the *walls* helps to reconstruct hypothetical developmental paths for primitive societies, by adding corners to the cube, as shown in Figure 3.3.

It is easy to imagine a primitive group of hunter-gatherers some 150 millennia ago starting on the "A" corner of hierarchy, harmony, and embeddedness. As in animal groups, an *alpha* male performed the leadership role stressing *authority* (a political dimension, although primitive groups were more *economically* and

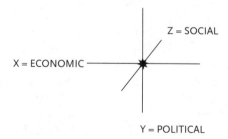

FIGURE 3.1 Three-dimensional space for economic, political, and social dimensions

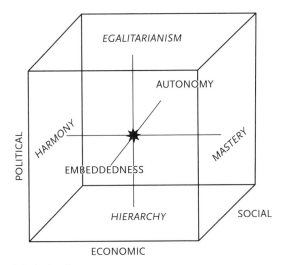

FIGURE 3.2 Six axiological *walls*

socially egalitarian). Because of the small size of the group, the *embeddedness* was concomitant to their daily lives. Finally, the relatively low technological level of their rudimentary tools meant that they had to adapt to the physical environment (*harmony*), with little capacity to alter nature.

The demographic explosion at the dawn of agriculture some 10 millennia ago and the associated creation of permanent settlements stimulated both economic and political growth, as well as a more complex network of social relations. Ancient civilizations took different paths of *development* within the cube as their own conditions allowed. Some grew richer from abundant agriculture

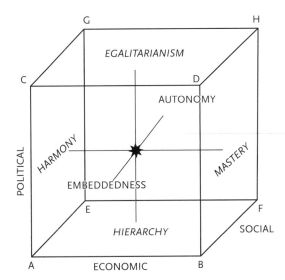

FIGURE 3.3 Eight axiology *corners*

(from A to B); others may have become more powerful as population and pyra-midal hierarchies grew (from A to C); consequently, social differentiation and *specialization* advanced (from A to E). All those simultaneous displacements were moving mankind toward the center of the cube at the core of the empires (China, Egypt, Babylon, Hindus Valley, Greece, Rome, Arabs, Mayans, Aztecs, and Incas).

The intellectual and technological revolution that began barely six centuries ago with the European Renaissance allowed the *mastery* of nature. The process began first by means of territorial expansion through advances in navigation, and later by means of the economic and political expansion spurred by the indus-trial revolution. The combination of these two forces produced an increasingly predominant role of the West over the rest of the world: first Spain and Portugal, then Holland, followed by England and France, and the United States today. By the middle of the 19th century, Europe had colonized practically the entire world.

The first important divergence in Europe was between two of the three legal systems of the world: the civil Roman and the common law traditions (Islamic law did not apply to Europe); the second divergence determined on which side of the Lutheran Reformation movement a country fell. These distinctions influ-enced which cultural zone a country and its colonies would gravitate toward: a culture of *achievement* (corner H) or culture of *honor* (corner A), as shown in Figure 3.4. Cultures of *joy* (at the center of the cube) appeared as such much later, as the next chapters explain.

In cultures in the *honor* corner, the incentives orient toward the political dimension: tradition, respect, hierarchy, discipline, loyalty, obedience, God, religion, and so on. The qualities of priests make a good fit. In the *achievement*

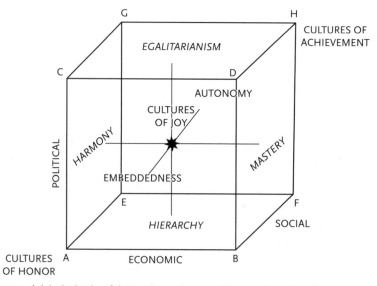

FIGURE 3.4 *Axiological cube* of three cultures: honor, achievement, and joy

corner, a person works within a culture that gives incentives toward the physical environment and economic production. Hence, the qualities of goal-oriented rationality, as practiced by the military or by businessmen, are highly useful; in the *joy* center are the cultures where the incentives orient toward human environments and social interaction that do not require greater congruence with the *outside* world, given the wealth and variety of the *internal* worlds. The qualities of artists make a better fit. In this respect, Douglass North makes a very insightful observation when he notes an element (the contrast between physical and human environment) that began separating the paths of cultures, and which lends support to my proposition. He states that

> [t]he contrasting [. . .] characteristics of economies geared to dealing with the *physical environment* and those constructed to deal with the *human environment* raise fundamental questions [. . .] that have evolved to result in economic growth on the one hand and stagnation on the other. [my emphasis] (North, 2005, p. 101)

Development is not an open continuum, and the points A and H in the three-dimensional space of Figure 3.4 represent hypothetical ends of the cultures of *honor* and cultures of *achievement* leaning to either side of the opposing corners. Each point has a finite end; cultures of *honor* are ultimately subservient to God, the ultimate *leader*, as in Islamic societies; while cultures of *achievement* are ultimately subservient to the carrying capacity of the physical environment (namely, the planet), which cannot sustain constantly increasing levels of consumption, as in consumerist American-style capitalism. But the limitations of these two cultures also highlight the need for balance—the location of the *cultures of joy,* somewhere midway between the two extremes in the center of the cube—what we might think of as the embodiment of Aristotle's *golden mean* or the Buddhist *middle path.*

Conventional Western thinking has assumed that the entire world should keep moving toward the H corner, seen as *progress*. Billions of dollars in aid programs and in military spending have gone to that end. But that is a *mirage,* founded in the success of past colonization, which is unsustainable in today's world.

International organizations and market forces for the several past decades have pushed countries to advance through material achievements, particularly along the economic scale—that is, by emphasizing movement from A to B. Those were the propositions of the early modernization theorists (Apter, 1965; Lipset, 1960; Rostow, 1960). The assumption has been that as a country gets closer to B, pressure mounts to advance along the political scale (i.e., from B to D) and also along the social scale (i.e., from D to H). Ultimately, a country should continue toward point H. Through this same logic, 10 basic hypothetical paths would be available: (1) ABDH; (2) ABFH; (3) ACDH; (4) ACGH; (5) AEFH; or (6) AEGH. Three other hypothetical options describe shorter possible journeys: (7) BH; (8) CH; (9) EH; but they all really are variations of the 10th one, AH, allegedly the *optimal* path. However, all those paths assume point H as the ultimate goal. And that's where the problem lies.

The three-dimensional representation allows us to visualize the 10 different hypothetical paths in the real world for the course of *development*, running from point A to point H. It is possible for a country, region, or city to advance greatly in social aspects (education and health, for instance) without achieving corresponding political development (Cuba) or economic development (Kerala, India). Similarly, a nation might advance politically without seeing parallel social (Barbados) or economic (India, 1950–1990) enhancement—or it might just as easily improve economically and remain behind politically (China) or socially (Russia). Indeed, some nations might show a more balanced location (France, Italy, Spain, Croatia, Israel) through the center of the three-dimensional space.

The countries that have arrived at point H in the *egalitarian, autonomous,* and *mastery* corner H of the cube (Figure 3.4), or the Confucian, Nordic, and some of the English Protestant clusters of Inglehart's map (Figure 2.4), clearly illustrate the price that must be paid in order to achieve that corner—ruthless and unremitting competition, with little free time and high levels of anxiety, which prevent the enjoyment of family and/or friends, and result in feeling in a permanent rush, with the need to do everything *fast* (fast food, fast talking, fast resting, fast interacting, fast living). There is often little or no time available to enjoy life—the difficult paradox of work–life balance. In return for that price, those countries have enjoyed for the past 50 years high levels of well-being: physical security, good and extended education and health systems, good job options, access to a home, and many other advantages. Many gladly pay this price when poverty is the alternative; however, in extreme cases, the suicide rates in achievement countries are alarming.

In the opposite corner of *cultures of honor* (A), individuals may have free time, but the price for large segments of population may be the absence of well-being, in many cases lack of essential material means of existence. That is clearly not the case for the small number of citizens of oil-rich Arab countries. They enjoy both leisure and well-being, but this is not sustainable in the long term.

All nations have their locations in the three-dimensional cultural space—locations dictated by their unique histories and circumstances. Some countries will be close to one of the diagram's eight corners, while others will be closer to the center. It is ultimately the responsibility of each society *to decide* for itself whether to continue on the path of its historic axiological inertia or to attempt axiological changes that might help it move onto a newly selected trajectory, if possible. However, the amount of effort and coordination required from political, intellectual, and business leaders to put in motion the right public policies, ideas, and market forces makes it highly unlikely that such deliberate shifts will occur—not that it is impossible under very special circumstances, as a few cases show: the Meiji restoration, Ataturk's Turkey, Gandhi's India, Lee Kuan Yew's Singapore, and Mandela's South Africa, among the most notable. Less well known but equally impressive is the case of Bogotá, Colombia, in the first decade of this century. I will discuss some of these cases in the next chapter.

Cultural Dissemination

Let's mentally rewind back some three thousand years, and imagine a primitive society on a small, far-off island in the middle of Polynesia, without any possible influence from or communication with the outside world. Let us imagine settlement that began with the arrival of a few young families navigating uncharted waters—say, a dozen couples. How would they have formed their values and beliefs? How would they have passed them on? How would they have reinforced and consolidated them?

Day-to-day problems—that is, the material conditions of survival—would have demanded day-to-day solutions for fetching water, finding food, and keeping a roof over their heads. Their ancestors would have done this for millennia and, accordingly, would have accumulated a very important body of knowledge. That is, these young couples would not have started *from scratch*, although the precise conditions of their new home would have required them to put this knowledge to new use. Three thousand years ago, just such a group did so, equipped with a high-powered evolutionary tool: language. Of course they lacked reading and writing skills, and would not come to know them until many centuries later.

If 10 couples arrived and each one produced 10 children, in 20–25 years the tribe would already have grown to more than a hundred, and in the next 20–25-year cycle there would be a thousand of them. Hypothetically at least, such a tribe could grow from 20 to 10,000 members within a century. But the central question is this: Can an island that size support them all? At some point they would have to realize that the island's carrying capacity would not tolerate such aggressive growth.

Jared Diamond (2005) has explored this subject convincingly. He began by studying birds in the Pacific islands before moving on to study the human race, surveying histories of success and failure in diverse populations around the world. He studied the population collapses of Easter Island, the Mayas, Anasazi, and Greenland, as well as success stories from New Guinea, Japan, and Tikopia, among others. He reaches a very thought-provoking conclusion regarding two opposite approaches that societies can take depending on the size of their territory: top-down public decision-making processes if the territory is large; and bottom-up processes if it is small.

Diamond takes the case of Tikopia, one of the Solomon Islands in Melanesia, as an environmental lesson in land size and cyclones that leaves no room for ambiguity. Its 1.8 square miles (4.7 square kilometers) cannot support a population greater than 1,200 inhabitants, and that is the population size that the island maintained for the last three millennia (Diamond, 2005, p. 286).

After centuries of trial and error, the inhabitants of Tikopia discovered seven inviolable methods of population control and came up with ways to pass them down from one generation to the next. These ranged from postponing the age of marriage to practicing *coitus interruptus*, from abortion to infanticide, and even war, suicide, and the elders' exiling themselves out to sea as a way to leave room for the youngest in case of drought or famine. The constraints imposed by the environment on Tikopia, specifically those of geography and climate, had to become part of their customs and rules, which were passed down through oral tradition, thus shaping their culture.

Tikopia did not face overpopulation problems for three millennia until the 20th century, when the arrival of the British government and Christian missions prevented the continuation of their traditional population-control customs. In 1952 the population had reached 1,753 inhabitants, when two cyclones in 13 months destroyed half their crops, leading to widespread famine. Today only 1,115 residents are allowed on the island, its millennia-old population level (Diamond, 2005, p. 291).

This process of natural, isolated culture formation is obviously no longer at work. The world today is a patchwork of thousands of overlapped and intermingled cultures. But understanding how cultures began may help to grasp where they stand today.

Historical Trajectory

About 5 millennia ago, humans had populated most landmasses, and writing was slowly beginning. The dispersion of micro-cultures was as numerous as the burgeoning of languages, though there is no possibility of tracing belief systems that far back. Organized religions began forming about the 8th to the 3rd centuries BC, starting a glacially paced process of cultural convergence from the thousands of micro-cultures toward the few hundreds of *national* mezzo-cultures, which merged into the handful of macro-cultures around belief systems. As powerful empires emerged in China, India, Egypt, Greece, Rome, and elsewhere, they were able to impose the belief system of their elites on the people of their controlled territories.

China and the Islamic societies had higher standards of living than Europe during the Middle Ages, but *cultures of honor* (typical of nomadic and agrarian, or Bell's *pre-industrial* societies) dominated everywhere, as status, hierarchy, expansion, domination, and the like were the prevailing rationality. In about the 12th century, the paths of the East and the West began diverging with the Renaissance, then the Lutheran and Reformation movement of the 16th century, and this divergence was accelerated by the discovery of the New World and the Enlightenment. Within Europe, two defining factors in each country's history became highly relevant causes of divergence: its religious roots and its legal codes.

The real jump-start to *cultures of achievement* began at the start of the Industrial Revolution. Many of the economic ideas and attitudes were already present in Confucian and Jewish ethics in the form of their high appreciation for learning and hard work, but their propagation in the dynamic countries of Europe ran through the Catholic–Protestant divide as they were preparing to colonize the world.

In the 16th century, Spain and Portugal, the first colonial empires, outperformed all the rest of Europe. They followed the civil Roman law and opposed the Protestant Reformation. Holland began expanding at the end of the 16th century, applying civil Roman law but in favor of the Reformation. England began expanding in the 17th century, also on the side of the Reformation and applying common law. France was under the civil Roman law, and by the end of the 17th century ended the French Reformation movement. From these facts one may conclude that there was no unique pattern, because both legal traditions and religions produced success stories. However, as time passed, the image began changing, and one lesson began dominating: material success was highly appreciated and enviable, paving the way toward the admiration of *achievement cultures*.

Britain was clearly moving in the direction of the H corner, drawn by the *mastery* the Industrial Revolution brought and the *autonomy* encouraged by the Protestant Reformation. In addition, the *Magna Carta* of 1215 had paved the road to *egalitarianism*. The United States in the 18th century basically followed the same path as Britain, highly favored by the conditions of the Americas. The Nordic countries were also heading toward the *achievement* corner, albeit with a greater leaning toward *egalitarianism*.

The Islamic, Catholic, and Christian Orthodox worlds did not embrace the Reformist movement, and they all remained in the *hierarchy, embeddedness*, and *harmony* corner A of *cultures of honor*. A polarization trend began both in the Western and Islamic worlds at the end of World War II and the fall of the Ottoman Empire: a rush to consumption in the West and a rush to hierarchies in the Islamic world. The *elites* all over (the 1%, in today's terms) and some of the colonial Catholic countries (Argentina in 1862–1930 and Mexico in 1933–1982, in particular) found a temporary spot at the center of the axiological cube as *cultures of joy*, for the relatively high levels of well-being they achieved in a balance between the two opposing corners.

The conventional linear concept of development and the *mirage* of achievement produce a false assumption that development is an open-ended continuum—that it goes on without limits. That is not true, as the three-dimensional space demonstrates. Development shows diminishing returns, particularly with regard to the limits of economic growth (Meadows, 1972), because the world cannot sustain the endless and universal expansion of the standard of living the West enjoys today. Equally, hierarchies cannot strengthen indefinitely, because they reach an ultimate limit once the honor culture escalates all the way up to what they believe is the final step: *God*.

In summary, the origins of cultural variation as shown in Table 3.2 come from three basic ethno-cultures: cultures of the **market** (work, saving, productivity), cultures of the **state** (honor, duty, discipline), and cultures of the **family** (joy, hospitality, indulgence). The basic idea is that the cultural values of a people are patterned by the historical institutional environment (market, state, or family) and what is rewarded by each environment. Most societies contain a combination of all three, including a combination of ethno-cultural groups

TABLE 3.2

A Summary of the Three Cultures

	Honor	Joy	Achievement
Drivers	The State (political)	The Family (social)	The Market (economic)
Period	Historic	Post–World War II	Industrial Revolution
Priorities	Dominance Tradition	Human relations Well-being	Wealth Efficiency, punctuality
Prevalent	Ancient empires	Catholic (and Buddhist) countries	Modern empires

from each type—so even in Latin America or Africa there exists a bureaucratic, state-oriented culture among a small minority, as well as market-dominant minorities, though neither is the dominant ethno-culture. Typically, social stratification also follows the logic of the cultural system; for example, in Europe the upper class might disproportionately have a culture of the state, the middle class a culture of the market, while the rest of society is mixed.

4

Cultural Geography

The three key cultures were disseminated throughout the world either by autonomous development, by adoption, or by external imposition through conquest or colonization. That is the way in which the cultural geography of the world was established. An outstanding empirical account of the world's cultural profile is presented by Michael Minkov, Geert Hofstede's associate, contrasting differences between rich and developing countries, across rich countries, between Eastern Europe and Latin America, as well as between the Arab world and sub-Saharan Africa (Minkov, 2013).

Cultures of *Honor:* Examples from the African Countries

Why is Africa, the cradle of humankind, today the least developed continent in the world? Over a very long historical horizon, the answers are geography and environment. While the largest landmass around the equator produced the best environment to jump-start *Homo sapiens* when most of the planet was covered in ice, in more recent times Africa's geography and environment have proven less conducive to development.

This section begins with the 54 African countries as an illustration of cultures of *honor,* with no intention of packaging them into a single monolithic culture, particularly because Africa's ethnic, linguistic, colonial, and religious diversity is enormous. The *ethnic* diversity originates in the eastern region around Kenya and Ethiopia, the focal point that DNA research pinpoints as the origin of all the world's migrations.[1] Humans began by following the contours of the continents, walking the lengths of the coastlines coming out of Africa, our original habitat, until we reached India, Southeast Asia, Europe, Australia, the Americas, and the Pacific Islands, as shown in Figure 4.1.

The combination of light soils, extended jungles, rich seeds, and lack of domestic animals was enough to sustain an adequate supply of humans to populate the planet, but not sufficient to generate demographic explosions *à la* China, Mesopotamia, India, or Mesoamerica. When the descendants of these migrants

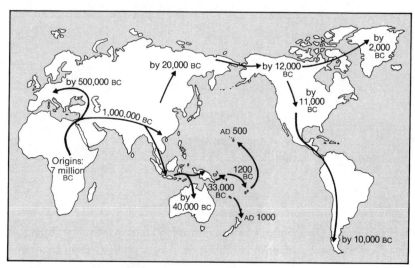

FIGURE 4.1 Continental migrations

The Spread of Humans Around the World, from *Guns, Germs and Steel: The Fates of Human Societies* by Jared Diamond. Copyright © 1997 by Jared Diamond. Used by permission of W. W. Norton & Company, Inc.

returned 150 millennia later, technological differences allowed the returnees to enslave, dominate, and subjugate the descendants of those who had stayed behind.

Two aspects in particular stand out in modern history as explanations of African underdevelopment. First is the pernicious effect imposed by waves of enslavement: under the Arabs from the 7th century onward, and under Europeans from the 15th century onward. It is estimated that Arabs may have taken as many as 18 million slaves and Europeans somewhere between 7 and 12 million. The arrival of Europeans and their diseases in Africa had an equally devastating effect demographically, but with different cultural implications. Second, the independence of the majority of African countries came quite late, after World War II.[2]

Hence, the average African country today has been independent for fewer than 50 years, a stretch of time equivalent to that of European countries in the 6th century as they began to pick up the pieces after the fall of the Roman Empire. Africa's relatively low development by today's standards is counterbalanced by the fact that it can leapfrog by adopting innovations already painstakingly achieved from around the world over the last millennium. That is, in five decades Africa may have reached development levels that took Europe five centuries to reach.

UNESCO has estimated that roughly a third of all the world's approximately 7,000 languages are spoken in Africa: over 2,000 languages derived from four great language families, spoken by the continent's more than one billion inhabitants. In terms of *colonial heritage*, seven European countries (France, England, Germany, Italy, Portugal, Belgium, and Spain) held dominion over Africa.

Finally, in *religions* 29 African countries have Christian majorities (especially in central, eastern, and southern Africa), while 16 are Islamic (predominantly in the north and west), and 9 are a mixture of both of these and/or other religions, as Table 4.1 shows.

Two other disturbing effects, not as far removed, which the Western world had on Africa were its arbitrary borders and Cold War alignments. The former was a product of colonization, which either split up ethnic groups and pitted them against each other, or took advantage of existing rifts in order to divide and conquer. The latter case was due to the multitude of reasons some countries aligned themselves with the United States and others with the Soviet Union. This translated into situations of internal instability and, in some cases, deadly conflicts.

One could argue that India also won its independence very late (1947), which is true. However, India's circumstances were very different and were not comparable to Africa's. This is above all due to the depth of a millennia-old shared system of meanings, values, and beliefs in India—that is, its culture—which was preserved throughout decades of foreign rulers, Britain the last on the list. By contrast, Africa is more of a patchwork of cultural influences, due both to its many different religious traditions (both indigenous and imported) and its experiences with different colonial rulers.

Analyzing the **population** of the African continent with Table 4.1 shows an enormous diversity on all fronts. By **size**, the top five largest countries are Nigeria (162 million), Ethiopia (85 million), Egypt (83 million), Democratic Republic of Congo (68 million), and South Africa (51 million), and the bottom five are Seychelles (86 thousand), São Tomé and Principe (169 thousand), Cape Verde (501 thousand), Equatorial Guinea (720 thousand), and Comoros (754 thousand), with an average of 19.5 k for the 54 countries (38 below and 16 above the average size). By population **density** per square kilometer, the top five countries are Mauritius (631), Rwanda (431), Comoros (395), Burundi (326), and Seychelles (188), and the bottom five are Namibia (3), Mauritania (3), Libya (4), Botswana (4), and Gabon (6), with an average density of 87 (41 below and 13 above the average). By the percent of **rural** population, the top five are Burundi (89%), Uganda (84%), Malawi (84%), Ethiopia (83%), and Niger (82%), and the bottom five are Gabon (14%), Libya (22%), Djibouti (23%), Algeria (27%), and Tunisia (34%), with an average of 58% (25 below and 29 above the average).

Analyzing the **economy** by **annual GDP** (in billions of US$), the top largest economies are South Africa ($576), Egypt ($534), Nigeria ($450), Algeria ($325), and Morocco ($173), and the bottom five are São Tomé and Principe ($0.3), Comoros ($0.9), Djibouti ($1.7), Cape Verde ($1.8), and Guinea-Bissau ($1.8), with an average of $67.4 for the 54 countries (12 above and 42 below the average). In terms of **GDP per capita**, the top five are Equatorial Guinea ($30k), Seychelles ($27k), Libya ($18k), Botswana ($16k), and Gabon ($16k), and the bottom five are Liberia ($639), Somalia ($600), Eritrea ($557), Burundi ($551), and Democratic Republic of Congo ($415), with an average of $4.7 k (14 countries above and 40 below the average).

TABLE 4.1

African Countries, 2014

Country	Population (Thousands)	Pop. Density	% Rural Pop.	GDP (billion US$)	GDP per Capita	Agr. % GDP	Ind. % GDP	Srvs. % GDP	Gini Index* Higher = unequal	Literacy % 15+ years old	GII Rank Higher = unequal	HDI Rank Lower = better	Freedom House Higher = better	Colonial BG **	Legal Tradition ***	ODI Rank **** Lower = better	Unsp. Christian	Protestant	Catholic	Islam	Orthodox	Indigenous	Other
Algeria	35,980	15	27	325.0	8,447	7	62	31	35.3	73	74	93	35	1	2/3	95				99			1
Angola	19,618	15	41	125.1	6,006	9	62	29	58.6	70		148	30	3	2	194		15	38			47	
Benin	9,100	80	55	15.7	1,557	32	13	54	38.6	42	135	166	82	1	2	139	5	10	27	24		17	17
Botswana	12,754	4	38	32.3	16,105	3	45	52	61	84	102	119	74	2	1/2	147	72					6	22
Burkina Faso	16,968	60	73	24.5	1,488	33	22	44	39.8	29	131	183	53	2/1	2	166		4	19	61		15	1
Burundi	8,575	326	89	5.4	551	35	19	46	33.3	67	98	178	34	6/5	2	157		21	61	3		15	
Cameroon	20,030	41	48	50.2	2,312	20	31	49	38.9	71	137	150	23	5/2/1	2/1	173	40		20			40	
Cape Verde	501	123	37	1.8	3,695	10	18	72	50.5	84		132	90	3	2	125	95		3			1	1
Cent. African Rep.	4,487	7	61	4.9	1,077	57	15	28	56.3	56		180	35	1	2	196		25	25	15		35	
Chad	11,525	9	78	26.6	2,135	14	49	38	39.8	34		184	21	1	2	192		14	20	53		7	6
Comoros	754	395	72	0.9	1,210	46	12	42	64.3	75		169	55	1	2/3	193			2	98			
Democratic Rep of Congo	67,758	29	66	27.3	415	46	22	33	44.4	67		186	20	6	2	195	10	20	50	10		10	
Côte d'Ivoire	20,153	62	49	39.8	2,006	24	30	45	41.5	56	138	168	34	1	2	177	33		39			12	16
Djibouti	906	38	23	1.7	2,170	4	17	79	40	68		164	29	1	2/3	169	6		94				
Egypt	82,537	81	56	533.9	6,614	14	37	49	30.8	72	126	112	38	2	2/3	119			90	9		1	
Equatorial Guinea	720	25	60	21.9	29,742	2	96	2	65	94		136	8	4	2	197	89		4		2	5	
Eritrea	5,415	52	79	3.4	557	15	22	63		68		181	3	7	2/3	186	48		50		1	2	
Ethiopia	84,734	83	83	101.7	1,109	46	11	43	29.8	39		173	18	7*	2	165		19	1	34	44	3	
Gabon	1,534	6	14	25.7	15,765	4	64	32	41.5	88	105	106	34	1	2	137	85		10			3	2
Gambia	1,776	173	43	3.4	1,917	19	13	68	47.5	50	128	165	23	2	1/3	189	8		90			2	
Ghana	24,966	107	48	51.1	2,014	26	26	49	42.8	67	121	135	84	2	1	115	11	46	13	18		5	7
Guinea	10,222	41	65	12.0	1,051	22	45	33	39.4	41		178	39	1	2	182	8		85	7			
Guinea-Bissau	1,547	54	56	1.8	1,101				35.5	54		176	30	3	2	176	10		50	40			
Kenya	41,610	71	76	75.0	1,737	28	18	54	47.7	87	130	145	55	2	1	162	12	47	23	11		2	5
Lesotho	2,194	72	72	4.0	1,931	8	34	58	52.5	90	113	158	72	2	1/2	158	80		20				
Liberia	4,129	41	52	2.7	639	53	10	37	38.2	61	143	174	60		1	161	86		12	1	1		
Libya	6,423	4	22	104.6	17,534	2	78	20	36	89	36	64	43	7	3	59			97		3		
Madagascar	21,315	36	67	21.5	962	29	16	55	44.1	64		151	35	1	2	167	41		7		52		
Malawi	15,381	158	84	12.0	753	30	19	50	39	75	124	170	60	2	1	153	83		13			4	
Mali	15,840	13	65	17.7	1,195	37	24	39	33	31	141	182	25	1	2	183	2		95		2	1	
Mauritania	3,542	3	58	9.7	2,561	16	46	37	40.5	58	139	155	34	1	2/3	171			100				
Mauritius	1,286	631	58	19.2	14,902	4	26	70	39	89	70	80	90	2	2	53	33		17			50	
Morocco	32,273	72	43	172.6	5,220	15	30	55	40.9	56	84	130	43	4/1	3	129			99			1	
Mozambique	23,930	30	69	25.4	1,007	32	24	44	45.7	56	125	185	59	3	2	172		28	28	18		26	
Namibia	2,324	3	62	16.8	7,442	8	20	73	63.9	89	86	128	76	5	1/2	151	91					6	3
Niger	16,069	12	82	13.2	769	40	17	43	34.6	29	146	186	56	1	2	170			80			20	
Nigeria	162,471	174	50	450.1	2,666	33	41	27	48.8	61		153	46	2	1/3	175	40		50	10			
Republic of Congo	4,140	12	36	18.9	4,354	3	77	20	47.3	84	132	142	29	1	2	179	50		2	48			
Rwanda	10,943	431	81	15.3	1,332	32	16	52	50.8	71	76	167	24	6/5	1	180	11	26	56	5		2	
São Tomé and Príncipe	169	172	37	0.3	1,822	16	17	67	50.8	89		144	81	3	2	149		7	70			23	
Senegal	12,768	65	57	26.2	1,908	15	24	61	39.2	50	115	154	75	1	2	127		5	94	1			
Seychelles	86	188	46	2.3	26,729	2	18	80	65.8	92		46	67	2	2/1	124	3	8	82	1		6	
Sierra Leone	5,997	82	61	8.0	1,337	44	18	37	42.5	42	139	177	70	2	1	163	10		60	30			
Somalia	9,557	15	62	5.9	600				30	38			2	7	2	181			100				
South Africa	50,587	41	38	576.1	11,255	3	31	66	63.1	89	90	121	81	2	1/2	144	36	37	7	2		18	
South Sudan	10,314	13	82	10.2	1,505				45.5	27			31			187							
Sudan	34,318	18	67	80.4	2,162	24	28	47	35.3	71	129	171	11	2	3	185	19		70	11			
Swaziland	1,068	69	79	6.4	5,161	7	50	42	51.5	87	112	141	21	2	1/2	184	88		1			10	1
Tanzania	46,218	51	73	73.1	1,575	28	25	47	37.6	73	119	152	66	5/2	1	135	30		35	35			
Togo	6,155	111	62	6.9	1,034	32	16	52	34.4	57	122	159	43	5/1	2	150	29		20	51			
Tunisia	10,674	68	34	103.8	9,636	8	33	58	41.4	78	46	94	58	1	2	67	1	0	98			1	
Uganda	34,509	170	84	48.3	1,330	23	25	51	44.3	73	110	161	40	2	1	164		42	42	12		4	
Zambia	13,475	17	61	23.7	1,684	20	37	43	54.6	71	136	163	62	2	1	178	86		1			11	2
Zimbabwe	12,754	32	61	9.8	714	17	29	53	50.1	92	116	172	25	2	1/2	190	25					24	51
Total/average Africa	**1,055,077**	**87**	**58**	**3,396**	**4,720**	**22**	**31**	**47**	**45**	**67**	**113**	**150**	**45**			**158**	**39**	**23**	**30**	**44**	**26**	**17**	**10**
Central Africa	129,981	35	49	301	7,070	19	48	33	49	73	132	150	31			179	55	16	41	16	0	26	9
East Africa	218,082	209	72	322	4,481	26	21	53	47	74	107	157	54			153	37	29	42	18	0	23	12
Horn of Africa	100,612	47	62	113	1,279	22	17	62	33	53		164	13			175	27	19	1	70	44	2	4
North Africa	212,519	43	47	1331	8,269	12	45	43	38	73	83	139	37			120	10	0	0	92	9	11	1
Southern Africa	81,681	37	58	645	8,379	8	35	57	57	89	103	154	58			162	65	35	7	2	0	13	19
West Africa	312,201	75	57	685	1,550	29	24	47	40	51	133	144	53			161	28	20	16	55	0	14	8

Sources and meanings: see appendix 3.
* Gini Index: 0 = zero wealth concentration; 1 = one person holds all the wealth.
** Colonial BG: 1 France; 2 Britain; 3 Portugal; 4 Spain; 5 Germany; 6 Belgium; 7 Italy.
*** Legal Tradition: 1 Common; 2 Civil; 3 Islamic.
**** Objective Development Index (ODI) combines Gini, GII, HDI, and Freedom House, and is explained in Chapter 10.

Analyzing the economy's **share in GDP** by **agriculture**, the top five countries are Central African Republic (57%), Liberia (53%), Comoros (46%), Ethiopia, (46%), and Democratic Republic of Congo (46%), and the bottom five with less than 3% each are South Africa, Republic of Congo, Equatorial Guinea, Seychelles, and Libya. The average is 22% (23 countries above and 28 below the average and no data for 3 countries). By **industry**, the top five countries are Equatorial Guinea (96%), Libya (78%), Republic of Congo (77%), Gabon (64%), and Angola (62%), and the bottom five are Benin (13%), Gambia (13%), Comoros (12%), Ethiopia (11%), and Liberia (10%), with an overall average of 31% (18 countries above and 33 below the average and no data for 3 countries). By **services**, the top five are Seychelles (80%), Djibouti (79%), Namibia (73%), Cape Verde (72%), and Mauritius (70%), and the bottom five are Central African Republic (28%), Nigeria (27%), Libya (20%), Republic of Congo (20%), and Equatorial Guinea (2%), with an average of 47% (26 above and 25 below the average and no data for 3 countries).

Analyzing the **social structure** by **income distribution**,[3] the top five countries on income equality are Burundi (.33), Mali (.33), Egypt (.31), Somalia (.30), and Ethiopia (.30), and the bottom five are Seychelles (.66), Equatorial Guinea (.65), Comoros (.64), Namibia (.64), and South Africa (.63), with an average of .45 for all (32 countries above and 21 below the average and no data for 3 countries). By **literacy** of the population 15 years of age and older, the top five countries are Equatorial Guinea (94%), Seychelles (92%), Zimbabwe (92%), Lesotho (90%), and Namibia (89%), and the bottom five are Chad (34), Mali (31), Burkina Faso (29), Niger (29), and South Sudan (27), with an average of 67% (24 countries on or above and 30 below the average). In the GII ranking of **gender equality**, the top five countries are Libya (36), Tunisia (46), Mauritius (70), Algeria (74), and Rwanda (76), and the bottom five are Niger (146), Liberia (143), Mali (141), Mauritania (139), and Sierra Leone (139), with no data for 18 countries, which shows the lack of priority on the topic.

By **colonial background**, there are 16 former French colonies, 17 British, 5 Portuguese, 1 Spanish, 1 German, 1 Belgium, 3 Italian, 8 mixed, and missing data on 2. By **legal tradition**, there are 9 common law, 25 Roman law, 3 Islamic law, 16 mixed, and 1 missing data. By **religion**, there are 21 majority Islam, 26 Christian, 4 indigenous or other, and 3 mixed.

With so much information, it is difficult to synthesize a measure that helps rank which countries are doing best or worst and why. To try to solve that puzzle, several indices have been developed: since 1990 the United Nations Development Program (UNDP) has run annually the Human Development Index (HDI), combining income, education, and health (see Appendix 6); Freedom House (FH), a bipartisan nonprofit organization established in 1941 in New York, has conducted since 1973 an annual survey of global political rights and civil liberties that measures political performance. Without demeaning the great contribution that these indices have made to measuring development over the old GDP rule established in 1934, a more complete index is offered in Chapter 10 as the ODI (Objective Development Index). The commission led by Joseph Stiglitz, Amartya Sen, and Juan-Paul Fitoussi in 2008 under the initiative of French president Sarkozy made the need for such an index very clear.[4]

In accordance with the commission's recommendations, a more complete index ought to include, at a minimum, monitoring political performance, income distribution, gender equality and environmental sustainability. Chapter 10 responds to this challenge with the Objective Development Index (ODI), combining them all (except environmental sustainability, for reasons explained in that chapter). The next paragraph shows African countries' rankings on all three aggregated indices—HDI, Freedom House, and ODI.

On the ranking from the UNDP, **Human Development Index (HDI)**, the top five countries are Seychelles (46), Libya (64), Mauritius (80), Algeria (93), and Tunisia (94), and the bottom five are Burkina Faso (183), Chad (184), Mozambique (185), Niger (186), and Democratic Republic of Congo (186), with no data for two countries. On **political performance** measured by the Freedom House index of political rights and civil liberties, the top five countries are Mauritius (90), Cape Verde (90), Ghana (84), Benin (82), and South Africa (81), and the bottom five are Ethiopia (18), Sudan (11), Equatorial Guinea (8), Eritrea (3), and Somalia (2), with an average of 45 (23 countries above and 30 below the average, and no data for 1 country). According to the **Objective Development Index (ODI)**, combining Gini, GII, HDI, and FH, the top five countries are Mauritius (53), Libya (59), Tunisia (67), Algeria (95), and Ghana (115), and the bottom five are Comoros (193), Angola (194), Democratic Republic of Congo (195), Central African Republic (196), and Equatorial Guinea (197).

Cultures of *Honor*: Examples from Islamic and Christian Orthodox Countries

Why is it that **Islamic countries**, which are heirs to the highly successful and millennia-old Persian, Babylonian, Assyrian, and Egyptian civilizations, followed by the Ottoman Empire, fall into the lower-middle development range in today's world, as Table 4.2 shows? To talk of the Islamic countries means focusing on the bottom-left half of the *Cultural Map of the World* shown in Chapter 2. The world's Muslim population is estimated at 1.6 billion—23% of the world's people—spread over 49 countries[5] in which more than 50% of the population follows Islam.

The Prophet Muhammad founded Islam in the 7th century AD, and his teachings were collected in the Koran in the form of verses organized into 114 chapters. These come out of his life along the western coast of the Arabian Peninsula, between Mecca and Medina. In the 20 years leading up to his death, his message spread rapidly and his following grew, enabling him to unify the tribes of Arabia.

Islam reached its golden age between the 9th and 13th centuries, and its geographic expansion spread from the Middle East to North Africa and Spain. Its rise was accompanied by developments in science, mathematics, and medicine, and the Islamic world maintained a constant exchange of ideas with Greeks, Christians, and Jews.

TABLE 4.2

Islamic and Christian Orthodox Countries, 2014

	Country	Population (Thousands)	Pop. Density	% Rural Pop.	GDP (billion US $)	GDP per Capita	Agr. % GDP	Ind. % GDP	Srvs. % GDP	Gini Index* Higher = unequal	Literacy % 15+ years old	GII Rank Higher = unequal	HDI Rank Lower = better	Freedom House Higher = better	Colonial BG **	Legal Tradition ***	ODI Rank **** Lower = better	Christian	Muslim	Sunni	Shiite	Orthodox	Other	Region	Corruption
	Muslim, Arab																								
1	Algeria	35,980	15	27	325	8,447	7	62	31	35.3	73	74	93	35	1	3/2	95			99			1	A	36
2	Ba hrain	1,324	1,660	11	32	24,590					92	45	48	20	2	3/2	78	9	81				10	A	48
3	Egypt	82,537	81	56	534	6,614	14	37	49	30.8	72	126	112	38	2	3/2	119	1	90			9		A	32
4	Iraq	32,962	74	33	136	4,177	9	70	21	30.9	78	120	131	25	3/2	2	143		97				3	A	16
5	Jordan	6,181	68	17	38	6,037	3	31	66	35.5	93	99	100	34	3/2	3/2	114	6		92			2	A	45
6	Kuwait	2,818	154	2	141	44,988	0	51	49		94	47	54	41	3/2	3	64		85				15	A	43
7	Lebanon	4,259	413	13	64	14,373	6	21	74		90	78	72	49	3/1	2	80	39	60				1	A	28
8	Libya	6,423	4	22	105	13,300	2	78	20		89	36	64	43	3/5	3	59			97			3	A	15
9	Morocco	32,273	72	43	173	5,220	15	30	55	40.9	56	84	130	43	1	3/2	129		99				1	A	37
10	Oman	2,846	9	27	78	25,806	2	55	43		87	59	84	23		3	99		75			25		A	47
11	Qatar	1,870	152	1	168	82,106				41.1	96	117	36	25	2	3/2	126	9	78				13	A	68
12	Saudi Arabia	28,083	13	18	883	31,214	2	60	38		87	145	57	8	3	3	154		100					A	46
13	Syria	20,820	111	44	120	5,347	23	31	46	35.8	83	118		7	3/1	3/2	155	10	90					A	17
14	Tunisia	10,674	68	34	104	9,636	8	33	58	41.4	78	46	94	58	1	2	67	1		98			1	A	41
15	United Arab Emirates	7,891	90	16	381	41,397	1	56	44		90	40	41	19	2	3/2	75		96				4	A	69
16	Yemen	24,800	46	68	58	2,448	8	29	63	37.7	64	148	160	25	3	3	188		99				1	A	18
	Subtotal/average	301,740	189	27	3,340	20,356	7	46	47	37	83	86	85	31			109	11	88	97		9	6		38
	Muslim, Non-Arab																								
1	Afghanistan	35,320	53	76	47	1,561	21	23	57	27.8	28	147	175	26		3/2	174			80	19		1	NA	8
2	Albania	3,216	117	47	30	9,403	19	16	66	34.5	96	41	70	63	3	2	49	10	70			20		NA	31
3	Azerbaijan	9,168	110	46	94	10,125	6	67	27	33.7	100	54	82	23	4	2	89		93			5	2	NA	28
4	Bangladesh	150,494	1,142	72	286	1,851	18	28	54	32.1	57	111	146	56	2	3/1	117		90				10	NA	27
5	Brunei	406	76	24	22	52,482	1	72	28		95			29	2	3/1	83	14	57				29	NA	60
6	Indonesia	242,326	132	49	1,204	4,876	15	47	38	34.0	93	106	121	65	6	2	88	9		87			4	NA	32
7	Iran	74,799	45	31	832	13,100	10	44	45	38.3	85	107		16		3	140			9	89		2	NA	25
8	Kazakhstan	16,558	6	46	230	13,667	6	40	54	29.0	100	51	69	26	4	2	70	2	47			44	7	NA	26
9	Kosovo	1,794	163			7,400	12	20	68	30.0	92			43	3	2	112	6	93				1	NA	33
10	Kyrgyzstan	5,507	28	65	13	2,370	20	29	51	36.2	99	64	125	41	4	2	100			75		20	5	NA	24
11	Malaysia	28,859	86	27	495	16,919	12	40	48	46.2	93	42		48	2	3/1	79	9	60				31	NA	50
12	Pakistan	176,745	225	64	491	2,741	22	25	53	30.0	55	123	146	42	2	3/1	138		96				4	NA	28
13	Tajikistan	6,977	49	73	18	2,192	20	20	60	30.8	100	57	125	24	4	2	103			94	4	2		NA	22
14	Turkey	73,640	95	29	1,358	18,348	9	28	63	39.0	91	68	90	61		2	72		100					NA	50
15	Turkmenistan	5,105	11	51	54	10,411	15	48	37	40.8	100		102	7	4	2	131			85	5		10	NA	17
16	Uzbekistan	29,341	67	64	105	3,533	19	36	45	36.7	99		114	4	4	2	141		88			9	3	NA	17
	Subtotal/Average	860,256	150	51	5,279	10,686	14	36	50	35	86	81	114	36			105	8	78	74	29	17	8		30
	Orthodox																								
1	Armenia	3,100	109	36	25	8,417	21	37	42	30.9	100	59	87	42	3	2	66	4				95	1	O	36
2	Belarus	9,473	47	25	145	15,327	10	44	46	27.2	100		50	14	4	2	62					80	20	O	29
3	Bulgaria	7,476	69	27	117	16,044	6	31	63	28.2	98	38	57	81	3	2	40			7	1	60	32	O	41
4	Cyprus	1,117	119	29	27	30,768	2	20	78	29.0	98	22	31	93	3/2	2	20			18		78	4	O	63
5	Georgia	4,486	78	47	26	5,806	9	23	67	41.3	100	81	72	60	4	2	84		10			84	6	O	49
6	Greece	11,304	88	39	286	25,331				34.3	97	23	29	83		2	34					98	2	O	40
7	Macedonia	2,064	82	41	25	11,834	11	27	61	43.2	97	30		64	3	2	55		33			65	2	O	44
8	Moldova	3,559	124	52	12	3,368				33.0	99	49		65	4	2	57					98	2	O	35
9	Montenegro	632	47	37	9	14,358	9	19	71	30.0	98		52	72	3	2	39	4	18			74	4	O	44
10	Romania	21,390	93	47	363	17,004	7	25	68	30.0	98	55	56	81		2	45	12				87	1	O	43
11	Russia	141,930	9	26	3,373	23,501	4	37	59	40.1	100	51		26		2	90		10			81	9	O	28
12	Serbia	7,261	83	44	85	11,801				27.8	98		64	78	3	2	42	7	3			85	5	O	42
13	Ukraine	45,706	79	31	333	7,298	10	32	59	26.4	100	57	78	57		2	48	12				83	5	O	25
	Subtotal/average	259,498	79	37	4,826	14681	18	41	41	32	99	47	58	63			52	8	16	12	1	82	7		40
	Total/average	1,421,494	144	38	13,445	15,279	13	41	46	34	89	72	89	42			91	9	73	67	24	58	7		36

Sources and meanings: see appendix 3.

* Gini Index: 0 = zero wealth concentration; 1 = one person holds all the wealth.

** Colonial BG: 1 France; 2 Britain; 3 Ottoman; 4 Russia; 5 Italy; 6 Dutch.

*** Legal Tradition: 1 Common; 2 Civil; 3 Islamic.

**** Objective Development Index (ODI) combines Gini, GII, HDI, and Freedom House, and is explained in Chapter 10.

But in the 12th century Al-Ghazali[6] sparked a debate over the preeminence of *revealed* knowledge versus *reasoned* knowledge—similar to that which exists today in the United States between young-Earth *creationism* and *evolution*. In Al-Ghazali's time, unfortunately, the former side won out (Hoodbhoy, 2002). The age of tolerance and science in the Islamic world came to an end and, to make matters worse for Islam, this doctrine was also incorporated into its legal system.

Meanwhile, Europe was waking up to the Renaissance. That awakening had been facilitated by Arab translations of Greek texts, but the scientific explosion that would come to dominate the world was to take place in Europe.

Today the majority (9 out of 10) of those who follow Islam belong to the Sunni branch (Pew Research, 2009), versus about 10% who belong to the Shiite branch, which is the majority faith in Iran, Iraq, Azerbaijan, and Bahrain. Another powerfully influential current, despite its relatively small number of adherents, is an orthodox sect within Sunni Islam: Wahhabism in Saudi Arabia.

Just as European colonial rule in Africa dissolved preexisting borders and fundamentally transformed the relationship between agricultural technology and population growth, it also altered the borders in the Middle East, though this was brought on by competition over the control of oil. Following the weakening and ultimate collapse of Ottoman imperial rule in 1923, Arab nationalist leaders came into conflict first with Britain and later with the United States.

International interests took priority, and governments in Iran, Egypt, and Indonesia were replaced with allies willing to deal with the superpowers. The incompetence and corruption of secular governments paved the way for religious movements to seize power toward the end of the 20th century.

In addition to the complexity of these situations, one must bear in mind the diversity of the Islamic world. In terms of population, Indonesia is the largest Muslim country. As a strategic economic powerhouse, Saudi Arabia's oil reserves put it on top. In terms of political conflict, Iran stands out. In terms of security risks, Pakistan dominates. Egypt had been the greatest cultural influence in the Arab Middle East. In sum, there is no single representative country that can speak for the world of Islam today.

While cultures emerge from individuals' systems of beliefs and values, once these value systems are shared, they rise to take on a collective nature at the national level. It is through leaders and parties—that is, the political process, be it democratic or authoritarian—that decisions are made into policies, laws, and institutions.

For the majority of Islamic countries, particularly in the Middle East, the clergy has a profound influence on the political process, and there is no separation of religion and state. Furthermore, since revealed truth is thought to be superior to discovered truth, there is no emphasis on science education.

Looking on the bright side, it is worth noting that Europe went through a similar situation for a thousand years from the 5th to the 15th centuries. The Vatican directed the Catholic Church to become deeply intertwined with the day-to-day politics of countries through the application of canon law. It was not until after the Protestant Reformation, begun in 1517 by Martin Luther, that corruption in the papacy was widely exposed and the Vatican's authority was seriously called into question.

An analysis of the **population** of Muslim countries as shown in Table 4.2 illustrates great diversity, as one might expect given their wide geographic distribution. The five largest countries by **population** (in millions) are Indonesia (242), Pakistan (177), Bangladesh (150), Egypt (83), and Iran (75), while the smallest five are Brunei (.406), Bahrain (1.3), Kosovo (1.8), Qatar (1.9), and Kuwait (2.8). Missing from this list is India, which although not a majority Muslim country has the third-largest population of Muslims in the world. The average size for the 32 countries is 36 million (6 countries above and 26 below the average). By **population density** per square kilometer, the top five countries are Bahrain (1,324), Bangladesh (1,142), Lebanon (413), Pakistan (225), and Kosovo (163), and the bottom five are Libya (4), Kazakhstan (6), Oman (9), Turkmenistan (11), and Saudi Arabia (13). The average density is 170 (4 countries above and 28 below the average). By percentage of rural population, the top five are Afghanistan (76%), Tajikistan (73%), Bangladesh (72%), Yemen (68%), and Kyrgyzstan (65%), while the bottom five are Qatar (1%), Kuwait (2%), Bahrain (11%), Lebanon (13%), and the United Arab Emirates (16%). The average is 39%, with 15 countries above and 16 below the average, and one country with no information available.

Analyzing the **economy** by **annual GDP** (in billions of US$), the five largest economies are Turkey ($1,358), Indonesia ($1,204), Saudi Arabia ($883), Iran ($832), and Egypt ($534), while the five smallest are Kyrgyzstan ($13), Tajikistan ($18), Brunei ($22), Albania ($30), and Bahrain ($32), with an average of $278 (10 countries above and 21 below the average, and one with no information available). In terms of **GDP per capita**, the five wealthiest countries are Qatar ($82,000), Brunei ($52,000), Kuwait ($45,000), the United Arab Emirates ($41,000), and Saudi Arabia ($31,000), while the poorest are Afghanistan ($1,561), Bangladesh ($1,851), Tajikistan ($2,192), Kyrgyzstan ($2,370), and Yemen ($2,448). The average is $15,500, with 9 countries above and 23 below the average.

Analyzing the sectors of their economies, the top five countries by **share of agriculture in GDP** are Syria (23%), Pakistan (22%), Afghanistan (21%), Kyrgyzstan (20%), and Tajikistan (20%), while the bottom five are Kuwait (0%), Brunei (1%), the UAE (1%), Oman (2%), and Libya (2%), with an average of 11% (14 countries above and 16 below the average, with no data for two countries). By **share of industry**, the top five are Libya (78%), Brunei (72%), Iraq (70%), Azerbaijan (67%), and Algeria (62%), and the bottom five are Albania (16%), Kosovo (20%), Tajikistan (20%), Lebanon (21%), and Afghanistan (23%). The average is 41% (12 countries above, 18 below, and 2 with no information available). By **share of services**, the top five are Lebanon (74%), Kosovo (68%), Jordan (66%), Albania (66%), and Turkey (63%), and the bottom five are Libya (20%), Iraq (21%), Azerbaijan (27%), Brunei (28%), and Algeria 31(%). The average is 48% (16 countries above, 14 below, and 2 with no data).

Analyzing the **social structure** by **income distribution**, the top five countries on income equality are Afghanistan (.28), Kazakhstan (.29), Pakistan (.30),

Kosovo (.30), and Egypt (.31), while the bottom five are Malaysia (.46), Tunisia (.41), Qatar (.41), Morocco (.41), and Turkmenistan (.41). The average is .35 (13 countries above and 11 below, and 8 with no data available). By **literacy rate**, the top five countries are Azerbaijan (100%), Kazakhstan (100%), Tajikistan (100%), Turkmenistan (100%), and Uzbekistan (99%)—all of which are former Soviet republics—while the bottom five are Afghanistan (28%), Pakistan (55%), Morocco (56%), Bangladesh (57%), and Yemen (64%). The average is 84% (22 above and 10 below the average). By the GII ranking of **gender equality**, the top five countries are Libya (36), the United Arab Emirates (40), Albania (41), Malaysia (42), and Bahrain (45), and the bottom five are Yemen (148), Afghanistan (147), Saudi Arabia (145), Egypt (126), and Pakistan (123), with no data for four countries.

By **colonial background**, there are 3 French, 8 British, 4 Ottoman, 6 Russian, 1 Dutch, 6 mixed, and 4 without data. By **legal tradition**, there are 13 Roman law, 6 Islamic law, and 13 mixed. By religion, all the countries are by definition majority Islamic, but 8 have substantial minority religious groups (20% or more of the population).

On the aggregated rankings of development, in terms of the **Human Development Index** the top five countries are Qatar (36), the United Arab Emirates (41), Bahrain (48), Kuwait (54), and Saudi Arabia (57), while the bottom five are Afghanistan (175), Yemen (160), Pakistan (146), Bangladesh (146), and Iraq (131), with no data for five countries. On **political performance** as measured by Freedom House, the top five countries are Indonesia (65), Albania (63), Turkey (61), Tunisia (58), and Bangladesh (56), while the bottom five are Uzbekistan (4), Syria (7), Turkmenistan (7), Saudi Arabia (8), and Iran (16). The average is 33, with 16 countries above and 16 below the average. According to the **Objective Development Index (ODI)**, the top five countries are Albania (49), Libya (59), Kuwait (64), Tunisia (67), and Kazakhstan (70), while the bottom five are Yemen (188), Afghanistan (174), Syria (155), Saudi Arabia (154), and Iraq (143).

Why is it that the **Orthodox countries**, which sprang from the cradle of Western civilization in Greece, also fall into the lower-middle development range in today's world? The Orthodox Church lists 43 countries where it has a presence, but it is only the majority faith in 13 of them, and in only two others (Ethiopia and Bosnia-Herzegovina) does it account for more than a third of the population. Six countries account for 80% of the world's Orthodox population: Russia (89 million or 63% of Russians), Ukraine (42 million), Ethiopia (36 million), Romania (19 million), Greece (11 million), and Egypt (5 million). Only three countries are more than 90% Orthodox: Moldova, Greece, and Ukraine.

Orthodox countries of the former Soviet Bloc attained a relatively high level of education, which increased secularism, as did decades of religious repression under communism. These factors explain their high position on the vertical axis of the *World Culture Map*.

Although Orthodox, Catholic, and Protestant religious traditions grew from the same Christian roots and share most of the same scriptures, the varieties of religious interpretation and rituals gave rise to different kinds of societies.

Eastern Orthodoxy operates within the typology of *cultures of honor*; colonial Catholicism, of *joy*; and Protestantism falls within the typology of *cultures of achievement*.

Following the division of the Roman Empire into Eastern and Western, Christianity eventually ended up mirroring this regional breakup. It was a long, drawn-out process, which emerged out of a series of seven ecumenical councils.[7]

Differences in doctrine and ritual are generally much smaller between Roman Catholicism and Eastern Orthodoxy than between the two of them and Protestantism, although papal authority ceased to have jurisdiction over the Orthodox Church. Today a sort of rapprochement is emerging on the basis of recognizing that, among the five Patriarchs (Rome, Constantinople, Alexandria, Antioch, and Jerusalem), Rome's holds a *place of honor*, though not one of *supremacy*.

Given the doctrinal similarity between Orthodox Christianity and Catholicism, it could be expected that the Orthodox countries would appear at the same level of the *Cultural Map of the World* on the secular-rational versus traditional values axis as the Catholic European countries. Given their lower level of economic development compared with Western Europe, they should appear, as they do, on the left side of the horizontal survival versus self-expression values axis.

Analyzing the **population size** of the world's Orthodox countries, the five largest are Russia (142 million), Ukraine (46 million), Romania (21 million), Greece (11 million), and Belarus (9 million), while the five smallest are Montenegro (632 thousand), Cyprus (1.1 million), Macedonia (2.1 million), Armenia (3.1 million), and Moldova (3.6 million). The average population size is 19.9 million (3 countries above and 10 below the average). By **density**, the top five are Moldova (124), Cyprus (119), Armenia (109), Romania (93), and Greece (88), while the bottom five are Russia (9), Belarus (47), Montenegro (47), Bulgaria (69), and Georgia (78). The average is 79 (8 countries at or above the average and 5 below). By the percentage of **rural inhabitants**, the top five are Moldova (52%), Romania (47%), Georgia (47%), Serbia (44%), and Macedonia (41%), while the bottom five are Belarus (25%), Russia (26%), Bulgaria (27%), Cyprus (29%), and Ukraine (31%). The average is 37% (7 countries at or above the average and 6 below).

Looking at the analysis of the economy, the five largest economies by **annual GDP** (billions of US dollars) are Russia ($3,373), Romania ($363), Ukraine ($333), Greece ($286), and Belarus ($145), while the smallest are Montenegro ($9), Moldova ($12), Macedonia ($25), Armenia ($25), and Georgia ($26). The average is $371, with 2 countries above and 11 below the average. In terms of **GDP per capita** (in thousands of dollars), the wealthiest five are Cyprus ($30.8), Greece ($25.3), Russia ($23.5), Romania ($17), and Bulgaria ($16), while the poorest are Moldova ($3.4), Georgia ($5.8), Ukraine ($7.3), Armenia ($8.4), and Serbia ($11.8). The average is $14.7, with six countries above and seven below that average, and noticeably less variation among the group than can be seen in Africa or the Islamic world.

By share of GDP in **agriculture**, the top five countries are Armenia (21%), Moldova (13%) Macedonia (11%), Belarus (10%), and Ukraine (10%), and the bottom five are Cyprus (2%), Greece (3%), Russia (4%), Bulgaria (6%), and Romania (7%), with an average of 9%. By share of GDP in **industry**, the top five countries are Belarus (44%), Armenia (37%), Russia (37%), Ukraine (32%), and Bulgaria (31%), while the bottom five are Greece (16%), Moldova (17%), Montenegro (19%), Cyprus (20%), and Georgia (23%), with an average of 27%. By share of GDP in **services**, the top five countries are Greece (80%), Cyprus (78%), Montenegro (71%), Moldova (70%) and Romania (68%), while the bottom five are Armenia (42%), Belarus (46%), Ukraine (59%), Russia (59%), and Macedonia (61%), with an average of 64%.

Turning to social structure, the most equitable five countries in terms of **income distribution** are Ukraine (.26), Belarus (.27), Serbia (.28), Bulgaria (.28), and Cyprus (.29), while the least equitable are Macedonia (.43), Georgia (.41), Russia (.40), Greece (.34), and Moldova (.33), with an average of .32 (8 countries above and 5 below this average). By **literacy rate**, the top five countries are Georgia, Ukraine, Belarus, Russia, and Armenia, all of which have 100% literacy, while the bottom five are Greece (97%), Macedonia (97%), Romania (98%), Serbia (98%), and Bulgaria (98%). All the countries in the group, however, boast high literacy rates, with little variation from their statistical average of 99%. In terms of **gender equality**, the top five countries are Cyprus (22), Greece (23), Macedonia (30), Bulgaria (38), and Moldova (49), while the bottom five are Georgia (81), Armenia (59), Ukraine (57), Romania (55), and Russia (51). We again see relatively little variation from their average ranking of 47.

By **colonial background**, five of the countries experienced Ottoman rule and three of them Russian rule, while one (Cyprus) experienced both British and Ottoman colonization. All the countries have a Roman law background. All of them have at least 60% of the population identifying as Orthodox.

In terms of the aggregated rankings of development, on the **Human Development Index** the top five Orthodox countries are Greece (29), Cyprus (31), Belarus (50), Montenegro (52), and Romania (56), and the bottom five are Armenia (87), Ukraine (78), Georgia (72), Serbia (64), and Bulgaria (57), with the remaining three (Macedonia, Moldova, and Russia) without data. On the Freedom House rankings of **civil and political rights**, the top five are Cyprus (93), Greece (83), Bulgaria (81), Romania (81), and Serbia (78), and the bottom five are Belarus (14), Russia (26), Armenia (42), Ukraine (57), and Georgia (60). The average is 63, with eight countries above and five below the average. According to the **Objective Development Index** (ODI), the top five countries are Cyprus (20), Greece (34), Montenegro (39), Bulgaria (40), and Serbia (42), and the bottom five are Russia (90), Georgia (84), Armenia (66), Belarus (62), and Moldova (57).

Cultures of *Achievement*: Examples from Asian and Confucian Countries

Confucian countries, with China at their core, were the most advanced civilization of antiquity, but lost their luster around the 19th century. Why? The central teachings of Confucius (551–479 BC) can be summed up as (1) the *Golden Rule* (one should treat others as one would like to be treated); (2) an emphasis on study and learning; and (3) the five key relationships (sovereign to subject, parent to child, husband to wife, elder sibling to younger sibling, and friend to friend), which establish mutual obligations of filial piety, upon which the veneration of ancestors is based.

The *Golden Rule* actually appears in most philosophies and religions of antiquity in one form or another as an ethical principle of reciprocity. An *emphasis on study* and learning had already been established by the Jews a millennium earlier, though it would not surface independently again for another two millennia after Confucius's time, in the form of European Protestantism. In any case, each of these teachings arose independently within Confucianism and were adopted and transmitted as a philosophy throughout a large region of East Asia.

After Confucianism at the axiological base of the countries of East Asia, other belief systems made their way into the region over the centuries: Buddhism, Daoism, and Shintoism (which do not insist that their adherents reject all other belief systems), as well as Christianity and Islam (which do). The Japanese, for example, observe Shinto rituals for life events (births and marriages) and Buddhist rituals for death. Two countries, China and Japan, provide a clear synthesis of these regional traits.

The modern social, economic, and political profile of China is primarily the result of a confluence of several factors: (1) great fertile plains, (2) trisected by two great rivers (the Yellow and the Yangtze), (3) where the world's cultivation of rice began, (4) which gave rise to an enormous growth in population over the millennia, (5) upon which one of the greatest and most advanced empires of antiquity was built.

China and Asia became better known in Europe at the end of the 13th century due to the Venetian Marco Polo (1254–1324), who traveled to China at the age of 20, accompanying his father and uncle. China by that time had become the most advanced country on Earth in terms of technology and recorded knowledge. By contrast, Europe was wandering through the very dark Middle Ages. Among great Chinese inventions were the compass, gunpowder, paper, and printing. The Chinese breadth of knowledge and navigation techniques regularly brought them to India, the Persian Gulf, and at least as far as Ethiopia and the coast of East Africa between the 7th and 15th centuries (Bowman, 2000; Levathes, 1994).

The centralization of imperial power that made China into one of the great empires of antiquity also prevented it from discovering the Americas or becoming the cradle of the industrial revolution. The centralized political system—so indispensable to the administration of irrigation in the Yellow and Yangtze River basins—also impeded individual innovation and entrepreneurship, because all decisions had to be approved by the central government. Another problem of imperial centralization were the nearly 2,000 famines over the course of 22 centuries—an average of almost one per year—typical of non-democratic regimes (Sen, 1999, chapter 7; and *Time*, 1928).

The complacency of the Chinese, along with their conviction that the rest of the countries in the world were *barbarians*, prevented them from realizing that Europeans had begun to experience an accelerated technological advancement during the 16th century. By the time they figured it out, it was already too late, and the powers of the West began to impose themselves on the *Celestial Empire* beginning with the First Opium War of 1839–1842.

Adverse domestic and international conditions led to a succession of rebellions, the product of the deleterious effects of opium and the spread of Christianity. As an outcome of the Second Opium War (1856–1860), China ceded Hong Kong to England and submitted to an inequitable treaty system that further weakened its economy.

China's rapid decline over the course of the 19th century led to a very large diaspora, which, two centuries later, would actually prove quite useful. While China was in decline, Japan was gathering strength, as I will discuss later, and the First Sino-Japanese War was fought over Korea (1894–1895), resulting in China's loss of Taiwan to Japan.

The last emperor of China, Pu Yi, was crowned in 1908, when he was just three years old, and was forced to abdicate in 1912 upon the proclamation of the Republic of China. Internal conflicts continued until 1920 when Chiang Kai-shek, leader of the Nationalist Party (Guomindang, or GMD), achieved a certain level of stability. The rise of the Soviet Union and of international communism opened a new front of opposition, which was temporarily postponed during World War II (1937–1945).

Hostilities between the Nationalist and Communist parties resumed after 1945, with the outbreak of civil war. In 1949 the Chinese Nationalist Party fled to Taiwan under Western protection. In 1966 Mao launched the Cultural Revolution while increasingly distancing China from the Soviet Union, and in 1972 he established diplomatic relations with the United States and took over Taiwan's seat at the United Nations.

Following Mao's death in 1976, the Communist Party loosened controls on land and the economy, and a period of recovery began under the new Constitution of 1982. In 2001 China joined the World Trade Organization. China went from a centrally planned economy to a mixed economy, or market socialism, which continues to this day.

Japan's economic success can be explained in the following nine points: (1) the location of the Japanese Archipelago, close enough to China to have reaped the benefits of the latter's developmental advances; (2) the ratio of agricultural land to forest; (3) the islands' sizes, being large enough to develop a complex political system (Diamond, 2005, p. 279); (4) the establishment of a single royal family line going back ten centuries; (5) the discovery of Spanish expansionist intentions and subsequent eradication of Christians beginning in 1597 (Landes, 1999, p. 354); (6) 250 years of stability and isolation under the Tokugawa Shogunate (1603–1867), which laid the groundwork for a demographic explosion of about 100 years in the first half of this time period, reflected in the fact that in 1720 Japan had the world's largest city,

Edo, now Tokyo (Diamond, 2005, p. 295); (7) the policy of protecting and managing its forests beginning in 1666, following the Great Fire of Meireki (p. 299); (8) its near-zero population growth rate for over a hundred years (1721–1828), when it went from 26.1 to 27.2 million inhabitants; and (9) the Meiji Restoration from 1867 onward, which triggered the modernization of Japan (see Chapter 7).

As can be seen, the first three causes of Japan's success were geographic,[8] the next three political,[9] and the last three environmental.[10] The axiological basis of Confucianism worked well in the structural conditions described here, which, in turn, reinforced the basic ideas of Confucianism. For this reason, Japan is a good illustration of the three sources of development: material and structural conditions, ideas, and their interaction, which I will discuss in Part VI.

Following this line of reasoning, it is interesting to note similarities and differences between the developmental histories of Japan, England, and the United States. All three grew up within an axiological infrastructure based on a culture of study and/or hard work, reinforced much earlier in Japan by Confucianism (5th century BC) and much later in the other two by the growth of Protestantism (15th–18th centuries AD). The initial economic development of all three was based on adequate climates for agriculture. All three share the effects of the distance provided by the sea between them and their powerful neighbors, although the United States is not an island.

As for their differences, Japan did not undergo a period of imperial domination the way England did under Rome or the United States did under England, but it did live under Chinese cultural dominance, as can be seen in its writing system, which, like Korean and Vietnamese, grew from the Chinese writing system (Kaiser, 1991). Japan and the United States were not beset with the same kinds of ongoing conflict and threats from their neighbors the way England was. But in Japan's case, centuries of feudalism led to intense competition and a warrior culture.

When comparing Japan with China, it is interesting to note that the decisions each made following the arrival of European ships in the 16th century had lasting and profoundly different effects on their future development. China underestimated European power and was more susceptible to religious and commercial infiltration. Japan was correct in its assessment of European power; it felt threatened and closed itself off.

China's *incidental* opening weakened it; while Japan's *intentional* isolation strengthened it. When both countries were forced to open their doors to increased trade with the West in the 19th century, they did so under diametrically opposed conditions—China from a position of weakness, and Japan from a position of strength.

Looking at the various South and East Asian countries on Table 4.3 (which includes both the Confucian countries of East Asia, the Hindu countries of South Asia, and some cities of China—Macao and Hong Kong—that have a very different historical background) by **population size** (in millions), the five largest are China (1,344), India (1,242), Indonesia (242), Japan (128),

TABLE 4.3

Asian and Confucian Countries, 2014

#	Country	Population (Thousands)	Pop. Density	% Rural Pop.	GDP (billion US $)	GDP per Capita	Agr, % GDP	Ind, % GDP	Srvs, % GDP	Gini Index* Higher = unequal	Literacy % 15+ years old	GII Rank Higher = unequal	HDI Rank Lower = better	Freedom House Higher = better	Colonial BG **	Legal Tradition ***	ODI Rank **** Lower = better	Unsp. Christian	Protestant	Catholic	Islam	Buddhism	Hindu	Chinese Universalist	Ethno-religionist	Other	Corruption
1	Cambodia	14.3	80	80	36	2,454	37	24	40	37.9	74	96	138	29	1	2	148				2	96				2	20
2	China	1,344.1	143	49	12,269	9,083	10	47	43	48	94	35	101	18		2	122	8				15		30	4	43	40
3	Hong Kong	7.1	6,783		366	51,103	0	7.1	93	43.4	94		13		2	1	44	14				15		46		25	75
4	India	1,241.5	412	69	4,716	3,813	17	26	56	33.4	63	132	136	76	2	1	107	2			13		81			4	36
5	Indonesia	242.3	132	49	1,204	4,876	15	47	38	34	93	106	121	65	6	2/3	88		6	3	86		2			3	32
6	Japan	127.8	350	9	4,487	35,178	1	27	71	37.6	99	21	10	88		2	29	2				71			84	8	74
7	Laos	6.3	27	66	19	2,879	31	35	35	36.7	73	100	138	11	1	2	159	2				67				31	26
8	Macao	0.6	19,416		48	86,341		7.4	93		93				4	2				15		50				35	35
9	Malaysia	28.9	86	27	495	16,919	12	40	48	46.2	93	42	64	48	2	1/3	79	9			60	19	6			6	50
10	Mongolia	2.8	2	32	15	5,374	14	36	49	36.5	97	56	108	86	7	2	54	6			4	50				40	38
11	Myanmar	48.3	73	67			48	16	35		92	80	149	29	2	1	152		3	1	4	89			1	2	21
12	Nepal	30.5	209	83	40	1,457	32	15	53	32.8	60	102	157	47		1	134				4	11	81		4		31
13	North Korea	24.5	202	40							100			3	3*	2	145					2			12	86	8
14	Philippines	94.9	313	51	420	4,339	13	31	56	43	95	77	114	63	5&8*	2/1	98	5	5	83	5					2	36
15	Singapore	5.2	7,252		323	60,800		27	73	47.3	96	13	18	52	2	1	46	10			5	15		43	4	23	86
16	South Korea	49.8	509	17	1,540	30,801	3	39	58	31.6	98	27	12	86	3*	2	25	24	8			24				44	55
17	Sri Lanka	20.9	329	85	125	6,146	12	30	58	40.3	91	75	92	43	2	2/1	101	6			8	69	7			10	37
18	Thailand	69.5	135	66	645	9,660	12	41	46	40	94	66	103	53		2/1	85	1			5	95					35
19	Vietnam	87.8	280	69	336	3,787	22	41	37	35.6	93	48	127	19	1	2	116	1		7		9				83	31
	Total/average	3,447	1,933	54	27,084	19,706	17	30	55	39	89	65	93	48			96	6	8	17	19	45	30	38	21	26	41

Sources and meanings: see appendix 3.

* Gini Index: 0 = zero wealth concentration; 1 = one person holds all the wealth.

** Colonial BG: 1 France; 2 Britain; 3 Japan; 4 Portugal; 5 Spain; 6 Dutch; 7 China; 8 US.

*** Legal tradition: 1 Common; 2 Civil; 3 Islamic.

**** Objective Development Index (ODI) combines Gini, GII, HDI, and Freedom House, and is explained in Chapter 10.

and Philippines (95), while the five smallest are Macao (.6), Mongolia (2.8), Singapore (5.2), Laos (6.3), and Hong Kong (7.1). The average is 181.4 million, with three countries above the average and 16 below, and enormous variation within the group. By **density** per square kilometer, the top five are Macao (19,416), Singapore (7,252), Hong Kong (6,783), South Korea (509), and India (412), while the bottom five are Mongolia (2), Laos (27), Myanmar (73), Cambodia (80), and Malaysia (86). By the percentage of **rural** inhabitants, the top five are Sri Lanka (85%), Nepal (83%), Cambodia (80%), Vietnam (69%), and India (69%), while the bottom five are Japan (9%), South Korea (17%), Malaysia (27%), Mongolia (32%), and North Korea (40%). Although formal data are unavailable for Macao, Singapore, and Hong Kong, these areas are essentially 100% urban. The average for all the countries is 54%, with 11 countries above and 8 below the average.

Moving to economic data, the countries with the largest **annual GDPs** (in billions of US$) are China ($12,269), India ($4,716), Japan ($4,487), South Korea ($1,540), and Indonesia ($1,204), while the smallest GDPs belong to Mongolia ($15), Laos ($19), Cambodia ($36), Nepal ($40), and Macao ($48). The average is $1,593, with three countries above the average, 14 countries below, and data unavailable for North Korea and Myanmar. Looking at **GDP per capita**, the five wealthiest countries are Macao ($86,000), Singapore ($61,000), Hong Kong ($51,000), Japan ($35,000), and South Korea ($31,000), while the five poorest are Nepal ($1,500), Cambodia ($2,500), Laos ($2,900), Vietnam ($3,800), and India ($3,800). The average is $19,706, with five countries above and 12 below the average, and data again unavailable for North Korea and Myanmar.

Analyzing the sectors of the economy, the top five countries by percentage of GDP from **agriculture** are Myanmar (48%), Cambodia (37%), Nepal (32%), Laos (31%), and Vietnam (22%), while the bottom five are Singapore (0%), Macao (0%) Hong Kong (.1%), Japan (1.2%), and South Korea (2.7%). The average is 17%, with 6 countries at or above the average and 12 below, and no data available for North Korea. By **industry**, the top five countries are Indonesia (47%), China (47%), Thailand (41%), Vietnam (41%), and Malaysia (40%), and the bottom five are Hong Kong (7.1%), Macao (7.4%), Nepal (15%), Myanmar (16%), and Cambodia (24%), with an average of 30%, 10 at or above the average, 8 below, and no data for North Korea. By **services**, the top five countries are Hong Kong (93%), Macao (93%), Singapore (73%), Japan (71%), and South Korea (58%), and the bottom five are Laos (35%), Myanmar (35%), Vietnam (37%), Indonesia (38%), and Cambodia (40%). The average is 55%, with 8 countries above the average, 10 below, and again no data for North Korea.

Turning to the **social structure** of the region, the top five countries in terms of **income equality** are South Korea (.32), Nepal (.33), India (.33), Indonesia (.34), and Vietnam (.36), while the five least equitable are China (.48), Singapore (.47), Malaysia (.46), Hong Kong (.43), and Philippines (.43). The average for all is .39 (9 countries above and 7 below the average, and no data available for 3 countries). By **literacy rate**, the top five countries are North Korea (a self-reported rate of 100%), Japan (99%), South Korea (98%), Mongolia (97%), and Singapore (96%), and the bottom five are Nepal (60%), India (63%), Laos (73%), Cambodia (74%), and Sri Lanka (91%). The average is 89% (15 countries above and 4 below the average). By **gender equality**, the top five countries are Singapore (13), Japan (21), South Korea (27), China (35), and Malaysia (42), and the bottom five are India (132), Indonesia (106), Nepal (102), Laos (100), and Cambodia (96), with no data for three countries.

Looking at the **colonial background** of the region, 3 countries were colonized by France, 6 by Britain, 2 by Japan, 1 by Portugal, 1 by Holland, 1 by China, and 1 by both Spain and the United States, while 4 countries were never colonized. By legal tradition, there are 5 common law, 9 Roman law, and 5 mixed. By **religion**, 2 are Muslim, 1 is Christian, 2 are Hindu, 8 are Buddhist, and 6 are other—bearing in mind that Confucianism, as an ethical code rather than a religion, is not included in these statistics, and influences most East Asian countries regardless of their stated religion.

Turning to the various aggregated rankings of development, according to the **Human Development Index** the top five countries are Japan (10), South

Korea (12), Hong Kong (13), Singapore (18), and Malaysia (64), while the bottom five are Nepal (157), Myanmar (149), Laos (138), Cambodia (138), and India (136), with no data for two countries. According to the Freedom House index of **political rights and civil liberties**, the top five countries are Japan (88), Mongolia (86), South Korea (86), India (76), and Indonesia (65), while the bottom five are North Korea (3), Laos (11), China (18), Vietnam (19), and Cambodia (29). The average is 48, with 9 countries at or above the average, 8 below it, and no information available for Hong Kong and Macao, which are part of China. According to the **Objective Development Index (ODI)**, the top five countries are South Korea (25), Japan (29), Hong Kong (44), Singapore (46), and Mongolia (54), and the bottom five are Laos (159), Myanmar (152), Cambodia (148), North Korea (145), and Nepal (134).

Cultures of *Achievement:* Examples from Western Countries and Their Offshoots

What explains the fact that the Protestant countries, which were considered barbarians by the Celestial Empire (China) until the 15th century and displayed a lower level of development than the Arab territories during the Middle Ages, have nonetheless been dominant for the last six centuries? Unlike the five blocs of countries already examined, the case of Western Europe, together with Israel and the former British colonies (Australia, Canada, the United States, and New Zealand), is unique.

First, over the millennia very different tribes peopled Europe, settling a highly differentiated territory divided by valleys and mountains. Second, Europe's geography kept together tightly knit populations, who were already split up according to ethnicity and language to begin with, thus facilitating the construction of strong identities. Third, geographic proximity of quite different tribes gave rise to frequent conflict, which molded a very competitive order between societies. And fourth, many of them were subjected to the homogenizing and civilizing influence of the Roman Empire.

Starting in the 6th century AD, with the collapse of the Roman Empire, Europe was deprived of the commercial center of gravity that was Rome, as well as of its centralized political authority.[11] Instead of having to struggle for its independence, Europe was simply left orphaned, which led to five centuries of regression, during which time Islam was in ascendancy. The empire was replaced by the rise of the feudal state, local agriculture, and the abandonment of trade. Angus Maddison handily sums up the first five centuries of Europe's Middle Ages:

> The main changes [. . .] were: a) the collapse of a large scale cohesive political unit which was never resurrected, and its replacement by a fragmented, fragile and unstable polity; b) disappearance of urban civilization and predominance of self-sufficient, relatively isolated and ignorant rural communities where a feudal elite extracted an income in kind from a servile peasantry; c)

the virtual disappearance of trading links between Western Europe, North Africa and Asia. (Maddison, 2006, p. 52)

A few dynamic centers slowly began to emerge. The first was Venice, with its strategic geographic position for East-West trade, which formed the basis for its success over 500 years (810–1324). Its relative independence from the Pope as well as the Patriarch allowed it a secular and tolerant atmosphere where local as well as foreign merchants could freely operate. In this environment, highly valuable institutional innovations emerged that secured property rights and the enforcement of contracts: credit, stock, and currency markets; banks; accounting systems; interest payments; tax system; land registries; and many more (Maddison, 2006, p. 54).

The second center of European economic dynamism was in Portugal and Spain, following the success of the crusades undertaken to reconquer territories held by the Arabs, particularly after the capture of Lisbon in 1147. They also held a geographic position, where the Atlantic coast meets the Mediterranean, which was strategically important in the development of the Age of Navigation. Due to their history, Spain and Portugal were able to bring together and use the knowledge, contributions, and intellectual and commercial networks of Jews and Muslims, as well as Christians. That combination gave them an advantage in maritime knowledge, made possible by their crowns' support. The outcome was a very active exploration of the seas, which led to the building of empires in the Americas and parts of coastal Asia and Africa, with a concomitant explosion in world trade.

The third center of European expansion was Holland, which began its rise in the 15th century on the basis of northern European trade and agricultural technology. The persecution of Moors and Jews by the Spanish Inquisition led to Holland becoming one of the countries that benefited most from the knowledge and skills of the new Jewish immigrants (Sombart, 1915, p. 13). The situation was consolidated upon Holland's independence from Spain in 1579, setting off a worldwide expansion in trade that made it the country with the highest level of income for two centuries (Landes, 1998, chapter 10).

The fourth and last center of European dynamism was England, triggered by its industrial revolution from the mid-18th century onward. The precursors to England's success were three key institutional innovations: the Magna Carta of 1215, which constituted the first recognition of basic rights; the English Civil War of 1639–1651, which led to the execution of King Charles I and established Parliament; and the *Glorious Revolution* of 1688, which consolidated these two prior advancements and eradicated the Counter-Reformation and Catholicism (Acemoglu and Robinson, 2012, chapter 7).

By the end of the second half of the 18th century, the British Empire had reached its zenith. It had taken territories from Holland and France in Asia and Africa and had explored Australia and New Zealand, despite having lost its American colonies. Its position as world leader would not end until after World War II, when it was replaced by the United States and the Soviet Union.

Outside Europe, possibly the most notable case of economic dynamism is that of Anglo America. Its colonization was not monolithic, and it had several false starts. Beginning in 1584 the English attempted to establish themselves on Roanoke Island (North Carolina) and at Jamestown (Virginia). From 1614 to 1664, the Dutch occupied the territory of New Netherland, centered on New Amsterdam, now Manhattan.

But real, major settlement began with the arrival in 1620 of Puritan migrants at Plymouth, Massachusetts; followed by that of noblemen and their servants in Virginia and Maryland; Quakers in Delaware; and by the 18th century, Scottish Highlanders and Northern Irish who spread out along the Appalachians (Fisher, 1989, p. 652). What is more, Spain held Florida and the central Gulf Coast region; and France controlled the North (present-day Canada) and the Louisiana Territory, which encompassed most of the watershed of the Mississippi River and its tributaries.

Overall, European countries were involved in five critical historical junctures: (1) the fall of the Roman Empire, which brought sudden changes in prevailing conditions from the 6th century onward; (2) the plagues, which profoundly altered the labor market; (3) the opening of world trade with the discovery of the Americas and the conquest of the Indian Ocean and the South Seas; (4) the English industrial revolution; and (5) the two World Wars of the 20th century. Those five *critical junctures* put Europe in an incremental and solid path of world domination for the last six centuries.

Looking at the data in Table 4.4, the top five Western countries by **population** are the United States (312 million), Germany (82 million), France (65 million), the United Kingdom (63 million), and Italy (61 million), while the smallest are San Marino (32 thousand), Monaco (35 thousand), Liechtenstein (36 thousand), Iceland (319 thousand), and Malta (419 thousand). The average is 24.6 million (with 8 countries above and 27 below the average). By population **density** per square kilometer, the top five are Monaco (17,704), Malta (1,300), San Marino (526), Netherlands (493), and Belgium (360), while the bottom five are Australia (3), Iceland (3), Canada (4), Norway (16), and New Zealand (17). In terms of the percentage of **rural inhabitants**, the top five countries are Liechtenstein (86%), Slovenia (50%), Slovakia (45%), Croatia (42%), and Poland (39%), and the bottom five are Monaco (0%), Belgium (3%), Malta (5%), San Marino (6%), and Iceland (6%). The overall average is 24% (with 16 countries above and 19 below the average).

According to the size of the economy, the largest **annual GDPs** (in billions of US$) belong to the United States ($16,244), Germany ($3,378), France ($2,372), the United Kingdom ($2,368), and Italy ($2,018). The smallest are Iceland ($12), Malta ($12), Estonia ($32), Latvia ($44), and Luxembourg ($47). The overall average is $1,132 (with 7 countries above and 25 below the average, and no data for 3). In terms of **GDP per capita**, the wealthiest countries are Luxembourg ($88,000), Norway ($66,000), Switzerland ($53,000), the United States ($52,000), and Australia ($45,000), and the poorest are Croatia ($21,000), Latvia ($22,000), Hungary ($22,000), Poland ($22,000), and Estonia ($24,000).

TABLE 4.4

Western Countries and Offshoots, 2014

#	Country	Population (Thousands)	Pop. Density	% Rural Pop.	GDP (billion US $)	GDP per Capita	Agr. % GDP	Ind. % GDP	Srvs. % GDP	Gini Index* Higher = unequal	Literacy % 15+ years old	GII Rank Higher = unequal	HDI Rank Lower = better	Freedom House Higher = better	Colonial BG **	Legal Tradition ***	ODI Rank **** Lower = better	Other Christian	Protestant	Catholic	Muslim	Jewish	Other	Corruption
1	Australia	22,621	3	11	1,011.6	44,598	2	20	78	35.2	99	17	2	97	1	1	14	11	27	26	2		34	81
2	Austria	8,419	102	32	369.5	43,661	2	29	69	29.2	98	14	18	96		2	8		5	74	4		17	69
3	Belgium	11,008	360	3	442.9	39,751	1	22	78	33.0	99	12	17	97		2	13			75			25	75
4	Canada	34,483	4	19	1,483.6	42,533	2	32	66	32.6	99	18	11	98	1/2	1	10	4	23	43	2		28	81
5	Croatia	4,407	79	42	89.5	20,964	5	26	68	33.7	99	33	47	86		2	37	5		88	1		6	48
6	Czech Republic	10,546	136	27	280.7	26,698	2	36	62	31.0	99	20	28	95		2	19		1	10			89	48
7	Denmark	5,574	131	13	235.8	42,173	1	22	77	24.8	99	3	15	98		2	3	3	95		2			91
8	Estonia	1,340	32	30	31.7	23,631	4	29	68	36.0	100	29	33	95		2	31	14	14				72	68
9	Finland	5,387	18	16	207.2	38,271	3	29	68	26.9	100	6	21	100		2	4	2	83				15	89
10	France	65,437	119	14	2,371.9	36,104	2	19	79	32.7	99	9	20	95		2	11		2	85	8	1	4	71
11	Germany	81,726	235	26	3,377.5	41,245	1	28	71	28.3	99	6	5	96		2	7		34	34	4		28	78
12	Hungary	9,971	110	31	218.4	21,959	4	31	65	31.2	99	42	37	88		2	36	4	19	52			25	54
13	Iceland	319	3	6	12.0	37,636	7	25	68	28.0	99	10	13	100		2	6	4	81	3			12	78
14	Ireland	4,487	65	38	200.5	43,683	1	32	67	34.3	99	19	7	97	1		17	2	3	87			8	72
15	Israel	7,766	352	8	252.0	31,869				39.2	97	25	16	81	3/1	1	35	2			17	76	5	61
16	Italy	60,770	206	32	2,018.4	33,134	2	25	73	36.0	99	11	25	88		2	28			80			20	43
17	Latvia	2,220	36	32	44.4	21,905	4	22	74	36.6	100	36	44	84		2	43	16	20				64	53
18	Liechtenstein	36	225	86							100		24	98		2	18		7	76			17	
19	Lithuania	3,203	52	33	72.8	24,374	4	28	68	37.6	100	28	41	90		2	38	4	2	79			15	57
20	Luxembourg	517	196	15	46.9	88,286		13	86	30.8	100	26	26	100		2	16			87			13	80
21	Malta	419	1,300	5	12.1	29,030	2	33	65	27.4	92	39	32	97	1	2/1	24			98			2	56
22	Monaco	35	17,704	0		0					99			87			27			90			10	
23	Netherlands	16,696	493	17	722.8	43,105	2	24	74	30.9	99	1	4	99		2	5		20	30	6		44	83
24	New Zealand	4,405	17	14	142.8	32,219	6	25	70	36.2	99	31	6	97	1	1	26	2	39	13			46	91
25	Norway	4,952	16	21	329.4	65,640	2	40	58	25.8	100	5	1	100		2	1	3	86	1	2		8	86
26	Poland	38,216	126	39	854.2	22,162	4	32	65	34.1	100	24	39	93		2	30	2		90			8	60
27	Portugal	10,637	116	39	267.3	25,389	2	23	74	38.5	95	16	43	97		2	33	2	85				13	62
28	San Marino	32	526	6							97			100			15	92					8	
29	Slovakia	5,440	113	45	136.2	25,175	4	35	61	26.0	100	32	35	92		2	21	4	11	69			16	47
30	Slovenia	2,052	102	50	56.5	27,474	2	32	66	31.2	100	8	21	91		2	12	3		58	2		37	57
31	Spain	46,235	92	23	1,480.9	32,043	3	26	71	34.7	98	15	23	96		2	22			94			6	59
32	Sweden	9,453	23	15	409.4	43,021	2	26	72	25.0	99	2	7	100		2	2		87				13	89
33	Switzerland	7,907	196	26	426.1	53,281				33.7	99	3	9	96		2	9	2	35	42	4		17	85
34	United Kingdom	62,641	257	20	2,368.2	37,456	1	22	78	36.0	99	34	26	97	1		32		72	3			25	76
35	United States	311,592	34	18	16,244.6	51,749	1	20	79	40.8	99	42	3	93	1	1	41	3	51	24	1	2	19	73
	Total/average	860,948	674	24	36,218	37,194	3	27	71	32	99	19	21	95			20	9	38	58	4	26	23	69

Sources and meanings: see appendix 3.

* Gini Index: 0 = zero wealth concentration; 1 = one person holds all the wealth.

** Colonial BG: 1 Britain; 2 France; 3 Ottoman.

*** Legal Tradition: 1 Common; 2 Civil; 3 Islamic.

**** Objective Development Index (ODI) combines Gini, GII, HDI, and Freedom House, and is explained in Chapter 10.

The average is $37,000 (with 16 countries above the average, 16 below it, and no data for 3).

Turning to an analysis of the sectors of the economy, the top five countries for share of GDP from **agriculture** are Iceland (7%), New Zealand (6%), Croatia (5%), Latvia (4%), and Slovakia (4%); the bottom five are Luxembourg

(0%), Monaco (0%), Belgium (1%), the United Kingdom (1%), and Germany (1%), with an average of 3% (11 countries at or above the average, 20 below it, and no data for 4). By **industry**, the top five countries are Norway (40%), the Czech Republic (36%), Slovakia (35%), Malta (33%), and Canada (32%), while the bottom five are Luxembourg (13%), France (19%), Australia (20%), the United States (20%), and the United Kingdom (22%). The average is 27% (with 14 countries above the average, 16 below it, and no data for 5). By **services**, the top five countries are Luxembourg (86%), France (79%), the United States (79%), Australia (78%), and the United Kingdom (78%), while the bottom five are Norway (58%), Slovakia (61%), Czech Republic (62%), Poland (65%), and Malta (65%). The average is 71% (with 14 countries at or above the average, 16 below, and no data for 5).

With regard to social structure, five countries with the most **equitable incomes** are Denmark (.25), Sweden (.25), Norway (.26), Slovakia (.26), and Finland (.27), while the five least equitable are the United States (.41), Israel (.39), Portugal (.39), Lithuania (.38), and Latvia (.37). The average overall is .32 (with 14 countries above and 18 below the average, and no data for 3). The **literacy rate** is 100% in 10 countries (Luxembourg, Finland, Norway, Liechtenstein, Estonia, Latvia, Lithuania, Slovenia, Slovakia, and Poland). The lowest literacy rates are found in Malta (92%), Portugal (95%), San Marino (97%), Israel (97%), and Spain (98%), but overall there is not much variation from the high average of 99%. In terms of **gender equality**, the top five countries on the GII index are the Netherlands (1), Sweden (2), Denmark (3), Switzerland (3), and Norway (5), while the bottom five are Hungary (42), the United States (42), Malta (39), Latvia (36), and the United Kingdom (34).

By **colonial background**, most of the Western countries were never colonized; however, the United States, Australia, New Zealand, and Malta were colonized by Britain; Canada was colonized by both Britain and France; and Israel was colonized by both Britain and the Ottoman Empire. By **legal background**, 7 countries use common law, 25 use Roman law, Malta uses a mixed system, and 2 have no data available. In terms of **religion**, 16 countries are primarily Catholic, 8 are primarily Protestant, 1 is Jewish, and 10 have no clear majority.

Turning to the ranking of these countries on the aggregated development indices, the top five countries according to the **Human Development Index** are Norway (1), Australia (2), the United States (3), Netherlands (4), and Germany (5), while the bottom five are Croatia (47), Latvia (44), Portugal (43), Lithuania (41), and Poland (39). According to Freedom House's index of **civil rights and political liberties**, six countries score a perfect 100—Luxembourg, Finland, Iceland, Sweden, Norway, and San Marino. The bottom five are Israel (81), Latvia (84), Croatia (86), Monaco (87), and Italy (88). The average for the region is 95 (with 24 countries at or above average and 11 below the average). The top five countries on the **Objective Development Index** (**ODI**) are Norway (1), Sweden (2), Denmark (3), Finland (4), and the Netherlands (5), while the bottom five are Latvia (43), the United States (41), Lithuania (38), Croatia (37), and Hungary (36).

Cultures of *Joy*: Examples from Latin American and Caribbean Countries

What has become of the colonial Catholic countries of Latin America and the Pacific? At the beginning of their three centuries of colonization (circa 1500–1800), many places in Latin America displayed a much higher level of development than the English colonies of North America. However, by the end of the 18th century, at the time of the American War of Independence, the tables had been turned. Why? Because the colonial Catholic elites looked down on education; hard work was left to servants and the indigenous population; and the colonizers established a hierarchical, status-oriented society on top of a set of extractive institutions (Acemoglu and Robinson, 2012).

At the time of the discovery of the Americas, the Aztec capital of Tenochtitlán, now Mexico City, had a population conservatively estimated at 212,500 inhabitants (Smith, 2005, p. 411), greater than that of the biggest European cities—Naples had a population of 150,000, and Venice and Milan had 100,000 each (Maddison, 2006, p. 56). Furthermore, the standard of living in New Spain was higher than that in New England until the end of the 18th century (Maddison, 2006, p. 492). Notwithstanding, beginning in the 19th century, this scenario radically changed. What caused the enormous advance of Anglo America and the stagnation of Latin America? The explanation lies in the preconditions and different processes of colonization of the two regions.

First, Columbus's voyage—at a time when the common people believed the world was flat—was made possible only with the financial and political backing of the king and queen of Spain. The English, almost a century after Columbus's trip, saw no need to fund an adventure into the unknown, so any would-be travelers had to find their own way. Second, those Spaniards who set out for New Spain were overwhelmingly young single men in search of fortune, sex, and power. The English traveled together in family units for the purpose of settling and working the land, and they were also fleeing from religious persecution. Third, in Latin America the land that was conquered became the property of the Spanish or Portuguese crowns; in Anglo America, the land became the property of those who worked it. Fourth, in Latin America, two *monopolies*—a hierarchical army and a hierarchical church—*imposed* social order; in Anglo America, the strong *axiology* of individuals around a plurality of Protestant churches was the foundation of society. Fifth, Latin America replicated the hierarchies and social classes of Spain and Portugal; in Anglo America, the absence of hierarchy and class was the dominant trend, at least among the white population. Sixth, in Latin America indigenous manual laborers were plentiful and miscegenation was pronounced; in Anglo America, manual laborers were scarce, and miscegenation scarcer still. Seventh, Latin America remained in the Catholic fold of Counter-Reformation Europe; Anglo America saw a redoubling of its commitment to European Protestant Reformation movements. Finally, the Catholic ethic conveyed a message of resignation and suffering as the path to *salvation*; the Protestant ethic, however, exhorted its followers to take the path of hard work, effort, and achievement as a sign that they were predestined, although not totally guaranteed, to earn *salvation.*

Interestingly, Latin America ended up, culturally speaking, as one big country, only artificially divided into nation-states, unlike the African case, where the Western powers scrambled ethnicities and territories during the colonial years.

In addition to the cultural traits outlined here, there were other key structural differences. Latin America offered vast reserves of minerals, particularly gold and silver, as well as enormous indigenous populations, which immediately made its economy ready to export goods. In the same way, the Caribbean and other tropical colonies were ideal for growing sugar cane and other cash crops, which were also labor-intensive. Anglo America, by contrast, bereft of minerals, tropical cash crops, or abundant manual labor, offered only small plots of land for the yeoman farmer (Sokoloff and Engerman, 2000), at least until the explosion of plantation agriculture in the early 18th century. Culture and structure created powerful feedback loops.

Institutions and the patterns of development they established responded to three distinct production structures: (1) the extraction of minerals for export, (2) the production and export of sugar, and (3) an agricultural smallholding economy. In the first two cases, institutions were set up to extract the maximum possible economic benefit for a tiny minority originating in Europe. The third case promoted institutions of equal treatment for the population. With the passage of decades, these cultural and structural differences would be expressed in the robust and plucky development of Anglo America and the relative stagnation of Latin America.

The Spanish conquest of Latin America under such circumstances was in many ways a disaster: the values that drove it and those that were forged by it were, in the ensuing centuries, passed to metropolis and colony alike. The question, therefore, is how from this disaster a *culture of joy* managed to flourish. It seems a contradiction.

Facing the small circle of colonizers were the great masses of the indigenous population that the Catholic Church attempted to look after. Paul III's papal bull, *Sublimus Dei*, declared in 1537 that indigenous Americans did indeed have souls and therefore, out of protection for their natural rights, they were not subject to slavery.

The conflict between human kindness and exploitation was resolved by Catholic missionaries, who offered a message of encouragement and hope that glorified poverty, sacrifice, and suffering as paths to salvation and eternal life. Hence, poverty and suffering were exalted, while wealth and hard work were despised in all of Latin America.

In this largely unavoidable, fatalistic cycle, the establishment of the Catholic priest as an intermediary between the individual and his God ultimately proved comforting: the priest could absolve men of their sins through confession, and they were then able to sin again, confess, and begin the cycle anew. Of course the availability of absolution resulted in conduct rather more libertine than was perhaps desirable, but it provided for an existence without the same level of obsessive worry and sense of duty created by Protestantism among European and Anglo American Reformists, where the relation between God and man was direct, with neither intermediaries nor absolution.

This worldview moved the individual away from any concern with the future and focused him on day-to-day survival. If submission to a life of grueling manual labor supplied the daily dose of suffering that would lead to religious glory, it remained possible for the individual to try to find regular joy in his or her daily life and circumstances. Clearly in this case the individual did not take control of his or her life, nor did he or she take full responsibility for his or her actions. It was a philosophical outlook that made it extraordinarily difficult for people to prosper economically, but somehow easier to find some joy every day.

While all this was occurring in the *rich* Catholic world of the 16th, 17th, and 18th centuries, the Protestant Reformation was sanctifying the ideas of hard work, entrepreneurship, and frugality, thereby unleashing productive forces in trade, industry, finance, and agriculture—and in short, creating prosperity.

The result is not difficult to anticipate: the treasures pouring out of Latin America barely ever reached Spain, as creditors from Holland, England, and France intercepted them in port as payment for Spain's prior borrowings. The industrial revolution that so benefited the countries of northern Europe passed unnoticed on the Iberian Peninsula.

By the end of the 18th century, the Spanish economy was unsustainable, having been shattered by foreign debt, inflation, waste, war, onerous relations with the Vatican, corruption, mismanagement, and political uprisings. The wars of independence fought in the Americas at the beginning of the 19th century effectively destroyed the political links between the colonizers and the colonized—and yet the axiological seed had been well planted: disdain for hard work and study, a fundamental mistrust of others, and the avoidance of entrepreneurial endeavors reigned in the New World, as they had in the Old. And eventually the movements advocating dissent, independence, and personal autonomy were beaten, burned, and hanged out of existence at the hands of the Inquisition, which helped replace them with the spirit of submission, obedience, and self-denial.

Latin America and the Caribbean are treated as a single region in international summits and conferences due to their geographic continuity. Following that geographic criterion here includes the former English colonies of the Caribbean, which really belong to the *achievement culture* group by their legal system and religious roots. They are nevertheless influenced by *cultures of joy*. Further research should explore the feasibility of a *sunshine bonus*—the idea that a country's level of happiness can be positively influenced by a warm, sunny climate. Table 4.5 breaks them up and, citing their colonial history, highlights the fact that the countries of mainland Latin America remained Spanish colonies, with the exception of Brazil.

By contrast, the majority of the Caribbean colonies did not belong to Spain, only Cuba, the Dominican Republic, and Puerto Rico. Two belonged to Holland (Aruba and Curacao), and one to France (Haiti). In terms of population and

TABLE 4.5

Latin American and Caribbean Countries, 2014

#	Country	Population (Thousands)	Pop. Density	% Rural Pop.	GDP (billion US $)	GDP per Capita	Agr, % GDP	Ind, % GDP	Srvs, % GDP	Gini Index* Higher = unequal	Literacy % 15+ years old	GII Rank Higher = unequal	HDI Rank Lower = better	Freedom House Higher = better	Colonial BG **	Legal Tradition ***	ODI Rank **** Lower = better	Protestant	Catholic	Other	Region	Corruption
1	Antigua and Barbuda	90	202	70	1.7	19,640	2	18	79		99		67	80	4	1	77	76	10	14	C	
2	Argentina	40,765	15	8	468.5	12,016	11	31	59	45	98	71	45	80	1	2	60	2	92	6	LA	34
3	Aruba	108	597	53		21,800					97				3	2		8	81	10	C	
4	Bahamas	347	34	16	11.6	31,116	2	16	82		96	53	49	96	4	1	51	68	14	18	C	71
5	Barbados	274	636	56	7.5	25,500	3	23	74		100	61	38	99	4	1	47	63	4	33	C	75
6	Belize	357	15	55	2.6	7,937	12	23	65	53	77	79	96	88	4	1	91	31	39	30	C	
7	Bermuda	65	1,285			69,900	1	8	91		98				4	1		49	15	36	C	
8	Bolivia	10,088	9	33	54.5	5,196	13	39	49	56	91	97	108	69	1	2	136	5	95		LA	34
9	Brazil	196,655	23	15	2,327.4	11,716	5	28	67	55	90	85	85	81	2	2	104	15	74	11	LA	42
10	Cayman Islands	57	234			43,800					99				4	1		68	13	19	C	
11	Chile	17,270	23	11	390.6	22,363	3	39	57	52	99	66	40	96	1	2	56	15	70	15	LA	71
12	Colombia	46,927	42	25	497.8	10,436	7	38	55	56	93	88	91	61	1	2	132		90	10	LA	36
13	Costa Rica	4,727	91	35	61.2	12,733	6	26	68	51	96	62	62	91	1	2	63	14	76	10	LA	53
14	Cuba	11,254	106	25		9,900	5	21	74		100	63	59	11	1	2	142		59	41	C	46
15	Curacao	146	324			15,000					99				3	2		11	80	9	C	
16	Dominica	68	90	33	0.9	12,426	14	15	71		94		72	95	4	1	65	21	61	18	C	58
17	Dominican Rep.	10,056	205	30	103.2	10,038	6	33	61	47	90	109	96	75	1	2	105		95	5	C	29
18	Ecuador	14,666	58	33	149.3	9,637	7	38	55	49	92	83	89	60	1	2	111		95	5	LA	35
19	El Salvador	6,227	299	35	44.0	6,991	13	27	60	48	84	82	107	77	1	2	97	21	57	22	LA	38
20	Grenada	105	307	61	1.2	10,928	5	17	78		96		63	89	4	1	68	47	53		C	
21	Guatemala	14,757	134	50	75.7	5,019	11	68	20	56	75	114	133	57	1	2	160	42	55	3	LA	29
22	Guyana	756	4	72	2.7	3,344	21	34	45	45	92	104	118	71	4	2/1	109	31	8	61	C	27
23	Haiti	10,124	363	47	12.3	1,208				59	49	127	161	43	5	2	191	16	80	4	C	19
24	Honduras	7,755	68	48	33.1	4,174	15	27	58	57	85	100	120	51	1	2	156	3	97		LA	26
25	Jamaica	2,709	250	48	18.8	9,100	7	22	72	46	87	87	85	73	4	1	87	63	3	34	C	38
26	Mexico	114,793	58	22	2,022.2	16,734	4	37	60	48	93	72	61	65	1	2	82	2	83	15	LA	34
27	Nicaragua	5,870	48	42	24.0	4,006	20	26	54	41	78	89	129	51	1	2	120	23	59	18	LA	28
28	Panama	3,571	47	25	62.2	16,346	4	17	79	52	94	108	59	82	1	2	93	15	85		LA	35
29	Paraguay	6,568	16	38	40.4	6,038	23	20	57	52	94	95	111	62	1	2	133	6	90	4	LA	24
30	Peru	29,400	23	23	322.8	10,765	6	36	57	48	90	73	77	71	1	2	81	13	81	6	LA	38
31	Puerto Rico	3,707	420	1		16,300	1	50	49		90				1	2/1			85	15	C	62
32	Saint Kitts and Nevis	53	202	68	1.0	18,384	2	23	75		98		72	91	4	1	69	60	5	35	C	
33	Saint Lucia	176	285	82	2.1	11,427	3	16	81	43	90		88	93	4	2/1	61	18	68	14	C	71
34	St Vincent and Grenadines	109	280	51	1.2	11,900	6	20	74		96			89	4	1	73	75	13	12	C	62
35	Suriname	529	3	30	4.7	8,722	11	38	51	53	95	94	105	77	3	2	113	25	23	52	C	36
36	Trinidad and Tobago	1,346	261	86	35.5	26,550	1	60	40	40	99	50	67	81	4	1	52	26	26	48	C	38
37	Turks and Caicos Islands	39	40	6		11,500					98				4	1		73	11	16	C	
38	Uruguay	3,369	19	7	53.6	15,776	10	25	65	45	98	69	51	97	1	2	50	11	47	35	LA	73
39	Venezuela	29,278	33	6	397.4	13,267	6	52	42	45	96	93	71	39	1	2	121	2	96	2	LA	20
	Total/average	595,160	183	37	7,232	14,862	8	30	63	50	92	84	84	74			96	30	56	20		43
	Caribbean	42,474	279	47	207	18,019	6	26	68	48	92	83	82	78			88	44	38	25		49
	Latin America	552,686	59	27	7,025	10,777	10	34	57	50	91	85	85	70			103	13	79	12		38

Sources and meanings: see Appendix 3.
* Gini Index: 0 = zero wealth concentration; 1 = one person holds all the wealth.
** Colonial BG: 1 Spain; 2 Portugal; 3 Dutch; 4 Britain; 5 France.
*** Legal Tradition: 1 Common; 2 Civil; 3 Islamic.
**** Objective Development Index (ODI) combines Gini, GII, HDI, and Freedom House, and is explained in Chapter 10.
† Geographically mainland countries: Belize, Guyana, Suriname.

economy, the Caribbean represents a tiny slice (8% and 5%, respectively) of the Latin American whole. Nonetheless, in terms of annual income per capita, the Caribbean is close to that of Latin America as a whole: US$6,245 versus US$8,828 per year, respectively. Religion is another area of contrast: 79% of the mainland is Catholic; it is just 39% on the islands, 38% of whose inhabitants are Protestant. This brief overview underlines the importance of colonial heritage's contrasts, law and religion (Acemoglu et al., 2005, p. 392).

In terms of **population size**, the five largest Latin American/Caribbean countries are Brazil (197 million), Mexico (115 million), Colombia (47 million), Argentina (41 million), and Peru (29 million), and the five smallest are the Caribbean nations of Turks and Caicos (39 thousand), Saint Kitts and Nevis (53 thousand), Cayman Islands (57 thousand), Bermuda (65 thousand), and Dominica (68 thousand). The average population is 15.3 million (7 countries above and 32 below the average). By **density** per square kilometer of population, the top five are Bermuda (1,285), Barbados (636), Aruba (597), Puerto Rico (420), and Haiti (363), while the bottom five are Suriname (3), Guyana (4), Bolivia (9), Argentina (15), and Belize (15). The average is 183 (16 countries above and 23 below the average). By percentage of **rural** inhabitants, the top five countries are Trinidad and Tobago (86%), Saint Lucia (82%), Guyana (72%), Antigua and Barbuda (70%), and Saint Kitts and Nevis (68%), while the bottom five are Puerto Rico (1%), Turks and Caicos (6%), Venezuela (6%), Uruguay (7%), and Argentina (8%). The average is 37%, with 16 countries above, 20 below, and no data for 3.

Analyzing the economy by **annual GDP**, the top five largest economies (in billions of US$) are Brazil ($2,327), Mexico ($2,022), Colombia ($498), Argentina ($469), and Venezuela ($397), while the smallest five are Dominica ($.9), Saint Kitts and Nevis ($1), Grenada ($1.2), Grenadines ($1.2), and Antigua and Barbuda ($1.7). The average is $226 (7 countries above the average, 25 below, and no data for 7). By **GDP per capita**, the five wealthiest countries are Bermuda ($70,000), Cayman Islands ($44,000), Bahamas ($31,000), Trinidad and Tobago ($27,000), and Barbados ($26,000), while the five poorest are Haiti ($1,200), Guyana ($3,300), Nicaragua ($4,000), Honduras ($4,200), and Guatemala ($5,000). The overall average income per capita is $14,900 (14 countries above and 25 below the average).

By share of GDP derived from **agriculture**, the top five countries are Paraguay (23%), Guyana (21%), Nicaragua (20%), Honduras (15%), and Dominica (14%). The bottom five are Puerto Rico (1%), Trinidad and Tobago (1%), Bermuda (1%), Saint Kitts and Nevis (2%), and Bahamas (2%). The average is 8% (12 countries above, 22 below, and 5 with no data). By share of GDP derived from **industry**, the top five are Guatemala (68%), Trinidad and Tobago (60%), Venezuela (52%), Puerto Rico (50%), and Chile (39%), and the bottom five are Bermuda (8%), Dominica (15%), Bahamas (16%), Saint Lucia (16%), and Grenada (17%). The average is 30% (14 countries above, 20 below, and no data for 5). By share of GDP derived from **services**, the top five countries are Bermuda (91%), Bahamas (82%), Saint Lucia (81%), Antigua and Barbuda (79%), and Panama (79%), while the bottom five are Guatemala (20%), Trinidad and Tobago (40%), Venezuela (42%), Guyana (45%), and Bolivia (49%). The average is 63% (16 above, 18 below, and no data for 5).

Turning to social indicators, the top five countries for equitable **income distribution** are Trinidad and Tobago (.40), Nicaragua (.41), Saint Lucia (.43), Guyana (.45), and Argentina (.45). The five most inequitable are Haiti (.59), Honduras (.57), Bolivia (.56), Colombia (.56), and Guatemala (.56). The average for the region is a very high .50, with 13 countries above average, 12 countries below, and no data for 14 countries. By **literacy rate**, the top countries are Cuba (100%), Barbados (100%), Antigua and Barbuda (99%), Cayman Islands (99%), Trinidad and Tobago (99%), and Chile (99%). The bottom five are Haiti (49%), Guatemala (75%), Belize (77%), Nicaragua (78%), and El Salvador (84%). The average is 92%, with 25 countries at or above the average, 13 below, and one with no data. By **gender equality**, the top five countries are Trinidad and Tobago (50), Bahamas (53), Barbados (61), Costa Rica (62), and Cuba (63), and the bottom five are Haiti (127), Guatemala (114), Dominican Republic (109), Panama (108), and Guyana (104).

Looking at **colonial background**, 19 countries were colonized by Spain, 1 by Portugal, 3 by the Netherlands, 15 by Britain, and 1 by France. By **legal tradition,** there are 13 common law, 23 Roman law, and 3 mixed systems. By **religion,** there are 25 Catholic countries, 8 Protestant countries, and 6 other or with no clear majority.

In terms of rankings on aggregated development indices, the top five countries on the **Human Development Index** are Barbados (38), Chile (40), Argentina (45), Bahamas (49), and Uruguay (51). The bottom five are Haiti (161), Guatemala (133), Nicaragua (129), Honduras (120), and Guyana (118), and seven countries have no data available. By **political rights and civil liberties**, the top five countries are Barbados (99), Uruguay (97), Bahamas (96), Chile (96), and Dominica (95), and the bottom five are Cuba (11), Venezuela (39), Haiti (43), Honduras (51), and Nicaragua (51). The average is 74, with 19 countries above the average, 14 below, and 6 lacking data. By the **Objective Development Index (ODI)**, the top five countries are Barbados (47), Uruguay (50), Bahamas (51), Trinidad and Tobago (52), and Chile (56). The bottom five are Haiti (191), Guatemala (160), Honduras (156), Cuba (142), and Bolivia (136).

CONTRASTING VALUES IN COLONIAL AMERICA

The key concepts of trust, hard work, and autonomy-dissent precipitated the development of cultures with deeply opposed values: cultures of achievement in the regions of colonial Anglo America, and cultures of honor in the colonial territories of Latin America, which boasted precious minerals and valuable crops (Sokoloff and Engerman, 2000). Very slowly, inadvertently, and mainly among the Latin American elites—later trickling down to the masses—a culture of honor began turning into a culture of joy.

The Anglo American ethic of egalitarianism and hard work turned out to be optimal for the colonization of what would become the United States: a small population, ample land, and a general absence of high-value natural resources. Both the spiritual world of the individual and the material conditions within the society benefited from the glorification of *hard work*.

That ethic, however, was not applied to colonial Latin America, where an enormous native population, as well as African slaves, could be used for manual labor, the extraction of vast quantities of mineral resources—gold, silver, copper, and the like—and the cultivation of sugar, cocoa, coffee, tobacco, and other products. The European minority had not gone to Latin America to work, but rather to become rich on the backs of servants and slaves. Hard work was not glory to them; instead, leisure became a symbol of status and respectability.

Of all the colonies wrought by empires since the beginning of the 16th century, those occupied by the English (particularly the United States, Canada, Australia, and New Zealand) would remain better positioned for global economic competition. They were favored by a particular combination of oral legal tradition and intense competition among Protestant religious groups—proponents of interpersonal trust and extreme horizontality in hierarchic relationships. The other homogeneous and powerful colonial world—that which was formed by Spain and Portugal—was weighted down by legal formalities and Catholic monopolies that fostered distrust and extreme verticality in hierarchical relationships.

In 1776 there were nine colleges serving a population of 2.5 million in the 13 British colonies, while in Latin America there were only two (in Mexico City and Guadalajara) for a population of 17 million (Maddison, 2006, p. 26). Historically speaking, the freewheeling and egalitarian sociopolitical ethic of Puritan New England was the order of the day in the United States. First came the Declaration of Independence and the Constitution, and later the settling of accounts in the Civil War.

It is in the contrast between Latin and Anglo America that we may see the full effect of *shared systems of meanings, values, and beliefs*, originally deriving from monopolistic Catholicism and pluralistic Protestantism, further reinforced by their diametrically opposed legal systems. The concepts of *trust, hard work*, and *autonomy-dissent* intertwine and gain strength as social, economic, and political institutions are created.

In the Anglo American concept, hard work was a *reward*; it was the center around which everything else revolved. Everything was subordinate to the necessities and requirements of hard work. It was the font of satisfaction, pride, and even, in some cases, pleasure. In the Latin American ethos, however, hard work was a necessity and an obligation; it did not carry the same connotation of *salvation*, much less of pleasure—and in the extreme, it was even seen as a *punishment*. Consequently, the organizing power that hard work had in Anglo America did not exist in Latin America.

In Latin America, interpersonal relationships served as the dominant structuring element. The concepts of family and friendship—the radius of identification and trust—were for Latin Americans what hard work was for Anglo Americans. The individual oriented his actions and opinions with his family and friends in mind; he gained satisfaction and pride from being useful or beneficial to them; and the well-being of his family circle was more important than his own.

In the Anglo American view, this was not the case. The well-being of the individual was the starting point and might extend to the family circle or to close friends, but that was not essential. Being useful and beneficial to a circle of friends and relatives yielded neither special satisfaction nor pride, and orienting one's opinions and actions around the group was similarly unfulfilling. Individuality and independence of thought were, in the Anglo American ethos, much more important. However, the lack of emphasis on personal relationships was as conspicuous in Anglo America as the lack of emphasis on hard work was in Latin America.

The concept of *dissent*—an element underlying the political dimension of *autonomy*—had very different connotations in Anglo and Latin America. In the former, critical thought and the free exchange of ideas was a healthy exercise of one's independence and autonomy. In Latin America, however, *dissent* was—indeed, still is—seen in a very different light. The Latin American exchange of ideas is an exercise in social bonding; it is subjective and emotional, and has no rational, objective, or intellectual connotation. In this frame, criticism has no positive connotation and confrontation yields no benefits; instead, Latin Americans are concerned with the construction of consensuses and the widening of the circle of friends. Independence, dissent, and autonomy are hence not esteemed in the Latin American ethos.

The lesson learned from comparing and contrasting the United States with Latin America is how the shaping of institutions and their expression in culture impacts the development of nations, as noted by Tocqueville. In other words, just as institutions respond to material conditions, so do the values that affect the construction of culture. Therefore, values and institutions are, in subjective and objective senses, reflections of each other.

Conclusions and Further Research

What is the message after reviewing these regional cases? Africa is the home of us all, the place from where we all came. It was there that humankind, and therefore the world as we know it, successfully incubated for millennia. However, the continent was greatly burdened by a legacy of colonialism, and came very late to independence as nation-states. When we compare the countries of Africa today with countries in Europe, for instance, it would be more appropriate to make the comparison with those periods in time when the Europeans were emerging as former imperial dependencies—say, the 6th century, following the dismantling of the Roman Empire.

Islam in its original Middle Eastern form was, for a longer time than any other empire, the driving force behind development in the Middle East, at least from the 7th through 12th centuries; Islam spread the values of bygone civilizations (Babylon, Syria, Persia), rather than wiping them out and replacing them with something new, as Catholicism did to indigenous colonial societies.

The Confucian countries have seen extraordinary rates of sustained economic growth in Japan, first, and China, in the last 30 years. Everything seems to indicate that if China continues on the path of economic prosperity it has been on since the end of the Cold War, within 10–15 years it will replace the United States as the world's single largest economy, with all the implications that carries with it. This civilization has been recovering its position over the past four decades, with its sphere of influence based in Confucianism encompassing Taiwan, Japan, Korea, Vietnam, and Singapore.

The Western countries, made up of an array of national cultures (Nordic Protestantism, European Catholicism, Anglo Protestantism, and Judaism, not to mention of course the many immigrant communities living in their midst), have been in the *driver's seat* of the world for the last six centuries. The United States has occupied this position for nearly seven decades, five of them (1945–1989) shared with the Soviet Union.

What message do we learn from Latin America? It is, above all, one of the powerful influences of a highly homogenized cultural zone forged over three centuries (16th to 18th), deeply rooted in Catholicism and the Roman law, with the paradoxical outcome of its preference for *joy* over *honor* or *achievement*.

As this review shows, the three cultures (honor, achievement, and joy) are only *ideal types*, meaning that no single country—and even less a group of countries—corresponds monolithically to the theoretical description. Japan is both *honor* and *achievement* among pockets of its population; while the United States shows the three by region: *honor* in the South, *achievement* in the Northeast, and *joy* on the West Coast. To return to the three-dimensions triangle described in the Introduction, each of the three cultures is located at each of the three corners of the triangle. Thus, countries may fall closer to the typological corners or into any space between two corners. Determining specific countries' locations will be a matter of future research.

Not only that, all populations have the capability of adopting a different culture, as is shown by the migrants that move from their original countries to an array of host countries mainly in search of employment and sometimes of survival. Stories of success abound among Hispanics in the United States, Indians in the United Kingdom, Muslims in Canada and the Nordic countries, and Turks in Germany, to mention just a few cases. There is also the case of a few minorities (Jews, Chinese, Lebanese, Spanish Basques, and Indian Sikhs) that seem to succeed wherever they go. Identifying the causes for such success, whether culture or simply the adversity derived from being a minority, requires further research.

A quantitative summary of all the regions reviewed in the five preceding tables is presented in Table 4.6. From the review of the *Objective Development Index* (ODI), it is the West (average 20) that comes out on top, followed by the Orthodox (52), Caribbean (88), and Asians (96). The next tier is of Latin Americans (103), non-Arab Muslims (105) and Arab Muslims (109), practically at the same level. The bottom region is Africa, with an average of 158.

TABLE 4.6

World Summary, 2014

Region	Population (Thousands)	Pop. Density	% Rural Pop.	GDP (billion US $)	GDP per Capita	Agr, % GDP	Ind, % GDP	Srvs, % GDP	Gini Index* Higher = unequal	Literacy % 15+ years old	GII Rank Higher = unequal	HDI Rank Lower = better	Freedom House Higher = better	ODI Rank **** Lower = better
West	861	674	24	36,218	37,194	3	27	71	32	99	19	21	95	20
Orthodox	259	79	37	4,826	14,681	18	41	41	32	99	47	58	63	52
Caribbean	42	279	47	207	18,019	6	26	68	48	92	83	82	78	88
Asians	3,447	1,933	54	27,084	19,706	17	30	55	39	89	65	93	48	96
Latin America	553	59	27	7,025	10,777	10	34	57	50	91	85	85	70	103
Non-Arab Muslims	860	150	51	5,279	10,686	14	36	50	35	86	81	114	36	105
Arab Muslims	302	189	27	3,340	20,356	7	46	47	37	83	86	85	31	109
Africa	1,055	87	58	3,396	4,720	22	31	47	45	67	113	150	45	158
World	922	431	41	87,375	17,018	12	34	54	40	88	72	86	58	91

* Gini Index: 0 = zero wealth concentration; 1 = one person holds all the wealth.

**** Objective Development Index (ODI) combines Gini, GII, HDI, and Freedom House, and is explained in Chapter 10.

This book makes the argument that all cultures are worthy of respect, but their inherent dignity should not prevent the frank analysis of the advantages and disadvantages that culture can impose on certain segments of the population. Of course, cultural relativity unleashes disgruntlement among those authors and practitioners who would like to see their schemes and solutions accepted universally. For example, *cultures of honor* tend not to place much value on gender equality; in some *cultures of achievement* (such as the US), there is less emphasis on income equality.

For Americans, income inequality is seen as a natural result of individuals' varying talents and abilities, while at the same time gender inequality as practiced in cultures of honor seems inexplicable. For individuals who belong to the cultures of honor, exactly the opposite happens: gender inequality is seen as natural and inherent, but it is difficult to understand why Americans allow such vast differences in income. In other words, there is no way of establishing a constructive and fruitful dialogue between nations without taking into account the historical patterns and unique characteristics of each country, in order to understand how their practices, customs, and institutions came to be.

Some leads for further research can be taken from this summary: (1) regardless of their current problems and the political performance deficit of the Orthodox, mainly former Soviet countries, their record in terms of ODI is remarkable. (2) The legacy left in the Caribbean countries is also worth noting. They are small and population dense, but nevertheless their overall performance is third in the world. (3) Asia is clearly rapidly catching up, as if the lost century will soon be part of the past—above all for China. (4) Africa is the region with the highest potential for economic growth and integral development.

A synthesis of this brief overview points to the alternating cycles of hard work and arrogance that propel the rises, apexes, and declines of different countries, regions, and civilizations. The history of the world is like a spiral, in which countries and civilizations rise and fall as time passes. Everyone gets their 15 minutes of fame.

PART III

Cultures of Honor, Achievement, and Joy

The social sciences do not have anything comparable to genes, protons, neutrons, elements to build upon [. . .] the culture of a society is the cumulative aggregate of the surviving beliefs and institutions.

—DOUGLASS NORTH, *UNDERSTANDING THE PROCESS OF ECONOMIC CHANGE*, P. 83

5

Empirical Profiles of the Three Cultures

The evolution of the three cultures was triggered by specific major events: the agricultural and industrial revolutions and World War II. It also replicates the socioeconomic unfolding described by Daniel Bell (1976) as pre-industrial, industrial, and postindustrial. It is a process linked to the cultural imprint left by the transition from nomadic and agrarian (rural) life to urban and industrial societies up to today's service and postmaterial societies. As we saw earlier, Inglehart's World *Cultural Map* (Figure 2.4 in Chapter 2) shows that cultures of *achievement* are located in the top, right, and upper right quadrants comprising the clusters of Nordic and English Protestants as well as the Confucian countries (shaped like a waxing crescent moon). In the opposite bottom left quadrant are found the cultures of *honor*, which include the Orthodox, African, and Islamic clusters (shaped like a waning crescent moon). In between appear the paradoxical cultures of *joy* along the Catholic and Buddhist cluster. Basically the same groupings are revealed when reviewing Schwartz's *Cultural Map* of Figure 2.11.

This broad characterization of cultures is supported by empirical survey data on values and attitudes. Table 5.1 shows the values that most separate cultures of honor from cultures of achievement, using data derived from the World Values Survey (WVS). Cultures of joy generally occupy an intermediate position with reference to each value. The data are ranked in descending order (column 1 of Table 5.1), with those values that most separate the cultures at the top. Column 2 shows the distance between the score for honor and achievement, and column 3, the WVS topic; column 4 shows the question number on the WVS sourcebook; the following six columns (5 to 10) show the score and the standard deviation for each of the three cultures (honor, joy, and achievement).

For example, row 1 shows a distance of 1.00 in column 2 for "Important in life: religion" (column 3), which is the WVS question A006 (column 4). The score for honor in column 5 (negative 0.43), as opposed to the score for achievement in column 9 (positive 0.57), explains the 1.00 distance. The positive and negative scores are related to the polarity of the original questions. Note that in item 1, religion is very important for honor cultures (whereas it is very unimportant in achievement cultures), while in item 2 the polarity is different. God is very

TABLE 5.1

Largest contrasts between cultures of *honor* and *achievement**

Rank	Distance	World Values Survey (WVS) topics	WVS Question	Honor	SD	Joy	SD	Achievement	SD
1	1.00	Important in life: religion	A006	(0.43)	0.80	0.35	0.98	0.57	0.97
2	0.98	How important is God in your life	F063	0.38	0.76	(0.34)	1.02	(0.60)	1.04
3	0.00	Justifiable: homosexuality	F118	(0.47)	0.67	0.29	1.04	0.49	1.08
4	0.96	Politicians who don't believe in God are unfit for public office	F102	(0.46)	0.94	0.44	0.84	0.49	0.83
5	0.95	Believe in: hell	F053	0.37	0.95	(0.18)	0.97	(0.52)	0.82
6	0.00	Better if more people with strong religious beliefs in public office	F104	(0.37)	0.89	0.68	0.85	0.52	0.93
7	0.00	Political action: signing a petition	E025	0.40	0.87	(0.27)	0.97	(0.47)	0.96
8	0.90	Get comfort and strength from religion	F064	0.34	0.79	(0.17)	1.05	(0.47)	1.06
9	0.89	One of main goals in life has been to make my parents proud	D054	(0.31)	0.89	0.31	0.97	0.51	1.02
10	0.87	Neighbors: homosexuals	A124_09	0.44	0.96	(0.34)	0.90	(0.38)	0.88
11	0.82	Believe in: God	F050	0.31	0.62	(0.14)	1.10	(0.50)	1.27
12	0.81	Requirements for citizenship: having ancestors from my country	G028	(0.29)	0.96	0.28	0.90	0.49	0.92
13	0.81	Important for successful marriage: adequate income	D028	(0.32)	0.88	0.08	1.00	0.44	1.01
14	0.80	Requirements for citizenship: being born on my country's soil	G029	(0.24)	0.95	0.11	0.92	0.51	0.95
15	0.00	Important child qualities: religious faith	A040	0.33	1.05	(0.26)	0.87	(0.42)	0.74
16	0.78	Women want a home and children	D062	(0.30)	0.92	0.06	0.96	0.45	1.01
17	0.76	Justifiable: euthanasia	F122	(0.35)	0.88	0.27	1.01	0.40	0.97
18	0.76	Men make better political leaders than women	D059	(0.37)	1.00	0.50	0.87	0.38	0.86
19	0.75	Men make better business executives than women	D078	(0.35)	1.03	0.50	0.84	0.37	0.84
20	0.75	Religious person	F034	(0.27)	0.75	0.11	1.09	0.44	1.17
21	0.75	Political action recently done: signing a petition	E025B	0.31	0.76	(0.19)	1.08	(0.40)	1.12
22	0.74	Confidence: churches	E069_01	(0.33)	0.92	0.32	1.00	0.38	0.91
23	0.72	Political system: having the army rule	E116	(0.33)	1.10	0.32	0.76	0.37	0.76
24	0.00	How often do you attend religious services	F028	(0.25)	0.95	0.13	1.01	0.44	0.91
25	0.72	Pray to God outside religious services	F066	(0.27)	0.95	0.11	0.98	0.43	0.94

important in honor cultures (positive 0.38) and very unimportant in achievement cultures (negative 0.60). In both cases, joy cultures are in between the other two (but closer to achievement).

The standard deviation (SD) in columns 6, 8, and 10 show the level of consensus or dissent among the countries' populations. For instance, *believe in God* (item 11) shows the lowest dissent among the *honor* cultures (0.62) and the highest dissent (1.27) among the *achievement* cultures. In other words, not only do many people *believe in God* in *honor* cultures, but also they tend to be uniform

TABLE 5.2
Authority and Hierarchy Values, % (*World Values Survey*, 2010)*

CULTURAL GROUPS (%):	1	2	3	4	5
1: Honor / 2: Achievement / 3: Joy (European Catholics) / 4: Joy (Latin America) / 5: World					
Respect and love for parents (A025)					
Always	85	56	74	96	74
Important child qualities:					
obedience (A042)	44	24	32	53	37
Political system: having a strong leader (E114)					
Very/fairly good	49	27	28	43	38
Political system: having the army rule (E116)					
Very/fairly bad	69	92	92	74	81
Future changes: greater respect for authority (E018)					
Good thing	63	53	64	83	62

* See Appendix 2 for methodology details.

in their belief, whereas in *achievement cultures* fewer people *believe in God* and there is also less consensus within the culture about *belief in God*.

A particular area of separation for cultures of honor versus cultures of achievement is **attitudes toward authority and hierarchy**, as Table 5.2 shows. Cultures of honor tend to accept greater levels of hierarchy, whereas cultures of achievement are more horizontal and egalitarian. These attitudes can be empirically measured using survey data. For example, when asked if children should always love and respect their parents, or if parents must earn their children's love and respect, respondents from cultures of honor are much more likely to respond that children should love and respect their parents regardless of how good or bad the parents are (85% in cultures of honor, compared with 56% in cultures of achievement). They also are more likely to believe that obedience is an important quality for parents to instill in children (44% in cultures of honor, compared with 24% in cultures of achievement and 32% in cultures of joy). In addition, they are much more likely to say that it is a good idea for their country to have a strong leader who does not have to bother with parliament and elections. They also tend to be more supportive of military rule. While 68% in cultures of achievement (and 64% in cultures of joy) say it would be very bad to have the army rule, only 37% in cultures of honor agree. In addition, the questions measuring gender attitudes, shown on Table 5.4, also show greater acceptance of hierarchy, because unequal gender roles are essentially a hierarchy of the sexes.

Another value separating cultures of honor from cultures of achievement is **religion**, as Table 5.3 shows, the highest submission to the authority and hierarchy of God. Of the top 10 values that most separate the cultural areas in Table 5.1, six deal specifically with religion. These include the percentage of respondents stating that religion is important in their life; how important respondents say that God is in their life; the percentage of respondents stating that politicians who don't believe in God are unfit for public office; the percentage of respondents who say they

TABLE 5.3

Religious Values, % (*World Values Survey*, 2010)*

CULTURAL GROUPS (%):	1	2	3	4	5
1: Honor / 2: Achievement / 3: Joy (European Catholics) / 4: Joy (Latin America) / 5: World					
Important in life (very important):					
Religion (A006)	57	17	22	49	39
How important is God in your life (F063)					
Very important (7–10)	82	40	52	91	66
Believe in: God (F050)	94	64	77	96	82
Believe in: hell (F053)	66	21	38	67	47
Politicians who don't believe in God are unfit for public office (F102)					
Agree/strongly agree	54	13	16	35	34
Better if more people with strong religious beliefs in public office (F104)					
Agree/strongly agree	59	21	14	44	43

* See Appendix 2 for methodology details.

TABLE 5.4

Gender Values, % (*World Values Survey*, 2010)*

CULTURAL GROUPS (%):	1	2	3	4	5
1: Honor / 2: Achievement / 3: Joy (European Catholics) / 4: Joy (Latin America) / 5: World					
Child needs a home with father and mother (D018)					
Tend to agree	92	76	82	85	85
Preschool child suffers with working mother (D061)					
Agree and strongly agree	63	39	54	NA	54
A woman has to have children to be fulfilled (D019)					
Needs children	80	36	51	64	60
Ideal number of children (D017)					
Mean	3.7	2.9	NA	2.9	3.4
Men make better political leaders than women (D059)					
Agree and strongly agree	63	29	24	29	46
Men better business executives than women do (D078)					
Agree and strongly agree	56	23	17	23	40
University is more important for a boy than for a girl (D060)					
Agree and strongly agree	30	12	9	15	21

* See Appendix 2 for methodology details.

believe in hell; the percentage of respondents who say that it is better if more people with strong religious beliefs are in public office; and the percentage of respondents saying that they get comfort and strength from religion.

In addition to the emphasis on religion, the data show that another area of separation between cultures of honor and cultures of achievement is how they view **gender roles,** as Table 5.4 shows. Cultures of honor tend to value traditional gender roles, with men as political and business leaders and women as the primary caretakers of home and children. Some of the survey data show a

TABLE 5.5

Family Values, % (*World Values Survey*, 2010)*

CULTURAL GROUPS (%):	1	2	3	4	5
1: Honor / 2: Achievement / 3: Joy (European Catholics) / 4: Joy (Latin America) / 5: World					
Goals in life: make my parents proud (D054)					
Agree strongly	53	18	22	37	38
How much freedom of choice and control (A173)					
A great deal (7–10)	55	68	59	76	61
Trust in people (A165)					
Most people can be trusted	21	47	26	14	28
Schwartz: A person who believes tradition is important is very much like me (A198)	39	16	19	24	29

* See Appendix 2 for methodology details.

wide gap between cultures of honor and those of achievement in the percentage of respondents agreeing that women want a home and children, that men make better political leaders than women, that men make better business executives than women, and that preschool children suffer if they have a working mother.

Other questions measuring attitudes toward gender inequality show somewhat less divergence, but still demonstrate that cultures of honor tend to be more traditional in this realm. They include whether men have more right to a job than women, whether a woman must have children to be fulfilled, whether it is justifiable for a man to beat his wife, if university education is more important for a boy than a girl, and whether women should have the same rights as men in a democracy. When asked if a woman has to have children to be fulfilled, 80% in cultures of honor agree, compared with only 36% in cultures of achievement and 51% in cultures of joy.

On the positive side, both men and women in honor societies argue that the role of women is so special as mothers that they deserve particular protection because of that special role. Hence, they have no need to get a job, or to bother with duties outside the home, as they always will have a man to provide, either their father, brothers, or husband. However, in many cases that arrangement turns into abuses from men over women, with little social or legal protection to correct for those cases. However, these concepts of gender roles are not monolithic. As families move from rural to urban areas, from less to more educated, from agriculture to service occupations, and from less to more income, particularly women but also men begin to relax these strict traditional values.

Finally, cultures of honor tend to enjoy **close family and social bonds**, as Table 5.5 shows, with less importance placed on individual desires. For instance, when asked about their primary goals in life, respondents from cultures of honor are much more likely to reply that one of their primary goals is to make their parents proud. As a reflection of this emphasis, they are also more likely to feel that they do not have a great deal of choice and control over their own lives. In cultures of honor, 55% say that they have control over their own lives, compared with 68% in cultures of achievement. This is an important value as an ingredient of entrepreneurship.

Cultures of *Honor*: Respect for Tradition and Authority

Cultures of honor have the longest history of any of the cultural clusters. For millennia, all human societies evolved as cultures of honor, from our roots in the animal kingdom, in which the alpha male is the leader, for purposes of evolutionary advantage. First as nomadic societies and later as agrarian, when societies settled down at the dawn of agriculture, respect for tradition was venerated, governance was generally authoritarian, and hierarchies as well as monarchies were absolute—nobles over peasants, man over wife, parents over children. It was not until the historical and intellectual European movements of the Protestant Reformation, the Enlightenment, and the industrial revolution took hold in some countries that their cultures began shifting toward achievement as the dominant value. But other areas—especially, although not exclusively, impoverished regions where people face strong competition for resources—remained culturally oriented toward respect for tradition and obedience. Today, *cultures of honor* are dominant in Africa, the Islamic world, the Orthodox world, and in Hinduism.

These cultures of honor are characterized, above all, by *adherence to tradition*. They are the polar opposite of cultures of *achievement*, and looking at their contrasts helps to understand their profile. The time-honored values, traditions, beliefs, and ways of living are generally considered superior to new ways of life, especially if the new ways are perceived as foreign. If we look empirically at their values, cultures of honor display a high level of religiosity, with virtually all members of society professing belief in God and saying that religion is important in their lives. In addition, these countries place a high value on established gender roles. A woman's place is thought to be in the home, and the dominance of men in the political, economic, and social spheres is taken for granted. Homosexuality is generally considered unacceptable. Perhaps most important, cultures of honor accept—even embrace—hierarchies and strong authority. Family and social bonds tend to be strong, and individual desires and aspirations are generally secondary to the well-being of the group, be it defined narrowly (as family) or more broadly (as tribe or sect). In these cultures, political rationality—the authority to dominate others—tends to prevail over economic or social rationality.

Table 5.3 shows that 57% of respondents from cultures of honor say that **religion** is very important in their lives, compared with 17% of those in cultures of achievement and 22% in cultures of joy. These figures illustrate, first, that people in cultures of honor are much more personally religious than those in cultures of achievement. They are much more likely than those in cultures of achievement or joy to say that God and religion are very important in their lives, to say that they believe in God, heaven, hell, and sin, to attend religious services often, and to pray outside religious services. Crucially, however, the data also show that cultures of honor are more likely to consider it natural and appropriate that religion should occupy a place in the public sphere. For instance, they are much more likely to believe that politicians who don't believe in God are unfit for public office; to say that it is better if more people with strong religious beliefs are in public office; and to say that in a democracy, religious leaders should interpret the law. In cultures of honor, 59% say they either agree or strongly agree that it would be better if more people with strong religious beliefs were in public office, compared to 21% for cultures of achievement and only 14% for cultures of joy.

Another aspect that shows a significant divergence between cultures of honor and achievement is attitudes toward **homosexuality,** one of the most powerful indicators of tolerance and predictors of openness to political rights and civil liberties. While cultures of achievement and joy have been moving rapidly toward increased acceptance of homosexuality, such a shift is not occurring in cultures of honor. Today, every survey question dealing with homosexuality shows a wide divergence between cultures of honor and those of achievement. For instance, when asked whether homosexuality is ever justified, 70% of respondents from cultures of honor say that it is never justified, compared with 29% in cultures of achievement and 35% in cultures of joy. They are also more likely to say that they would not like to have homosexuals as neighbors.[1]

Table 5.6 presents the **cultures of honor** ranking based on the data gathered by the World Values Survey. It takes the two axes from Inglehart's *World*

TABLE 5.6
Countries of *Honor* and Respect for Tradition and Authority (Highest to Lowest), 2010*

1	Zimbabwe	27	Venezuela	53	Ukraine	79	Japan
2	Pakistan	28	Zambia	54	Macedonia	80	Slovenia
3	Jordan	29	Mali	55	Malaysia	81	Canada
4	Morocco	30	Philippines	56	Thailand	82	Galicia
5	Ghana	31	Indonesia	57	Lithuania	83	Greece
6	Iraq	32	Albania	58	Bulgaria	84	East Germany
7	Algeria	33	South Korea	59	India	85	Czech Republic
8	Rwanda	34	Saudi Arab.	60	Vietnam	86	New Zealand
9	Trinidad	35	Armenia	61	Hong Kong	87	Britain
10	Bangladesh	36	Moldova	62	Brazil	88	Luxemburg
11	Tanzania	37	Turkey	63	Portugal	89	Austria
12	Romania	38	South Africa	64	Bosnia	90	Belgium
13	Egypt	39	Hungary	65	Serbia	91	Australia
14	Guatemala	40	Kyrgyzstan	66	Cyprus	92	France
15	Uganda	41	Latvia	67	Argentina	93	West Germany
16	El Salvador	42	Ethiopia	68	Slovenia	94	Iceland
17	Burkina Faso	43	Montenegro	69	Moscow	95	Finland
18	Azerbaijan	44	Belarus	70	Ireland	96	Netherlands
19	Iran	45	Poland	71	Slovakia	97	Andorra
20	Malta	46	China	72	United States	98	Switzerland
21	Colombia	47	Chile	73	Croatia	99	Denmark
22	Puerto Rico	48	Mexico	74	Northern Ireland	100	Norway
23	Georgia	49	Singapore	75	Uruguay	101	Sweden
24	Nigeria	50	Dominican Republic	76	Israel		
25	Russia	51	Taiwan	77	Spain		
26	Peru	52	Estonia	78	Italy		

* The ranking is derived from the World Values Survey map (Figure 2.4) as described in Appendix 5.

Cultural Map shown in Figure 2.4 in Chapter 2 (survival–self-expression and traditional–secular/rational), and combines them back into a single line, with a score for each country measuring the distance to the bottom left corner of the *cultural map*, as shown in Appendix 5.

Of course, the foregoing analysis is not to suggest that all cultures of honor hold exactly the same values. On the contrary, there are important differences among the various geographic and historical groups that comprise cultures of honor. Perhaps most important is the difference between the Islamic world and Africa, on the one hand, and the Orthodox world, on the other hand, on the question of religion. The Orthodox world tends to be much more secular than Africa or Islamic countries. There are lower rates of belief in God, less personal importance placed on religion, and less attendance at religious services. For instance, 42% of Orthodox respondents say that religion is very important in life, compared with 57% in cultures of honor overall. This is very likely a remnant of 70 years of communist rule, during which these countries' leaders actively tried to suppress religion. Notwithstanding this difference, the primacy of political rationality—the importance of the authority to dominate—within the Orthodox world means that they can properly be classified as cultures of honor.

Cultures of *Achievement*: Punctuality and Efficiency

Cultures of achievement are the polar opposite of cultures of honor. Egalitarianism, individualism, and orientation toward economic productivity are their hallmarks. This group, which has its modern roots in the Protestant Reformation, the Enlightenment, and the industrial revolution, gives priority to economic productivity and today finds its outlet in Protestantism (northern Europe and the English-speaking world), Confucianism, and Judaism. Tradition is given relatively little weight. The predominant values of cultures of achievement are **individualism** and **secularism**. Relatively few people actively practice a religion (except in the US), and, if they do, they share a widespread belief that religion is purely a personal matter. The idea that religion has any place in the public sphere is anathema to the values of these societies. Gender equality is valued in principle, even if it may not have been achieved in practice. Homosexuality is rapidly growing in acceptance, so that in recent waves of survey data there is a large gap between cultures of achievement and honor in this respect. The individual's well-being usually takes priority over that of the family or group, and personal qualities such as independence and perseverance are valued, whereas maintaining one's role in the family or group is secondary. In cultures of achievement, economic rationality is dominant, taking priority over social or political rationality. Pursuit of material well-being is given highest priority, as is the education necessary to achieve a high level of economic productivity.

As with cultures of honor, empirical data derived from survey research allow us to demonstrate that these broad generalizations are rooted in the actual values and beliefs of individuals. For instance, let us examine the value of **secularism**, one of the distinguishing characteristics of cultures of achievement. In any question that measures people's individual religious beliefs, people in cultures of achievement show the lowest levels of religious belief and participation of any of the three main clusters. They are the least likely to say that religion or God is important in their lives, to believe in God, hell, heaven, or sin, to say that they get comfort and strength from religion, to attend religious services, and to pray outside religious services. In comparison with cultures of honor, they also strongly reject the influence of religion and religious authorities in the public sphere.

Cultures of achievement are also widely divergent from cultures of honor when it comes to their attitudes toward **gender equality** and the role of women. Respondents from cultures of achievement are much less likely to agree that women want a home and children, that men make better political leaders or business executives than women, and that preschool children suffer with a working mother.

Cultures of achievement also display a wide divergence from cultures of honor when it comes to **acceptance of homosexuality**. Respondents in these cultures are much more likely to say that homosexuality is justifiable, and to say that they would not mind having homosexuals as neighbors. It is important to note that attitudes toward homosexuality have changed rapidly in cultures of achievement over the past few decades, so this wide discrepancy between cultures of honor and achievement is a relatively recent phenomenon.

While cultures of honor, as previously described, tend to be hierarchical, cultures of achievement are much more **horizontal** and **egalitarian**, and individual needs and desires are more important. For instance, whereas respondents in cultures of honor tend to consider obedience a value that parents should teach children, respondents from cultures of achievement tend to prefer teaching independence. They are much more likely to reject authoritarian governing methods, such as the army taking over when the government is incompetent, or having a strong leader who doesn't bother with parliament and elections. They are also more likely than those in cultures of honor to believe that *parents must earn their children's love and respect*. As a further illustration of their individualist ethos, they are the most likely to reject the notion that service to others is important in life. Only 5% call service to others "very important," while fully 41% say that it is "not at all important." They are also more likely to believe that they have freedom of choice and control over their own lives.

As with cultures of honor, cultures of achievement are not monolithic. Crucial differences exist within the larger cluster. Nordic Protestants are different from English-speaking Protestants, and even more so than American Protestants. Also, differences arise with Confucians and Jews. However, when seen in the world landscape, they are closer to each other.

One difference that merits further study is the Confucian attitude toward hierarchy and obedience. While most cultures of achievement are highly egalitarian, Confucian society remains quite hierarchical. Individual well-being is generally considered subservient to that of the group as a whole. It may be that this is one reason that Confucian societies such as China and North Korea retain an authoritarian political system, while other cultures of achievement have successfully implemented democratic governance. Another important distinction among cultures of achievement is the United States' religious tradition. Whereas most cultures of achievement are quite secular in their beliefs, the United States remains very religious. In the United States 96% believe in God—well above the 86% average worldwide, and much more than the 72% of Britons, 69% of Danes and Norwegians, and 53% of Swedes who say they do (Inglehart, Basáñez, et al., 2004, table F050). Americans, however, share the egalitarianism, individualism, and orientation toward economic productivity that are the hallmarks of cultures of achievement.

Cultures of *Joy*: Family and Friendship

It was not until after World War II and the subsequent period of peace and prosperity that a few countries (Nordic and European Catholic above all), as well as a postmaterialist public, began questioning the rationality of cultures of achievement. Why should you work that hard, without time to enjoy your family, your friends, your meals, and yourself, just in order to make extra income, even though all your material needs are already met? Why not escape from the obsessions of prestige and material accumulation and devote some time to *quality of life?*

Cultures of joy might be best characterized as reflecting Buddhism's *middle path* or Aristotle's *golden mean*. On most values, they occupy the middle ground between cultures of achievement and cultures of honor, while avoiding the extremes of either. Cultures of joy predominate in Catholic Europe and in Latin America, which is also historically a strongly Catholic region. Like cultures of achievement, they have a high degree of secularism: while people in these cultures may be personally religious, they reject the idea that **religion** should play a role in the public sphere. In their attitudes toward hierarchy and individualism, they are intermediate between cultures of honor and achievement, with the belief that the **well-being** of individuals and families or groups must be balanced. They share a strong sense of **social responsibility** (72% of Latin Americans [a *joy* culture] versus 5% of respondents from cultures of *achievement* say service to others is very important) and a belief that **quality of life** is essential. In cultures of joy, social rationality takes priority over economic or political rationality.

In looking at the divergence of World Values Survey responses, cultures of joy tend to fall closer to the mean, while cultures of honor and achievement cluster at opposite ends. Such is the case for measures of **religiousness**, which as we have seen is one of the most important factors separating the cultural clusters. Respondents from cultures of joy are less religious than those from cultures of honor, but more religious than those from cultures of achievement. For example, as mentioned earlier, 22% of those from cultures of joy say that religion is very important in their lives, as compared to 57% in cultures of honor and only 17% in cultures of achievement. However, when we look at acceptance of religion in the public sphere, we see an important distinction.

Cultures of joy reject the role of religion in the public sphere just as strongly—or even more so—as cultures of achievement. They are nearly as likely to reject the statement that politicians who don't believe in God are unfit for public office. In answering the survey questions regarding whether it is better if more people with strong religious beliefs are in public office and whether religious authorities should interpret the law in a democracy, they are even more secular than those in cultures of achievement. For instance, only 14% of respondents in cultures of joy agree or strongly agree that it would be better if more people with strong religious beliefs were in public office, compared with 21% in cultures of achievement and fully 59% in cultures of honor.

With regard to questions dealing with the role of women and families, people from cultures of joy tend to be **relatively egalitarian**. To draw a somewhat finer distinction, they seem to be just as—or even more—egalitarian than cultures of achievement when it comes to questions dealing specifically with the rights of men and women. For instance, only 24% agree or strongly agree that men make better political leaders than women, compared with 29% in cultures of achievement and fully 63% in cultures of honor. However, when the questions involve children, they tend to be a bit more conservative, landing somewhere in between cultures of honor and those of achievement. They give intermediate answers as to whether women want children and a home, if a preschool child suffers with a working mother, whether children are important to a successful marriage, and whether a woman has to have children to be fulfilled. For example, 51% say a woman has to have children to be fulfilled, compared with 36% in cultures of achievement and 80% in cultures of honor.

When it comes to measures of **hierarchy** and **obedience**, cultures of joy, as we would expect, are between those of honor and achievement. They are also between the two other cultural clusters in the value they place on obedience versus independence in children, and in whether children should always love and respect their parents regardless of whether the parents have earned it. In cultures of joy 26% say that parents must earn their children's love and respect, compared with 15% in cultures of honor and 44% in cultures of achievement. However, they are relatively attached to democratic governance and generally reject the notion that the army should take over if the government is incompetent or that it is good to have a strong leader who doesn't bother with parliament and elections. In cultures of joy 72%, compared with 73% in cultures of achievement and only 51% in cultures of honor, say that it is bad or very bad to have a strong leader who doesn't need to bother with parliament or elections.

Although both Catholic Europe and Latin America are considered cultures of joy due to the influence of Catholicism, there are very significant differences between the two. In many respects, Latin America has a great deal in common with cultures of honor. It tends to be quite hierarchical, and to place a strong emphasis on obedience. It also is much more religious than Catholic Europe. Finally, it has very low levels of trust, which is also more similar to cultures of honor. So great are these differences that, in the previous empirical analysis, cultures of joy are considered to consist of Catholic Europe, which is the fullest expression of a culture of joy (statistics for Latin America, with its strong *culture of honor* component, are given separately).

Most of the differences between Catholic Europe and Latin America stem from the fact that Latin America remains at a fairly low level of economic development, which tends to reinforce those cultural traits that are similar to cultures of honor. Its essential similarity with Catholic Europe lies in the relative absence of *guilt* brought about by Catholicism's emphasis on confession and forgiveness. Finally, survey data show that Latin Americans place a high priority on **quality of life** and social interactions, one of the defining characteristics of cultures of joy. For instance, the percentage of Latin Americans saying that they are *very happy* with their lives in general is the highest of all the clusters (41%, compared with 21% in cultures of honor, 32% in cultures of achievement, and 24% in Catholic Europe). They also rank highest in percentage of respondents saying that they are overall *very satisfied with their life* (28%, compared with 11% in cultures of honor, 12% in cultures of achievement, and 13% in Catholic Europe). A similar trend shows up with respect to *freedom of choice and control over their lives*: 76% say they hold a great deal, compared to 55% in cultures of honor, 68% in cultures of achievement, and 59% for Catholic Europe.

The top four countries in Table 5.8 share a legacy of European Catholicism (and the fifth is the Latin American Catholic country of Uruguay), while the bottom five are geographically diverse—Sweden, Zimbabwe, Estonia, Pakistan, and Jordan. The second-highest scoring group is also primarily Catholic, both European and Latin American, except for Israel, while the second-lowest scoring group is quite diverse, comprising East Asian, former communist, Northern European, Islamic, and African countries. This geographical diversity is perhaps not surprising given the methodology behind this index, which measures distance from the cultural map's center (Figure 2.4) in any direction.

Particularly remarkable is finding Sweden—a country that generally tops international rankings—at the bottom of the list, closely followed by Estonia and Norway and surrounded by Zimbabwe and Pakistan, among the least joyful countries. However, a further complexity arose within the cultures of *joy*: the existence of at least three different meanings of joy. The first—the *work hard, play hard* type—was more common among cultures of achievement. Another, *contemplative joy*, was more common among cultures of honor. Finally, prevalent among cultures of joy was a *carefree* type of joy, which remains difficult to understand for cultures of both achievement and honor. Furthermore, younger postmaterialist generations everywhere, but particularly in the Nordic countries, have begun to question the meaning of material accumulation at the expense of personal joy.

Further Research

After reviewing the empirical characteristics of the three cultures, the profile of each seems clear. However, it is critical to realize that the three cultures represent ideal types, and nearly all countries in reality represent a *blend* of different characteristics. For instance, within the United States, the culture of Massachusetts is very different from that of Texas or California. Among cultures of joy, Catholic Europe tilts toward achievement, while Latin America leans more toward honor. Simply listing them in tables, as in Tables 5.6, 5.7, and 5.8, can actually make understanding more difficult. There is no easy way to synthesize the three lists in one, or to represent those countries that contain elements of multiple cultures.

One way to resolve this difficulty is by adapting the Lewis triangle (Lewis, 1996[2012]), as shown in Figure 5.1. In the three vertices, the three cultural types are represented, while countries or regions appear on the corresponding sides. This is a conceptual hypothetical exercise without any pretense of empirical precision, although it would certainly be a fruitful topic for further research.

TABLE 5.7
Countries of *Achievement*, Punctuality and Efficiency (Highest to Lowest), 2010*

1	Sweden	27	Uruguay	53	Singapore	79	Georgia
2	Norway	28	Northern Ireland	54	Mexico	80	Colombia
3	Denmark	29	Croatia	55	Chile	81	Puerto Rico
4	Switzerland	30	United States	56	China	82	Malta
5	Andorra	31	Slovakia	57	Poland	83	Iran
6	Netherlands	32	Ireland	58	Belarus	84	Azerbaijan
7	Finland	33	Moscow	59	Montenegro	85	Burkina Faso
8	Iceland	34	Slovenia	60	Ethiopia	86	El Salvador
9	West Germany	35	Argentina	61	Latvia	87	Uganda
10	France	36	Cyprus	62	Kyrgyzstan	88	Guatemala
11	Australia	37	Serbia	63	Hungary	89	Egypt
12	Belgium	38	Bosnia	64	Turkey	90	Tanzania
13	Austria	39	Portugal	65	South Africa	91	Romania
14	Luxemburg	40	Hong Kong	66	Armenia	92	Bangladesh
15	Britain	41	Brazil	67	Moldova	93	Trinidad
16	New Zealand	42	Vietnam	68	Saudi Arabia	94	Rwanda
17	Czech Republic	43	India	69	South Korea	95	Algeria
18	East Germany	44	Bulgaria	70	Albania	96	Iraq
19	Greece	45	Lithuania	71	Indonesia	97	Ghana
20	Galicia	46	Thailand	72	Philippines	98	Morocco
21	Canada	47	Malaysia	73	Mali	99	Jordan
22	Slovenia	48	Macedonia	74	Zambia	100	Pakistan
23	Japan	49	Ukraine	75	Venezuela	101	Zimbabwe
24	Italy	50	Estonia	76	Russia		
25	Spain	51	Taiwan	77	Peru		
26	Israel	52	Dominican Republic	78	Nigeria		

* The ranking is derived from the *World Values Survey* map (Figure 2.4) as described in Appendix 5.

TABLE 5.8

Countries of *Joy* and Friendship (Highest to Lowest), 2010*

1	Italy	26	Finland	51	Slovakia	76	Iraq
2	Spain	27	Singapore	52	Philippines	77	Trinidad
3	Northern Ireland	28	Canada	53	Mali	78	Russia
4	Croatia	29	Australia	54	Peru	79	Bangladesh
5	Uruguay	30	Chile	55	Ukraine	80	China
6	Israel	31	Poland	56	Zambia	81	Rwanda
7	Galicia	32	Iceland	57	Albania	82	Lithuania
8	Argentina	33	Netherlands	58	Slovenia	83	South Korea
9	Brazil	34	Ethiopia	59	Georgia	84	Latvia
10	Portugal	35	Germany	60	Switzerland	85	Algeria
11	Luxemburg	36	Kyrgyzstan	61	Azerbaijan	86	Ghana
12	Cyprus	37	Macedonia	62	El Salvador	87	Japan
13	Greece	38	Czech Republic	63	Malta	88	Montenegro
14	Belgium	39	Mexico	64	Iran	89	Belarus
15	Austria	40	Saudi Arabia	65	Burkina Faso	90	Bulgaria
16	Vietnam	41	Venezuela	66	Hungary	91	Morocco
17	India	42	Serbia	67	Puerto Rico	92	Hong Kong
18	Slovenia	43	South Africa	68	Guatemala	93	Norway
19	Britain	44	Bosnia	69	Denmark	94	Moscow
20	Thailand	45	Turkey	70	Uganda	95	Taiwan
21	France	46	United States	71	Romania	96	Jordan
22	Malaysia	47	Nigeria	72	Moldova	97	Pakistan
23	Dominican Republic	48	Colombia	73	Tanzania	98	Estonia
24	New Zealand	49	Indonesia	74	Egypt	99	Zimbabwe
25	Ireland	50	Andorra	75	Armenia	100	Sweden

* The ranking is derived from the World Values Survey map (Figure 2.4)
as described in Appendix 5.

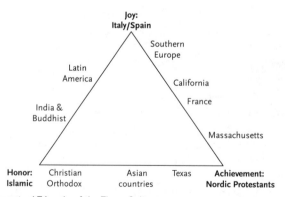

FIGURE 5.1 Conceptual Triangle of the Three Cultures

6

The Three Cultures in the World Values Survey

The preceding chapter analyzed the highest contrasts between cultures of honor and cultures of achievement. In this chapter I will discuss a selection of the World Values Survey (WVS) values that appear in the *World Cultural Map* of Figure 2.3 in Chapter 2. These focus on issues of happiness, respect for parents and authority, gender, religion, national pride, trust, life satisfaction, income equality, competition, and acceptance of homosexuality. They are taken from the 1990–2000 World Values Survey waves (Inglehart, Basáñez, et al., 2004). The cultures of joy remain in a sort of balance between extremes. Perhaps the main element that distinguishes the culture of *joy* from the other two is a contradictory absence of guilt in adults, produced by the ease with which the Catholic priests historically granted forgiveness. A culture of joy is also promoted by the sense of balance that Buddhism teaches; or the postmaterialist awakening among European populations, particularly in the Nordic countries.

On the *survival* end of the map (left-hand side), low levels of happiness combine with high levels of appreciation for hard work, respect for authority, and obedience to parents. On the *self-expression* end (right-hand side), high levels of trust in people, life satisfaction, and acceptance of homosexuality blend together. The *traditional* end (bottom) shows high national pride, and importance of god and religion. Similarly, the *secular-rational* end (top) shows high determination and acceptance of divorce and abortion.

The reader will get a clearer sense of the distinctions between the cultures of honor and the cultures of achievement by looking in the following tables at the variation by percentages among different countries, as well as from the 1990–2000 wave, or the differences by gender, age, education, income, or materialism-postmaterialism. All the data are taken from national representative samples following conventional standards for public opinion research. Technical details and full documentation are available at www.worldvaluessurvey.org.

Table 6.1, *Feeling of Happiness*, lists 81 countries alphabetically from Albania to Zimbabwe (except for the last column on the right, which is ranked from the highest to the lowest percentage). The question reads: "Taking all things together, would you say you are very happy, quite happy, not very happy, not at all happy?"

TABLE 6.1

Feeling of Happiness

Taking all things together, would you say you are

Very happy (%)

(WVS: V11)

Country	Wave 1990	Wave 2000	Gender Male	Gender Female	Age 16-29	Age 30-49	Age 50+	Education Lower	Education Middle	Education Upper	Income Lower	Income Middle	Income Upper	Values Mat	Values Mixed	Values Postm.
Albania	na	10	10	10	11	11	7	6	9	20	7	9	14	8	11	13
Algeria	na	17	14	19	16	18	15	14	18	18	15	15	21	18	15	23
Argentina	33	33	31	35	39	33	28	30	37	37	31	33	37	28	35	33
Armenia	na	6	6	6	6	7	5	5	6	9	7	4	9	7	6	4
Australia	na	43	40	46	43	44	42	41	47	40	38	44	45	46	44	41
Austria	30	36	35	37	45	36	31	36	37	34	29	32	44	33	37	34
Azerbaijan	na	11	13	10	15	10	7	20	11	10	10	9	16	11	12	16
Bangladesh	na	15	15	15	15	13	22	13	17	18	6	12	27	14	15	11
Belarus	6	5	4	6	8	4	4	3	7	5	4	6	8	4	8	4
Belgium	40	43	42	44	48	43	40	35	44	48	29	43	52	37	45	42
Bosnia and Herz.	na	22	22	22	28	21	17	17	21	28	17	20	32	22	22	15
Brazil	21	22	24	20	23	23	19	23	21	20	21	19	26	25	21	21
Bulgaria	7	8	8	8	17	7	5	2	11	13	4	9	11	7	9	13
Canada	30	44	43	46	43	42	47	49	43	41	40	45	46	44	44	44
Chile	33	36	34	39	44	32	36	33	36	43	33	36	40	41	35	32
China	28	13	11	12	0	13	11	12	12	5	8	14	15	11	11	13
Colombia	na	47	45	49	52	45	44	44	51	44	45	49	46	50	49	52
Croatia	na	13	14	12	21	11	10	14	11	18	11	14	14	11	14	14
Czech Rep.	5	11	9	13	16	11	8	10	11	16	8	11	13	11	11	13
Denmark	43	45	46	44	47	46	43	45	40	48	37	49	55	43	46	46
Dominican Rep.	na	32	28	35	36	27	18	32	31	33	38	25	37	42	28	34
Egypt	na	18	19	17	18	18	18	15	22	20	16	18	21	16	21	19
El Salvador	na	56	58	54	61	53	52	51	60	63	45	57	67	na	na	na
Estonia	3	7	6	7	9	7	5	6	7	8	5	7	7	6	7	na
Finland	20	24	25	24	29	23	23	22	26	29	17	26	33	24	23	30
France	25	31	31	32	41	32	26	30	36	31	25	30	39	28	33	32
Georgia	na	12	11	12	16	10	9	13	11	13	9	12	14	11	12	12
Germany	14	20	16	22	19	21	18	13	23	29	15	21	26	22	19	18
Great Britain	38	na	na	na	na	na	na	na	na	na	na	na	na	na	na	na
Greece	na	19	21	18	19	19	18	25	18	19	19	13	24	19	20	15
Hungary	11	17	16	18	25	16	13	17	18	16	12	16	23	15	19	13
Iceland	41	47	44	50	43	51	44	43	48	52	33	50	57	50	47	37
India	24	26	27	24	25	27	23	22	29	30	24	19	33	23	33	42
Indonesia	na	21	18	24	19	25	17	17	21	24	17	23	25	19	23	25
Iran	na	25	20	31	27	23	24	24	28	23	20	24	31	29	25	22
Ireland	44	42	40	45	34	47	42	45	42	40	32	48	46	38	43	43
Israel	na	28	25	30	35	24	22	24	29	28	22	26	27	25	28	23
Italy	16	18	19	18	25	19	15	16	21	18	15	17	22	17	18	19
Japan	18	29	22	34	28	31	27	25	31	27	27	29	31	31	29	25
Jordan	na	13	11	15	13	13	14	12	11	16	14	10	16	12	14	5
Korea, South	10	10	9	10	9	10	10	7	10	9	8	9	11	9	10	9
Latvia	2	7	5	8	12	4	7	7	6	8	6	7	9	7	7	4
Lithuania	4	5	6	4	10	4	2	2	5	9	2	6	6	1	4	25
Luxembourg	na	36	39	33	34	36	36	34	35	39	36	37	39	38	35	40
Macedonia	na	19	20	18	27	16	17	13	22	25	12	20	29	18	21	18
Malta	na	31	32	31	38	28	29	33	33	28	28	35	34	25	34	33
Mexico	26	57	58	56	58	59	52	53	62	61	49	64	61	55	58	64
Moldova	na	6	6	6	11	4	4	5	6	7	4	5	9	6	7	11
Montenegro	na	9	7	10	8	10	8	7	10	10	5	8	12	8	9	13
Morocco	na	26	26	27	27	26	25	27	24	28	17	21	26	27	27	25
Netherlands	48	46	44	48	55	49	38	44	49	44	34	46	55	46	47	44
New Zealand	na	33	29	36	27	34	35	31	38	32	30	27	41	31	32	32
Nigeria	40	67	66	67	70	64	58	62	70	70	61	67	74	67	67	69
Northern Ireland	37	47	45	48	47	50	47	41	52	52	35	52	58	46	49	47
Norway	29	30	29	31	34	31	26	26	29	36	na	na	na	28	30	31
Pakistan	na	20	21	19	27	19	8	16	23	26	15	20	26	20	20	25
Peru	na	31	29	32	33	31	27	29	30	33	28	33	33	25	31	38
Philippines	na	38	37	40	45	37	32	35	38	42	30	38	47	35	41	38
Poland	10	18	18	18	27	17	13	17	20	13	12	20	23	16	18	25
Portugal	13	18	19	18	30	21	8	14	25	27	4	19	24	9	23	20
Puerto Rico	na	54	57	51	55	53	53	51	51	56	46	59	56	52	54	52
Romania	6	4	4	4	5	2	4	5	4	1	7	2	2	4	3	3
Russian Fed.	6	6	7	5	9	7	3	4	6	7	4	7	7	5	7	9
Serbia	na	12	13	11	12	13	12	9	15	12	9	11	17	12	13	16
Singapore	na	29	27	31	25	33	29	27	28	38	27	27	34	24	31	25
Slovakia	na	8	8	8	12	8	5	6	9	10	4	9	10	6	10	6
Slovenia	9	16	16	15	20	17	11	11	18	16	11	19	21	12	17	17
South Africa	24	39	35	43	39	36	45	35	43	37	31	37	49	39	40	25
Spain	20	20	21	19	23	20	18	19	22	21	16	20	21	21	20	18
Sweden	41	37	33	40	35	36	38	44	33	37	27	41	44	41	37	34
Switzerland	36	40	37	43	44	38	40	40	41	35	35	41	41	41	41	37
Taiwan	na	30	26	33	28	33	22	25	37	30	22	31	36	31	32	28
Tanzania	na	57	57	58	66	50	58	57	60	48	59	53	55	52	60	67
Turkey	29	31	26	36	30	31	32	34	27	27	31	31	31	32	32	27
Uganda	na	26	26	26	29	24	25	22	27	35	32	28	31	21	27	37
Ukraine	na	6	7	7	10	6	4	2	6	10	3	5	10	4	7	10
United States	41	39	37	42	38	36	44	42	36	41	35	41	43	37	39	40
Uruguay	na	21	17	24	24	20	20	20	22	21	16	19	28	19	21	19
Venezuela	na	57	57	57	59	55	56	50	58	62	49	56	64	52	59	57
Vietnam	na	49	49	50	46	53	47	47	54	43	42	50	52	52	51	49
Zimbabwe	na	20	18	22	25	16	15	18	24	10	17	21	24	19	20	27
Total	23	27	26	27	30	26	23	25	26	30	22	27	30	21	28	31

RANKING

Country	2000
Nigeria	67
Tanzania	57
Mexico	57
Venezuela	57
El Salvador	56
Puerto Rico	54
Vietnam	49
Colombia	47
Iceland	47
Northern Ireland	47
Netherlands	46
Denmark	45
Canada	44
Australia	43
Belgium	43
Ireland	42
Switzerland	40
United States	39
South Africa	39
Philippines	38
Sweden	37
Chile	36
Austria	36
Luxembourg	36
Argentina	33
New Zealand	33
Dominican Rep.	32
France	31
Malta	31
Turkey	31
Peru	31
Norway	30
Taiwan	30
Singapore	29
Japan	29
Israel	28
Morocco	26
Uganda	26
India	26
Iran	25
Finland	24
Brazil	22
Bosnia and Herz.	22
Uruguay	21
Indonesia	21
Zimbabwe	20
Pakistan	20
Spain	20
Germany	20
Macedonia	19
Greece	19
Italy	18
Egypt	18
Portugal	18
Poland	18
Hungary	17
Algeria	17
Slovenia	16
Bangladesh	15
Croatia	13
Jordan	13
Serbia	12
Georgia	12
China	12
Azerbaijan	11
Czech Republic	11
Korea, South	10
Montenegro	9
Slovakia	8
Bulgaria	8
Estonia	7
Latvia	7
Armenia	6
Moldova	6
Russian Fed.	6
Ukraine	6
Belarus	5
Lithuania	5
Romania	4
	27

Variation goes from the very high of Nigerians (67%), Tanzanians and Mexicans (57%), or Salvadorians (56%) and Puerto Ricans (54%) replying they are *very happy* to the very low 4% to 6% of the former Soviet Republics of Romania, Lithuania, Belarus, Ukraine, Russia, Moldova, and Armenia. There is a strong contrast between the happy Catholic and the unhappy Orthodox countries, as indicated in Figure 2.4. The grey row at the very bottom shows an average percentage of 27%.

The second column from left to right shows that the world became very slightly happier from 1990 to 2000, from 23% to 27%, although some countries report a much higher increase rate—Mexico went from 26% to 57%, Nigeria 40% to 67%, South Africa 24% to 39%, Canada 30% to 44%, and Japan 18% to 29%.

Happiness is a feeling that correlates with optimism and also responds to external conditions, but it does not correlate with development. Countries rich and poor, egalitarian and non-egalitarian, educated and non-educated, highly developed and underdeveloped, can be happy or unhappy. In 2000 Mexico elected the first president from a different party than the one in power for 72 years; South Africans were excited about Mandela's victory. In the opposite direction, the Chinese lowered their happiness rate from 28% to 12%. Was that the outcome of rapid change shaking the traditional way of life (Steele and Lynch, 2012)?

Looking into the differences by **gender** (third column from left to right) it is clear that males and females shared practically the same opinions (26%–27%), except in three countries, Japan, Iran, and Turkey, where women reported being 10% happier than men. By **age** a slight diminishing trend is clear: 30% of the younger (18–29 years old), 26% of the middle-aged (30–49), and 23% of those older than 50 said they were *very happy*. However, 17 countries showed a difference larger than 10%, and in one country (Portugal) happiness declined by age even further, from 30% to 8%.

Education increases happiness slightly from 25% to 30%, but in 14 countries it made more than a 10% difference, except in Azerbaijan, where it decreased from 20% to 10%. **Income** had a similar effect as education, raising happiness from 22% to 30%. Thirty countries showed an increase of over 10%, and seven of those over 20% (Bangladesh, Belgium, El Salvador, Iceland, Netherlands, Northern Ireland, and Portugal). Finally, **postmaterialists** ranked themselves happier than materialists (21% to 31%), with Lithuania showing a big difference (1% to 25%) and the reverse trend in Iceland and South Africa.

Respect for parents was the question that back in 1993 during my summer stay at the University of Michigan showed the largest difference between Catholics and Protestants. The question was worded as follows: "With which of these two statements do you tend to agree? A. Regardless of what the qualities and faults of one's parents are, one must always love and respect them; or B. One does not have the duty to respect and love parents who have not earned it by their behavior and attitudes." It's taken as a proxy of autonomy-dissent versus obedience, and as expected, it appears the farthest in the bottom left position in the Inglehart's *World Cultural Map* of Figure 2.3. Schwartz also arrived through quite a different method into a much more elaborate axis of *embeddedness-autonomy* to reveal what this powerful item conceals.

When examining Table 6.2, *Respect for Parents*, a world average of 82% diverges into the highest rates of Confucian, Islamic, and colonial Catholics countries with over 90% agreement, as opposed to the lower rates of Protestant countries of under 63%, with the lowest in the Netherlands (32%), Sweden (44%), and Norway (52%). Two Catholic countries stand as outliers within the under-average group: Austria at 65% and Ireland at 71%. Japan is also an outlier of the Confucian group at 72%.

The second column shows that from 1990 to 2000 the world slightly increased its *respect for parents* by 8% (from 74% to 82%). Four countries went even further: Argentina (75% to 88%), China (75% to 95%), Finland (40% to 63%), and Mexico (78% to 90%). However, another four countries showed the reverse trend: Austria (75% to 65%), Belarus (83% to 71%), Belgium (77% to 65%), and Germany (76% to 53%). By **gender** the world average shows no variation at 82% with all the countries under 10% variation one way or the other, except Sweden where men are 12% higher than women (50% to 38%). By **age** there is only a 3% difference between the young (81%) and the old (84%), but 26 mostly European countries (with Uruguay and South Korea as outliers) show a difference of more than 10%, and three show more than 20% (Croatia, Greece, and Japan).

Education lowers parental respect 9% from 86% to 77%; in 32 countries it lowered more than 10% and in 12 of those more than 20% (Austria, Bulgaria, Croatia, Greece, Ireland, Iceland, Luxembourg, Netherlands, Romania, Slovenia, Sweden, Switzerland, and Turkey). Uganda, on the contrary, showed an increase from 85% to 96% with increase in education. Increase in **income** correlates with a slighter decrease in parental respect from 85% to 80%, but in 22 countries the decrease was more than 10%, roughly following the age profile. Finally, **postmaterialists** were 13% less respectful than materialists (71% vs. 87%) with eight countries showing more than 20% difference (Georgia, Greece, Island, Luxembourg, Netherlands, Northern Ireland, Spain, and Sweden) and a reverse trend of 11% in Lithuania.

The high *respect for parents* that Confucian countries show is remarkable, which explains the high scores those countries get in the Schwartz's *hierarchy* axis. The high scores of Islamic and colonial Catholic countries lean them toward Schwartz's embeddedness. On the other end, the lower scores among Protestants connect with Schwartz's *autonomy* axis, a value essential for dissent, critical thinking, and freedom of thought, all-powerful tools for knowledge production. Freedom of thought is indispensable to questioning established ideas (critical thinking), which leads to creative autonomy and dissent.

Table 6.3, *Men Have More Right to a Job*, captures respondents' attitudes toward one measure of gender equality. The question asks respondents to agree or disagree with the following statement: "When jobs are scarce, men should have more right to a job than women." Countries where many people agree with this proposition appear on the *survival* end of the World Culture Map, whereas high levels of disagreement place a country on the *self-expression* side of the map.

pect for Parents

ich of these two statements do you tend to agree? A. Regardless of what the qualities and faults of one's parents are, st always love and respect them (%)

Country	Wave 1990	Wave 2000	Gender Male	Gender Female	Age 16-29	Age 30-49	Age 50+	Education Lower	Education Middle	Education Upper	Income Lower	Income Middle	Income Upper	Values Mat	Values Mixed	Values Postm.
a	na	87	86	88	84	88	88	84	88	89	85	85	91	88	86	87
a	na	93	92	94	93	91	97	95	93	92	93	94	91	93	93	91
ina	75	88	88	88	83	89	92	90	86	79	91	88	85	93	90	81
ia	na	93	95	91	91	93	94	95	93	91	92	94	92	95	92	80
lia	na	74	75	73	72	72	79	82	76	65	78	72	69	83	77	67
a	75	65	61	69	60	59	73	73	60	46	73	68	60	72	68	55
aijan	na	92	92	91	89	93	94	94	92	91	91	93	91	92	90	88
adesh	na	90	90	90	90	90	92	91	90	88	93	89	89	90	90	85
s	83	71	73	69	69	68	77	77	71	59	76	69	67	73	71	62
m	77	65	65	65	57	60	74	75	66	56	72	68	58	71	65	58
a and Herz.	na	91	91	91	88	93	92	93	92	87	92	90	92	94	90	93
	90	93	93	93	92	92	96	95	92	87	96	95	89	96	93	85
ia	83	82	81	83	77	80	86	90	81	70	86	82	75	86	78	71
lia	69	78	77	78	73	76	82	85	78	70	83	79	71	84	80	71
	88	87	87	87	84	87	91	87	89	84	89	84	89	89	86	86
	75	94	95	94	89	96	96	96	93	93	94	96	93	94	94	90
bia	na	91	90	92	91	91	93	91	92	90	92	91	90	91	91	89
a	na	72	72	71	59	71	81	83	65	60	81	71	67	72	75	58
Republic	67	74	73	75	63	73	80	77	70	73	80	73	68	77	74	64
ark	47	na	na	na	na	na	na	na	na	na	na	na	na	na	na	na
ican Rep.	na	86	82	88	85	87	82	81	85	87	87	86	78	86	87	83
ador	na	95	95	95	94	95	96	95	95	95	95	96	96	96	95	93
a	na	94	93	94	94	94	93	94	93	93	93	94	93	na	na	na
a	62	72	69	75	68	71	75	72	72	71	77	72	67	77	69	65
d	40	63	65	62	59	59	71	67	60	55	63	62	65	63	65	59
e	77	75	75	74	71	71	80	80	68	67	77	80	69	84	76	58
ia	na	91	92	91	89	91	95	92	91	92	91	91	91	92	91	93
any	76	53	52	54	46	49	61	62	46	44	60	53	45	58	54	44
Britain	68	65	65	65	66	60	69	78	57	60	70	63	56	na	na	na
e	na	69	69	69	59	75	81	84	74	63	73	68	69	79	69	58
ary	81	83	81	85	79	79	89	86	73	81	87	80	83	85	81	72
d	61	61	63	59	55	59	68	68	60	48	55	67	57	70	59	50
	84	89	89	89	90	88	89	91	88	85	90	93	85	91	85	88
esia	na	90	88	92	88	91	90	90	89	92	89	89	93	90	90	96
	na	89	89	90	89	89	90	90	87	91	90	88	88	94	87	84
d	78	71	73	69	68	67	78	81	69	59	80	71	63	76	72	57
	na	na	na	na	na	na	na	na	na	na	na	na	na	na	na	na
	84	79	79	80	67	80	86	86	75	71	86	80	76	88	80	72
	79	72	72	71	55	71	78	81	72	65	76	74	66	72	70	69
	na	94	93	95	94	94	94	96	94	90	96	92	94	95	93	92
, South	94	92	93	92	87	93	97	96	93	91	91	94	93	93	93	84
	72	77	78	77	72	82	75	79	77	76	78	79	74	75	79	74
nia	80	83	81	85	79	83	85	84	83	82	82	87	79	80	83	91
bourg	na	59	63	55	52	54	69	70	56	46	62	63	45	67	60	40
donia	na	91	91	91	89	89	96	95	89	89	92	89	93	89	92	92
	na	91	91	92	85	90	96	97	90	81	93	95	87	95	90	84
o	78	90	90	90	90	91	89	90	91	87	88	91	91	92	91	89
va	na	90	88	93	87	92	92	92	91	88	93	90	89	89	92	85
enegro	na	87	85	89	80	86	93	92	86	80	94	91	81	91	86	77
cco	na	97	97	98	97	98	98	98	96	94	97	98	96	99	97	91
rlands	38	32	33	31	24	27	41	45	30	21	39	31	24	51	32	20
ealand	na	62	64	61	62	56	68	69	62	55	69	64	52	65	60	55
a	87	94	94	95	93	95	97	96	94	94	95	95	92	95	94	89
ern Ireland	80	78	79	77	75	73	84	84	74	71	80	78	79	87	79	62
ay	45	52	53	51	44	48	63	61	53	42	na	na	na	60	52	41
an	na	94	94	95	94	94	97	95	93	96	95	94	94	95	94	100
	na	91	91	91	89	92	90	89	90	93	90	91	92	89	91	94
ines	na	94	92	95	93	94	94	92	94	95	94	95	92	95	93	92
d	84	87	85	88	82	88	87	89	87	76	88	86	84	88	86	81
gal	77	83	81	84	79	80	87	83	83	82	86	81	84	84	84	80
o Rico	na	98	98	97	95	96	100	97	98	97	98	98	96	98	97	97
nia	83	84	82	85	76	81	90	92	83	69	91	86	78	86	82	68
an Fed.	76	84	84	85	79	85	86	84	85	82	84	85	84	85	84	83
a	na	87	86	88	81	83	93	90	87	83	89	87	85	90	84	88
pore	na	93	92	94	93	93	93	94	94	91	93	94	93	94	94	87
kia	na	74	70	77	64	73	82	80	70	74	77	74	71	75	73	61
nia	82	78	77	79	72	75	86	90	77	63	84	85	65	86	77	72
Africa	87	91	91	91	90	92	88	90	92	90	86	94	94	93	89	92
	80	83	82	85	74	81	91	90	78	73	87	86	77	89	86	68
en	51	44	50	38	33	43	51	59	43	33	49	45	36	65	45	35
erland	70	66	68	65	58	64	75	76	65	55	73	72	56	70	69	57
n	na	93	91	95	91	94	94	94	90	94	93	95	91	93	93	94
nia	na	91	90	91	91	89	95	90	92	90	90	90	93	91	91	96
y	83	86	85	87	83	87	89	92	81	69	91	85	74	89	87	78
da	na	90	91	89	90	90	89	85	91	96	85	94	93	94	91	75
ne	na	86	84	87	84	83	90	93	85	85	88	83	84	85	87	89
d States	75	77	77	78	77	78	77	82	81	73	80	79	74	81	79	72
aay	na	78	75	80	69	75	84	82	74	65	77	79	78	84	77	74
zuela	na	94	93	95	93	95	94	94	95	93	95	92	95	94	94	93
am	na	99	99	99	100	99	99	99	100	100	99	99	100	100	99	100
abwe	na	96	97	96	95	97	98	96	97	100	97	96	97	98	95	99
	74	82	82	82	81	82	84	86	81	77	85	83	80	87	81	71

(WVS: V13; EVS: V162)

RANKING

Country	2000
Vietnam	99
Puerto Rico	98
Morocco	97
Zimbabwe	96
Egypt	95
China	95
Pakistan	94
Nigeria	94
Venezuela	94
Jordan	94
Philippines	94
El Salvador	94
Singapore	93
Taiwan	93
Algeria	93
Armenia	93
Brazil	93
Korea, South	92
Azerbaijan	92
Georgia	91
Bosnia and Herz.	91
Malta	91
Colombia	91
Macedonia	91
South Africa	91
Peru	91
Tanzania	91
Moldova	90
Mexico	90
Bangladesh	90
Uganda	90
Indonesia	90
Iran	89
India	89
Argentina	88
Chile	87
Montenegro	87
Serbia	87
Poland	87
Turkey	86
Dominican Rep.	86
Ukraine	86
Russian Fed.	84
Romania	84
Spain	83
Hungary	83
Lithuania	83
Portugal	83
Bulgaria	82
Italy	79
Slovenia	78
Northern Ireland	78
Uruguay	78
Canada	78
United States	77
Latvia	77
France	75
Australia	74
Czech Republic	74
Slovakia	74
Estonia	72
Japan	72
Croatia	72
Belarus	71
Ireland	71
Greece	69
Switzerland	66
Belgium	65
Great Britain	65
Austria	65
Finland	63
New Zealand	62
Iceland	61
Luxembourg	59
Germany	53
Norway	52
Sweden	44
Netherlands	32
Total	82

TABLE 6.3
Men Have More Right to a Job

Do you agree or disagree with the following statements?
"When jobs are scarce, men should have more right to a job than women."
Agree (%)

(WVS: V78; EVS:

Country	Wave 1990	Wave 2000	Gender Male	Gender Female	Age 16-29	Age 30-49	Age 50+	Education Lower	Education Middle	Education Upper	Income Lower	Income Middle	Income Upper	Values Mat	Values Mixed	Values Postm.	RANKING Country
Albania	na	47	55	38	34	48	56	56	44	30	51	46	43	48	47	31	Egypt
Algeria	na	68	80	54	69	65	69	76	67	62	68	64	67	71	66	64	Morocco
Argentina	24	26	30	22	22	22	33	34	17	8	35	28	14	35	26	16	Jordan
Armenia	na	60	71	50	54	64	63	63	61	54	54	61	69	68	56	38	Iran
Australia	na	26	27	24	12	20	44	35	27	16	35	24	16	37	27	20	Philippines
Austria	50	27	28	26	16	22	37	35	21	14	37	28	19	35	29	18	Bangladesh
Azerbaijan	na	64	70	57	66	63	61	67	64	63	67	63	63	65	62	64	Algeria
Bangladesh	na	68	76	58	61	72	76	72	64	63	82	61	65	71	67	57	Pakistan
Belarus	38	25	31	20	21	23	31	33	24	15	26	24	25	27	23	17	Georgia
Belgium	38	25	22	28	10	21	36	46	25	10	41	27	14	37	24	13	Azerbaijan
Bosnia and Herz.	na	27	31	23	23	25	32	33	27	18	34	27	20	31	24	25	Turkey
Brazil	38	36	41	31	30	38	44	50	27	16	49	30	25	48	32	22	Nigeria
Bulgaria	46	39	45	33	33	37	44	47	40	24	48	33	34	42	36	43	Armenia
Canada	19	15	14	15	8	11	22	28	11	9	23	14	7	25	16	9	India
Chile	37	25	31	20	22	24	30	32	23	17	29	24	22	28	24	26	Taiwan
China	41	45	47	43	27	50	48	51	43	23	45	48	42	45	43	40	Indonesia
Colombia	na	29	30	28	28	28	36	46	31	15	44	32	18	41	34	34	Vietnam
Croatia	na	29	32	27	13	34	34	38	27	11	52	28	18	27	33	16	Malta
Czech Republic	55	18	17	20	14	14	25	24	14	8	25	17	14	25	17	9	Albania
Denmark	11	6	7	5	4	2	11	9	1	2	12	5	na	14	6	1	China
Dominican Rep.	na	15	22	10	13	19	20	29	23	11	23	14	6	17	15	14	Moldova
Egypt	na	90	93	86	86	91	92	92	87	89	90	89	91	92	88	82	Macedonia
El Salvador	na	27	28	26	26	27	29	36	23	8	44	22	12	na	na	na	Uganda
Estonia	45	14	18	10	14	12	15	16	13	11	19	13	12	13	13	14	Zimbabwe
Finland	15	10	13	7	5	9	13	14	5	4	8	13	8	14	9	4	Bulgaria
France	33	22	21	22	13	18	30	30	12	9	26	23	18	31	22	8	Korea, South
Georgia	na	65	74	56	64	63	67	63	67	57	67	66	60	66	63	63	Romania
Germany	31	27	33	22	17	22	37	38	17	17	36	30	19	35	28	13	Russian Fed.
Great Britain	34	23	25	21	14	17	34	35	16	8	25	21	17	22	21	13	Brazil
Greece	na	20	28	14	13	21	35	44	25	12	27	18	19	22	21	13	Poland
Hungary	42	25	25	25	18	25	28	32	11	11	26	27	22	27	21	13	Mexico
Iceland	6	4	4	3	4	3	4	6	2	1	5	2	4	7	3	1	Japan
India	49	57	61	52	53	59	58	62	59	46	68	61	49	65	50	41	South Africa
Indonesia	na	52	61	43	53	52	52	62	52	47	54	49	57	54	50	57	Venezuela
Iran	na	73	80	65	69	75	80	80	69	68	76	74	68	81	70	62	Serbia
Ireland	36	15	14	16	4	12	28	29	9	6	28	14	7	22	16	7	Ukraine
Israel	na	na	na	na	na	na	na	na	na	na	na	na	na	na	na	na	Singapore
Italy	43	27	27	27	13	20	41	42	18	9	40	26	15	43	28	17	Montenegro
Japan	34	32	33	31	20	25	43	56	30	24	37	32	28	37	31	21	Portugal
Jordan	na	80	87	74	78	82	84	85	82	70	84	81	77	87	78	66	Colombia
Korea, South	42	39	44	33	14	42	60	62	43	30	41	37	38	45	35	19	Croatia
Latvia	34	20	20	19	18	16	24	27	19	15	22	16	16	19	21	11	Uruguay
Lithuania	66	24	30	20	22	19	32	33	23	15	30	27	24	27	23	16	Switzerland
Luxembourg	na	26	30	22	18	22	36	37	23	16	34	31	17	34	28	14	El Salvador
Macedonia	na	43	46	40	40	43	45	55	41	26	51	42	33	44	40	42	Tanzania
Malta	na	47	49	46	28	46	62	68	44	14	60	53	30	52	47	30	Italy
Mexico	23	34	37	31	29	34	40	43	25	15	42	32	23	40	31	26	Germany
Moldova	na	45	46	44	43	38	55	55	46	35	56	43	37	45	42	42	Austria
Montenegro	na	30	43	16	22	26	39	40	26	15	35	22	28	31	28	22	Bosnia and Herz.
Morocco	na	83	88	78	81	83	88	86	76	55	90	84	79	85	82	74	Luxembourg
Netherlands	22	12	11	13	4	8	21	26	10	3	19	9	6	28	13	4	Argentina
New Zealand	na	13	12	13	2	9	20	17	12	8	17	10	10	14	13	8	Australia
Nigeria	48	60	73	47	60	60	60	61	61	58	64	59	58	57	61	68	Chile
Northern Ireland	34	16	17	15	7	11	25	22	10	12	17	16	7	18	16	11	Belgium
Norway	16	14	15	14	8	11	24	22	15	7	na	na	na	24	14	5	Belarus
Pakistan	na	67	71	63	65	65	80	74	64	50	74	69	56	70	65	64	Hungary
Peru	na	15	18	13	13	17	17	21	16	9	20	13	13	19	14	13	Lithuania
Philippines	na	69	72	66	61	72	75	75	71	58	74	68	66	70	69	63	Slovakia
Poland	55	35	36	34	17	32	48	47	21	18	37	34	33	41	32	28	Great Britain
Portugal	34	30	32	28	15	29	39	35	20	13	42	37	20	34	27	30	France
Puerto Rico	na	21	22	20	17	17	25	30	26	16	28	20	14	28	21	14	Puerto Rico
Romania	42	38	38	38	34	32	45	58	31	17	57	42	20	45	33	15	Greece
Russian Fed.	40	36	43	31	37	36	36	40	39	27	36	39	34	37	35	38	Latvia
Serbia	na	31	37	27	22	29	37	46	29	15	39	29	27	37	28	17	Spain
Singapore	na	30	33	27	21	37	43	41	27	15	41	31	23	37	29	18	Czech Republic
Slovakia	na	24	29	20	17	22	32	33	21	12	29	25	20	29	22	14	Slovenia
Slovenia	29	18	18	18	8	16	27	34	14	5	25	18	8	28	16	15	Northern Ireland
South Africa	45	32	43	18	30	32	38	39	23	17	38	28	27	28	34	35	Ireland
Spain	31	19	19	19	10	14	29	27	13	9	29	17	14	28	17	8	Dominican Rep.
Sweden	8	2	3	2	1	1	4	4	3	1	4	2	1	3	3	na	Peru
Switzerland	na	27	29	26	17	22	41	43	25	15	34	32	17	37	30	14	Canada
Taiwan	na	57	56	58	41	57	67	70	57	45	64	67	44	62	53	53	Norway
Tanzania	na	27	33	20	28	24	34	30	25	21	36	22	25	28	26	41	Estonia
Turkey	51	60	67	54	55	62	67	71	50	34	72	56	41	69	60	47	New Zealand
Uganda	na	41	58	25	42	39	42	47	36	59	51	50	29	35	44	42	Netherlands
Ukraine	na	31	35	27	25	30	34	43	33	19	33	30	30	35	25	35	Finland
United States	24	10	11	9	7	8	14	12	10	9	12	11	6	11	12	5	United States
Uruguay	na	28	33	24	27	17	37	37	15	14	37	30	16	44	28	14	Denmark
Venezuela	na	31	36	27	30	30	36	38	33	18	38	30	29	39	31	22	Iceland
Vietnam	na	48	54	43	45	49	50	53	45	32	56	42	51	54	48	43	Sweden
Zimbabwe	na	40	51	31	42	35	46	43	36	30	49	41	27	42	39	42	
Total	35	34	39	30	32	34	38	44	32	24	42	34	29	44	32	21	Total

Overall, 34% of interviewees agreed that men have more right to a job than women, which means that gender equality is far from achieved around the world, although there is a great deal of variation among regions. Middle Eastern and Islamic countries tended to have the highest levels of agreement, with 90% in Egypt, 83% in Morocco, and 80% in Jordan. African and East Asian countries also tended to agree at rates above the world average. Agreement was lowest in Western Europe and English-speaking Protestant countries and especially so in Scandinavia, where only 2% in Sweden, 4% in Iceland, and 6% in Denmark agreed.

The world overall showed little movement on this question between 1990 and 2000, with the percentage who agreed that men have more right to a job than women dropping only one point, from 35% to 34%. However, some countries showed greater movement, particularly in Eastern Europe. Support dropped from 50% to 27% in Austria, 38% to 25% in Belarus, 55% to 18% in the Czech Republic, 45% to 14% in Estonia, 42% to 25% in Hungary, 66% to 24% in Lithuania, 55% to 35% in Poland, and 29% to 18% in Slovenia. Spain, Ireland, and South Africa also showed a large drop. On the other hand, some countries showed retrenchment in their attitudes toward gender equality, with agreement rising from 23% to 34% in Mexico and 48% to 60% in Nigeria.

It is important to note that the increase in gender equality worldwide over time may be understated, as many countries lack data from 1990. Data are especially missing for those countries least supportive of gender equality, including all of the top 10 countries that agreed that men have more right to a job than women (Egypt, Morocco, Jordan, Iran, Philippines, Bangladesh, Algeria, Pakistan, Georgia, and Azerbaijan). Had respondents from those countries been asked this question in 1990, the overall world agreement in 1990 would probably have been much higher than its actual 35%, and thus the change to the 2000 level of 34% would likely have been more dramatic.

With regard to **gender**, it is perhaps not surprising that fewer women than men agreed that men have more right to a job, as overall 39% of men agreed, compared with 30% of women. In a number of countries (Algeria, Armenia, Montenegro, Nigeria, South Africa, Uganda, and Zimbabwe), the gap between men and women on this question was at least 20 percentage points. Surprisingly, in a few countries (Belgium, Canada, Czech Republic, France, Ireland, the Netherlands, New Zealand, and Taiwan) women were actually more likely than men to agree that men had more right to a job, although the difference was never more than a few percentage points. By **age**, there was a trend for the young to be more egalitarian than the old, with only 32% of the youngest generation (16–29) agreeing that men have more right to a job, compared to 34% of the middle-aged (30–49) and 38% of those 50 and older.

By **education** we can see a movement from survival to self-expression values with increasing education, as 44% of the least educated, 32% of the middle group, and only 24% of the most educated agree that men have more right to a job than women. **Income** tells a similar story, with 42% of the poorest, 34% of the middle group, and 29% of the richest agreeing. Postmaterialists tended to be more egalitarian, with only 21% (compared with 44% of materialists) agreeing that men have more right to a job.

Table 6.4, *Respect for Authority*, is derived from a World Values Survey question that reads: "I'm going to read out a list of various changes in our way of life that might take place in the near future. If it were to happen, do you think it would be a good thing, a bad thing, or don't you mind? Greater respect for authority." The numbers in the columns indicate the percentage of respondents who answered that greater respect for authority would be a good thing. This value is associated with both survivalism and traditionalism on the World Cultures Map (lower left corner).

Overall, the world appears fairly respectful of authority, with 61% agreeing that greater respect for authority would be a good thing. Generally, European countries tended to agree less, while African, Middle Eastern, and Latin American countries tended to agree more, but there was considerable variation in these regional patterns. The Japanese were actually the least likely to agree that more respect for authority would be desirable (perhaps as an indication of the already high level of respect they grant to authority), with only 4% agreeing. South Koreans (17%), Indonesians (37%), Indians (43%), and Taiwanese (45%) were also relatively unlikely to wish for more respect for authority. On the other hand, the Irish (76%) and the French (69%) were above the world average in their desire for greater respect for authority.

Over time, the world on average appeared slightly more desirous of greater respect for authority, with 61% agreeing in 2000, compared with 58% in 1990. However, many countries lacked data for 1990, so one should not attempt to read too much into the change over time. Interestingly, desire for more respect for authority skyrocketed in China from 24% to 64%.

In terms of gender, men and women appeared virtually identical in their desire for greater respect for authority, with 61% of both groups agreeing. Older generations (65% of those 50 and up) appeared to desire greater respect for authority more than younger ones, which was 59% both for those 16–29 and 30–49. The difference between generations was greater than 20 percentage points in several countries, including Austria, Bulgaria, Dominican Republic, Germany, Great Britain, Greece, Ireland, Moldova, Montenegro, New Zealand, Pakistan, Poland, Slovenia, Spain, Switzerland, and Uruguay. Increasing education and income both appear to make people somewhat less desirous of greater respect for authority, as agreement declined from 68% to 58% to 55% with increasing education, and from 64% to 62% to 59% with increasing income. Materialists were also more respectful of authority, with 65% agreeing, than postmaterialists, with 50% agreeing.

Table 6.5 addresses the question of **religion**, asking specifically "Do you belong to a religious denomination?" The table records the percentage of respondents who answered this question affirmatively, without attempting to measure the actual strength of their beliefs or practices. This table shows the world to be quite religious, as in all but five countries (China, Estonia, the Czech Republic, Japan, and the Netherlands) the percentage answering "yes" is above 50%. In

ect for Authority

g to read out a list of various changes in our way of life that might take place in the near future.
to happen, do you think it would be a good thing, a bad thing, or don't you mind? Greater respect for authority.

(WVS: V130; EVS: V196)

Country	Wave ###	###	Gender Male	Female	Age 16-29	30-49	50+	Education Lower	Middle	Upper	Income Lower	Middle	Upper	Values Mat	Mixed	Postm.
a	na	34	35	34	30	33	41	34	33	38	35	33	35	37	35	23
	na	63	62	63	59	63	68	67	63	59	66	59	63	66	65	47
ina	69	72	72	73	66	73	77	80	62	58	81	74	60	82	76	58
ia	na	63	63	63	60	61	70	67	62	64	56	70	63	61	64	58
lia	na	73	71	75	68	69	82	80	78	61	79	72	67	92	78	61
a	47	39	35	42	30	34	50	49	32	23	52	37	33	59	43	25
ijan	na	61	62	59	62	59	65	72	58	65	53	68	68	59	61	83
adesh	na	92	92	91	91	92	91	89	95	92	92	90	94	93	91	93
s	71	72	73	72	71	70	76	68	73	79	72	73	73	73	73	63
m	50	63	60	67	55	56	73	76	65	52	70	67	56	79	65	41
and Herz.	na	26	27	26	21	26	33	34	24	26	29	29	21	28	27	21
	81	83	84	82	78	85	89	88	82	72	87	85	77	90	82	70
ia	78	69	73	65	51	72	75	76	65	68	74	71	62	69	70	66
a	64	66	64	69	59	63	75	76	69	55	67	72	60	72	70	59
a	80	56	56	56	53	55	61	61	57	44	61	55	49	60	57	48
	24	64	59	69	68	61	68	74	59	54	67	62	61	61	65	74
oia	na	89	89	88	86	90	88	90	87	90	88	87	91	89	87	89
	na	56	59	53	50	55	61	66	52	43	66	56	51	56	59	47
Republic	65	52	54	51	45	46	62	55	50	46	58	57	44	57	53	44
ark	35	38	40	36	45	34	39	49	29	23	45	38	23	54	40	17
ican Rep.	na	56	58	54	56	54	90	57	56	57	53	61	65	57	59	51
	na	86	87	85	86	86	88	86	85	85	88	85	85	85	88	81
ador	na	86	86	85	85	85	87	88	87	79	91	85	80	na	na	na
a	na	44	45	43	35	40	53	45	43	46	46	48	41	44	44	38
d	26	39	39	40	40	35	44	42	37	35	43	40	38	38	41	31
	59	69	66	71	61	64	77	76	61	57	72	67	66	82	70	46
a	na	75	76	75	68	77	81	77	75	74	77	77	73	78	73	71
ny	57	46	46	45	26	42	58	52	40	42	49	47	43	57	47	25
Britain	72	71	67	75	59	69	82	75	70	63	71	74	68	na	na	na
	na	17	18	16	11	16	32	30	18	14	18	17	16	22	16	13
ry	61	69	68	69	72	61	74	73	65	52	66	70	68	72	68	57
d	42	47	49	44	40	46	54	55	43	36	47	47	46	54	47	27
	54	43	48	38	45	44	41	41	43	49	37	45	45	49	47	36
sia	na	37	36	39	31	43	34	34	38	39	33	44	38	35	40	36
	na	71	72	70	73	72	66	66	75	74	70	71	71	77	71	72
l	83	76	75	77	66	73	86	87	73	66	84	75	69	84	75	69
	na	58	57	60	55	57	64	68	59	52	67	58	55	44	61	65
	49	51	53	50	42	47	61	57	47	46	55	51	49	65	53	40
	6	4	3	5	4	3	5	7	4	2	6	5	3	4	4	2
	na	90	91	90	89	93	87	92	90	88	89	91	90	94	89	78
South	14	19	18	21	14	20	24	34	21	16	22	16	19	20	19	21
	na	49	50	48	42	44	56	52	46	55	50	46	52	50	49	41
nia	53	44	46	43	46	41	46	51	40	47	40	40	45	48	42	55
bourg	na	53	55	51	50	46	62	62	51	42	63	53	44	63	57	30
onia	na	49	48	49	44	47	54	44	54	43	55	44	48	49	50	32
	na	92	93	92	91	90	95	93	93	88	91	93	93	93	93	86
	65	76	74	77	71	78	80	79	72	74	77	75	76	77	77	68
ya	na	48	48	48	39	46	59	52	49	43	57	50	43	51	44	41
negro	na	45	44	47	33	46	53	55	40	35	42	42	51	53	39	29
co	na	89	87	91	85	91	95	92	80	74	89	82	86	93	87	72
lands	51	67	66	68	58	64	74	82	66	53	71	68	59	89	72	41
ealand	na	50	48	52	37	44	60	55	53	41	51	47	51	57	55	35
	91	83	83	83	82	83	84	82	82	85	83	82	84	85	82	77
rn Ireland	82	77	75	78	70	71	86	80	73	76	85	77	76	85	78	59
y	32	32	30	33	30	29	36	34	30	30	na	na	na	50	30	22
an	na	62	63	61	51	64	77	71	52	52	71	64	49	66	57	67
	na	80	79	82	78	83	79	83	81	78	80	80	82	78	82	82
ines	na	70	71	68	69	72	67	69	71	68	72	70	68	71	70	65
	73	55	60	49	44	50	68	56	53	51	53	58	49	54	55	58
al	74	78	75	80	70	74	85	83	72	51	88	75	74	83	76	66
Rico	na	93	92	95	90	92	97	94	94	93	97	93	92	99	94	94
ia	na	85	83	86	78	83	89	87	82	88	85	85	84	84	87	74
an Fed.	68	56	54	58	49	55	62	59	54	62	55	55	59	58	55	55
	na	55	56	54	46	49	65	61	53	51	60	59	49	59	52	52
ore	na	52	53	51	52	52	52	55	52	47	57	51	48	51	54	45
ia	na	68	65	71	63	67	74	68	69	64	72	67	68	72	67	56
ia	66	43	40	44	28	38	60	56	41	30	54	43	39	51	44	33
Africa	88	73	70	76	75	71	73	71	74	78	69	73	77	77	72	62
	69	59	56	63	46	55	72	68	51	50	64	59	56	69	60	41
en	22	22	24	21	26	21	21	29	25	12	23	25	17	27	24	15
rland	46	31	32	29	20	28	41	37	30	20	36	34	26	44	32	17
	na	45	42	47	43	46	44	48	46	42	51	45	40	43	49	38
nia	na	82	82	83	82	81	87	86	80	75	86	83	76	84	83	79
	65	68	67	69	65	68	75	76	62	43	77	64	53	72	70	54
e	na	73	77	70	72	73	82	77	72	69	76	70	69	74	74	66
e	na	64	62	66	56	62	70	70	64	62	66	62	63	67	63	62
States	78	70	65	76	61	71	77	69	75	68	75	70	64	73	73	61
y	na	58	61	56	44	48	72	69	45	37	65	60	49	76	59	42
uela	na	91	93	90	90	91	93	92	92	90	90	90	93	87	92	95
m	na	80	82	79	75	82	82	77	86	84	78	80	83	82	87	86
owe	na	90	87	92	90	89	90	89	89	92	94	88	91	89	90	94
	58	61	61	61	59	59	65	68	58	55	64	62	59	65	61	50

RANKING Country	2000
Puerto Rico	93
Malta	92
Bangladesh	92
Venezuela	91
Jordan	90
Zimbabwe	90
Morocco	89
Colombia	89
Egypt	86
El Salvador	86
Romania	85
Brazil	83
Nigeria	83
Tanzania	82
Peru	80
Vietnam	80
Portugal	78
Northern Ireland	77
Ireland	76
Mexico	76
Georgia	75
Uganda	73
Australia	73
South Africa	73
Belarus	72
Argentina	72
Iran	71
Great Britain	71
United States	70
Philippines	70
Bulgaria	69
France	69
Hungary	69
Slovakia	68
Turkey	68
Netherlands	67
Canada	66
Ukraine	64
China	64
Belgium	63
Armenia	63
Algeria	63
Pakistan	62
Azerbaijan	61
Spain	59
Israel	58
Uruguay	58
Russian Fed.	56
Chile	56
Dominican Rep.	56
Croatia	56
Serbia	55
Poland	55
Luxembourg	53
Czech Republic	52
Singapore	52
Italy	51
New Zealand	50
Latvia	49
Macedonia	49
Moldova	48
Iceland	47
Germany	46
Montenegro	45
Taiwan	45
Lithuania	44
Estonia	44
India	43
Slovenia	43
Finland	39
Austria	39
Denmark	38
Indonesia	37
Albania	34
Norway	32
Switzerland	31
Bosnia and Herz.	26
Sweden	22
Korea, South	19
Greece	17
Japan	4
Total	61

TABLE 6.5
Belong to Religious Denomination

Do you belong to a religious denomination?

Yes (%)

(WVS: *V184; EVS

Country	Wave 1990	Wave 2000	Gender Male	Gender Female	Age 16-29	Age 30-49	Age 50+	Education Lower	Education Middle	Education Upper	Income Lower	Income Middle	Income Upper	Values Mat	Values Mixed	Values Postm.	RANKING Country
Albania	na	87	85	89	85	84	93	89	84	89	89	88	84	91	83	92	Jordan
Algeria	na	na	na	na	na	na	na	na	na	na	na	na	na	na	na	na	Moldova
Argentina	84	87	84	90	83	87	91	87	87	89	90	85	87	87	89	82	Morocco
Armenia	na	87	82	91	86	88	85	88	86	86	85	86	88	87	88	75	Zimbabwe
Australia	na	81	77	85	77	78	89	86	82	76	85	81	76	85	84	76	Switzerland
Austria	86	88	86	90	91	88	86	88	88	88	86	88	89	89	89	86	Egypt
Azerbaijan	na	94	94	94	93	95	94	97	96	90	97	97	86	95	91	94	Bangladesh
Bangladesh	na	100	100	100	100	100	100	100	100	100	100	100	100	100	100	100	Israel
Belarus	30	52	41	61	51	49	57	61	51	43	61	49	43	54	51	50	Indonesia
Belgium	68	64	59	68	53	57	74	72	61	61	66	63	60	72	64	54	Nigeria
Bosnia and Herz.	na	75	75	76	79	74	73	83	75	69	74	75	77	79	73	79	Uganda
Brazil	88	88	84	92	83	90	94	88	88	89	89	89	86	91	87	89	Iran
Bulgaria	34	70	65	75	62	64	79	81	64	65	79	66	65	72	70	71	Malta
Canada	74	69	64	73	55	67	79	75	68	65	72	71	62	71	74	59	Tanzania
Chile	82	66	60	72	65	61	75	72	63	63	69	65	63	73	67	53	Turkey
China	4	6	5	7	6	6	6	5	7	9	5	6	8	5	7	3	Romania
Colombia	na	92	89	95	88	94	95	93	92	90	92	93	90	91	93	87	Montenegro
Croatia	na	89	87	90	88	89	90	97	85	80	88	89	89	94	91	78	Greece
Czech Republic	56	34	28	39	21	23	50	35	34	25	43	32	25	39	31	36	Iceland
Denmark	92	90	88	92	90	88	92	92	90	87	91	91	88	94	93	78	Poland
Dominican Rep.	na	76	71	80	75	78	91	74	70	79	77	76	76	77	74	85	Peru
Egypt	na	100	100	100	100	100	100	100	100	100	100	100	100	100	100	100	Azerbaijan
El Salvador	na	84	82	86	81	83	90	83	85	86	82	83	88	na	na	na	Serbia
Estonia	13	25	18	30	14	23	33	29	22	25	30	30	18	28	23	20	Georgia
Finland	89	88	84	91	92	85	88	88	88	89	90	85	88	92	89	80	India
France	62	58	55	60	46	54	67	60	53	55	54	61	54	65	59	43	Colombia
Georgia	na	94	93	95	94	95	92	92	94	94	93	94	94	94	93	100	Ireland
Germany	35	77	73	79	73	72	83	83	73	67	76	76	83	78	77	75	Norway
Great Britain	58	83	80	87	76	84	89	83	86	78	82	83	86	na	na	na	Philippines
Greece	na	96	94	97	95	96	97	98	97	95	97	96	95	98	97	92	Denmark
Hungary	58	57	53	61	43	54	68	61	48	54	61	59	53	64	51	46	Portugal
Iceland	98	96	96	95	93	95	99	97	98	90	97	96	95	98	96	89	Croatia
India	99	93	94	92	95	93	92	94	92	93	90	94	94	94	92	93	Puerto Rico
Indonesia	na	100	100	100	100	100	100	100	100	100	100	100	100	100	100	100	Austria
Iran	na	99	99	99	99	99	99	99	99	99	99	99	99	100	99	100	Finland
Ireland	96	91	88	93	86	89	96	89	92	92	91	92	90	91	91	87	Brazil
Israel	na	100	100	100	100	100	100	100	100	100	100	100	100	100	100	100	Albania
Italy	85	82	78	87	80	80	86	88	79	74	83	82	78	90	82	79	Argentina
Japan	na	41	43	39	19	32	59	56	42	34	45	46	37	43	41	36	Armenia
Jordan	na	100	100	100	100	100	100	100	100	100	100	100	100	100	100	100	South Africa
Korea, South	72	63	57	69	60	63	69	64	65	60	60	63	68	63	63	62	Northern Ireland
Latvia	37	59	53	64	44	54	70	67	54	66	63	60	54	63	59	57	Macedonia
Lithuania	63	81	72	89	72	75	94	92	77	81	88	79	78	83	82	74	El Salvador
Luxembourg	na	72	70	74	59	71	82	78	69	72	69	77	71	76	73	63	Great Britain
Macedonia	na	86	88	84	85	86	86	92	85	79	89	83	85	89	85	90	Spain
Malta	na	99	97	100	97	99	100	99	99	96	100	99	98	98	99	97	Italy
Mexico	85	81	78	83	76	80	88	85	76	72	83	80	77	84	80	67	New Zealand
Moldova	na	100	100	100	100	100	100	100	100	100	100	100	100	100	100	100	Lithuania
Montenegro	na	97	97	98	97	97	97	98	96	97	97	99	99	98	97	95	Australia
Morocco	na	100	100	100	100	100	100	100	100	100	100	100	100	100	100	100	Mexico
Netherlands	51	45	42	48	34	38	58	49	44	43	43	45	43	58	46	34	Singapore
New Zealand	na	82	80	84	64	80	90	86	83	76	84	80	82	78	84	77	Taiwan
Nigeria	95	99	99	99	99	99	99	99	99	99	99	99	99	98	100	100	United States
Northern Ireland	91	86	83	89	81	78	95	91	81	84	88	86	85	88	86	87	Slovakia
Norway	90	91	89	93	90	89	93	92	93	86	na	na	na	95	92	78	Germany
Pakistan	na	71	69	73	69	71	74	79	70	41	78	70	63	73	68	67	Dominican Rep.
Peru	na	95	94	97	93	97	97	95	97	94	96	96	94	96	95	97	Sweden
Philippines	na	90	92	89	89	90	92	89	89	92	92	90	90	88	92	91	Bosnia and Herz.
Poland	na	96	95	97	95	96	97	98	95	87	97	96	94	98	95	92	Venezuela
Portugal	72	89	84	94	82	93	91	93	82	79	94	92	85	92	89	75	Luxembourg
Puerto Rico	na	88	87	90	83	86	93	90	90	88	89	90	88	88	90	85	Pakistan
Romania	94	98	97	99	98	97	98	99	97	97	97	98	97	98	98	92	Bulgaria
Russian Fed.	37	51	39	60	43	46	61	62	49	50	61	50	42	55	46	36	Slovenia
Serbia	na	94	93	95	94	95	94	97	93	91	96	93	94	96	93	87	Canada
Singapore	na	80	78	82	78	79	92	87	79	67	92	80	73	88	78	69	Chile
Slovakia	na	77	71	82	66	74	88	83	76	65	85	78	73	79	76	69	Belgium
Slovenia	74	70	69	71	65	66	78	82	70	50	76	71	59	78	68	70	Korea, South
South Africa	na	86	79	94	85	84	96	85	87	88	85	92	80	86	87	86	Latvia
Spain	85	83	77	89	74	81	91	88	78	77	87	81	81	90	84	68	France
Sweden	82	76	74	78	76	73	78	79	74	76	75	76	78	70	77	74	Hungary
Switzerland	92	100	100	100	100	100	100	100	100	100	100	100	100	100	100	100	Ukraine
Taiwan	na	79	72	86	67	81	83	89	79	70	82	82	72	81	79	62	Vietnam
Tanzania	na	98	99	99	99	99	99	99	99	98	98	99	99	100	99	100	Belarus
Turkey	97	98	98	98	97	98	100	99	98	90	99	98	94	99	98	94	Uruguay
Uganda	na	99	98	100	100	99	97	98	99	100	99	99	99	99	99	99	Russian Fed.
Ukraine	na	56	43	67	53	53	62	77	53	52	59	56	55	57	53	64	Netherlands
United States	77	79	73	84	65	80	88	70	75	84	74	78	85	84	80	73	Japan
Uruguay	na	52	40	61	43	47	60	57	45	48	55	51	50	61	54	42	Czech Republic
Venezuela	na	73	69	77	65	76	83	76	70	78	71	70	73	76	72	70	Estonia
Vietnam	na	54	50	58	54	51	57	62	43	45	48	57	52	62	49	40	China
Zimbabwe	na	100	100	100	100	100	100	100	100	100	100	100	100	100	100	100	
Total	70	80	78	83	79	79	83	84	78	79	81	80	78	82	80	75	Total

nine countries (Jordan, Moldova, Morocco, Zimbabwe, Switzerland, Egypt, Bangladesh, Israel, and Indonesia), the percentage stating that they belonged to a religious denomination was 100%. Some strong regional trends appear, with Middle Eastern and African countries among the most religious, with East Asian and Eastern European among the least religious, with English-speaking Protestant, Latin American, and Western European countries generally around the middle of the pack. The world average is 80%. Females were more likely than males to belong to a religious denomination overall (83% of women vs. 78% of men). The gap between women and men was particularly large (more than 20%) in Belarus, Russia, Ukraine, and Uruguay. In a few countries (Philippines, Macedonia, Japan, India, and Iceland) men reported belonging to a religious denomination at higher rates than women, although the difference was never more than a few percentage points.

With regard to **age**, older generations were more likely to belong to a religious denomination than younger ones, although the difference was not large (79% of those 16–29 and 30–49, versus 83% of those 50 and up). The difference between generations appeared especially pronounced in Europe and English-speaking Protestant countries, as well as Japan, while the rest of the world saw greater agreement between generations. Overall, increasing education and income appeared to make people less likely to belong to a religious denomination, although this pattern was reversed in the United States, where those of higher income and education were actually more likely to belong to a religious denomination. Finally, those with postmaterial values were less likely to belong to a religious denomination (75%) than those with material values (82%).

Table 6.6, *Believe in God*, forms an interesting contrast with the previous one. Respondents were asked "Which, if any, of the following do you believe in?" and offered "God" as one possible answer. The table measures the percentage of respondents who indicated that they believed in God. Overall, 86% of respondents indicated that they believed in God, with the highest levels of belief in the Middle East and African countries, and lower levels of belief in Europe (especially Eastern Europe).

It is interesting to note that the percentage of respondents reporting belief in God is 6 percentage points higher than the percentage who reported belonging to a religious denomination. This appears to show that many people have spiritual faith without actually taking part in organized religious practice (a notable pattern in Belarus, Bosnia, Brazil, Canada, Chile, Dominican Republic, El Salvador, Estonia, Hungary, Italy, Japan, Latvia, Mexico, Netherlands, Pakistan, Puerto Rico, Russia, South Africa, Ukraine, United States, and Uruguay, which all had a 10% or greater gap). However, in many countries the reverse was true: respondents reported belonging to a religious denomination although they didn't actually believe in God. This would appear to indicate that they viewed their religion more as a cultural and traditional matter than as a spiritual matter. Countries where at least 10% belonged to a religious denomination, yet did not believe in God, include Denmark, Germany, Great Britain, Iceland, Montenegro,

TABLE 6.6

Believe in God

Which, if any, of the following do you believe in? Believe in God.
Yes (%)

(WVS: V191; EVS: V

Country	Wave 1990	Wave 2000	Male	Female	16-29	30-49	50+	Edu Lower	Edu Middle	Edu Upper	Inc Lower	Inc Middle	Inc Upper	Mat	Mixed	Postm.
Albania	na	92	88	96	90	93	92	94	91	88	92	91	92	91	92	87
Algeria	na	100	100	100	100	100	100	100	100	99	100	100	99	100	100	99
Argentina	92	96	94	98	95	97	97	98	95	91	98	97	94	99	97	93
Armenia	na	86	80	91	89	84	82	83	87	83	84	86	88	85	88	70
Australia	na	80	75	86	79	77	85	86	78	78	84	80	73	83	82	76
Austria	87	87	83	90	80	87	91	87	88	83	86	88	86	90	88	82
Azerbaijan	na	98	97	99	98	98	97	97	99	96	99	99	95	98	98	97
Bangladesh	na	100	99	100	99	100	100	100	99	99	100	99	100	100	99	100
Belarus	43	83	72	91	79	82	86	90	82	73	86	83	75	85	82	69
Belgium	69	71	65	76	56	67	81	79	69	69	76	71	66	79	71	62
Bosnia and Herz.	na	88	86	90	93	90	81	94	90	78	88	88	87	90	87	88
Brazil	99	99	99	100	99	99	100	100	99	98	99	100	99	99	99	99
Bulgaria	40	66	60	72	66	61	71	77	61	59	73	68	60	68	64	67
Canada	89	89	86	93	84	88	94	92	91	85	92	90	86	94	92	82
Chile	95	97	96	98	97	97	97	98	97	93	99	97	94	98	98	91
China	na	na	na	na	na	na	na	na	na	na	na	na	na	na	na	na
Colombia	na	99	99	100	99	99	99	100	99	98	100	100	98	100	99	98
Croatia	na	93	92	95	89	96	93	96	94	85	93	94	92	98	93	89
Czech Republic	na	39	32	46	34	31	49	40	38	40	46	36	32	43	37	40
Denmark	64	69	61	77	55	67	79	74	55	64	72	70	63	64	71	59
Dominican Rep.	na	93	95	91	95	89	91	87	94	93	90	93	95	92	93	92
Egypt	na	100	100	100	100	100	100	100	100	100	100	100	100	100	100	100
El Salvador	na	99	99	100	99	100	99	100	99	99	100	99	100	na	na	na
Estonia	na	51	40	61	43	46	61	58	49	45	61	58	44	54	51	31
Finland	76	83	73	91	73	79	91	83	83	83	83	75	89	81	85	74
France	62	62	58	64	53	60	67	63	59	60	61	61	61	67	63	48
Georgia	na	93	90	96	96	94	89	92	94	93	92	94	94	94	92	99
Germany	36	68	61	73	56	63	78	74	62	66	64	70	71	68	69	65
Great Britain	78	72	63	80	64	71	76	74	71	62	68	74	67	na	na	na
Greece	na	91	88	93	90	91	95	97	95	87	93	91	89	96	93	80
Hungary	65	68	56	79	53	63	82	74	57	52	76	71	62	75	62	54
Iceland	85	84	78	90	76	86	89	87	84	80	85	87	82	88	85	73
India	94	95	94	96	94	96	94	95	93	94	93	96	95	96	93	93
Indonesia	na	100	100	100	99	100	100	100	100	100	100	100	99	100	100	99
Iran	na	99	99	100	99	100	99	100	100	99	99	100	99	100	100	99
Ireland	98	96	93	98	93	94	98	95	95	97	96	96	95	99	95	90
Israel	na	na	na	na	na	na	na	na	na	na	na	na	na	na	na	na
Italy	91	94	90	97	94	92	95	96	92	90	94	94	90	97	94	89
Japan	65	53	46	59	47	55	53	56	53	49	55	55	49	54	52	51
Jordan	na	100	100	100	100	100	100	100	100	99	100	100	100	100	100	100
Korea, South	na	na	na	na	na	na	na	na	na	na	na	na	na	na	na	na
Latvia	58	80	67	90	75	79	82	83	78	80	82	80	76	80	80	80
Lithuania	na	87	75	95	80	83	93	95	83	85	95	82	86	88	87	68
Luxembourg	na	73	67	79	63	73	81	73	74	73	70	74	71	75	73	67
Macedonia	na	91	89	92	91	92	88	98	87	86	96	89	85	92	90	89
Malta	na	100	99	100	100	99	100	100	99	100	99	100	99	100	99	99
Mexico	93	98	98	98	98	98	99	99	97	97	99	98	97	98	98	97
Moldova	na	96	94	98	94	97	97	98	97	92	97	96	95	97	96	96
Montenegro	na	83	80	86	77	84	86	89	80	75	84	87	83	85	83	72
Morocco	na	100	100	100	100	100	100	100	100	100	100	100	100	100	100	100
Netherlands	64	60	55	64	50	54	70	66	58	56	58	62	52	76	57	58
New Zealand	na	78	74	81	76	73	83	77	82	77	79	79	74	84	80	71
Nigeria	100	100	100	99	100	100	100	100	100	100	100	100	100	100	100	99
Northern Ireland	97	93	90	96	89	94	95	95	92	92	95	94	92	96	92	92
Norway	65	69	60	77	55	68	80	74	68	65	75	70	na	75	70	53
Pakistan	na	100	100	100	100	100	100	100	100	100	100	100	100	100	100	100
Peru	na	99	98	99	98	99	99	98	99	97	99	99	97	99	98	98
Philippines	na	99	99	100	100	99	99	99	100	99	100	99	99	99	100	100
Poland	97	97	97	98	97	98	97	99	96	93	98	97	95	99	96	95
Portugal	86	96	94	98	92	98	98	99	94	82	100	97	94	97	97	90
Puerto Rico	na	99	99	99	99	99	99	100	99	99	99	100	99	99	99	99
Romania	94	96	94	99	94	98	97	98	96	94	97	97	96	96	97	92
Russian Fed.	44	70	57	81	70	66	75	80	69	68	76	68	66	75	66	55
Serbia	na	83	76	88	86	82	81	90	78	79	86	83	78	85	81	75
Singapore	na	87	84	90	84	89	94	90	86	83	89	89	84	92	86	76
Slovakia	na	83	77	88	76	80	91	87	82	72	89	85	78	84	82	85
Slovenia	63	65	61	69	59	64	71	81	64	41	76	62	50	81	62	62
South Africa	98	99	98	100	99	99	99	99	99	99	99	100	98	99	99	99
Spain	86	85	79	90	73	84	93	91	80	75	89	83	81	92	84	72
Sweden	45	53	46	61	43	50	63	61	49	54	52	57	50	58	54	47
Switzerland	na	83	78	89	66	85	91	86	82	85	84	86	82	89	83	82
Taiwan	na	76	70	83	79	74	82	81	76	72	77	78	71	78	75	68
Tanzania	na	99	99	99	100	99	100	99	100	99	99	100	99	100	100	100
Turkey	na	98	97	99	97	98	99	100	97	91	99	98	94	100	98	94
Uganda	na	99	99	100	99	100	97	98	100	100	100	100	100	99	100	99
Ukraine	na	80	68	90	80	81	80	85	79	80	82	81	79	81	77	83
United States	96	96	94	98	93	97	96	94	97	95	96	95	96	97	96	95
Uruguay	na	87	81	91	81	83	92	91	83	71	91	85	86	87	89	80
Venezuela	na	na	na	na	na	na	na	na	na	na	na	na	na	na	na	na
Vietnam	na	19	14	24	22	19	17	25	10	15	15	19	20	32	15	17
Zimbabwe	na	99	100	99	99	100	100	99	99	100	99	99	100	99	100	100
Total	76	86	83	89	86	85	87	89	85	84	88	87	84	89	85	81

RANKING

Country
Morocco
Pakistan
Egypt
Algeria
Jordan
Nigeria
Bangladesh
Indonesia
Malta
El Salvador
Iran
Philippines
Zimbabwe
Uganda
Tanzania
Brazil
Colombia
South Africa
Puerto Rico
Peru
Mexico
Turkey
Azerbaijan
Poland
Chile
Argentina
Portugal
Romania
Moldova
United States
Ireland
India
Italy
Croatia
Georgia
Northern Ireland
Dominican Rep.
Albania
Greece
Macedonia
Canada
Bosnia and Herz.
Singapore
Austria
Uruguay
Lithuania
Armenia
Spain
Iceland
Switzerland
Montenegro
Belarus
Slovakia
Finland
Serbia
Ukraine
Australia
Latvia
New Zealand
Taiwan
Luxembourg
Great Britain
Belgium
Russian Fed.
Denmark
Norway
Hungary
Germany
Bulgaria
Slovenia
France
Netherlands
Sweden
Japan
Estonia
Czech Republic
Vietnam
Total

Norway, Serbia, Sweden, Switzerland, and Vietnam, a predominantly Western European group.

Overall, belief in God is shown to have increased from 76% in 1990 to 86% in 2000, although these results are likely skewed by the fact that respondents in many countries were not asked this question in 1990. It is interesting to note that reported belief in God jumped 20% or more in Belarus, Bulgaria, Germany, Latvia, and Russia, very likely as a result of the fall of the Soviet Union, which repressed religious practice.

Overall, females were more likely than males to say that they believe in God (89% vs. 83%), with particularly large gaps in Estonia, Hungary, Latvia, Lithuania, Russia, and Ukraine, all former Soviet states or satellites. Age did not appear to have a strong effect on belief in God, with 86% of 16–29-year-olds, 85% of 30–49-year-olds, and 87% of those 50+ years old acknowledging belief. Increasing levels of income and education did have a negative impact on belief, dropping from 89% to 85% to 84% from the lowest to the highest education group, and from 88% to 87% to 84% from the lowest to the highest income group. Finally, with regard to values, materialists were more likely to believe in God than post-materialists (89% to 81%).

Table 6.7 addresses the question of **national pride**, tabulating the percentage of respondents who answered "Very proud" when asked "How proud are you to be [nationality]?" In the World Cultures Map, national pride is associated with traditional values. Overall, 56% of people answered that they were very proud of their nationality. The highest rates of pride were found in Puerto Rico,[1] Iran, and Venezuela (all above 90%), and the lowest in Taiwan, Germany, and South Korea (all below 20%). In terms of regional groupings, national pride seems to be the most common in Latin America, the Middle East, and Africa, and the least common in the Confucian countries and in Europe.

National pride appears to have increased in recent years, with the number saying they are very proud of their nationality rising from 47% in 1990 to 56% in 2000, although once again this may be misleading, as many countries lacked data for 1990. Several countries experienced significant shifts in their levels of pride: large increases for South Africa, Portugal, Mexico, Iceland, Finland, Chile, and Argentina; and large decreases for China, Germany, South Korea, Lithuania, and Northern Ireland. Males and females were almost equally proud, with men at 57% and women at 56%, although men were much prouder than women in Uganda (80% to 54%). With regard to age, overall older generations were the proudest (59%), followed by the youngest generation (56%), with the middle generation the least proud (54%).

Some countries showed large generation gaps, with older generations much prouder in Croatia, Great Britain, Israel, Italy, Japan, Latvia, Luxembourg, Malta, Romania, Serbia, Slovenia, the United States, and Uruguay. Income and education are both negatively associated with national pride, as the percentage who are very proud declined from 63% to 53% to 52% with increasing education, and 59% to 56% to 54% with increasing income. Finally, materialists (57%) were slightly more likely to feel proud of their nationality than postmaterialists (53%).

TABLE 6.7

National Pride

How proud are you to be [NATIONALITY]?
Very proud (%)

(WVS: V216; EVS:

Country	Wave ##	Wave ##	Gender Male	Gender Female	Age 16-29	Age 30-49	Age 50+	Education Lower	Education Middle	Education Upper	Income Lower	Income Middle	Income Upper	Values Mat	Values Mixed	Values Postm.	RANKING Country
Albania	na	73	74	71	67	71	81	72	73	74	74	65	78	77	71	74	Puerto Rico
Algeria	na	74	73	74	68	75	83	80	73	71	75	71	72	78	71	71	Iran
Argentina	55	68	69	67	65	66	73	72	65	54	74	68	61	69	70	62	Venezuela
Armenia	na	44	46	41	39	48	45	50	44	39	47	36	46	42	44	52	Morocco
Australia	na	73	73	74	68	72	81	83	74	65	75	72	73	73	75	72	Philippines
Austria	53	53	52	53	47	49	59	57	52	35	51	50	57	55	59	39	El Salvador
Azerbaijan	na	64	66	61	64	62	66	75	59	71	55	60	76	69	55	57	Colombia
Bangladesh	na	73	75	71	71	73	79	75	71	72	71	71	77	77	71	67	Egypt
Belarus	35	27	25	28	22	23	34	32	26	21	29	28	20	29	27	16	Tanzania
Belgium	29	23	23	23	18	17	30	33	24	14	31	26	17	28	22	17	Pakistan
Bosnia and Herz.	na	38	37	39	36	32	47	49	36	33	47	41	29	34	39	33	Mexico
Brazil	64	65	67	62	64	63	69	66	67	49	68	65	62	68	65	58	Portugal
Bulgaria	39	34	32	37	28	27	44	36	33	36	36	33	34	32	36	38	Vietnam
Canada	61	67	66	67	62	65	72	74	64	64	64	67	68	68	66	68	Zimbabwe
Chile	53	72	70	73	69	69	79	79	71	59	75	71	67	78	70	67	Peru
China	43	26	27	25	29	25	26	20	30	24	20	29	29	27	27	28	Dominican Rep.
Colombia	na	85	85	85	83	85	87	86	85	84	85	85	84	83	85	87	South Africa
Croatia	na	42	42	41	31	39	52	47	41	32	56	40	36	50	41	37	Uruguay
Czech Republic	25	26	24	28	23	22	32	28	25	22	29	27	23	28	26	23	Malta
Denmark	42	48	49	47	50	43	52	59	41	32	52	48	43	55	50	39	Algeria
Dominican Rep.	na	76	76	76	72	83	73	81	76	76	80	72	76	72	74	86	Australia
Egypt	na	82	84	80	82	82	83	82	84	79	86	79	79	78	84	87	Bangladesh
El Salvador	na	86	84	87	82	87	90	87	86	82	89	86	84	na	na	na	Albania
Estonia	30	24	23	25	25	20	26	27	20	27	29	22	21	22	25	22	United States
Finland	38	56	53	59	53	58	57	53	61	58	49	61	61	59	56	48	Nigeria
France	35	40	40	40	34	32	49	46	34	29	48	37	32	46	41	27	Chile
Georgia	na	65	70	60	64	64	66	73	64	61	65	70	60	67	63	69	Ireland
Germany	29	17	19	15	9	13	23	19	14	16	18	20	15	18	17	14	Poland
Great Britain	54	51	54	48	36	44	62	56	46	43	49	50	47	na	na	na	India
Greece	na	55	54	55	50	54	68	68	57	51	59	52	53	63	56	48	Argentina
Hungary	47	49	48	50	40	45	59	53	45	37	50	54	44	50	48	42	Jordan
Iceland	54	67	65	69	68	66	66	74	65	54	64	70	65	75	66	55	Canada
India	75	71	74	66	73	70	69	66	73	78	66	67	76	70	73	76	Iceland
Indonesia	na	48	53	44	43	48	51	54	48	44	50	47	49	54	47	43	Uganda
Iran	na	92	92	93	91	93	95	96	91	89	92	92	92	96	92	83	Georgia
Ireland	77	72	72	71	65	71	79	77	69	69	76	73	65	77	71	63	Brazil
Israel	na	54	51	57	46	52	66	69	54	45	61	54	48	32	59	56	New Zealand
Italy	41	39	39	40	30	34	50	48	35	24	45	44	29	49	40	33	Azerbaijan
Japan	29	23	24	22	14	13	34	39	23	16	29	21	20	26	21	15	Turkey
Jordan	na	68	72	64	65	68	72	73	66	61	73	67	63	68	68	59	Macedonia
Korea, South	45	17	20	15	11	16	29	34	20	12	22	13	15	19	16	15	Finland
Latvia	49	40	38	43	21	35	54	41	38	48	43	40	39	37	43	33	Slovenia
Lithuania	41	22	20	23	21	18	26	23	21	21	27	24	18	21	21	27	Greece
Luxembourg	na	49	52	47	40	38	63	59	51	25	65	48	35	66	50	27	Israel
Macedonia	na	61	60	61	50	61	69	54	65	59	63	57	62	62	61	34	Spain
Malta	na	75	72	77	63	72	84	83	74	55	77	75	69	80	74	59	Austria
Mexico	56	80	81	79	75	80	85	82	76	81	78	77	80	83	77	84	Great Britain
Moldova	na	23	25	22	18	21	29	23	25	19	26	23	20	25	17	31	Norway
Montenegro	na	33	33	32	26	30	39	35	32	30	30	34	29	31	34	52	Hungary
Morocco	na	89	86	92	86	90	94	91	81	77	93	87	85	93	86	78	Luxembourg
Netherlands	21	20	18	22	16	16	26	29	21	11	23	15	21	29	22	11	Indonesia
New Zealand	na	64	64	64	58	63	69	68	64	61	61	62	67	63	65	60	Denmark
Nigeria	68	72	74	70	73	72	66	71	73	71	69	75	72	71	72	76	Romania
Northern Ireland	54	28	31	27	25	23	33	32	30	19	30	32	22	29	30	22	Singapore
Norway	45	50	48	53	48	51	51	57	53	40	na	na	na	55	53	27	Armenia
Pakistan	na	81	79	83	79	80	91	87	76	71	85	80	79	84	77	100	Serbia
Peru	na	77	75	78	72	80	79	79	77	74	76	79	75	77	77	75	Croatia
Philippines	na	87	87	87	84	90	86	85	90	85	88	87	87	88	86	86	Sweden
Poland	69	72	72	71	69	67	79	75	73	54	72	71	71	71	71	81	Latvia
Portugal	42	79	75	83	71	80	83	84	71	56	84	84	74	88	75	70	France
Puerto Rico	na	95	94	96	94	91	98	94	97	94	97	94	94	94	95	96	Italy
Romania	48	47	49	46	29	42	61	58	41	41	57	43	44	52	44	27	Bosnia and Herz.
Russian Fed.	26	31	30	31	25	28	38	39	31	26	33	31	28	32	29	31	Bulgaria
Serbia	na	42	40	44	30	36	53	50	41	31	50	45	38	46	38	38	Montenegro
Singapore	na	44	42	46	45	42	42	45	44	38	46	45	42	41	47	27	Russian Fed.
Slovakia	na	25	26	24	21	22	32	27	24	22	28	23	23	28	23	20	Northern Ireland
Slovenia	59	56	53	58	46	52	67	68	53	45	61	54	50	59	56	54	Belarus
South Africa	64	75	75	75	78	75	68	78	72	67	76	82	67	73	77	74	Czech Republic
Spain	45	53	51	54	43	51	61	61	44	47	54	56	53	58	55	40	China
Sweden	41	41	42	41	38	40	44	52	39	36	43	40	41	42	42	39	Switzerland
Switzerland	38	25	25	25	18	20	36	34	24	12	26	26	24	34	27	13	Slovakia
Taiwan	na	15	14	16	8	16	17	19	17	10	18	16	12	13	15	22	Ukraine
Tanzania	na	82	81	83	76	80	92	85	76	82	87	80	83	83	81	92	Estonia
Turkey	67	63	60	66	57	65	73	67	61	46	62	65	54	70	65	48	Belgium
Uganda	na	66	80	54	71	64	57	65	67	70	79	73	70	54	72	78	Moldova
Ukraine	na	24	25	23	18	23	28	23	25	23	22	17	33	22	25	38	Japan
United States	76	72	72	72	61	71	83	76	75	69	71	71	76	74	74	68	Lithuania
Uruguay	na	75	72	77	61	70	84	77	73	66	78	76	71	76	77	70	Netherlands
Venezuela	na	92	92	92	91	92	95	95	91	91	92	93	92	88	93	95	Korea, South
Vietnam	na	78	82	75	76	75	86	76	83	77	81	76	80	79	82	79	Germany
Zimbabwe	na	78	78	78	78	78	79	80	76	52	80	77	78	76	79	87	Taiwan
Total	47	56	57	56	56	54	59	63	53	52	59	56	54	56	56	53	Total

Table 6.8 examines the idea of **trust**, asking "Generally speaking, would you say that *most people can be trusted* or that you need to be very careful in dealing with people?" High levels of trust are associated on the World Cultures Map with both secular-rational and self-expression values, and many researchers have theorized that they are conducive to economic development and to democratic governance. In the world overall, just 28% of respondents believed that most people could be trusted. This ranges from a low of 3% in Brazil to a high of 67% in Denmark. Latin American and African countries generally showed low levels of trust, while trust was highest in Scandinavia (along with Iran, which appears to be an outlier with a very high 65% level of trust). East Asia also showed fairly high levels of trust, while Muslim countries were very varied in their trust levels, ranging from just 11% in Algeria to 65% in Iran.

Trust has declined, according to the survey, from 35% in 1990 to 27% in 2000. In many countries it dropped sharply, including Canada, Great Britain, Ireland, Mexico, Poland, Portugal, Russia, South Africa, and the United States. However, a few countries enjoyed a significant increase in trust, including Belarus, Denmark and Germany.

Males appeared slightly more trusting than females (29% vs. 27%). With regard to age, the youngest generation appeared to be the least trusting, at 25%, while both the middle and older generations showed 29% levels of trust. However, in a few countries, including Taiwan, Pakistan, Norway, the Netherlands, and Denmark, the young were more trusting than their older counterparts. Income and education both positively correlated with trust: levels rose from 24% to 27% to 36% with increasing education, and from 25% to 27% to 31% with increasing income. The rise in trust with increasing income and education was particularly strong in some countries, including Austria, Belgium, Canada, China, Czech Republic, Denmark, France, Great Britain, Iceland, Israel, Italy, Japan, the Netherlands, Norway, Slovenia, Sweden, Switzerland, and Taiwan—mostly the European and Confucian groups. Postmaterialists (37%) were also significantly more trustful than materialists (24%).

Table 6.9 shows respondents' self-reported **life satisfaction**. The question asks "All things considered, how satisfied are you with your life as a whole these days?" with respondents ranking their satisfaction on a scale of 1–10. The table shows the percentage of respondents who answered 7, 8, 9, or 10. Life satisfaction is associated in the World Cultures Map with self-expression values. However, it is important to note that the World Values Survey asked this question immediately after one asking participants about their satisfaction with their financial situation. Therefore, the data may be somewhat skewed toward greater satisfaction for respondents from more prosperous countries.

The overall world satisfaction level is 56%; but there are significant differences between countries. Perhaps not surprisingly, people in prosperous, democratic countries tended to be more satisfied with their lives than those in poor, autocratic ones. The highest level of life satisfaction was in the Netherlands (90%), followed by Iceland, Malta, Denmark, Ireland, Puerto Rico, Colombia,

TABLE 6.8

Trust in People

Generally speaking, would you say that most people can be trusted or that you need to be very careful in dealing with people?
Most people can be trusted (%)

(WVS: V25; EVS: V6)

Country	Wave ###	Wave ###	Gender Male	Gender Female	Age 16–29	Age 30–49	Age 50+	Education Lower	Education Middle	Education Upper	Income Lower	Income Middle	Income Upper	Values Mat	Values Mixed	Values Postm.	RANKING Country
Albania	na	24	24	25	25	25	24	27	23	24	24	27	22	22	24	42	Denmark
Algeria	na	11	11	11	8	12	16	16	10	10	12	10	13	12	11	10	Sweden
Argentina	23	15	16	15	10	18	18	14	17	21	15	14	18	15	15	17	Iran
Armenia	na	25	24	25	26	26	22	26	24	28	26	24	22	23	26	31	Norway
Australia	na	40	41	39	32	45	41	31	38	50	35	44	47	28	39	45	Netherlands
Austria	32	34	37	31	31	40	30	24	38	58	25	33	44	20	30	44	Finland
Azerbaijan	na	21	21	20	21	19	24	21	19	24	20	19	24	19	23	33	China
Bangladesh	na	24	24	23	22	23	31	30	17	15	23	26	21	21	25	29	Indonesia
Belarus	26	42	41	43	37	43	44	38	43	44	39	43	46	39	44	46	New Zealand
Belgium	33	31	34	28	29	34	28	18	27	47	22	28	41	21	31	46	Japan
Bosnia and Herz.	na	16	16	15	15	15	17	19	15	16	21	13	16	16	16	11	Belarus
Brazil	7	3	3	2	2	4	1	2	3	5	3	2	3	2	3	6	Vietnam
Bulgaria	30	27	29	25	27	26	27	23	26	34	25	23	30	24	31	24	Iceland
Canada	52	39	41	37	36	40	39	30	34	54	28	37	51	36	37	43	India
Chile	23	23	22	24	20	22	26	20	24	26	19	24	29	24	22	23	Switzerland
China	60	55	53	56	48	56	55	50	57	74	52	56	58	53	55	69	Australia
Colombia	na	11	13	9	9	12	10	9	8	17	9	9	16	10	11	11	Northern Ireland
Croatia	na	18	21	16	17	23	14	14	19	30	17	16	23	16	18	19	Canada
Czech Republic	28	24	23	25	21	24	25	20	25	40	22	23	27	16	24	39	Taiwan
Denmark	58	67	68	66	68	75	57	56	79	83	58	70	83	58	65	82	Egypt
Dominican Rep.	na	26	25	28	26	26	55	19	17	32	22	31	25	16	29	26	Spain
Egypt	na	38	37	39	34	37	46	45	34	26	41	41	35	40	38	24	United States
El Salvador	na	15	16	14	15	15	13	15	13	15	15	15	15	na	na	na	Ireland
Estonia	28	23	23	22	29	18	24	19	22	33	23	17	29	19	25	27	Germany
Finland	63	58	56	60	61	55	59	53	63	70	53	56	62	49	60	69	Austria
France	23	22	22	23	23	24	21	14	27	41	18	20	35	14	20	41	Montenegro
Georgia	na	19	17	20	19	18	19	16	19	21	18	17	22	16	21	26	Italy
Germany	26	35	37	33	44	32	34	28	41	46	31	33	40	35	33	40	Pakistan
Great Britain	44	30	31	29	25	32	32	21	31	50	24	36	38	na	na	na	Belgium
Greece	na	24	25	23	20	29	20	13	20	30	19	21	31	21	23	33	Great Britain
Hungary	25	22	23	21	24	21	22	16	31	35	19	18	28	19	25	18	Jordan
Iceland	44	41	40	42	33	44	44	32	38	67	35	44	43	34	40	64	Korea, South
India	35	41	42	40	40	40	43	45	36	37	41	45	38	46	34	33	Ukraine
Indonesia	na	51	53	50	49	51	54	56	49	52	43	56	62	52	50	52	Bulgaria
Iran	na	65	66	65	63	68	66	65	63	68	66	67	64	64	65	68	Dominican Rep.
Ireland	47	35	41	30	30	39	36	33	33	45	25	36	45	28	38	34	Luxembourg
Israel	na	23	22	25	24	23	22	11	21	36	18	18	33	23	24	19	Nigeria
Italy	34	33	34	31	33	36	29	21	37	55	25	33	45	15	31	44	Lithuania
Japan	42	43	42	44	45	46	40	30	42	54	36	48	47	45	42	60	Armenia
Jordan	na	28	30	26	27	28	29	28	23	33	28	31	24	28	27	20	Albania
Korea, South	34	27	27	28	27	27	29	23	26	29	22	32	30	27	28	28	Czech Republic
Latvia	19	17	17	17	18	18	16	13	17	23	18	14	19	14	19	16	Greece
Lithuania	31	25	29	21	30	26	20	21	25	33	20	23	28	22	26	24	Russian Fed.
Luxembourg	na	26	27	25	21	28	27	20	28	35	16	29	35	23	25	34	Bangladesh
Macedonia	na	14	16	11	16	13	12	14	12	18	13	15	15	14	12	24	Morocco
Malta	na	21	21	20	20	20	22	18	20	31	15	21	28	21	20	29	Israel
Mexico	34	21	23	20	22	20	23	22	18	28	23	22	21	25	19	25	Chile
Moldova	na	15	15	14	14	13	17	16	14	14	12	17	14	15	16	9	Estonia
Montenegro	na	34	33	34	37	36	30	29	36	39	31	32	34	28	37	61	Puerto Rico
Morocco	na	24	21	26	23	22	29	25	18	23	26	17	25	24	24	23	France
Netherlands	56	60	62	58	67	63	53	38	62	79	50	58	76	43	56	78	Uruguay
New Zealand	na	48	49	48	38	51	49	43	41	61	43	50	54	53	48	53	Hungary
Nigeria	23	26	26	25	25	26	28	28	24	24	27	25	24	24	26	35	Slovenia
Northern Ireland	44	40	42	37	30	42	44	40	38	43	38	41	42	36	38	54	Mexico
Norway	65	65	64	67	69	74	52	46	65	84	na	na	na	49	66	80	Malta
Pakistan	na	31	33	29	35	32	21	31	32	27	30	28	38	28	35	55	Azerbaijan
Peru	na	11	11	10	10	12	9	8	9	15	9	10	15	8	11	13	Poland
Philippines	na	8	9	8	8	9	9	8	9	8	9	7	10	9	8	10	Serbia
Poland	35	19	19	21	17	18	21	16	20	26	16	20	25	17	19	25	Georgia
Portugal	21	10	12	9	9	11	10	9	12	14	7	13	12	10	10	13	Croatia
Puerto Rico	na	23	25	21	15	21	27	13	18	27	15	25	28	24	22	24	Latvia
Romania	16	10	11	10	11	9	10	10	9	13	9	9	12	7	13	13	Singapore
Russian Fed.	38	24	23	24	22	24	25	21	24	25	24	23	25	22	26	25	Venezuela
Serbia	na	19	19	19	17	20	18	21	18	18	17	19	22	16	21	25	Bosnia and Herz.
Singapore	na	17	19	14	20	15	10	11	18	29	11	14	23	16	17	23	Slovakia
Slovakia	na	16	16	15	16	18	13	12	17	17	11	15	19	13	17	29	Turkey
Slovenia	17	22	23	21	21	23	21	7	23	46	13	24	34	19	22	28	Argentina
South Africa	28	12	13	11	11	12	13	12	12	12	16	7	12	13	10	15	Moldova
Spain	32	36	36	36	38	39	33	33	37	45	33	35	39	33	37	39	El Salvador
Sweden	66	66	66	67	67	68	65	53	63	82	63	60	80	57	62	81	Macedonia
Switzerland	43	41	40	42	35	40	45	32	41	57	37	39	47	33	39	54	Zimbabwe
Taiwan	na	38	39	38	56	38	29	27	40	48	33	33	48	37	38	47	South Africa
Tanzania	na	8	9	7	6	10	7	9	5	9	11	7	7	9	6	21	Algeria
Turkey	10	16	18	14	15	15	18	15	14	25	16	15	16	16	15	18	Colombia
Uganda	na	8	9	7	9	6	8	7	8	9	9	11	3	7	8	8	Peru
Ukraine	na	27	29	26	27	28	27	24	27	29	24	31	27	27	26	27	Romania
United States	52	36	34	38	24	35	47	24	33	42	28	41	40	37	35	40	Portugal
Uruguay	na	22	23	21	20	24	22	19	25	32	21	23	23	25	21	25	Philippines
Venezuela	na	16	18	14	16	16	15	11	16	22	18	16	16	14	17	15	Tanzania
Vietnam	na	41	43	40	41	39	46	42	39	48	39	45	40	32	42	42	Uganda
Zimbabwe	na	12	11	13	10	12	17	14	10	na	18	11	6	13	11	12	Brazil
Total	35	28	29	27	25	29	29	24	27	36	25	27	31	24	28	37	Total

E 6.9

Satisfaction

...s considered, how satisfied are you with your life as a whole these days?
...ed (7-10)

(WVS: V81; EVS: V68)

	Wave		Gender		Age			Education			Income			Values		
	###	###	Male	Female	16–29	30–49	50+	Lower	Middle	Upper	Lower	Middle	Upper	Mat	Mixed	Postm.
	na	30	33	26	32	31	26	21	35	39	19	25	46	29	31	39
	na	44	39	49	42	45	44	40	45	45	37	42	55	44	43	47
...na	69	69	69	69	73	68	66	67	71	77	61	69	77	65	69	71
	na	19	21	18	25	17	15	26	18	21	28	14	10	16	23	16
...ia	na	77	76	79	75	78	79	72	79	79	70	78	86	77	77	78
	64	83	85	81	87	84	80	79	84	91	76	81	88	73	81	89
...jan	na	32	34	30	39	27	30	34	30	35	22	27	46	33	30	32
...desh	na	32	32	34	36	29	36	28	40	33	17	28	55	37	30	35
	33	24	25	24	34	20	22	18	26	27	16	24	40	19	27	53
...n	79	79	78	79	84	77	78	70	78	86	64	78	88	76	79	80
...and Herz.	na	38	38	38	46	38	30	28	37	52	25	33	61	34	40	36
	68	63	68	57	62	62	67	65	61	61	60	64	64	66	60	66
...a	25	36	39	33	51	40	25	21	40	53	21	35	49	32	40	46
	84	81	81	81	82	79	82	79	79	87	71	82	88	78	80	83
	70	63	62	64	65	62	63	57	62	79	56	62	76	58	66	64
	68	53	52	55	54	51	58	55	53	51	46	56	61	51	54	63
...ia	na	85	86	84	85	86	82	82	84	91	79	86	90	84	84	83
	na	54	53	55	67	54	45	49	53	69	50	53	57	46	54	57
...Republic	50	67	67	67	70	68	64	61	71	81	57	66	76	60	68	73
...rk	86	86	87	84	88	88	82	83	90	88	77	89	94	86	86	91
...can Rep.	na	68	72	65	67	68	70	66	60	71	61	68	84	68	67	66
	na	44	43	44	44	44	43	43	44	45	44	43	43	43	45	40
...ador	na	71	73	69	76	67	69	65	76	79	63	68	84	na	na	na
...a	45	44	44	44	54	41	40	39	42	56	31	41	52	36	49	54
	79	84	84	85	86	84	84	79	91	90	75	88	92	85	84	88
	59	66	68	64	71	66	63	63	67	71	51	67	77	66	66	65
	na	25	26	24	31	24	20	26	24	26	17	26	35	23	27	27
...ny	59	79	78	79	84	78	77	76	81	79	70	81	83	82	78	78
...ritain	74	73	77	69	78	74	71	75	72	76	66	73	80	na	na	na
	na	61	62	60	57	64	63	54	58	65	52	60	69	61	61	59
...y	44	37	37	37	47	35	33	31	45	58	20	29	55	35	41	30
	85	87	86	88	87	91	82	82	88	96	77	90	94	89	87	82
	53	28	31	24	28	28	28	22	33	35	22	21	37	28	32	33
...sia	na	62	62	62	59	66	59	53	64	68	45	69	84	59	64	71
	na	52	48	57	53	53	49	46	52	58	41	48	63	49	54	57
	80	85	87	84	83	87	85	83	87	87	80	87	91	88	84	86
	na	65	64	67	75	64	56	53	65	75	48	59	80	69	65	70
	71	70	72	67	68	72	68	65	73	75	63	68	79	65	70	72
	53	53	52	54	51	50	57	44	52	61	46	51	65	51	54	54
	na	37	33	42	39	37	35	33	33	51	28	37	50	35	39	48
...South	61	47	46	49	44	48	49	34	47	49	36	45	61	46	48	48
	40	33	32	34	48	29	30	26	34	40	27	32	43	30	34	36
...ia	44	33	35	31	52	24	26	25	34	42	23	23	40	30	31	47
...ourg	na	82	83	81	81	81	84	76	85	86	76	84	89	82	80	90
...nia	na	31	30	32	38	31	25	19	35	41	16	32	53	29	33	28
	na	86	86	86	88	87	84	82	88	86	82	88	89	84	87	88
	72	80	80	79	81	78	81	78	81	86	75	80	82	80	80	78
...a	na	19	19	19	26	19	14	12	19	26	8	16	29	17	21	27
...egro	na	41	40	43	43	42	39	32	45	52	24	38	54	32	51	44
...co	na	38	37	40	38	39	38	36	45	53	22	40	37	42	36	36
...lands	85	91	91	89	93	92	86	82	94	92	80	93	95	86	90	91
...ealand	na	77	77	77	76	74	80	73	75	82	68	76	85	72	77	82
	54	64	63	65	68	59	60	57	65	72	54	63	80	65	65	54
...rn Ireland	83	85	84	85	87	83	88	83	87	86	77	86	92	85	85	85
...r	78	79	82	76	82	82	73	75	79	83	na	na	na	75	80	79
...an	na	10	10	9	12	10	5	5	13	20	2	10	18	8	12	17
	na	50	49	51	51	48	54	48	46	56	44	53	52	47	51	54
...ines	na	53	53	54	57	49	57	53	49	61	40	49	72	55	53	50
	57	51	51	50	61	48	47	46	56	59	38	54	66	47	51	62
...al	63	62	64	61	80	64	51	56	74	82	35	59	78	58	65	67
...Rico	na	85	87	85	88	83	86	82	82	88	79	88	89	80	85	90
...ia	44	38	37	39	45	36	39	34	36	51	36	29	44	35	38	38
...n Fed.	32	27	31	24	42	26	19	20	25	37	20	24	35	25	28	46
	na	40	41	39	50	40	35	30	43	48	30	41	50	34	45	51
...ore	na	71	70	71	71	70	71	66	73	74	60	67	83	71	71	68
...a	na	47	47	46	51	48	42	38	49	62	36	42	57	46	49	52
...ia	47	67	68	67	78	66	60	55	71	77	59	69	78	64	68	69
...Africa	51	42	45	38	37	45	46	35	50	62	21	47	66	42	44	31
	66	65	65	65	68	66	63	61	69	71	56	69	70	63	66	70
...n	84	80	81	78	79	80	80	79	78	83	71	83	87	77	79	81
...rland	86	85	88	82	85	84	86	81	85	92	75	85	91	81	85	85
	na	50	47	52	52	53	40	41	46	60	36	51	63	52	49	54
...ia	na	21	19	24	23	19	24	21	20	22	20	22	19	20	22	30
	48	39	33	45	41	36	41	39	36	38	34	39	50	41	38	35
...a	na	36	30	41	38	32	42	36	35	43	38	35	39	40	33	41
...e	na	25	26	23	36	25	17	13	23	34	12	22	44	21	26	36
...States	81	79	79	78	79	76	83	74	77	82	72	79	90	75	79	80
...ay	na	63	62	63	63	60	65	60	64	72	53	65	70	56	65	63
...uela	na	70	73	68	71	70	69	65	69	78	59	69	77	67	71	71
...m	na	44	45	44	41	46	45	40	50	55	29	36	62	46	48	49
...owe	na	18	16	20	22	16	12	16	21	39	15	18	29	19	18	16
	62	56	56	56	57	55	56	51	55	65	45	54	65	48	50	60

RANKING

Country	2000
Netherlands	90
Iceland	87
Malta	86
Denmark	86
Ireland	85
Puerto Rico	85
Colombia	85
Switzerland	85
Northern Ireland	85
Finland	84
Austria	83
Luxembourg	82
Canada	81
Sweden	80
Mexico	80
Norway	79
United States	79
Germany	79
Belgium	79
Australia	77
New Zealand	77
Great Britain	73
El Salvador	71
Singapore	71
Venezuela	70
Italy	70
Argentina	69
Dominican Rep.	68
Slovenia	67
Czech Republic	67
France	66
Israel	65
Spain	65
Nigeria	64
Chile	63
Brazil	63
Uruguay	63
Portugal	62
Indonesia	62
Greece	61
Croatia	54
China	53
Philippines	53
Japan	53
Iran	52
Poland	51
Peru	50
Taiwan	50
Korea, South	47
Slovakia	47
Vietnam	44
Estonia	44
Algeria	44
Egypt	44
South Africa	42
Montenegro	41
Serbia	40
Turkey	39
Morocco	38
Bosnia and Herz.	38
Romania	38
Jordan	37
Hungary	37
Uganda	36
Bulgaria	36
Latvia	33
Lithuania	33
Bangladesh	32
Azerbaijan	32
Macedonia	31
Albania	30
India	28
Russian Fed.	27
Georgia	25
Ukraine	25
Belarus	24
Tanzania	21
Armenia	19
Moldova	19
Zimbabwe	18
Pakistan	10
Total	66

and Switzerland, all 85% or higher. The lowest level of life satisfaction was found in Pakistan (10%), followed by Zimbabwe, Moldova, Armenia, Tanzania, and Belarus, all less than 25%.

Overall, males and females had identical life satisfaction rates, 56% for both. However, significant gender differences were seen in Algeria, Iran, Jordan, Turkey, and Uganda, in all of which women were significantly more satisfied. Age did not appear to have a strong impact on life satisfaction, as rates were 57% for the youngest, 55% for the middle, and 56% for the oldest generation.

However, in Armenia, Belarus, Bosnia and Herzegovina, Bulgaria, Croatia, Estonia, Georgia, Hungary, Israel, Latvia, Lithuania, Macedonia, Moldova, Poland, Portugal, Russia, Serbia, Slovenia, Taiwan, Ukraine, and Zimbabwe, the young were much more satisfied than the old. The predominance of former communist countries on this list perhaps indicates that the older generations were having a more difficult time adjusting to a capitalist system than their younger counterparts. It is perhaps not surprising that more income and education tend to increase life satisfaction, as levels increase from 51% to 55% to 65% with rising education and 45% to 54% to 65% with rising income. Postmaterial values were strongly correlated with life satisfaction, at 68% in contrast to 46% for materialists.

Table 6.10 seeks to capture **feelings of freedom,** or respondents' attitudes toward destiny versus self-control. The relevant question asks "Some people feel they have completely free choice and control over their lives, while other people feel that what they do has no real effect on what happens to them." Participants are asked to rank how much control they feel they have over their lives on a scale from 1–10 (1 being none at all, and 10 being a great deal), and the table shows the percentage of respondents who answer 7, 8, 9, or 10.

In the world overall, 58% of people felt that they have control over their own lives, but there is significant regional variation. People in the English-speaking democracies, northern Europe, and Latin America generally tended to feel greater levels of control over their own lives than those in Africa, South Asia, or the Orthodox or Islamic worlds. Puerto Rico ranked the highest in self-reported control, with 83%, followed by the United States, Venezuela, Iceland, Mexico, Colombia, and Finland, all 78% or higher. Of all regions, South Asia tends to be the most fatalistic, with the three lowest-ranked countries on the scale, Bangladesh, India, and Pakistan, with 33%, 22%, and 11%, respectively, feeling they had control over their lives.

Males tended to feel that they were more in control of their lives, with 60% saying that they had a great deal of control, compared with 56% for females. Young people also tended to feel more in control, with 61% of the youngest group, 58% of the middle, and 55% of the oldest responding that they had a great deal of control over their lives. In general, increasing levels of education and income correlated with a greater feeling of control over one's life, as did an orientation toward postmaterialist values.

Table 6.11 presents respondents' views on **income equality.** The question asks respondents to rank their beliefs on a scale of 1–10, with 1 being "Incomes should be made more equal" and 10 being "We need larger income differences as

E 6.10

ng of Freedom

ople feel they have completely free choice and control over their lives; while other people feel
t they do has no real effect on what happens to them.
deal (7-10)

	Wave		Gender		Age			Education			Income			Values		
	###	###	Male	Female	16-29	30-49	50+	Lower	Middle	Upper	Lower	Middle	Upper	Mat	Mixed	Postm.
a	na	46	47	44	50	49	37	42	47	53	41	45	51	45	49	44
a	na	56	55	58	50	63	58	53	56	59	49	59	61	53	58	61
ina	68	68	68	69	72	68	65	67	71	66	64	67	73	59	70	72
ia	na	36	42	31	43	34	29	34	36	37	43	31	30	33	39	35
lia	na	76	76	76	74	76	78	71	76	80	72	78	80	68	77	76
a	57	70	72	68	79	64	70	68	71	72	67	67	75	62	70	71
aijan	na	41	48	34	39	38	50	45	38	44	28	37	53	41	38	41
adesh	na	33	34	30	30	32	45	31	33	37	28	25	47	42	27	22
s	40	37	42	32	48	40	24	19	42	46	28	37	50	32	41	64
m	57	59	60	58	66	58	56	46	61	66	49	57	70	55	58	66
a and Herz.	na	47	48	47	54	47	41	42	46	58	41	43	61	44	50	53
	63	66	73	58	69	62	68	65	68	63	66	66	65	68	64	66
ia	28	46	52	41	58	49	39	35	50	57	37	45	57	46	47	49
a	77	77	75	78	82	76	76	72	76	82	71	77	82	75	75	82
	61	65	66	64	64	64	66	60	62	81	57	67	75	59	66	71
	63	64	67	61	61	65	65	67	63	56	61	67	68	61	65	71
bia	na	78	82	74	79	78	75	72	76	85	69	78	84	80	77	70
a	na	60	63	57	61	62	57	57	59	73	56	55	68	55	61	57
Republic	42	59	63	56	65	63	54	53	64	74	51	56	69	56	59	71
ark	64	72	73	71	80	76	63	63	81	85	62	72	90	60	72	83
ican Rep.	na	70	72	69	71	70	55	53	58	75	69	70	80	65	69	76
	na	43	42	44	44	43	40	40	45	45	40	43	46	43	41	49
vador	na	70	76	64	71	66	75	63	75	81	61	70	84	na	na	na
a	50	43	42	43	53	43	36	38	41	56	33	37	47	37	47	49
d	79	78	80	76	85	83	71	70	86	92	70	79	85	76	77	85
e	45	51	53	49	51	50	52	50	50	53	44	51	56	50	51	52
ia	na	49	58	42	53	52	41	46	49	51	41	52	59	47	52	50
any	53	73	76	71	70	70	77	71	75	69	71	68	77	82	72	67
Britain	65	67	67	68	71	67	65	67	66	72	66	60	75	na	na	na
e	na	65	69	62	66	64	65	60	63	67	62	61	69	58	66	69
ary	50	44	48	41	54	46	37	38	56	57	32	42	54	41	49	43
d	70	81	81	81	90	85	67	73	86	89	71	81	92	80	83	77
	50	22	26	16	26	22	17	17	25	29	20	18	27	24	23	21
esia	na	67	65	69	66	69	65	65	66	72	52	76	85	66	69	70
	na	55	54	55	55	55	52	50	56	58	48	55	59	57	54	57
d	65	70	70	69	77	70	63	60	72	81	57	67	82	63	70	76
	na	na	na	na	na	na	na	na	na	na	na	na	na	na	na	na
	52	51	56	46	68	51	41	36	60	69	41	51	62	41	50	58
	29	39	39	39	54	40	32	30	38	48	35	38	41	34	40	47
	na	65	76	55	62	66	70	63	62	72	60	68	75	64	67	70
, South	73	64	61	66	73	63	54	43	62	68	58	60	73	59	66	83
	48	42	45	39	52	45	34	30	45	46	38	40	46	41	40	53
ania	55	50	50	49	61	50	41	41	51	57	45	48	54	47	48	70
nbourg	na	64	67	61	68	62	64	59	66	70	64	65	72	68	63	71
donia	na	42	40	44	48	42	36	30	44	55	31	43	57	41	43	51
	na	75	77	73	78	78	71	72	77	76	68	77	78	72	78	73
o	70	79	81	78	79	79	80	77	80	87	76	81	82	79	81	80
va	na	46	48	43	49	48	39	40	43	54	34	49	52	42	50	43
enegro	na	45	51	38	51	48	37	32	49	59	30	45	59	36	54	54
cco	na	46	51	42	46	46	47	45	54	51	38	49	44	46	48	35
rlands	52	65	70	60	75	71	53	50	68	75	58	66	75	54	66	69
Zealand	na	77	76	78	81	78	74	73	79	80	67	78	84	77	77	80
a	57	67	68	66	68	66	66	61	69	73	62	64	79	72	65	59
ern Ireland	75	74	72	75	72	75	76	73	79	70	74	75	78	79	76	65
ay	67	71	69	72	79	73	61	62	71	79	na	na	na	60	71	77
an	na	11	13	9	7	12	15	9	14	12	7	11	15	12	10	10
	na	64	67	61	63	64	69	65	62	68	61	66	67	61	65	71
ines	na	55	53	57	56	53	55	49	53	63	46	57	60	51	58	56
d	52	48	51	45	58	47	42	44	52	52	36	52	64	41	50	66
gal	52	55	59	50	61	54	52	49	65	70	44	53	62	49	57	70
o Rico	na	83	80	85	83	80	84	80	78	85	80	81	85	77	85	83
	49	58	61	54	63	61	51	46	61	67	54	56	62	57	57	60
an Fed.	47	38	45	32	49	39	29	25	36	52	27	37	49	34	41	45
a	na	44	49	39	55	43	40	33	47	54	36	44	52	37	50	59
pore	na	69	68	69	70	67	67	66	69	75	65	64	74	63	70	75
kia	na	50	53	48	54	49	45	42	52	65	41	48	58	44	54	64
nia	44	64	65	63	75	66	53	48	67	80	52	67	81	55	65	68
Africa	57	55	57	52	51	57	59	49	61	81	41	56	73	53	57	53
	56	58	58	58	62	59	55	54	62	64	53	58	61	53	60	61
en	74	74	74	74	83	77	66	63	74	82	67	75	83	62	74	77
erland	66	70	69	72	79	69	67	68	71	72	64	63	80	70	69	70
n	na	68	68	69	71	70	62	63	71	71	59	68	77	66	74	65
nia	na	41	44	37	42	38	47	45	37	35	48	43	32	41	41	42
y	31	39	45	34	42	39	33	31	49	57	30	42	54	34	38	52
da	na	51	52	49	50	54	56	49	52	45	44	57	48	49	52	49
ne	na	34	38	31	47	36	25	17	34	42	24	31	50	30	39	39
d States	77	82	83	81	85	80	82	78	79	85	76	84	89	75	82	85
ay	na	60	63	58	61	57	62	59	61	70	51	64	67	56	57	70
zuela	na	82	85	78	85	80	78	75	84	84	74	81	88	75	84	85
am	na	66	71	61	59	70	64	67	65	70	50	64	77	74	67	60
abwe	na	44	45	43	43	45	42	45	41	44	38	47	50	42	46	35
	57	58	60	56	61	58	55	53	58	66	51	57	65	51	60	67

(WVS: V82; EVS: V67)

RANKING	
Country	2000
Puerto Rico	83
United States	82
Venezuela	82
Iceland	81
Mexico	79
Colombia	78
Finland	78
Canada	77
New Zealand	77
Australia	76
Malta	75
Northern Ireland	74
Sweden	74
Germany	73
Denmark	72
Norway	71
Switzerland	70
El Salvador	70
Dominican Rep.	70
Austria	70
Ireland	70
Singapore	69
Argentina	68
Taiwan	68
Great Britain	67
Nigeria	67
Indonesia	67
Brazil	66
Vietnam	66
Jordan	65
Netherlands	65
Greece	65
Chile	65
China	64
Peru	64
Luxembourg	64
Korea, South	64
Slovenia	64
Uruguay	60
Croatia	60
Czech Republic	59
Belgium	59
Spain	58
Romania	58
Algeria	56
South Africa	55
Philippines	55
Portugal	55
Iran	55
France	51
Italy	51
Uganda	51
Slovakia	50
Lithuania	50
Georgia	49
Poland	48
Bosnia and Herz.	47
Bulgaria	46
Morocco	46
Albania	46
Moldova	46
Montenegro	45
Hungary	44
Serbia	44
Zimbabwe	44
Estonia	43
Egypt	43
Macedonia	42
Latvia	42
Tanzania	41
Azerbaijan	41
Turkey	39
Japan	39
Russian Fed.	38
Belarus	37
Armenia	36
Ukraine	34
Bangladesh	33
India	22
Pakistan	11
Total	58

TABLE 6.11

Income Equality

Now I'd like you to tell me your views on various issues. How would you place your views on this scale?
% "We need larger income differences as incentives for individual effort" (codes 7-10)

(WVS: V141; EVS: o)

Country	Wave ###	Wave ###	Gender Male	Gender Female	Age 16-29	Age 30-49	Age 50+	Education Lower	Education Middle	Education Upper	Income Lower	Income Middle	Income Upper	Values Mat	Values Mixed	Values Postm.	RANKING Country
Albania	na	49	54	43	53	50	43	40	52	62	43	43	61	48	51	44	Egypt
Algeria	na	77	76	78	78	80	69	66	78	84	76	82	77	68	81	85	Algeria
Argentina	65	35	38	32	35	37	33	29	45	39	28	38	39	28	35	41	Dominican Rep.
Armenia	na	53	57	49	54	58	45	47	52	61	62	46	47	51	56	52	Morocco
Australia	na	41	43	39	38	43	41	38	42	43	35	44	45	51	43	36	Jordan
Austria	42	26	32	20	31	26	23	18	29	44	16	23	38	20	27	26	Georgia
Azerbaijan	na	43	44	43	39	47	44	38	39	52	36	36	60	38	52	50	Peru
Bangladesh	na	67	67	66	64	68	70	62	70	74	65	59	79	73	63	58	Puerto Rico
Belarus	71	36	42	31	49	35	26	21	37	57	30	35	49	27	40	80	Uganda
Belgium	50	42	46	39	43	43	41	36	43	47	41	41	47	39	44	39	Bangladesh
Bosnia and Herz.	na	46	49	43	49	44	44	34	44	60	40	44	54	50	43	51	Ukraine
Brazil	48	47	48	46	42	50	51	44	47	57	42	45	53	42	49	51	Indonesia
Bulgaria	61	48	52	44	61	56	33	23	56	72	28	49	64	37	59	70	Russian Fed.
Canada	63	40	43	37	36	43	39	38	39	44	36	38	46	43	42	36	El Salvador
Chile	47	22	22	22	23	24	18	21	22	25	21	23	23	21	21	24	Singapore
China	80	56	59	53	55	56	58	58	54	60	62	53	55	54	58	61	Zimbabwe
Colombia	na	52	53	51	52	53	48	45	52	55	47	50	57	51	47	54	Luxembourg
Croatia	na	22	23	22	27	21	21	19	22	35	20	21	27	12	23	27	Estonia
Czech Republic	78	42	48	37	43	47	37	34	49	60	33	41	51	28	46	52	Korea, South
Denmark	57	na	na	na	na	na	na	na	na	na	na	na	na	na	na	na	Moldova
Dominican Rep.	na	75	76	74	74	76	82	75	69	77	80	70	79	75	73	79	China
Egypt	na	87	87	87	87	87	86	85	88	91	87	88	89	88	87	88	Nigeria
El Salvador	na	63	64	61	62	62	66	58	65	70	55	64	71	na	na	na	Armenia
Estonia	77	62	63	61	60	68	58	59	62	68	55	61	65	56	66	72	Colombia
Finland	61	28	31	25	29	28	27	20	38	42	25	23	34	19	32	25	Poland
France	40	34	36	31	31	31	37	32	35	37	29	32	41	31	35	33	Netherlands
Georgia	na	72	73	72	73	75	68	75	70	75	70	74	74	72	72	75	Philippines
Germany	74	na	na	na	na	na	na	na	na	na	na	na	na	na	na	na	Vietnam
Great Britain	58	39	43	35	33	43	39	34	43	47	29	37	56	na	na	na	Ireland
Greece	na	na	na	na	na	na	na	na	na	na	na	na	na	na	na	na	Italy
Hungary	49	na	na	na	na	na	na	na	na	na	na	na	na	na	na	na	Albania
Iceland	47	44	46	43	52	44	39	41	51	40	42	39	53	48	46	29	Bulgaria
India	47	31	33	27	32	32	25	24	35	36	23	31	34	32	31	48	Serbia
Indonesia	na	65	65	66	68	69	61	55	68	71	58	72	79	66	68	64	Brazil
Iran	na	33	32	34	33	34	32	39	32	28	37	29	32	35	32	34	Taiwan
Ireland	58	50	53	47	56	50	46	42	50	63	42	47	62	44	52	48	Bosnia and Herz.
Israel	na	12	13	12	13	13	10	10	11	16	11	13	13	8	14	5	Iceland
Italy	47	49	53	45	51	54	43	40	54	59	40	48	59	43	50	50	Northern Ireland
Japan	34	35	42	30	35	33	38	35	32	46	34	32	44	33	36	42	United States
Jordan	na	72	76	69	71	72	77	65	80	77	67	74	78	72	72	77	Venezuela
Korea, South	39	60	60	60	60	60	61	59	59	62	55	61	65	57	62	63	Azerbaijan
Latvia	68	na	na	na	na	na	na	na	na	na	na	na	na	na	na	na	Belgium
Lithuania	73	34	34	33	41	39	23	18	36	51	27	24	46	24	35	54	Czech Republic
Luxembourg	na	62	62	62	64	63	61	55	64	68	60	61	68	58	65	61	Australia
Macedonia	na	35	35	36	35	36	34	29	35	47	31	34	42	36	36	27	Canada
Malta	na	na	na	na	na	na	na	na	na	na	na	na	na	na	na	na	Montenegro
Mexico	50	39	42	36	42	38	38	35	41	51	30	38	50	34	41	40	Mexico
Moldova	na	58	57	59	60	59	54	53	55	67	64	57	54	51	61	75	South Africa
Montenegro	na	40	44	36	55	42	29	26	45	61	42	29	53	38	44	42	Great Britain
Morocco	na	73	72	74	74	72	72	73	73	74	61	73	72	75	70	74	Tanzania
Netherlands	48	51	55	47	44	53	52	53	52	47	43	49	61	54	54	40	Uruguay
New Zealand	na	35	42	29	32	39	32	32	35	39	25	34	47	41	36	32	Belarus
Nigeria	74	55	56	54	56	54	54	55	53	56	54	54	59	53	56	58	Japan
Northern Ireland	67	44	46	42	47	41	45	36	48	55	39	43	50	47	44	40	Macedonia
Norway	47	34	37	30	32	34	34	25	34	40	na	na	na	33	35	26	Spain
Pakistan	na	11	12	11	13	10	13	4	19	16	3	10	23	7	17	50	New Zealand
Peru	na	70	69	71	68	72	72	70	71	71	71	73	66	68	71	74	Argentina
Philippines	na	51	52	49	51	50	51	46	49	57	48	50	54	50	51	49	Switzerland
Poland	79	51	53	49	52	55	46	42	59	73	41	58	60	44	54	68	Lithuania
Portugal	25	na	na	na	na	na	na	na	na	na	na	na	na	na	na	na	France
Puerto Rico	na	70	71	70	68	70	72	66	69	72	66	70	74	74	72	65	Norway
Romania	55	20	18	22	19	21	19	20	17	27	23	19	18	18	20	28	Iran
Russian Fed.	63	65	68	63	72	67	58	57	65	68	60	65	70	62	69	61	India
Serbia	na	47	50	44	52	51	42	35	48	62	35	46	59	40	53	63	Finland
Singapore	na	63	62	63	61	66	59	61	62	68	58	64	65	63	64	53	Austria
Slovakia	na	na	na	na	na	na	na	na	na	na	na	na	na	na	na	na	Turkey
Slovenia	48	20	21	20	21	21	19	10	22	35	15	20	30	19	21	17	Croatia
South Africa	37	39	43	34	45	36	33	33	45	59	31	38	50	37	40	48	Chile
Spain	32	35	36	35	39	33	35	34	34	42	34	37	35	36	37	29	Slovenia
Sweden	58	na	na	na	na	na	na	na	na	na	na	na	na	na	na	na	Romania
Switzerland	na	35	38	31	36	36	31	28	35	45	26	31	41	42	34	29	Israel
Taiwan	na	46	46	47	38	48	49	50	39	47	44	44	51	52	42	44	Pakistan
Tanzania	na	38	41	35	41	36	37	36	40	39	39	33	43	39	38	46	
Turkey	31	25	25	25	25	26	25	25	25	28	23	26	27	25	26	25	
Uganda	na	67	60	74	65	69	72	65	69	63	63	76	63	66	67	75	
Ukraine	na	66	67	65	66	68	63	63	64	71	64	65	68	62	69	80	
United States	62	44	45	42	39	43	48	43	42	45	42	40	55	39	46	38	
Uruguay	na	36	36	36	36	34	38	34	38	38	31	31	46	28	37	39	
Venezuela	na	44	44	43	45	44	39	34	44	55	34	41	53	41	44	47	
Vietnam	na	50	55	46	54	54	41	45	55	61	46	45	58	32	57	52	
Zimbabwe	na	63	63	62	59	64	70	63	62	70	66	59	67	57	68	52	
Total	56	47	49	46	50	48	43	41	48	55	44	46	53	46	48	45	Total

incentives for individual effort." The table shows the percentage of respondents who replied 7, 8, 9, or 10, indicating that they prefer larger income differences.

The overall world rate is 47% of respondents who would prefer less equality of income. Interestingly, there does not appear to be a strong regional pattern for which countries tend to share this value. The country with the highest level of agreement (Egypt, 87%) and lowest level of agreement (Pakistan, 11%) are both Islamic countries. Egypt, Algeria, Morocco, and Jordan tended to support less income equality, while Turkey and Iran join Pakistan in wanting more income equality. Europe generally tended to be more supportive of income equality, but by no means was this universal. Likewise, there was a lot of variation among Latin American countries, former communist countries, and African countries.

The world seems to have become more egalitarian over the past recent decades, as the percentage wanting greater income differences dropped from 56% to 47% between 1990 and 2000. The drop was particularly large in Argentina, Austria, Belarus, Bulgaria, Canada, Chile, China, Czech Republic, Estonia, Finland, Great Britain, India, Lithuania, Mexico, Nigeria, Northern Ireland, Norway, Poland, Romania, Slovenia, and the United States. Many of these countries did in fact experience an increase in inequality during those years, and it may be that the change to more egalitarian values was a result of that.

With regard to gender, females were slightly more egalitarian than males (46% vs. 49%), except in Uganda, where the pattern was reversed. In general, the young were more supportive of large income differentials than their elders, with 50% among the youngest group, 48% among the middle, and 43% among the oldest generation. Increases in education and income both tended to increase support for large income differentials (from 41% to 48% to 55% for education, and 44% to 46% to 53% for income). This perhaps shows that the wealthy and well educated believed they achieved their positions through their own efforts and should be rewarded accordingly. With regard to values, there was not much effect on responses to this question, with 46% of materialists and 45% of postmaterialists supporting larger income differentials.

Table 6.12 presents respondents' beliefs about **competition**. The question asks respondents to rank their beliefs on a scale of 1–10, with 1 being "Competition is good. It stimulates people to work hard and develop new ideas." and 10 being "Competition is harmful. It brings out the worst in people." The table shows the percentage of respondents who replied 1, 2, 3, or 4, indicating that they believe competition is good.

Overall, 66% of respondents agreed that competition is good. This ranges from a high of 84% in Iceland to a low of 46% in both Chile and France. In general, there was not a very strong regional pattern to the responses, although it is interesting to note that the countries least supportive of competition tended to be Roman Catholic. On the other hand, the countries most supportive of competition (Iceland, Morocco, Zimbabwe, China, and Albania) showed great cultural and geographic diversity.

With regard to gender, men tended to see competition more favorably than women, with 69% of men agreeing that it is good, compared with 62% of women.

TABLE 6.12

Competition (is Good)

Now I'd like to tell me your views on various issues. How would you place your views on this scale?
% Competition is good. It stimulates people to work hard and develop new ideas (codes 1–4)

(WVS: V144; EVS: V186)

Country	Wave		Gender		Age			Education			Income			Values		
	###	###	Male	Female	16–29	30–49	50+	Lower	Middle	Upper	Lower	Middle	Upper	Mat	Mixed	Postm.
Albania	na	80	83	78	84	81	76	76	82	86	79	79	82	79	80	84
Algeria	na	na	na	na	na	na	na	na	na	na	na	na	na	na	na	na
Argentina	11	59	64	54	50	63	63	54	65	68	52	59	64	57	59	59
Armenia	na	56	58	54	50	63	54	52	53	64	55	56	55	52	59	57
Australia	na	76	76	75	71	77	78	74	74	80	72	79	79	75	76	75
Austria	7	74	78	71	74	75	74	73	74	79	73	72	79	65	76	74
Azerbaijan	na	64	67	60	63	65	62	59	64	64	64	62	71	59	73	60
Bangladesh	na	71	72	70	70	70	78	69	72	74	74	69	70	78	67	60
Belarus	13	65	69	61	75	64	56	51	68	72	60	63	76	62	65	93
Belgium	16	48	52	44	50	45	45	41	50	50	44	44	49	46	51	41
Bosnia and Herz.	na	74	75	73	75	74	71	65	74	79	70	73	80	77	73	79
Brazil	18	69	72	66	63	72	77	65	70	81	62	66	77	65	69	81
Bulgaria	7	66	70	61	72	70	59	52	69	77	58	65	72	62	70	84
Canada	10	70	75	66	68	70	71	68	69	73	63	72	75	72	70	70
Chile	21	46	48	45	49	44	48	42	48	50	42	50	48	43	49	46
China	5	80	82	78	79	78	88	83	79	83	81	79	84	76	85	77
Colombia	na	na	na	na	na	na	na	na	na	na	na	na	na	na	na	na
Croatia	na	75	79	71	69	79	74	76	73	78	68	75	76	71	77	71
Czech Republic	5	77	77	76	79	78	75	73	80	84	74	75	82	69	79	87
Denmark	13	61	68	55	71	62	55	60	76	55	54	61	70	54	65	52
Dominican Rep.	na	72	75	70	70	74	82	68	67	74	65	76	75	65	71	77
Egypt	na	na	na	na	na	na	na	na	na	na	na	na	na	na	na	na
El Salvador	na	66	68	64	66	64	68	63	68	72	62	65	76	na	na	na
Estonia	8	52	56	49	56	55	47	47	50	64	44	47	59	48	55	54
Finland	8	59	63	55	66	56	57	53	67	65	53	57	63	61	59	54
France	16	46	45	46	45	43	49	44	44	51	44	42	53	45	48	39
Georgia	na	73	76	71	75	75	68	71	73	76	70	72	78	71	75	78
Germany	8	66	69	64	65	64	69	65	66	73	69	74	66	71	66	59
Great Britain	15	59	61	57	53	58	63	57	56	68	55	58	64	na	na	na
Greece	na	55	55	55	49	58	62	58	60	51	57	56	55	61	57	45
Hungary	13	61	65	59	66	61	58	56	69	70	57	59	66	57	65	74
Iceland	5	84	87	81	88	87	75	80	88	83	75	86	88	87	85	71
India	7	64	65	63	62	65	64	64	64	63	64	64	64	64	64	61
Indonesia	na	na	na	na	na	na	na	na	na	na	na	na	na	na	na	na
Iran	na	na	na	na	na	na	na	na	na	na	na	na	na	na	na	na
Ireland	13	65	67	62	67	65	62	59	64	77	59	61	74	62	68	61
Israel	na	na	na	na	na	na	na	na	na	na	na	na	na	na	na	na
Italy	18	57	62	53	58	55	58	54	60	61	55	57	61	59	57	58
Japan	13	56	62	51	54	55	58	54	53	64	56	52	64	57	56	62
Jordan	na	na	na	na	na	na	na	na	na	na	na	na	na	na	na	na
Korea, South	9	58	61	54	58	57	58	38	57	60	58	57	57	54	60	63
Latvia	8	68	71	65	69	67	69	57	71	71	69	64	68	63	71	63
Lithuania	10	60	62	57	68	59	54	41	63	69	43	58	68	53	62	69
Luxembourg	na	52	57	47	48	49	57	49	55	50	51	53	56	50	51	56
Macedonia	na	77	78	76	78	75	80	71	78	84	73	77	82	73	80	74
Malta	na	76	79	74	78	76	75	68	78	83	73	76	79	69	80	81
Mexico	16	60	66	54	59	62	55	55	61	75	54	62	68	56	61	67
Moldova	na	61	65	59	65	63	57	59	61	64	61	57	63	58	65	59
Montenegro	na	73	72	74	80	74	67	71	72	81	80	73	71	74	73	64
Morocco	na	83	86	81	82	85	81	83	84	90	74	82	86	82	84	92
Netherlands	14	50	58	43	50	51	49	53	45	53	44	50	57	51	52	44
New Zealand	na	69	72	66	70	69	69	67	67	73	62	68	78	70	72	65
Nigeria	7	na	na	na	na	na	na	na	na	na	na	na	na	na	na	na
Northern Ireland	16	64	64	64	63	63	68	62	66	67	64	64	66	67	66	55
Norway	7	70	78	63	69	73	68	65	71	75	na	na	na	67	72	61
Pakistan	na	na	na	na	na	na	na	na	na	na	na	na	na	na	na	na
Peru	na	67	67	67	65	69	69	64	65	72	64	69	69	59	68	73
Philippines	na	55	56	55	55	56	55	54	51	63	60	56	50	54	57	49
Poland	12	59	62	56	63	60	55	57	60	65	55	60	69	53	61	62
Portugal	19	49	49	50	47	49	51	48	49	60	44	44	47	55	47	41
Puerto Rico	na	73	78	70	61	74	78	71	70	75	72	73	74	63	76	71
Romania	6	79	82	76	83	77	78	72	79	89	75	76	84	78	80	80
Russian Fed.	12	58	63	53	65	58	52	46	55	72	51	53	69	54	62	57
Serbia	na	70	72	69	73	68	71	63	73	75	69	69	75	65	76	68
Singapore	na	75	79	71	78	75	66	72	75	87	67	75	82	70	77	75
Slovakia	na	68	70	66	71	69	65	62	69	82	64	68	72	64	70	80
Slovenia	9	73	74	72	75	73	70	72	70	83	71	73	79	70	74	71
South Africa	14	65	62	68	66	63	67	60	70	83	62	66	65	71	60	64
Spain	22	52	55	48	50	50	54	51	52	53	52	49	55	56	51	47
Sweden	7	74	79	68	75	72	75	69	75	74	69	73	82	80	75	66
Switzerland	na	75	79	72	71	75	79	70	76	79	67	74	80	76	77	67
Taiwan	na	60	66	54	56	63	56	55	60	64	55	60	66	58	62	62
Tanzania	na	75	80	69	67	78	84	75	75	78	75	80	81	76	76	57
Turkey	23	65	69	59	61	68	64	59	71	72	59	65	73	55	67	69
Uganda	na	78	85	72	81	77	67	73	79	90	83	71	78	78	76	85
Ukraine	na	62	72	54	73	68	50	36	63	72	53	65	69	56	66	66
United States	10	71	75	67	67	69	77	60	73	74	64	72	81	72	71	73
Uruguay	na	50	53	47	51	46	52	48	51	53	45	48	57	47	50	51
Venezuela	na	65	68	62	63	67	65	63	63	72	67	65	69	63	66	64
Vietnam	na	59	63	54	57	59	60	57	61	58	53	57	63	56	61	55
Zimbabwe	na	82	86	79	80	82	87	81	83	70	79	86	86	82	83	87
Total	12	66	69	62	66	66	64	62	67	69	62	65	70	64	67	64

RANKING

Country
Iceland
Morocco
Zimbabwe
China
Albania
Romania
Uganda
Macedonia
Czech Republic
Malta
Australia
Switzerland
Singapore
Tanzania
Croatia
Austria
Bosnia and Herz.
Sweden
Georgia
Montenegro
Puerto Rico
Slovenia
Dominican Rep.
United States
Bangladesh
Serbia
Norway
Canada
Brazil
New Zealand
Slovakia
Latvia
Peru
Germany
El Salvador
Bulgaria
Venezuela
Belarus
Ireland
South Africa
Turkey
Northern Ireland
India
Azerbaijan
Ukraine
Hungary
Moldova
Denmark
Taiwan
Lithuania
Mexico
Great Britain
Poland
Finland
Argentina
Vietnam
Russian Fed.
Korea, South
Italy
Japan
Armenia
Philippines
Greece
Estonia
Luxembourg
Spain
Netherlands
Uruguay
Portugal
Belgium
Chile
France
Total

Age had only a mild effect on attitudes toward competition, but in general the younger generation saw it more favorably. Sixty-six percent of both the youngest and the middle agree it was good, compared with 64% of the oldest. (In a few countries, including Argentina, Brazil, Dominican Republic, Great Britain, Greece, Puerto Rico, Tanzania, and the United States, older people were more supportive of competition.) Education and income both correlated with more favorable attitudes toward competition. Support rose from 62% to 67% to 69% with increasing education and from 62% to 65% to 70% with increasing income. Values did not appear to affect attitudes toward competition, with 64% of both materialists and postmaterialists agreeing that competition is good.

Finally, Table 6.13 deals with respondents' attitudes toward **tolerance of homosexuality**. The question asks "Please tell me for each of the following statements whether you think it can always be justified, never be justified, or something in between," offering "homosexuality" as one of the choices. The table lists the percentage of respondents who believed that homosexuality can never be justified. In the world overall, 56% of respondents said that homosexuality could never be justified. There was a strong regional pattern to the responses, with homosexuality viewed most negatively in the Middle East and Africa (100% in Egypt said it could never be justified), compared with European and English-speaking Protestant countries, where it was much more accepted (only 7% in the Netherlands said it could never be justified).

Over the 10 years between 1990 and 2000, the percentage viewing homosexuality as never justifiable dropped from 63% to 56%. However, the total worldwide percentage understates the change in opinion over that time period, as most of the countries that were least accepting of homosexuality have no data from 1990. What the data actually show is that acceptance of homosexuality is increasing rapidly, particularly in the West. For the 41 countries that have data for both waves of the World Values Survey, 22 showed a drop of 20% or more in the percentage who said that homosexuality is never justifiable. Another 11 had a drop of between 10% and 20%, and five countries had a drop of less than 10%. In only three countries (Hungary, Nigeria, and Turkey) was there an increase or no change in the percentage of people who think homosexuality is never justifiable.

In terms of gender, females tended to be more accepting of homosexuality than males, with 53% of women and 59% of men calling it "never justifiable." Younger generations were more accepting of homosexuality, with 52% of the youngest calling it "never justifiable," compared with 55% of the middle and 61% of the oldest generations. Education and income both tended to make people more accepting of homosexuality. With increasing education, the percentage saying homosexuality is never justifiable dropped from 63% to 55% to 46%, whereas with increasing income it dropped from 63% to 57% to 50%. Values also strongly correlated with attitudes toward homosexuality; 68% of materialists, but only 36% of postmaterialists, said that it is never justifiable.

TABLE 6.13

Tolerance (of Homosexuality)

Please tell me for each of the following statements whether you think it can always be justified, never be justified, or something in between: Homosexuality

Never justifiable (%)

(WVS: V208; EVS: V2…)

Country	Wave		Gender		Age			Education			Income			Values			RANKING Country
	1990	2000	Male	Female	16-29	30-49	50+	Lower	Middle	Upper	Lower	Middle	Upper	Mat	Mixed	Postm.	
Albania	na	81	81	81	70	83	88	82	82	74	84	79	80	83	80	74	Egypt
Algeria	na	93	93	94	92	93	96	95	93	92	94	94	91	95	92	95	Bangladesh
Argentina	63	40	45	35	32	37	52	50	28	23	49	41	30	53	42	27	Jordan
Armenia	na	71	75	68	60	75	83	87	71	67	68	73	75	74	70	58	Pakistan
Australia	na	31	38	25	23	25	46	49	30	17	40	33	16	51	32	24	Zimbabwe
Austria	52	26	30	23	13	22	37	37	19	5	36	27	21	54	26	19	Indonesia
Azerbaijan	na	89	90	88	86	90	93	94	90	85	93	91	80	91	85	95	Tanzania
Bangladesh	na	99	99	99	98	100	99	100	98	98	100	98	100	99	99	99	Iran
Belarus	84	57	57	58	39	59	72	73	53	50	62	58	48	66	51	40	Algeria
Belgium	46	27	31	23	19	20	36	41	26	16	37	30	16	34	26	17	China
Bosnia and Herz.	na	72	76	69	63	72	82	85	72	63	80	75	64	74	72	60	Uganda
Brazil	73	56	62	50	54	55	61	63	52	46	61	56	51	67	52	45	Azerbaijan
Bulgaria	81	60	64	56	49	55	70	75	57	42	74	61	45	67	53	61	Hungary
Canada	40	27	29	24	21	22	35	42	26	15	32	28	17	31	29	18	Montenegro
Chile	78	37	41	34	33	34	46	45	36	24	43	38	25	44	38	22	Turkey
China	93	92	93	91	87	93	96	93	93	86	88	95	94	92	92	88	Georgia
Colombia	na	61	62	60	54	63	72	72	59	48	69	62	51	67	60	51	Vietnam
Croatia	na	70	71	69	54	69	81	78	68	53	78	68	67	77	71	61	El Salvador
Czech Republic	39	27	31	23	18	21	37	33	21	15	32	28	19	36	25	19	Albania
Denmark	44	21	27	15	6	12	39	31	9	6	29	17	12	41	22	6	Romania
Dominican Rep.	na	53	57	50	49	58	70	77	63	46	62	50	38	53	52	49	Lithuania
Egypt	na	100	100	100	100	100	100	100	100	100	100	100	100	100	100	100	Nigeria
El Salvador	na	81	83	79	75	83	88	86	79	69	87	80	76	na	na	na	Latvia
Estonia	78	57	60	54	42	51	71	61	56	53	62	64	51	59	55	49	Macedonia
Finland	36	29	38	20	17	21	44	38	19	15	32	31	22	33	28	25	Serbia
France	42	23	28	18	12	17	35	30	15	12	29	23	20	33	22	11	Bosnia and Herz.
Georgia	na	82	84	80	79	81	87	87	83	76	88	84	71	80	83	80	Armenia
Germany	50	19	21	17	10	12	29	27	11	16	25	17	12	27	17	10	Ukraine
Great Britain	42	25	30	19	12	20	33	28	20	21	24	28	17	na	na	na	India
Greece	na	24	29	20	13	24	51	60	27	15	33	24	19	30	24	18	Russian Fed.
Hungary	85	88	89	88	86	87	91	91	86	76	89	87	87	89	88	78	Croatia
Iceland	30	12	17	7	3	11	23	15	13	3	16	12	9	15	11	7	Taiwan
India	94	71	71	70	66	74	70	67	75	74	70	67	73	76	72	83	Moldova
Indonesia	na	95	94	96	91	95	97	97	95	93	97	94	94	97	94	89	Venezuela
Iran	na	94	94	94	92	96	96	95	95	92	95	95	92	97	93	92	Colombia
Ireland	52	37	39	35	20	26	62	64	26	15	60	34	21	46	38	19	Malta
Israel	na	38	39	37	32	36	46	61	37	23	51	39	19	51	34	35	Poland
Italy	49	30	35	26	17	22	44	45	19	16	43	26	19	49	30	18	Bulgaria
Japan	61	30	33	27	12	18	49	50	30	21	36	26	30	35	27	22	Belarus
Jordan	na	98	99	98	98	98	99	99	99	96	98	100	97	99	97	96	Estonia
Korea, South	91	53	56	50	29	58	69	79	59	41	56	53	49	56	52	34	Peru
Latvia	84	77	81	74	64	73	86	85	75	70	83	76	70	82	75	64	Brazil
Lithuania	89	78	79	77	61	76	92	92	73	72	89	77	73	81	78	76	Singapore
Luxembourg	na	20	23	18	12	18	29	32	15	14	22	26	15	26	21	12	Mexico
Macedonia	na	76	80	71	66	78	80	89	72	62	87	73	65	72	76	78	Dominican Rep.
Malta	na	61	61	60	44	57	76	77	57	39	74	59	51	69	59	37	Korea, South
Mexico	58	53	57	49	40	56	66	65	43	29	59	52	44	64	51	33	Puerto Rico
Moldova	na	65	66	63	51	68	73	74	65	57	81	66	49	66	65	43	South Africa
Montenegro	na	86	88	83	81	82	93	93	85	71	93	86	83	92	81	73	Uruguay
Morocco	na	na	na	na	na	na	na	na	na	na	na	na	na	na	na	na	Portugal
Netherlands	20	7	9	5	6	5	9	14	5	3	11	5	3	12	7	5	Northern Ireland
New Zealand	na	30	39	22	18	21	42	40	32	17	38	28	21	41	30	18	Slovenia
Nigeria	73	78	78	77	78	78	74	75	79	80	79	76	76	76	79	78	Argentina
Northern Ireland	65	42	46	39	31	33	55	52	38	26	49	41	26	56	43	26	Israel
Norway	53	27	36	19	18	22	41	39	26	18	na	na	na	36	28	9	Chile
Pakistan	na	96	96	97	94	97	99	98	94	95	99	96	94	97	96	92	Ireland
Peru	na	57	55	58	53	60	59	62	59	50	65	51	49	57	56	59	United States
Philippines	na	29	28	30	28	29	32	26	30	32	31	31	24	29	30	24	Australia
Poland	81	60	65	55	38	59	74	72	50	34	67	55	54	64	57	64	Italy
Portugal	67	43	43	44	30	41	55	50	35	22	58	42	37	49	42	32	Japan
Puerto Rico	na	50	55	48	36	46	61	67	56	45	60	52	43	61	51	45	New Zealand
Romania	87	80	81	78	70	75	91	92	75	71	88	83	73	86	77	57	Philippines
Russian Fed.	89	71	73	69	56	69	83	80	71	64	77	72	63	73	68	70	Finland
Serbia	na	75	77	73	60	70	87	86	77	55	84	74	68	81	71	56	Norway
Singapore	na	55	58	52	48	62	61	58	56	41	54	59	50	58	54	48	Czech Republic
Slovakia	na	24	23	25	18	21	33	33	22	9	32	26	18	27	21	14	Canada
Slovenia	66	42	47	37	26	42	53	59	40	18	54	43	25	59	39	33	Belgium
South Africa	78	48	51	43	51	45	46	48	46	60	47	48	47	52	47	30	Austria
Spain	46	17	18	16	7	10	28	24	10	9	25	12	13	25	16	5	Great Britain
Sweden	45	9	12	5	5	5	15	21	5	4	10	12	4	17	10	3	Greece
Switzerland	49	17	20	15	11	14	25	25	16	13	23	19	11	21	19	8	Slovakia
Taiwan	na	65	66	65	52	66	74	70	72	58	68	67	63	66	65	65	France
Tanzania	na	94	95	94	96	93	96	93	97	95	93	96	93	96	95	96	Denmark
Turkey	85	85	84	86	79	89	91	91	80	59	90	88	69	87	86	80	Luxembourg
Uganda	na	91	92	90	90	92	94	93	90	93	92	94	90	91	92	86	Germany
Ukraine	na	71	74	68	53	71	82	81	72	65	78	67	65	73	68	69	Switzerland
United States	57	32	34	30	28	35	31	45	33	26	36	29	29	38	33	27	Spain
Uruguay	na	46	49	44	35	38	57	55	33	32	49	47	41	56	46	33	Iceland
Venezuela	na	62	63	60	59	62	66	69	64	47	64	60	62	66	62	52	Sweden
Vietnam	na	82	83	81	83	78	87	82	83	76	80	86	79	90	79	83	Netherlands
Zimbabwe	na	96	95	97	95	97	97	98	94	92	98	95	92	98	95	99	
Total	63	56	59	53	52	55	61	63	55	46	63	57	50	68	53	36	Total

Final Remarks and Guides for Future Research

The analysis focuses on the three key dimensions (economic, political, and social) and the three key associated values: work, autonomy, and trust. In *cultures of achievement* people consider *work* as a prize; they are high on *autonomy* and *dissent*; and their radius of *trust* is wide. Their strength lies in the economic dimension and their weakness in the social dimension. In *cultures of honor* the opposite is true: *work* is considered a *deserved* punishment; they are high on obedience and low on *autonomy and dissent*; and the radius of *trust* is tight, constrained to relatives and close friends only. Their strength lies in the political dimension and their weakness in the economic dimension. These two polar opposites leave *cultures of joy* somewhere in between both ends: neither too committed to *achievement* nor too committed to *honor*. They pursue an existence much less driven by anguish and anxiety.

Another element to keep in mind is that although a culture may be dominant at the national level because of the legal system, institutions, and religious roots in which the country was founded, there are nevertheless regional variations due to migration inflows and the resulting ethnic origins of the population. In the case of the United States, it belongs to the achievement group at the national level, but the South has pockets of *honor* culture, and the coastal areas are more influenced by *joy*.

At the personal level, an individual can also display either a consistent and monolithic profile or any paradoxical combination of values: socially *joy*; psychologically *achievement*; rationally *freethinking*; or any other combination. Such an individual will be subject to the tensions arising from the inherent contradictions that ensue. He or she will have to choose which type of rationality to employ in any given situation, depending on the circumstances.

Returning to the national level, all three cultures show upsides and downsides. This book has concentrated mainly on the upsides, but a thorough exploration of the downsides is also important. Some worrying signs among *cultures of achievement* are the high anxiety rates (Wilkinson and Pickett, 2010, p. 33), as well as suicide and rape rates, long studied and highly prevalent in some East Asian and Nordic countries; also, the absurdity of constant American killings of students and young children. But perhaps more worrisome are the emerging trends in Japan of female rejection of marriage (*The Economist*, August 20, 2011), or even worse, youth abandonment of sex (Waldman, 2013).

In *cultures of honor* the values of obedience, loyalty, and respect for the extended family are very strong. A recent *Romeo and Juliet*-type tragedy in Afghanistan emphasizes it (*New York Times*, June 8, 2014, p. 130). Such behavior translates into a political demand for an often unaccountable political leader of the town, all the way up to the region or the nation. The levels of authority continue to ascend until they reach the concept of God as supreme authority, quite similarly to Europe's utter reverence for the Pope in the Middle Ages. In the *cultures of joy* the people are more likely to err on the side of lack of achievement than to commit excesses for the sake of honor. But all this exploration will have to wait for further research.

Consequently, *cultures of achievement* are oriented toward the physical environment, economic activity, and the production of goods and services. Incentives reward pragmatic and utilitarian actions; individuals in these cultures are highly conscientious of the most efficient usage of time, hence punctuality and productivity are quite high priorities; independence and innovation are highly valued, which leads to a high sense of and pride in agency. Along with these qualities there is a strong emphasis on learning and studying. However, these advantages also have some downsides: the social and economic pressure force people to live under a permanent time obsession, reinforced by feelings of guilt when they fall behind in their duties. Hence, they have relatively less leisure and less ability to enjoy relaxed social interactions with family, relatives, and friends. Family relations are relatively more distant.

On the other hand, *cultures of honor* are oriented toward the social environment, the enjoyment of human interaction, and relaxed living, even in precarious economic conditions; families and close friends tend to get together more frequently and in more intimate circumstances; kind manners and charm are appreciated, and there is no great sense of urgency at work; hence, the concept of time is quite relaxed. But there are some downsides: breaking a promise or other form of social misconduct is seen as damaging to the honor of those involved (person, family, group, or nation); the relaxed sense of time leads to unpunctuality and unproductiveness; distrust of others and demanding obedience and loyalty are very high; because the physical environment does not play much of a role, the individual's sense of agency and independence are low; and because work is perceived as a deserved punishment, innovation and learning are less common.

PART IV

Cultural Change

When comparing the time scales of genetic and cultural evolution, it is useful to bear in mind that we today—every one of us—can *easily* understand many ideas that were simply unthinkable *by the geniuses* in our grandparents' generation!

—DANIEL DENNETT, *DARWIN'S DANGEROUS IDEA*, P. 377

7

Six Agents of Cultural Change

Cultures are not static; they keep slowly changing all the time, adjusting to the variability of circumstances by generational replacement. But the change can be either virtuous or vicious, depending on the decisions made in response to those circumstances. This chapter discusses six agents of cultural transmission and change: family, school, religion, media, leadership, and the law.

The monopoly that *families* held on the dissemination of values for millennia was transformed by the appearance of organized *religion* starting in the eighth century BC. The resulting family–church duopoly reigned for centuries, until the expansion of *education* and of public schooling during the industrial revolution narrowed the scope of the church's influence. In addition, exchanges of opinion within groups (which would eventually become *media*), structures of *leadership*, and systems of rules (which would evolve into *laws*) allowed societies to adapt ideas and structures to suit changing conditions.

The power of the *media* to transmit values was boosted by the introduction of the printing press in the 15th century, and later by the advent of the movies (1896), radio (1909), television (1948), the Internet (1992), and now social media (2004), outcompeting families, schools, and churches on value dissemination to children and youth. The impact of *leadership* and *the law* on children and youth, however, is remote and indirect, because it runs mainly through adults and institutions.

The discussion that follows shows that the structure of values within the individual is influenced by the combined actions of these six agents of cultural transmission. It also presents some cases of cultural change in Japan, Turkey, Singapore, Ireland, Spain, Mexico, and Colombia, as well as a typology of values.

The Power of Family

For thousands of years, *families* were responsible for passing knowledge, values, skills, and customs to new generations. Crucially, these cultural transmissions contained the two forces that move the world: ideas and structures.

Throughout most of the world, parents continue to be the most important transmitters of values, habits, beliefs, lifestyles, and social norms. However, in less developed societies, or in severe conditions of poverty or excessive violence, there is less likelihood that the family structure will survive; indeed, in many cases, children in such societies are left to fend for themselves in the streets. At the same time, the stereotypical nuclear family structure of a father, mother, and two children is also disappearing from postindustrial societies, albeit for different reasons. In the United States, for example, nuclear families of two parents and two children, allegedly *typical*, comprise only 12.2% of families as of 2010 (US Census Bureau, 2012, table 64).[1] The causes for these changes are connected to demographic transitions, to the incorporation of women into the labor force and to an increase in their empowerment, as well as to the cultural shifts that give legitimacy to couples without children, to single mothers, and to the idea of an independent life.

In our species, the capacity for learning as well as for expressing elevated intelligence becomes evident around the 18-month mark. The innate ability to identify similarities and differences and to identify what is known and unknown first manifests itself in the construction of identity: children first recognize traits they share with their family members, and later, similarities with a particular gender.

Family identity and *gender identity* are topics of importance in the formation of values, and particularly for the notions of obedience, autonomy-dissent, and trust. These three values lay the foundation for children's understanding of democracy, fairness, prosperity, and justice.

An examination of large families shows that children absorb ideas in different and sometimes unique ways. Parents who hope to pass their own behavior patterns to their children typically find that the effect of their teachings varies widely.

Studies reveal that even children as young as 18 months old begin to assimilate the repetitive behaviors of their family members, particularly those exhibited in emotional displays (Kagan, 2010b, p. 2). These behaviors can be reinforced or curtailed by mechanisms of punishment and reward. In traditional families, the burden of transmitting behavioral patterns is largely borne by the mother, as it is she who typically spends the most time with the children, but that is rapidly changing as more fathers take on caregiving responsibilities.

Although parents are undoubtedly cultural agents—that is, transmitters of ideas, beliefs, concepts, attitudes, values, and the like—what they transmit is profoundly influenced by the structural conditions in which the family lives. Structural conditions may include whether the child is an only child; whether he is older or younger than his siblings; whether both parents are present; whether grandparents, aunts, uncles, or other relatives reside in the same house; what level of education the parents achieved; how much money the parents earn; whether the family lives in a rural, urban, or suburban setting; whether the parents belong to any religious group; whether the family lives in a country that is rich or poor, democratic or authoritarian. Under normal conditions, parents raise their children using the repertoire they learned from their own parents—a repertoire filtered through the light of their own experiences and modified to suit the dominant conditions.

In a hypothetical average family, and mainly out of social prejudice, boys will more readily absorb behaviors exhibited by older males, and girls will more readily absorb behaviors exhibited by older females. Both male and female children closely observe how adults treat each other; how they treat younger people; how they encourage others to treat them; how adults react to threats and/or the unexpected (thunder, lightning, danger, etc.); what type of games and tasks they expect children to engage in; what reactions they anticipate the children having; who wields authority within the family; the degrees of participation allowed in the family's decision-making processes; the honesty of older people when dealing with others; how responsible they are in their work; how much discipline they need to meet their obligations; what items constitute financial priorities; and so on.

A traditional family in a *culture of honor* teaches children that the father is the head of the household, and that he expects to be attended to by his wife and daughter(s) but not by his son. Similarly, children will see that they are compelled to play games that are typical for their gender. They will see that girls are allowed to cry, but boys are not. They will see that while the mother may participate in decision-making, it is the father who ultimately makes decisions. They will see that both expect total obedience from the children.

Children whose families live in a *culture of achievement* are less likely to see top-down demonstrations of authority at home and are more likely to see horizontal interactions. The higher the level of education achieved by the parents, the less likely it is that the children will play gender-specific games. The family's decision-making processes are more inclusive, and the children participate with greater creativity and less deference. Parents are more open with strangers. If they are given a choice between prolonging enjoyment and completing unfinished work, they typically choose work. Parents promote taking personal responsibility and eschew excuses. Overall, leisure (i.e., recreation, pleasure, enjoyment) and camaraderie are subordinate to job, school, and study.

The point here is that parents make no special effort to pass their own values to their children; instead, they merely go about their lives and unconsciously replicate the behaviors of their own parents. One Sunday in 1996 in Princeton, New Jersey, my wife and I drove with our two younger children—Pamela, 10, and Nicolas, 9—to buy a book at the now defunct Borders bookstore. On such trips we used to sing, joke, laugh, hug, touch, and talk a lot. Clearly, we had an intense, close, and noisy relationship, the kind we experienced with our own parents. After a while browsing books, we entered the Borders cafeteria and sat at a table. There we came upon a scene that, while common in the United States, is rather rare in cultures of joy. Another family of four was sitting nearby. In sharp contrast to us, they did not talk to or even look at each other at all. Instead, they were reading, separately and in total silence. We looked at each other and thought: What's going on with this family's communication? We were shocked!

A more frequent alternative that replicates the pattern of education described in the preceding may be found in the single-mother families who remain embedded in large families (i.e., those with grandparents, aunts, uncles, and cousins in the immediate vicinity), which is a typical circumstance in poor circles within cultures of *honor*. In these cases, children treat the mother and/or grandmother with veneration. When the children move on and become parents themselves, they carry with them behaviors of the previous generation.

The importance of good parenting practices is recognized in many countries, and consequently many societies offer training courses for first-time parents that cover every imaginable topic. In the United States alone there are more than 50,000 such courses (Kagan, 2006, p. 43). It should be noted, though, that their principal emphasis is not on the transmission of values, but on aspects of health, nutrition, security, emotional and cognitive development, the importance of reading to children before bed, the importance of openly expressing affection, and other such topics. In cultures oriented toward traditional values and toward *honor*, groups that train parents are often influenced by religious doctrines or even notions of self-help: they more frequently promote the sense of predestination, prayer before bed, and the sacredness of the family bond.

Any family will inevitably pass on to its children the realities of its existence. As a family's conditions change, its dominant values will also change. For instance, a family that moves from a rural area to an urban area will necessarily adjust its values. Sparsely populated rural areas promote little human interaction but extensive contact with nature. People living in such areas are therefore less exposed to diverse ideas, and as a result are often less tolerant of viewpoints differing from their own. Densely populated urban areas, however, typically cause people to want to fit in, which leads to *value adjustment*—a phenomenon also seen in families that move from their home countries to nations with entirely different cultures. Value adjustments may take years or even generations, but they will certainly occur eventually. Interestingly, children adopt new values more quickly than their parents, often doing so as soon as they become part of a school environment.

The power of family remains through *identity*, which will endure in children as they mature through *peer pressure* to fit in with the group at school or in the neighborhood, through sharing the support of a sports team or musical group or a political party or an ethnicity or a religion, all the way up to identification with a national anthem or a *flag* as symbol of nationality.

The sort of upward social mobility that can be brought about by education or the attainment of wealth might precipitate a more rapid change in values, but the process of value adjustment is basically the same.

All of this underscores the fact that preparing for parenting is a gradual, structural process that may be enhanced through direct training, religion, and media products (including health campaigns, movies, soap operas, etc.). If educational, religious, and media messages are aligned, families begin to internalize encouragement from their environments—and when this occurs, the transmission of consistent values is a natural consequence. However, this alignment rarely happens, and when it does, it is most likely mere coincidence.

The Power of School

After families, school systems are the second most important source of value transmission and change throughout the world. Traditionally, the influence of schools has started at around five years of age; however, as more mothers enter the job market and children attend day care or nursery schools at younger ages, the influence of caretakers and teachers is expanding. First, simply by teaching reading and writing to children, schools open a life-changing experience. Additionally, along with the formal knowledge and social skills needed to prepare children for adult life, schools also transmit the underlying societal values.

Modern education is especially useful at facilitating the rise of an individual in society: in just five or six years of primary school, an individual gains knowledge that it took humans 10,000 years to acquire. The next five or six years of middle and high school prepare the individual to navigate the complexities of the modern world. The final four to 10 years of college and graduate studies prepare the individual to innovate, as well as to expand the knowledge base.

Some would characterize modern educational processes as invasive and disrespectful of the cultural identities of some groups (as is, for example, an education that indoctrinates one into a political ideology or a specific religion). Debates like those surrounding bilingual education or teaching evolutionary theory or global warming in US schools illustrate this point. These views may simply reflect resistance to change or ideological positions that obstruct social mobility. Furthermore, scientific and humanist education allows for dissent and rebuttal, and encourages the construction of solid, verifiable arguments.

In 1946 the United Nations established what is today known as the United Nations Children's Fund (UNICEF), one of the most important international organizations for the advancement of education. Its original purpose was to help provide emergency food and healthcare to children in war-torn countries. Although its mission creates ample opportunities to enhance education in the world's developing countries, its low budget (US $3.7 billion in 2010, equivalent to US $0.53 per capita worldwide) limits its scope and potential impact.

In addition to institutional and budgetary problems that inhibit the spread of education worldwide, we must also note cultural difficulties: many countries give little importance to schooling within their respective value systems.[2] However, this does not necessarily depend upon limited wealth. In the opposite direction, most Christian Orthodox nations, for example, as well as Cuba and the Indian state of Kerala, boast high education levels as a public policy decision, despite suffering the effects of harsh poverty.

However, schools tend to perpetuate the cultural patterns of their societies—especially when national education systems discourage the appropriation of standards and practices used in other countries. In *authoritarian* societies, teaching techniques typically reproduce authoritarian dynamics: obedience, discipline, and rote memorization are emphasized, while questions, dissent, and critical thinking are effectively discouraged.

Values transmission runs also from school extracurricular activities, such as sports or the arts. Again in Princeton, New Jersey, in 1996, my wife and I took our children Pamela and Nicolas to join the school soccer team, assuming it would be a *fun* activity to share, according to our cultural mindset. What a surprise we got when the coach recited a long list of duties and strict discipline the whole family had to commit to in order to *achieve success* in the competitions. We reluctantly agreed for their sake. Clearly, the coach took away all the fun for us. We were shocked!

Among the many reactions to the traditional and authoritarian teaching style are methods developed by a variety of pedagogues, such as Pestalozzi in Switzerland (1780), Fröbel in Germany (1837), Montessori in Italy (1897), and Steiner (Waldorf schools) in Austria (1919), which accentuate respect for the child, exercising freedom within certain parameters, and encouraging values of participation, independence, tolerance, respect, autonomy, dissent, and trust.[3] However, one problem with the international replication of teaching best practices is that almost all countries have politically powerful teachers' unions that resist change. In some countries, the existence of strong parents' associations that link families with schools sometimes helps to alleviate such resistance.

One effort to improve education is through standardized testing, which is somewhat useful for evaluating the educational achievements of states, cities, schools, or particular demographics. SATs, ACTs, and other private tests are required in the United States for college admission. Nevertheless, the data stemming from these exams is of limited usefulness because it does not allow for international comparison.

Since 2000, the Organisation for Economic Co-operation and Development (OECD) has been conducting the Program for International Student Assessment (PISA). The PISA test measures the achievement of 15-year-olds in reading, mathematics, and science. The introduction of this comparative international evaluation is increasing pressure for the betterment of education in various countries.

The 2013 PISA test (covers 75 countries and economies [34 OECD country members and 41 non-OECD member economies]). The test shows an overall average for the 34 OECD countries of 493 points, ranking students in Shanghai (556), Korea (539), and Finland (536) the highest, while US students (500) ranked 17th and Kyrgyzstan (314) ranked 75th.[4] How are countries like Korea and Finland able to generate such high scores? Are their teachers better paid? Do they spend more money on education? Do they have superior curricula? Apparently, the answers to these questions have less to do with the characteristics of education systems or education funding, and more to do with the social prestige enjoyed by teachers and the quality of educators that such prestige attracts.

Finally, the school years are also accompanied by negative forces such as bullying, low-quality television, the Internet, peer pressure, and so on, which make the role of parents and teachers essential in helping children navigate to adulthood. Quality education is not only important for the transmission of values to the youth, but it is also associated with higher levels of development for the country as a whole.

The Power of Religion

This section is dedicated to an agent of cultural change whose influence is felt around the world: religion. The origins of religious sentiments can be traced back about 40 millennia when humans became aware of *death* (Diamond, 1997, p. 39). *Belief systems* first developed in response to the needs and fears of the group, to explain the occurrences of everyday life: day, night, sun, moon, stars, snow, thunder, wind, fire, and so on.

The development of writing in the third millennium BC allowed the formation of more elaborate belief systems, which in turn gave rise to the religious and philosophical explosion that began around the 8th century BC. Table 7.1 shows the main eight religions today and their influence on some indicators of development.

The world's eight main systems of beliefs in terms of their influence today—Catholicism, Protestantism, Orthodoxy, Islam, Judaism, Hinduism, Buddhism, and Confucianism—may expand to as many as 20 if other belief systems with fewer followers are included (Barrett et al., 2001). In turn, the count of religions more than doubles if national faiths are incorporated, and can further subdivide into hundreds of denominations and religious groups.

When comparing the world's major religions through these statistics, it becomes clear that some have more positive effects on the indicators than others. For example, Protestant and Orthodox nations boast 99% literacy rates, while Islamic nations show 65% literacy and Hindu nations only 57%. In Catholic countries, only 16% of people believe that others can be trusted, while in Confucian nations 51% hold that belief. In the Human Development Index, Judaism in Israel achieves a favorable score of 22, while Buddhism and Hinduism are at the opposite end of the spectrum, with scores of 92 and 115, respectively.

Correlation is not causation, and the high literacy rates in Protestant countries might be due to their comparatively substantial wealth, while literacy rates in Orthodox countries might be connected to the communist emphasis on education. Similarly, low levels of trust in Catholic countries could be an effect of rampant income inequality. However, the data are consistent with the general findings of this book.

Many of the practices and teachings of religions were designed to respond to some need that existed at a particular historic moment. For instance, practices of hygiene and health in Judaism, like washing hands (Leviticus 15:11) or not mixing dairy and meat (Exodus 34:26), were developed in order to prevent the spread of disease. Confession and celibacy in Catholicism were instituted in the 13th century in response to the financial crisis of the Vatican (Laveaga, 2006). The

TABLE 7.1

Influence of Religions on Development*

Religions in Countries (over 50% of Members or Largest Minority Religion)

Religion	1. Population, millions (total)	2. HDI Rank (average)	3. Literacy % (average)	4. Freedom House (average)	5. GDP per capita (average)	6. GINI (average)	7. Corruption (average)
Protestant	621	48	95	91	$31.4	36	69
Jewish (Israel)	8	16	97	81	$31.9	39	61
Confucian	1,622	47	96	53	$31.8	41	60
Buddhist	163	121	88	42	$18.8	38	30
Catholic	1,039	78	90	75	$17.1	44	46
Islam: Arab	302	85	83	31	$20.4	37	38
Islam: Non-Arab	1,190	147	68	36	$6.2	38	28
Orthodox	344	68	94	60	$13.7	32	39
Hindu	1,272	147	62	62	$2.6	33	34

* Based on Harrison (2006), p. 88, updated for this research.

1: Total population (millions), World Bank World Development Indicators, 2011 or latest available data

2: Human Development Index, UN Development Programme, 2012 (Human Development Reports); lower rank = more developed

3: Percentage of adults who are literate, World Bank World Development Indicators and CIA Factbook, latest available data

4: Freedom in the World Sub-scores (Civil Liberties and Political Rights), 2013; higher rank = more free

5: GDP per capita, PPP in current international dollars, WB, World Development Indicators, 2012 or latest available data

6: A measure of income inequality that technically ranges from 0 to 100, WB, World Development Indicators, latest available data and supplemented by data from CIA Factbook; smaller value = more equal

7: Transparency International Corruption Per ception Index, 2013; higher values = "cleaner"

importance placed on women's chastity and fidelity stemmed from males' desire to ensure the purity of their bloodlines (Engels, 1884, p. 92).

The conditions that brought about such practices have changed over time. Although they no longer serve their original purpose, they continue to be part of religious practice today. Religions become rigid because of the paradigms set in place by the dogma that erected them. To change a traditional belief or practice is seen as challenging the infallibility of God, or the Prophet, or the religious chief, as the case may be. Hierarchical churches (as the Catholic and Orthodox), particularly in those countries where they reach the majority of the population, are a very powerful political force—most of the time, dedicated to preserving the status quo.

Earlier in this chapter, I referred to parents and families as the most significant and powerful transmitters of values from one generation to the next.

The second most important influence on the axiological base of an individual today remains schools and teachers—although the media is vying to take over second place any day. In third place comes religion, which in many countries still substitutes for public schools. The full effect of religion on the individual begins as maturation develops with the onset of adolescence (Schwartz, 2012, p. 104).

However, religion is powerful, because it acts not just directly on the individual, but also indirectly as the institutional root and background, as well as axiological frame, of the other five agents of cultural transmission. The history of world religions illustrates the power of ideas to mobilize entire societies.[5] Today the advancing religious movements in Latin America and Africa—for example, the Evangelical and Pentecostal movements—are extremely powerful.

Most philosophies and religions began from a *teacher's* life narrative and lessons: Socrates, Confucius, Buddha, Jesus, or Muhammad. Frequently, these lessons are summarized in short lists of values. An example is the biblical Ten Commandments of the Judeo-Christian tradition (as taken from the Protestant Bible): (1) You shall have no other gods but me; (2) You shall not make unto you any graven images; (3) You shall not take the name of the Lord your God in vain; (4) You shall remember the Sabbath and keep it Holy; (5) Honor your *father and mother*; (6) You shall not *murder*; (7) You shall not commit *adultery*; (8) You shall not *steal*; (9) You shall not bear *false* witness; and (10) You shall not covet anything that *belongs to your neighbor*. The first four reinforce the faith, and the last six refer to day-to-day ethics.

However, it is difficult to explain differences in human behavior around the world with these Ten Commandments because Jews, Protestants, Catholics, and in most ways Muslims all share these values. Similar sentiments appear in the *Analects* of Confucius, the teachings of Buddha, and Aristotle's *Nicomachean Ethics*. It is not then the content of the *teachings* that matters, but their interpretation and usage that makes the difference.

In summary, religions as doctrines carry a positive educational weight, but when they turn into international business or into political parties, they can end up as powerful political actors quite far away from their original mission. Hence, religion lies at the root of culture formation, alongside law and language.

The Power of the Media

Religion is not the only agent of cultural transmission with the power to trigger collective action and shape public opinion; communications media wield this power as well. Social changes instigated by the increased availability of information and the widespread sharing of knowledge have occurred since mid-15th century AD, the date that marks the introduction of the *printing press*. Perhaps the most prominent examples of social changes prompted by communications media are the Lutheran and Calvinist Reformation in the 16th century and the French Enlightenment in the 18th.

Europe's ideological wars and the Americas' wars for independence were in great part produced by this ideological awakening. But if one speaks of cultural transmission—that is, of determining which values to promote and which to stifle in the modern world—religions, like the media, confront a similar problem: they lack a clear understanding of what to do. Religions uncritically propose doctrines of moral or social value to attract as many followers as possible, whereas communications media are merely guided by business concerns to achieve audience expansion and financial success (Schonfeld, 2006, p. 318).

Since 1987, when the *Fairness Doctrine* introduced in 1949 was eliminated,[6] media outlets have been free to advocate the political opinions of their owners. Outstanding examples of these *media wars* in the United States are two cable news channels: Fox and MSNBC. However, their impact on political polarization, particularly among younger, educated populations, seems limited (Prior, 2007).

Analyzing the transmission of values by the media has become increasingly complicated and difficult, as technological advances have transformed communications into a worldwide industry with the power to inform almost instantaneously. However, there exist important measurements showing that in many countries soap operas, entertainment novels, plays, television series, and the like can have a strong impact, either negative or positive, on the public. Consider education on health issues; or the use of the media in Hitler's Germany; or the Soviet Union's ideological goals; or the use of print and electronic media in political campaigns around the world today that may bend the truth and facts about issues.

Unlike religions, which are rigid, media are flexible and fluid, particularly in countries with free markets and strong competition. In order to attract readers, listeners, and viewers, they try to appeal to the tastes of the majority; unfortunately, in the battle for wider audiences, media often exploit the prurient interests and the fears of those people they seek to attract—horoscopes, vampires, and gossip about celebrities are hence common. While there are exceptions, such practices do not always serve the collective good.

Reese Schonfeld, founder of CNN, tells an excellent story of the global battle for cultural domination (Schonfeld, 2006, p. 305). He describes with extensive internal information the effects—both beneficial and detrimental—of electronic media. He laments how American television programs no longer try to be instructive as much as

> ... sensational, populated by vampires, voodoo, reincarnations, psychics, and miracles. Rich people seduce and backstab their way to even greater fortunes. Pleasure is everything, sex is routine and drug use is rampant. Evil triumphs as often as not, crimes go unpunished, and there is no moral compass—all in an attempt to attract the largest, youngest audience. (2006, p. 318)

Schonfeld also sees a formidable power to influence, even in the simple transmission of television images, which project distinctly Western values all over the world. His comments about cultural domination bring to mind the dialogue between Toyotomi Hideyoshi and the Spanish captain that led to the expulsion of the Christians from Japan in 1597. Hideyoshi asks how it was that Spain, which was so small, controlled such an extensive territory. The captain replied that ". . . His Very Catholic Majesty would first send our priests to Christianize the population, and these converts would then help the Spanish forces in their conquest" (Landes, 1999, p. 354).

By and large, however, cultural and ideological penetration comes about more through entertainment than news: soap operas, for example, are used around the world to transmit subliminal messages about health, education, and civic culture. Interestingly, the dominance enjoyed by Hollywood for much of the twentieth century is now challenged; the American film and television industries must now compete with Bollywood (India), Nollywood (Nigeria), and, with regard to the production of soap operas, Mexico, Brazil, and Colombia.

Finally, the growing media influence on youth has been impressive, and is a topic of considerable debate in the academic literature. Just consider, from a dated statistic, the amount of time young people spent in 2009 with electronic devices (10:45 hours a day) as a measure of the influence of communications media on the dissemination of values, as shown in Table 7.2.

The Power of Leadership

Parents, school, religion, and communications media have distinct influences and varying levels of importance during the course of a person's life. They are more relevant in childhood and adolescence, while local or national leadership,

TABLE 7.2
Youth and the media

	Among all 8- to 18-year-olds, average amount of time spent with each medium in a typical day:		
	2009	2004	1999
TV content	4:29[a]	3:51[b]	3:47[b]
Music/audio	2:31[a]	1:44[b]	1:48[b]
Computer	1:13[a]	1:02[b]	:27[c]
Video games	1:13[a]	:49[b]	:26[c]
Print	:38[a]	:43[ab]	:43[b]
Movies	:25[a]	:25[ab]	:18[b]
TOTAL MEDIA EXPOSURE	10:45[a]	8:33[b]	7:29[c]
Multitasking proportion	29%[a]	26%[a]	16%[b]
TOTAL MEDIA USE	7:38[a]	6:21[b]	6:19[b]

Victoria Rideout, Ulla Foehr, and Donald Roberts, *Generation M2: Media in the Lives of 8- to 18- Year Ol*ds. The Henry J. Kaiser Family Foundation, 2010, p. 2. Available at https://kaiserfamilyfoundation.files.wordpress.com/2013/04/8010.pdf.

as well as the law (discussed in next section), are more important in adult life. The leader of a group, a city, a region, or a country has the tools to introduce change in his or her environment (Lamm, 2006, p. 334), but those changes are typically ephemeral if they do not change the underlying culture: only rarely do they extend beyond the leader's term in office or outside his or her geography. One example of short-range but immediate change linked to a leader's behavior is encoded in a passage from an American commander in Iraq (Shultz, 2013). After having tried many solutions to achieve peace in the region, he walked through the middle of the town holding hands with the town leader. That ended the conflicts in that particular spot.

The following paragraphs review examples of cultural changes achieved by national political leaders in three different countries. However, business leaders can also trigger cultural change: think of Henry Ford or Steve Jobs, to name just two. Also, intellectual leaders can ignite change: think of Lenin or Friedrich Hayek (1899–1992). Role models from the arts, media, or sports can also trigger change, even more so in today's social media world—game-changing leaders can appear almost overnight, as the Tunisia and Egyptian Arab Spring movements of 2011 showed.

For changes promoted by political leaders to endure, it is generally necessary for them to be incorporated into the existing legal framework or set of rules. But even then, the next leader is usually empowered to reverse the changes made by his or her predecessor. Additionally, if changes made to rules on a low level (e.g., changes made to state laws) are not supported by rules at a higher level (e.g., federal laws), those changes can ultimately be reversed. In short, it is possible for a leader to directly effect cultural change, but this is the exception rather than the rule.

The dynamic actions of leaders and of law—the processes of negotiation, decision-making, and change—are all part of the interplay between ideas and structures. It is this interplay that generates new norms, which in turn generate new institutions—and institutions that endure become structures. And the interplay begins anew. Just as empires and religions have put their stamp on cultural geography, it is also possible to identify a positive cultural effect from leadership.

The three cases in the following sections about Japan, Turkey, and Singapore are examples of leadership in which major changes were achieved in a relatively short time, facilitated by unique historical circumstances. However, in most of the world today, the imposition of change by authoritarian leaders—or even worse, human rights violators—meets with ever less recognition from the international community.

LEADERSHIP SUCCESS CASE: THE MEIJI RESTORATION IN JAPAN (1867)

Ever since the second half of the 19th century, Japan has lived under the restoration of the emperor's power. It is a success story of collective leadership, embodied in and vouchsafed by the symbolic figure of the Emperor Meiji in 1867, who was only a teenager at the time.

The lineage of today's imperial family can be traced with certainty back to the 8th century (Diamond, 1997[2005], p. 443). Beginning in the year 1180, Japan was governed for the first time by a *shogun*, or commander-in-chief of the armed forces, but without dethroning the emperor; he was merely confined, along with his family, to his palaces, temples, and symbolic functions.

The last of these interregnums, the Tokugawa Shogunate (a feudal Japanese military government), governed Japan for two and a half centuries (1603–1868). The achievement of stability and political order during this period, which included the expulsion of foreigners, the mass execution of Japanese Christians, and isolation from the West, was very important for Japan's pre-industrial development. Nonetheless, those provinces that did maintain contact with the West could see the widening technological gap between the West and Japan, above all in terms of weaponry.

When Commodore Matthew Perry arrived in Japan in 1853 to propose the signing of a trade agreement, it was evident that the power of his four American ships and their cannons was far superior to anything in Japan. Upon his return the following year with twice as many ships, he obtained the shogun's signature for the treaty he sought in the Convention of Kanagawa. Europeans reached similar agreements in 1858.

These events heightened domestic tensions. In Satsuma province in 1862 and in Choshu province in 1864, there were incidents and confrontations with the West. These incidents led to an alliance between Satsuma and Choshu in favor of Emperor Komei, Meiji's father, with support from a broad coalition of other provinces.

Upon the death of his father, Emperor Meiji ascended the Japanese throne on February 3, 1867, at the age of 12, and reigned for 45 years. The last Tokugawa finally gave up power by the end of that year, thus ensuring the restoration.

An imperial Japanese delegation traveled for two years between 1871 and 1873, compiling the experiences and advancements of the world's most developed countries. The journey provided them with exclusive insights. Japan, unlike Europe or the United States, could pick and choose from among those technological and institutional innovations it wished to apply to its own development: postal service, standard time, public education, military organization, and the German legal system, among many others. Japan became a veritable sponge for innovations, which formed the basis of its rapid industrialization and the economic success it achieved from the beginning of the 20th century onward.

One example of this can be seen in the speed with which Japan brought electricity to its population, which surpassed that of the United States, as well as that of England.[7] In 1920 electricity reached 52% of Japanese manufacturers, while in the United States it was just 32%; the United States would not reach 53% coverage until 1929. England in 1924 had only 28% coverage (Landes, 1998, p. 381).

Something similar occurred in cotton and textiles, at that time the cutting edge of industrial technological development. Japan went from importing 62% of its textiles in 1886 to 0% in 1902, and by 1913 it was producing a quarter of the world's fabrics. It was the first non-Western country to industrialize. This explains the power play that led it to enter World War II on the German side, given its conflicts with China, which fought on the side of the Soviet Union and the Allied forces.

All of these dramatic developments were initiated by the constitutional, political, social, economic, and public policy changes introduced during the 45-year reign of Emperor Meiji.

LEADERSHIP SUCCESS CASE: TURKEY AND ATATÜRK (1923)

Another case study in which leadership succeeded in changing a society's culture and values is that of Turkey in 1923 under the guidance of Mustafa Kemal Pasha, later known as Atatürk.

Turkey lies in the region of the Earth that was home to some of its earliest civilizations and empires of antiquity. It formed part of the Assyrian, Babylonian, Greek, Roman, and Arab civilizations and, from 1299 onward, gave rise to the Ottoman Empire, after having adopted Islam between the 8th and 11th centuries. It consolidated its power with the fall of the Eastern Roman Empire and the conquest of Constantinople in 1453, which led to the Ottoman golden age (1453–1566), followed by another century of unrest (1566–1683).

Following its defeat at Vienna in 1683, the Ottoman Empire entered into a period of stagnation (1683–1827), harried by the Austro-Hungarian Empire and later by the Russians, until the independence of Greece and the Peloponnese. Its final stage (1828–1918) included an important hundred years of modernization, which laid the foundation for Atatürk's success. It then entered World War I (1914–1918) on the side of the Central Powers, whose defeat marked the end of the Ottoman Empire, when the Allied forces occupied Istanbul.

The Allied occupation sparked the formation of a nationalist movement under the leadership of Mustafa Kemal Pasha. He managed to expel the occupying forces in 1922 and establish the Republic of Turkey, which was recognized by the international community in 1923—hence the title given to him of Atatürk ("Father of the Turks").

The following list gives an idea of the enormous changes Turkey underwent. They would scarcely have been possible were it not for Atatürk's strong leadership and the modernizing trend that had already begun a century earlier:

1. Removing religious instruction from the public school curriculum (1924);
2. Prohibition of religious orders (1925);
3. Replacing the turban in favor of Western dress (1925);

4. Adopting the time zone system, whose Prime Meridian runs through Greenwich, England (1926);
5. Adoption of the Swiss Civil Code (1926);
6. Amending the Constitution to eliminate Islam's status as the state religion (1928);
7. Removal of the phrase "in the name of Allah" from the presidential and parliamentary oaths of office (1928);
8. Adoption of the Roman alphabet and prohibition of the Arabic alphabet (1928) (Esmer, 2006, p. 224).

LEADERSHIP SUCCESS CASE: SINGAPORE AND LEE KUAN YEW (1959)

Given the successful example set by Singapore, it is common to hear people asking why more developing countries don't follow its lead. Nonetheless, it is important to bear in mind the conditions that made its success possible and to wonder about their transferability.

The first condition is Singapore's strategic location on the sea routes between the South China Sea and the Indian Ocean. It was for this reason that the British East India Company founded a commercial port there in 1819. Second, the port's favorable conditions led it to grow within 50 years from a thousand Malay inhabitants and a few dozen Chinese families to a population of 100,000—mostly Chinese immigrants and some from India. Its demographic makeup today: 75% Chinese, 13% Malay, 9% Indian, and 3% other.

The third condition is a favorable mix of the Confucian work and study ethic with the flexibility and pragmatism of Anglo-Saxon common law, as seen in the country's culture and institutions. A fourth condition was the opportune time during which independence came to the city-state. It became self-governing in 1959 and fully independent from the United Kingdom in 1963—that is, during the postwar period and within the context of the Cold War, as embodied in that region by the Korean War (1950–1953), which led to the Peninsula's division between the Communist North and the capitalist South. For this reason, Singapore was seen as a high-value strategic, military, and commercial player.

A fifth condition was the rise to power of Lee Kuan Yew, who remained for nearly 40 years (1954–1992) as chairman of the official party, the PAP (People's Action Party), and for 30 years as prime minister of Singapore (1959–1988). Both of these tenures of leadership exemplified a certain kind of legitimacy, albeit one won through improvements made to the country's economy and a public perception of the prime minister and his family's honesty and competence, rather than through the ballot box.

The first four conditions for the case of Singapore are also applicable to some extent to Hong Kong, the East's other success story, which also tends to be regarded as a model to follow.

The Power of the Law

There are three main legal systems used in the world today: Anglo-Saxon common law, Roman civil law, and Islamic law.[8] Each of these traditions has a different impact on the development of the countries that adopt them. The more rigid and dogmatic the legal system, the more difficult it is to achieve development; on the other hand, flexibility and pragmatism facilitate it. The most rigid system is the Islamic, where the Koran is law; the most flexible is Anglo-Saxon common law, where judges practically make law orally, based on precedent. The Roman civil law system is an intermediate case, and varies according to the region in question: more flexible in its German and continental European tradition; more dogmatic in the French and, particularly, the Latin American tradition.

Institutions solidify the interaction between structures and culture—and the law, in turn, is the best way to build public institutions. The roots of the three different legal systems in the world (Anglo Saxon, Roman, and Islamic) exercise influence over countries much as their religious roots do.

The Middle East is the religious cradle of Judaism, Christianity, and Islam, just as Greece and Rome are the cultural and legal cradle of the West. Anglo-Saxon common law seems a distant reflection of the pre-Empire early laws of Rome, namely of the Roman *Republic*, influenced by Greek philosophy: no codes, oral, horizontal, informal, precedential. Continental French and German Roman law systems would be the product of the triumph of the Roman *Empire*: codified, written, vertical, authoritarian, rigid, formal: the same root, but at different times—one, republican; the other, imperial. Two millennia would pass before these two sources of modern Western legal systems would reveal their influence.

The two main structural forces that make the world go round today—demography and technology—would first have to reach critical mass. World population remained relatively stable during the first 17 centuries of our era. Without the pressure of population growth that leads to *new* conditions and problems, there was little demand for new solutions, and technology advanced very slowly then. Beginning with gradual improvements in hygiene, health, nutrition, material well-being, knowledge, and business, which gave rise to the demographic explosion of the 18th century, a technological takeoff also began: the industrial revolution.

The Anglo-Saxon legal system's deep roots are manifested in specific institutions, as shown in Figure 7.1 and these roots lead to outcomes associated with their origins (La Porta, Rafael et al., 2008, p. 292). The Roman civil law tradition is both the oldest and the most widespread. What is truly transcendent about the power of law comes not from its judicial forms, nor from its procedural efficiency, but from the set of cultural values that underlie each system, which are transmitted to the rest of the society through the law's application. Roman civil law is authoritarian, written, dogmatic, and rigid, with a formal vertical hierarchy. It is the heir of Rome's *imperial* period. Anglo-Saxon common law is egalitarian, flexible, and oral, with horizontal hierarchies, and seems to be the heir of the Roman *Republic*.

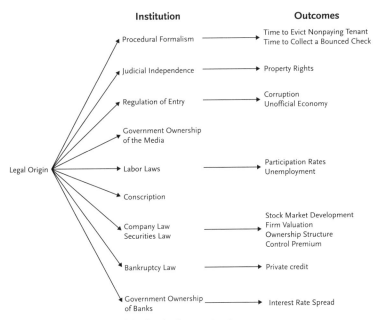

FIGURE 7.1 Anglo-Saxon legal origin, institutions and outcomes

Rafael La Porta et al. (2008). "The Economic Consequences of Legal Origins," *Journal of Economic Literature*, 46(2), p. 292.

The flexibility and pragmatism of the Anglo-Saxon legal system are reflected not only in law and business; they permeate behaviors throughout society. In 1973, as I was starting my master's degree at the University of Warwick in England—then newly opened and under construction—I looked out my window on the fourth floor of the library, and noticed that the paths which crisscrossed the central campus had not been paved. Curious, I asked one of the builders why this was, and he replied that they were waiting for the students to finish delineating—*with their footprints*—the best routes across campus, after which the builders would pave them. In my Latin mentality, I would have expected some engineer, working in his office away from the campus, to decide on the best routes for the paths, which students would then be forced to use.

A more modern, pragmatic, civilized legal system should be able to help economic development and employment. But it would not be able to alleviate insecurity or solve crime, much less organized crime. Law's application is reactive, not preventive. Laws cannot substitute for sound public policy and good government.

The main key to explaining countries' differing economic, political, and social circumstances lies in understanding how adaptable and flexible their legal systems are. Systems that rely on oral arguments and case law, such as the Anglo-Saxon common law model, are constantly being remade and are therefore more flexible. The laws that are applied are in reality the work of judges. Written and formal systems such as the Roman civil law and Islamic law are difficult to adapt. The legislators make laws. Greater flexibility, confidence, and ease of trade and business translate into economic and social improvement; greater rigidity translates into greater difficulty and lesser well-being (Sánchez, 2010). Hence, cultures of achievement are more flexible; cultures of honor more rigid; and cultures of joy are somewhere in between the two.

The preceding assessment has led international organizations to try to make known the importance of improving the quality of legal systems in different countries, with varying degrees of success. One case worthy of mention is that of Chile, which in the space of a decade successfully transitioned from an inquisitorial system belonging to the Roman (civil law) tradition to an adversarial system belonging to the Anglo-Saxon (common law) tradition.

An empirical study conducted some years ago by the World Bank, *Where Is the Wealth of Nations?* (2006), helps clarify the dilemma of the wealth of nations by identifying and quantifying the input of three sources of wealth: natural, produced, and intangible. **Natural wealth** is the sum total of natural resources in a given country: its land, seas, mountains, minerals, oil, water, forests, and so on. **Produced wealth** is that which derives from the primary sector of the economy (agriculture, livestock, and forestry), the secondary sector (industry and manufacturing), and the tertiary sector (services). **Intangible wealth** comes from the quality of education (one-third) and the quality of the justice system (two-thirds).

Through a review of 120 countries, the study found, on average across the world, that natural wealth accounts for 5% of the total, produced wealth for 18%, and intangible wealth for a remarkable 77%. Of course, these percentages vary between poor and rich countries. Natural wealth in the former accounts for 29%, whereas in the latter it accounts for just 2%. By the same token, intangible wealth among poor countries makes up 55% of all wealth, while in rich countries it is 80%. Detailed figures are available for each of the 120 countries in the study.

LEGAL CHANGE IN LATIN AMERICA: THE FLETCHER PROGRAM

Identifying best practices around the world may pay handsomely, as the Meiji experience shows. That is the case with the promotion of the adversarial legal system and oral trials, which have been going on in the world for quite some time. In Mexico the transition from the inquisitorial to the adversarial tradition in criminal law began in 2008.

What follows is the story of 110 Mexican judges who attended the Fletcher School of Law and Diplomacy at Tufts University in the summer of 2010, to participate in a weeklong field visit to the court system in Boston. The program was planned as a culture-shock experience, followed by two more weeks spent visiting the court systems of Chile and Colombia. The program included going to courts every morning and returning to classroom discussions in the afternoon.

From the beginning, the other participating professors and I agreed that the group of judges arriving would be skeptical, if not openly hostile, to the visit to Boston. As with any human group, identity formation feeds a sense of pride, whether in one's country, state, hometown, family, sports team, or profession.

Mexican lawyers are steeped in the conviction that there was no better legal system than the Roman, with its millennia-old tradition, its noble principles, its majestic codes—Justinian and Napoleonic—and its elegant theoretical construction, to name but a few of its features. By contrast, the Anglo-Saxon system was not even centered on written procedure and was based entirely on precedent. It was pedestrian and pragmatic, rather than governed by noble principles. It trusted verdicts of guilt or innocence to common citizens instead of learned judges. And it allowed smooth-talking, articulate lawyers to manipulate the truth, to name but a few criticisms.

Furthermore, lawyers, just like priests, are among society's most conservative actors in most of Latin America. True guardians of tradition, they are quite resistant to change, all the more so if those changes, such as moving from written-inquisitorial trials to oral-adversarial ones, require them to go back to school to relearn certain subject matter.

In order to neutralize this hostility, we figured that in the first two substantive workshops the judges would talk about the strengths of the Mexican legal system and the weaknesses of the American system. It would be a kind of *catharsis*. Professors would say nothing positive about the American system, but only describe it factually. Participants would have to make their own discoveries through asking questions about their own subjects of interest.

Boston Visit

At the welcome dinner the day of their arrival, each judge introduced him- or herself and said, in a couple of minutes, what he or she hoped to get out of the visit. It was the first time ever that federal and state judges traveled together in the same group.

Culture shock would come at them from all sides. Perhaps the first was breaking down the belief that a federal judge, by definition, is better than a local one. Obviously, the participants had been carefully selected, and the qualifications of one were as good as those of any other. It came as a surprise to the professors and must have surprised the judges themselves that the introductions and expectations coming from them were less hostile than we had anticipated.

The second shock had to do with the program's punctuality. Starting at the welcome dinner, upon going over the itinerary timing in detail, we warned them about our need to arrive promptly at the scheduled time given the intensive nature of the visit: 75 hours in 6 days. If the bus was scheduled to leave at 8:00 in the morning, by 8:01 it should already be on its way. Except for a few on the initial day, the group had no problem understanding the seriousness and exactness of the schedule.

The barrage of culture shocks hit each person differently. I will share a few that I noticed from the group's questions and in our conversations. None of them was prepared for the shows of respect and admiration they received as judges. Each time that they mentioned they were judges, be it at the hotel, in the restaurant, while taking transportation, or wherever, people responded in a very flattering way, showing great respect to them. Such a level of social appreciation for their line of work, such deference toward judges, is unknown in Mexico.

A justice of the Supreme Court of Massachusetts gave a lecture for them. They asked him what happened in the United States when an attorney advised his or her client to lie in court. The judge had to think about it and answered that in his 30 years of experience he had never seen it personally, but that when something like that happens the attorney is reported to the bar association and disbarred, so that he or she can no longer practice law in the country. The group could see just how important bar associations were as levers of control over the profession's ethics and code of conduct.

In Mexico today, attorneys are accountable to no one for their actions as professionals, and that impunity makes corrupt practices easy and attractive. Demanding handsome sums from clients for real or fictitious bribes is an everyday practice. How many of these demands are of which type is impossible to say. From this point of view, it is possible that lawyers are at the base of the corruption pyramid.

At the end of one of the sessions, a trial judge continued talking with the group, and they asked him, "How often do you believe the jury gets the verdict right or gets it wrong?" "When I was a trial lawyer," he said, "I was convinced that the ratio was 50–50. The jury was right when they found in favor of my client and wrong when they decided against him or her—no doubt about it. However, now that I've been a judge for over 15 years, I realize that 95% of the time I concur with the jury's finding."

The role of the jury is perhaps the hardest for Mexicans to understand, coming from the Latin world of vertical and elitist authority. Knowledge, character, and importance are erroneously believed to be concentrated at the top of the social pyramid and absent or lacking at the base, be it due to education, wealth, or social status. Juries are drawn overwhelmingly from the base. "Keeping the lawyers from manipulating the jury's perceptions is perhaps one of the most important tasks for an American judge," the group was told later: hence the importance of oral argument, public trials, transparency, and the right to an attorney in the adversarial system. The prosecution keeps an eye on the defense and vice versa, and the judge keeps an eye on them both.

Furthermore, the notion of a *jury* stems from the fact that, statistically speaking, innate intelligence and talent follow a normal distribution pattern throughout the social pyramid. That is, the base—making up 90% of the population—accounts for 90% of the talent, and the apex accounts for just 10% of society's talent. This is the essence of the democratic principle.

Whenever a trial is shown in American films or television programs, members of the public all rise when the judge enters the courtroom. The group obviously knew this, and we followed this ritual when the trial we were observing began. The judge welcomed those present, gave instructions to the parties, and, once everything was ready, asked the bailiff to call the jury in.

When the bailiff opened the door and announced the arrival of the jury, he also called for those in attendance to all rise. To the enormous surprise of the Mexican judges, the judge also stood up! The question afterward was unavoidable: Why? "A citizen jury is the most important part of a trial," replied the judge, "which furthermore allows for healthy and positive citizen participation in the affairs of government."

In another session, they asked one of the officers from the state police if he wouldn't rather work for the Federal Bureau of Investigation (FBI). In the Latin concept of vertical hierarchies, once again, a federal officer is the most important, and a local one, the least important. Horizontal hierarchies are difficult for a Latin American to grasp.

The state police officer knew the answer quite well, since he had one brother in the FBI and another on the local police force. He explained that the three of them had received basically the same kind of training, performed similar duties, and received salaries commensurate with their age and seniority. Their reasons for picking one organization over the other depended on their personal preferences. The youngest brother was single and enjoyed being able to travel freely around the country; for him, the FBI was ideal. The other brother had young children and preferred being able to spend time with them and his wife; for him, the local police force was best. In the case of the officer addressing us, his children were already teenagers, so he was freer to move around within Massachusetts. Working for the state police gave him all that he wanted.

As the hours went by, I began to slowly perceive how the group was taking in the experience and modifying their initial conceptions. Toward the end of the sixth day, and with the deadline looming for submitting their essays on the lessons learned from the trip, the general conclusion was: "Very interesting, but not applicable to us. Mexico is a totally different culture. Clearly this system can't be applied."

Chile Visit

Arriving at the Palace of Justice in Santiago makes for a very powerful visual impact and transmits better than in the United States the essence of the adversarial system. Surrounding the enormous square stand, to the right, the public defenders' building; to the left, the public prosecutors' and the attorney-general's office; and toward the back, between them both, the imposing judges' building. A visit to a courtroom—smaller than in the United States but built with the same basic concept in mind, albeit without a jury—is surprising for the agility, precision, professionalism, respect, dignity, and fluid nature with which matters are carried out. Obviously, the group of judges no longer needed simultaneous interpretation. Notwithstanding, they frequently commented on the difficulty, in Spanish, of keeping up with the line of reasoning, due to the fast-paced use of jargon as Chileans rattled off arguments concerning sets of facts.

Visiting Chile was a great experience. The Mexican group's reception at the Catholic University, and everywhere else, could not have been warmer. We gained entry without hindrance and spoke with everyone involved. Each judge, speaking in his own language, participated as actively as he could. Evidently the adversarial system had been transplanted successfully, after a 10-year process that started in 2000, improving upon the original model in many respects. This surprise disproved the judges' conclusion in Boston that "it can't be done." How did the Chileans do it? What was the secret to their success?

Of course, the Pinochet dictatorship was the first answer to come to mind, but that was not sufficient. The excellent training, organization, professionalism, team spirit, pride, and heritage of the national police, the Carabineros, was doubtless a very important factor, but that wasn't sufficient either. The group was confronted with the task of trying to find the rhyme and reason for Chile's success.

Political support from the highest levels and abundant resources also helped to guarantee the process's full implementation. Based on the expenditures made in Chile toward the system's full implementation, Mexico would need the equivalent of US $6 billion over a 10-year period, starting in 2016.

The Mexican judges also marveled at the excellent technological platform that allows the Chileans to control a case, from the moment when the "911 emergency call" is first made until the accused is acquitted or found guilty.[9] An integrated computer system links police, investigators, prosecutors, defense attorneys, judges, administrators, and prisons, with different filters and access levels. It is impressive. This political, economic, and technological support was also indispensable, but it was not sufficient by itself.

The judges also looked into the gradual nature of the process's implementation. It had taken the Chileans nearly 10 years to reach the level of excellence we observed. The first legal modifications to the new system were made not fully but piecemeal—that is, they were not parceled out according to subject matter, but in terms of geography. They were carried out, during the first year, in those regions furthest from the capital and with the smallest population, in a kind of pilot program, which gave them space for troubleshooting and making improvements.

In the second stage, the modifications were extended to the next geographic ring inward, and they repeated the process, until some four or five years later they reached the capital, with a system more refined than in its original form. Legislation was continuously adapted in accordance with how the system kept learning from itself.

Another factor worthy of mention was the involvement and active participation of universities and law schools. The profession's educational programs were continually adjusted in order to train the new batches of lawyers that the reform would necessitate. It was yet another indispensable link in the chain.

One more factor that neither we, nor the professors, nor the judges had thought of was the active participation of Chilean civil society in adopting, implementing, and defending the judicial reforms, as well as an intensive effort aimed at saturating the media with the spirit of the reforms and shaping their expectations. Oral trials civilize the administration of justice, but they can do nothing to combat organized crime or social injustice. The Blanco family, founders of Fundación Paz Ciudadana (Citizens' Peace Foundation), explained to the judges the battles the citizenry fought in those 10 years to implement the system successfully.

The group also uncovered what might have been considered a failure in the system. Its implementation proved so successful—with 95% to 97% of cases settled before going to trial—that the prisons were filled well beyond capacity. The organized crime rings spend their time stealing cell phones! Nevertheless, the country's crime rate continues to be high, and a question began to form in my mind that I will barely sketch out here. Chile's level of economic inequality is among the highest in Latin America, and it would be interesting to explore, in future research, the link between high crime rates and inequality.

As the group approached the end of their stay and came under increasing pressure to submit the corresponding essay, a conclusion diametrically opposed to that reached in Boston seemed to circulate among them: "So then, it can be done and it is not so difficult to adapt the system to our culture after all." I felt pleased and encouraged by their preliminary conclusion, but that was not the end of the story. They were still to see a third and totally different case that would shake their perceptions about the ease of the cultural change. Yes, cultural change is possible; but it is not easy and it is not overnight. It requires understanding, commitment, continuity, and perseverance.

Colombia Visit

The Universidad Externado de Colombia: (Open-Campus University of Colombia) in Bogotá is impressive for the quality of its teachers, students, and facilities. Here as well, the Mexican group was wonderfully received. The number of high-ranking officials among its instructors is quite noteworthy and explains, in part, the high jurisprudential caliber of the profession in Colombia. Its scholars and experts in legal theory, in a wide range of subject areas, are frequent participants in conferences in Latin America and Europe.

The Mexican judges' attention was caught by the exceedingly high opinion in which Colombians—be they professors, attorneys, or government officials—hold their legal system. From our very first meetings and exchanges, they shared their pride and enthusiasm with us, as well as the latest jurisprudential developments they are undertaking.

The second day of our stay, the group went to the Paloquemao Judicial Complex to sit in on hearings. Upon arriving punctually at the courtroom for the first hearing, they informed us quite nicely that there was a delay and asked us to move to another courtroom. When we got to the second courtroom, they informed us again that that hearing was not going to take place because the expert witnesses were nowhere to be found.

We then proposed splitting the group up so they could sit in on hearings in different courtrooms throughout the complex; we would meet back together an hour later in order to tour the case management center in the basement. After we split up, the scenario of finding many hearings canceled played out again.

The group made another interesting observation: the pace of case assignment, management, and resolution was much more halting than the frenzy we had observed in Chile. It led us to think that the difference surely had to do with some connection between output and economic incentives, as well as with the professionalism and specialized administrative design of courts.

The tour of the case management center proved quite revelatory and enabled us to understand the reasons behind the deferrals of the hearings. Along a broad workspace, densely populated by industrious administrative workers who toiled away tirelessly, the whole case process is managed on paper, at the same time the public is received and other workers are attended to.

The enormous piles of files—which are moved about in large boxes on *dollies* due to their heavy weight—are made up of the printouts furnished by the system's various computers. They explained to us that this cannot be avoided because they must keep a written record of everything and all notices to appear must be delivered in person, be they for prosecutors, defense attorneys, expert witnesses, lawyers, or judges, and, "sometimes notices to appear get misplaced."

The Mexican group observed the Colombian system's problems with sympathy and understanding, since they are the same ones that have dogged the Mexican system for many years: the paper-trail jungles. Upon analyzing the matter in discussions at the university, we learned that the situation is so serious that standards of judicial efficiency[10] had been adjusted from an initial projection of 95% down to 80% two years later, but that by this time they were saying a 60% rate of efficiency might be more realistic.

As the end of our stay drew near, and once again the pressure of preparing the essay on the lessons learned from Colombia grew, the judges reached their conclusions about transitioning from the written-inquisitorial system to the oral-adversarial. It was clear to them that, although it involved different cultures, the switch is indeed possible, as Chile demonstrated for us. But they also became convinced that it is no easy task, as we could see in Colombia.

We decided to grade the systems of the three countries we visited, as well as the Mexican system. In order to avoid bias, we agreed to submit our grading anonymously. During our last session in Bogotá, before the farewell dinner, we passed out blank cards on which each participant wrote down a grade from 0 to 10, just like the grading system in Mexican schools, for the four legal systems. These four numbers represented the average grade, a synthesis of the hands-on learning over the course of three months in the summer of 2010: 8.5, 8.1, 6.7, and 6.8, respectively, for the United States, Chile, Colombia, and Mexico.

What we have seen thus far is cause for optimism concerning the possibilities for improvement. One must not assume that it will be easy to get lawyers to change their traditions and training. Nonetheless, unlike the serious conflicts that arise from the propagation of alien religious doctrines, above all in countries with a state religion, differences between legal systems need not generate such thoroughgoing conflict. Therefore, change is possible despite the enormous challenges it faces: witness the Chilean case.

8

Processes of Change

The previous chapter focused on the transmission and preservation of values from one generation to the next. But all cultures and values change along with modifications in their physical and social environments. The change happens slowly, as countries modernize, or sometimes rapidly from catastrophic or high-impact events of history (for example, World Wars I and II), as well as when other forces act as catalysts (for example, when political leaders try to speed up change).

Some theorists think that value change is just a matter of teaching *good* values to people. That is the case with lists of values and proselytism—whether religious or non-religious. Examples of non-religious **lists of values** are found in Benjamin Franklin's 13 *virtues*. He combined the best of the Puritan ethos with the curiosity and scientific openness of the Enlightenment: temperance, silence, order, resolution, frugality, industry, sincerity, justice, moderation, cleanliness, tranquility, chastity, and humility. These ideas were very influential and popular in the 13 colonies through the annual publication of Franklin's *Poor Richard's Almanac*, between 1732 and 1758, and also through their appearances in his *Pennsylvania Gazette*.

Within the United States today as well, many schools, colleges, initiatives, and coalitions have sought to emphasize the role of *lists of values* in the formation of character (Lickona, 2006, p. 61). Along the same lines, a program was created in Peru in 1990 to teach the so-called *Ten Commandments of Development*: order, cleanliness, punctuality, responsibility, achievement, honesty, respect for the rights of others, respect for the law, work ethic, and frugality—deliberately chosen to echo the culture of Japan. Octavio Mavila, a Honda distributor in Peru for 32 years, was committed to instilling these values in young people and in business, and founded the Institute of Human Development (Harrison, 2006, p. 185). More than two million people participated during the lifetime of the program, which no longer exists, but little if any change is detectable. The experiment underlines that change is not only a matter of recognizing a collection of positive values, but also knowing whether they play a beneficial role in improving individual well-being.

The main criticism of this line of thinking is that it is difficult to deny the validity of any of the items in the several *lists of values* presented in the preceding paragraphs; indeed, when considered separately, all seem entirely legitimate. However, what happens when there is a clash between two prescribed virtues? For example, truth versus friendship, achievement versus humility? Which will prevail—and why? And how? The problem with axiological prescriptions such as these is that cultures are not mere *lists* of values; they are *dynamic systems*. Whenever a hierarchy of values is established, some values are inevitably seen as more important than others—something that would not occur if culture were merely a static *list* of virtues.

It is also important to recognize that adherence to values is easily affected by the functionality of those values within a particular culture and at a particular time—a point illustrated by the behavior of people who transition from a culture of joy to a culture of achievement. Take punctuality, for example: neither *cultures of honor* nor *cultures of joy* particularly prize punctuality, and anyone living in such a culture will rarely arrive on time, except in settings linked to modern foreign business. But if that person visits a country with a *culture of achievement*, he or she will change his or her behavior to suit the host country's standards. Peer pressure and enforcement are powerful agents to change behavior.

Slow Change: The Modernization of Ireland, Spain, and Mexico

Unlike the cases of Japan, Turkey, and Singapore, in which leaders brought about cultural change under special historical circumstances, Ireland, Spain and Mexico illustrate the outcome of slower changes brought about by the modernization process, propelled by the national leadership. Ireland and Spain—before the 2008 crisis—were frequently cited in the Latin world to illustrate the feasibility of development in traditional Catholic countries. Similarly, Mexico, before the 1971 OPEC oil crisis, was also cited as a *miracle* after four decades of rapid economic growth—above 6% annually since 1933. For all three countries, change was an outcome of national leadership creating institutions through the intensive use of public policy.

The near simultaneous developmental takeoffs of both Spain and Ireland are recent examples of the interaction between *structures* and *ideas*. They shared with the colonial Catholic countries a history of coming down on the side of the European Counter-Reformation, which goes a long way toward explaining their backward states of development at the dawn of the 20th century. But these two countries experienced an accelerated development in the last quarter of the century: Ireland as a Catholic country under the influence of the Protestant United Kingdom until joining the European Union; and Spain, also deeply Catholic until Franco's death in 1975, under the influence on the European Union since then.

The case of Ireland is very straightforward. It won partial independence from Great Britain in 1921 in a process that would drag on until 1949. In 1955 it finally joined the United Nations and in 1959 it elected its first president. The country's precarious economic situation began to improve in 1966 with the signing of a trade agreement with England, but its later takeoff was really based on its 1973 entry into the European Community, which from 1990 onward resulted in prosperity.

A combination of (1) responsible leadership, (2) foreign investment, (3) the European Development Fund, (4) remittances from the diasporas, and (5) appropriate government policies in the areas of budgeting, finance, and education together explain the success it enjoyed until the global economic crisis of 2008.

The case of Spain was a bit more complicated, as it was under the autocratic rule of Francisco Franco for three and a half decades (1939–1975). Spain embarked on a bloody civil war (1936–1939) that broke out after Franco and the other Nationalist generals in North Africa rebelled and attacked the elected government of the Second Republic. It cost the lives of half a million Spaniards and generated a comparable number of émigrés, most of whom went to Latin America.

Because Spain remained formally *neutral* during World War II, Franco survived the defeat of fascism, but Spain did not join the United Nations until 1955. The country's opening up to trade initiated a period of economic growth from 1960 onward. Nonetheless, the dictatorship was an obstacle to Spain's political development.

Franco's death in 1975 precipitated Spain's democratization on the basis of a fortuitous combination of factors, which included steps taken—unintentionally—by Franco himself, the international climate, and the mood of Spanish society and its ruling class.

Franco's contribution consisted of his attempt to perpetuate himself through the virtual adoption of his political godson Juan Carlos, grandson of the deposed King Alfonso XIII, at the age of 10, and later designation as head of state at the age of 30. Franco's aversion to the Spanish Republic led him to the conclusion that the return of the monarchy was the best vehicle for the perpetuation of his political *vision*.

The international climate's contributions were (1) the dawn of the Cold War, which led the United States to establish military bases in Spain in 1953; (2) the Marshall Plan's success in reconstructing Europe after World War II, which did not include Spain; (3) the positive example set by the European Economic Community and its refusal to admit Spain in 1962; (4) the rise of Euro-communism as a movement independent from the Soviet Union and adapted to the democratic rules of the game; and (5) the change in the Vatican's position toward political openness following the Second Vatican Council (1962–1965).

Spanish society and its ruling class had been deeply affected by the Civil War and by the four decades of the Franco dictatorship, which accounts for their justified aversion to violence. The defeat of fascism in Europe, under whose banner they had originally begun supporting Franco and his autarchic utopia, also affected them. Another element that impacted Spain's culture was the growth of a broad middle class that, upon Franco's death, was ripe for modernity.

Spain attained democratic normalcy in the relatively short time period of seven years, between 1975 and 1982, as highlighted by the following timeline:

1975–1976: (1) Juan Carlos de Borbón is proclaimed King of Spain by the Parliament in November of 1975; (2) the king appoints Adolfo Suárez head of the government in July of 1976; (3) Suárez proposes deep political reforms to Parliament, which are approved in November 1976; (4) a nationwide referendum is held on December 15, 1976, which overwhelming ratifies the reforms (with a voter turnout of 78%, and 97% voting in favor).

1977: (5) The Communist Party is legalized in April; (6) a general election is held in June, confirming Adolfo Suárez in his position of leadership; (7) Suárez invites the main political parties and trade groups to discuss and establish core political and economic agreements for the transition, which culminates in the signing of the Moncloa Pact on October 25.

1978–1979: (8) A new constitution is issued in December 1978; (9) Suárez is reelected in Spain's second national election, in March 1979.

1981–1982: (10) Upon Suárez' enigmatic resignation in January 1981, there is a failed coup attempt against Vice President Calvo Sotelo during his inauguration ceremony as president in Congress on February 23; (11) 1.2 million Spaniards take to the streets to celebrate the coup's defeat on February 27; and (12) the Socialist Party wins Spain's third national ection, with Felipe González elected prime minister in October 1982, and subsequently re-elected for a total of four terms lasting until 1996.

The success stories of Spain and Ireland before the 2008 world economic crisis make for interesting case studies, since they were both developmentally backward Catholic countries in which a combination of preexisting cultural and structural causes played a role in their turnarounds. But although these conditions were necessary, they would not have been sufficient without the sequence of events described here, which led to their intensive interaction.

The political, economic, and social changes that Mexico's modernization unleashed led not only to culture shocks but also to generation gaps within families living under the same roof: grandparents, children, and grandchildren displayed quite different worldviews. Each of them grew up in very different times during their formative stages of preadolescence. These culture shocks of deconstruction and reconstruction of a culture are expressed in an axiological ferment.

The process of constructing the traditional Mexican system of values—which changed the pre-Hispanic indigenous culture—took four centuries, while its deconstruction took just about four decades. What were the traditional values that were constructed so slowly, and what are the new ones that are changing so rapidly? The three cultural pillars of the traditional values and ideologies can be summarized as (1) Catholic, (2) nationalist (anti-Spain and anti-US), and

(3) revolutionary. The new ones are still in formation. However, they seem to be moving toward a more tolerant, global, market-oriented, and democratic society.

Mexico went through a rapid modernization process from 1933 to 1982, which led to a deep shift in values from traditional to modern. The stagnation of real GNP per capita for two decades since 1982 paradoxically propelled an acceleration of the trend toward modernization. The acceleration is a byproduct of (1) an increase in documented and undocumented migration to and trade with the United States, which brought an enormous influx of revenues, a development incompatible with the old anti-US ideology; (2) women's participation in the labor force, which propelled gender equality and, in turn, pushed for changes in family structure and values; and (3) the explosion of the informal economy. The rapid change in new cultural values has resulted in a strong convergence of values between Mexico, Canada, and the United States. These conditions provided the background for the implementation of the North American Free Trade Agreement (NAFTA) in 1994.

Analyzing changes in values over time used to be very difficult due to the lack of consistent and reliable measures. The World Values Survey (WVS) fills that void, and gives us a unique opportunity to track changes in values after 1980. In 31 out of 34 WVS variables used to measure changes in values between Canada, Mexico and the United States, the three countries converged at the close of the 20th century. Interestingly, none of the three countries really led the change. It seems as if a new entity is in formation (Inglehart, Nevitte, and Basáñez, 1996, p. 162).

A preliminary review of the 2000 WVS data suggests that the convergent trend continues. Willingness to do away with the border increased in Mexico from 22% in 1990 to 36% in 2000. In the United States, it grew from 37% to 42% over the same period in relation to the Canadian border. Unfortunately, the survey does not have a question in the United States about the Mexican border. Similarly, readiness to form one country with the United States increased in Mexico from 21% to 31% over that decade, even when the question was posed under a very unappealing condition—adding one more state to the United States. However, if the question is posed under an appealing condition—to improve quality of life—the readiness to form one country goes up to 58%. For the United States, with respect to Canada, the value is an impressive 76% (Basáñez and Reyes Heroles, 2003, p. 258).

Historically, Mexico was, above all, structured around a Catholic value system that started with the Spanish colonization. The War of Independence of 1810 understandably aroused an anti-Spain ideology. The loss of half of Mexico's territory to the United States in 1848 produced a similar anti-US ideology, further reinforced by many more grievances throughout the history of both countries. Those two "anti-" sentiments were at the core of Mexico's nationalism. Finally, the civil war of 1910 justified the *revolutionary* ideology that validated the government and its lineage of successive political parties that remained in power for 71 years: the 1929 Partido Nacional Revolucionario (PNR), the 1938 Partido de la Revolución Mexicana (PRM), and the 1946 Partido Revolucionario

Institucional (PRI). These three cultural pillars (Catholicism, nationalism, and revolutionary) deeply shaped Mexicans' values, and they still are at the foundation of the belief system of many groups in Mexico.

It is important to note that the old values system fits a traditional society well. Mexico in the 1930s was a traditional society. It was thinly populated, rural, employed in the agrarian sector, illiterate, and had poor communications and little mobility. The leadership that handled this social, political, and economic structure was institutionalized into a set of laws and power coalitions that produced a network of monopolies in politics, business, and religion at the federal, state, and local levels. This institutional arrangement still remains and today constitutes the status quo, in which the conservative forces resist change.

In 1933, the country entered into a 50-year accelerated modernization process powered by an average 6.3% annual constant GDP growth; those years are referred to as the Mexican miracle (INEGI, 1998, pp. 311–312). The outcome of that growth was a 20-fold increase in the size of the Mexican economy and a nearly fivefold (4.8) increase in income per capita. Similarly, the country's population increased fourfold, and became more urban, employed in the service sector, literate, and highly mobile, thanks to an interstate highway system. That is, Mexican society became in many ways the opposite of what it had been 50 years earlier. The old system of values did not fit the new society well.

Some could say that the deconstruction of the old values system started in the middle of the 19th century, when the Mexican government expropriated the Catholic Church's land holdings and real estate property. However, despite major efforts by liberal governments following the 1857 Constitution to separate church and state and to counterbalance the influence of the Catholic Church, the impact of these efforts on the values of the masses was negligible.

The process of dismantling the traditional values system really started in 1968 with the student movement protests, which ended with the Tlaltelolco Massacre (the Mexican version of Tiananmen Square) when troops sent by the federal police fired on student demonstrators. Thirty-six people were killed[1] and over 1,500 imprisoned. The bottom line is that this violent clash was the first open and extended challenge to the contradictory elements of the official *revolutionary* ideology. On that occasion, Nobel Prize–winner Octavio Paz, then ambassador to India, resigned his post in protest. However, references by government officials to the Revolution continued for 20 years, until President Salinas took office in 1988.

The contradictions within the revolutionary ideology and its distinction from nationalism are important. The Mexican Civil War was not between the North and the South, but between the masses and the elite. That is why in Mexico it was referred to as a *revolution*, rather than as a *war*. Being revolutionary meant having an open preference for peasants, blue-collar workers, the urban lower class, and a detachment from businessmen. Nationalism was also an ingredient, but it predated the revolution. The contradictions were built into the 1917 Constitution, because of its origin in concern for the masses and its commitment to the rationale—if not the agents or institutions—of capitalism. This explains why the Mexican government, trying to escape being labeled, used to say that the country was neither a capitalist nor a communist system, but a *mixed economy*. The contradictions hidden in those two elements did not surface until the 1968 movement exploded, which highlighted new currents of thinking. The new counter-intelligentsia was born.

The weakening of nationalist ideology started a decade after the Tlaltelolco Massacre, when Mexico re-established relations with Spain in 1977 and the government's anti-Spain rhetoric stopped. When President Miguel de la Madrid, a Harvard graduate, came to power (1982–1988), the government's anti-US rhetoric decreased sharply, and eventually disappeared as NAFTA negotiations advanced (1990–1994), although anti-US rhetoric continued among union (though not peasant) leaders and some left-wing opposition groups. It also continued among faculty and students of the National Autonomous University of Mexico (UNAM), but not among those of private universities.

A remarkable trend, largely neglected in many analyses, is the increase of Protestantism in Mexico, at all income levels, which is altering the deepest pillar of the old Catholic value system. It is introducing competition for adherents among religions, in addition to providing an influx of different values. Despite Mexico's re-establishing diplomatic relations with the Vatican in 1992, Catholicism is in decline today. It has fallen as low as 81% of the population (Inglehart, Basáñez, et al., 2004, Table F024), down from an almost totally Catholic society a few decades earlier. As of today, Catholicism remains at the core of the Mexican values system, but the ideological constructs that validated the old regime—nationalism and revolution—are weakening by the day.

The shift in values implied by such a structural change explains why tensions in Mexican society started *boiling* at an increasingly powerful rate from 1968 onward. Demands for political, social, and economic changes were an outcome of the new values. However, the government tightly controlled the supposed agents that would transmit change—the media, elections, and the intelligentsia—from society up to the centers of power. The *boiling* brought the country into a period of five cyclical crises in 1968, 1976, 1982, 1987, and 1994, geared to an excessive presidential power (Basáñez, 1993, p. 95). The vicious cycle finally ended in the year 2000 with the democratic opening implied in the first electoral victory of an opposition presidential candidate in seven decades.

Fast Change: Local Leadership in Bogotá, Colombia, 1995–2003

A recent case that probably illustrates most clearly the effect of leadership on value change and, in turn, behavioral change, is that of Bogotá between 1995 and 2003 under the leadership of Mayor Antanas Mockus (1995–1997), followed by Enrique Peñalosa (1997–2001), and Mockus once again (2001–2003).

I traveled to Bogotá, commissioned by the Fletcher School, Cultural Change Institute, to evaluate just how genuine the supposed cultural change was that had taken place during this period. What follows is the report I produced from this visit.[2] I arrived on a Sunday night—November 21, 2004—17 years after my first visit. I had very fond memories of Bogotá and its courteous people—a friendly, peaceful city of fresh air and pleasant architecture, albeit rather chaotic in terms of traffic, as with any good Latin American city. Above all, the image of a city of small buildings had been impressed upon me: white houses with peaked red-tile roofs, the vast majority of them no more than two stories tall.

Notwithstanding this, from the time I landed that night—as would be confirmed the next morning—something didn't fit right with the original picture I had of the place. Bogotá was now an impressive city of tall, modern, well-designed buildings with very wide streets. It was very clean and orderly, with no billboards, with large sidewalks and crosswalks that people actually used on its street corners. What had happened? Of course this piqued my curiosity and lent greater interest to my visit. This image did not fit a country with a per capita income of around US $2,000. I decided I needed to find the answers to three questions. First, had there truly been a change in the mentality of Bogotá residents? If so, what was it all about? Second, how could it be explained? And third, what could other countries learn from this? Was it transferable?

The general perception of the people with whom I spoke was one of consensus concerning the city's transformation and the change in attitude this generated in Bogotá's residents. They spoke of a *new culture* of respect for life, law, and other people. The majority of those interviewed attributed the transformation to the fortuitous succession of the three administrations of Mockus, Peñalosa, and Mockus again.

Both politicians ran for office as independents, rather than aligning themselves with the traditional political parties. The first of these two was obsessed with the idea of a new citizen culture of respect for others and abiding by the law ("Law, Mores, and Culture" was his slogan). The second was obsessed with the idea of respect for public spaces, leisure, and with taking back the city for its residents, particularly those with few resources. Both of them enjoyed a high degree of prestige due to their honesty, their obsession with ideas, and their knack for bringing people together to do worthwhile things as a team.

Mockus was seen as a planner and a teacher, an irreverent *magician* and great communicator. A mathematician-philosopher, academic, and former president of the National University, he had done his graduate studies in France. His Lithuanian father died when he was very young. His Polish mother, of great artistic sensibility through her work in sculpture, was also a major influence. He was eccentric in the extreme. He went from being a total unknown to becoming a recognizable figure when he was broadcast on television mooning a group of art students during a debate at his university.

His wedding was held in a circus, at which he arrived accompanying his bride on the back of an elephant. He was not afraid to dress up as a *superhero*, complete with cape and boots (as Super-citizen or Jiminy Cricket), if doing so would help him get his point across. Through the use of mimes, he educated citizens on the proper use of *crosswalks*. Through children's games (spinning tops, or chutes and ladders), he raised awareness concerning paying taxes and the importance of *everyone paying their share*. He was called a civic priest who communicated in religious ways: "Life is sacred; public resources are sacred."

Peñalosa, in turn, was seen as an efficient manager who got things done, with a great gift for public administration. He was a historian and economist with a political and business background who was born in Washington (as his father was the Colombian ambassador) and renounced his US citizenship, and he attended school in the United States and France. His father, who was well-known in Colombian politics, and who distinguished himself as secretary-general of Habitat for Humanity's 1974–1976 world conference, died just days before his son was to take office as mayor. His mother, also a woman of great sensibility—a student of art with a passion for flowers and garden design—must have passed on her taste (or better yet, obsession) for trees and parks to her son.

He built his reputation through tenacity. He ran for mayor three times before winning and, from the moment he took office, worked tirelessly on high-impact public projects to promote the general welfare. It has been said of him that such were the fruits of his labor that in three years he went through the resources that under traditional rates of expenditure would have lasted the city for 20 years. Out of his sense of the need for greater social equality, he placed great importance on the construction of symbols, rituals, meanings, and names that emphasized this priority. His time in office included such accomplishments as traffic reduction programs (*Pico y Placa*: Rush Hour and License Plates), sidewalks with posts to prevent illegal parking, bicycle ridership and the creation of bike paths; the creation of a public transportation system with dedicated lanes (bus rapid transit or BRT), known as TransMilenio; the building of giant libraries, huge children's parks, and the Third Millennium Park; and the relocation of street vendors, to name just a few.

The achievements of both mayors probably gained support from Bogotá's democratization process, which began in 1988 with the first election for the office; together with the new Constitution of 1991, the judicial and institutional constitution; Bogotá Organic Statute #1421 of 1993, which provides for fiscal autonomy; and the reallocation and reinforcement of the city's finances; among many other positive influences.

The following is a list of their most relevant changes:

- Banning the use of gunpowder and fireworks
- A closing time of 1:00 a.m. for restaurants and night clubs (*Carrot* Law)
- Replacing corrupt traffic agents with the National Police
- Use of crosswalks for crossing the street, in the face of high mortality rates of pedestrians jaywalking
- Voluntary estimate and payment of property taxes, which increased revenue substantially
- An excise tax on gasoline
- Energy utility privatization
- Banning parking on sidewalks

- Widening sidewalks
- Expulsion of street vendors
- Use of eminent domain to reassert control over public squares and gardens, previously overwhelmed by squatters and unregistered private parties
- Large-scale tree planting and the restoration of 4,548 parks
- 195 kilometers (122 miles) of interconnected bike routes used by more than 60,000 riders daily
- Privatization of waste services (trash collection)
- Reduction in the homicide rate: from 81 per 100,000 residents in 1993, to 31 in 2003
- Sunday bike roads for one and a half million recreational users.

This list gives an idea of the cumulative and surprising effects of actions taken by city hall on a citizenry unaccustomed to receiving attention from the government.

Bogotá's experience is an example of the powerful influence not only on individuals' perceptions and attitudes, but of taking things to the next level, to the realm of their values. This does not mean having to discover previously unknown values. It means simply giving these values meaning and functionality in new circumstances. These new values had been latent but suppressed in a culture of *el vivo vive del bobo* (catch as catch can, or literally, "the living make their living off the fools"), in which only suckers would try to live according to principle.

Tracking the Gallup survey data from 1993 to 2003 for the question, "In your opinion, are things in Bogotá getting better or worse?" the public approval trend was clearly on the rise from 15% to 54% (see Figure 8.1), with some ups and downs evidently influenced by the media and political conflicts. In December 1993, 72% of respondents were pessimistic and 15% optimistic, whereas in 2003, 24% were pessimistic and 54% optimistic. In April 1999 there was enormous opposition to the sidewalk-parking ban, which led to a media campaign to recall the mayor, which explains the spike of pessimism (69%).

In the *Quality of Life* poll carried out by the National Department of Statistics in 2003, respondents were asked which public works and actions they perceived to have improved their lives in the past five years. Entertainment venues (parks: 73%) and improved mobility (65% +) were among the top responses, rated higher than libraries (56%) and schools (38%). Among those measures and actions named by the public, the reclamation of public spaces was the one that received the highest rate of responses (76%).

It is difficult to overstate the changes in Bogotá as a result of the reclamation of public spaces, and the pride of city residents as a result. Plaza San Victorino, the main plaza in the city, had previously been jammed with 1,500 street vendors, and as a result looked like a cross between a flea market and a shantytown. After the reforms, it became a sunny, wide-open space dominated by public art and strolling families. Some of those interviewed mentioned the date of the

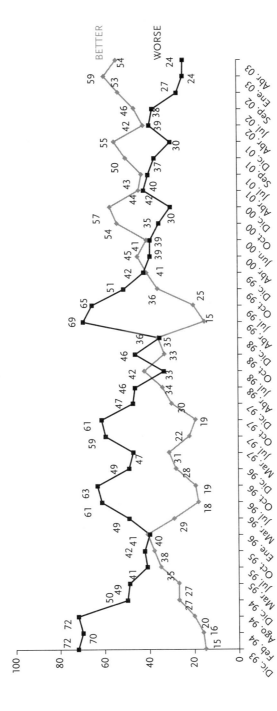

FIGURE 8.1 Is Bogotá getting better or worse? Gallup poll, 1993–2003

Reprinted with permission of Gallup, Inc. This graph is an interpretation of data compiled by Gallup, Inc. However, Gallup, Inc. had no part in the creation of this graphic interpretation.

agreement on clearing the plaza (in August 1999) as a watershed moment in city planning, which solidified the administration's prestige.

A similar change occurred as a result of Bogotá's sidewalk-parking ban. Prior to the ban, the city's sidewalks were chaos, with cars parked everywhere and pedestrians forced to walk in the streets. After the ban was implemented, the sidewalks were again unimpeded, allowing for easier flow of traffic and the safe passage of pedestrians.

Another source of pride for Bogotá residents is the new public transit system, TransMilenio or *metrobus*. It offers some of the features of a subway, but at a tenth of the construction cost, given that it runs *on* rather than *under* the streets. Also, the construction of three giant libraries, two of them in areas greatly affected by urban blight, and connected to the network of bike paths, has had a tremendous impact on children and young people, particularly students.

Part of the explanation no doubt lies, first, with the ability of mayors Mockus and Peñalosa to correctly perceive the needs of the city and the desires of the citizenry, and to respond to both. The majority of Bogotá residents take this view regarding the success of their capital city, except perhaps a third or fewer of them who were not directly benefited by these public works and development projects.

Another part of the explanation lies, second, in the long-term social, economic, and political modernization processes (Lipset, 1960; Rostow, 1960)—that is, the changes that come with the move from rural to urban life, from illiteracy to literacy, from low- to high-density living, from an agrarian to an industrial or service-sector way of life, from being a city made up of new arrivals to one of people born and raised there (Dávila, 2004, p. 419). In the space of 50 years the city grew from less than one million residents to almost seven million. Although per capita income in the capital hardly grew at all between 1980 and 2003 (around US $2,600 in constant dollars), total available public resources grew simply because of population growth. The coverage of public services (water, sewage, energy, transportation, etc.) was already decent by the standards of other large Latin American cities in the 1960s. By the end of 2003, coverage was near universal (though it left something to be desired in terms of quality).

Since the mid-1990s, the pressure on service provision and the financial burden of these concepts began to diminish, freeing up resources for education, public spaces, transportation, and culture (Dávila, 2004, p. 431).

Third, some credit is also due to the maturing of the citizens, as reflected in their choice of mayors. These new civic values were finding expression, but that does not mean that all the credit is due to civil society. One must not forget that important and influential segments of Bogotá society tenaciously opposed many of the measures implemented by these innovative mayors. Put another way: civil society was not the only author of these changes. But once their benefits were realized and appreciated, residents took ownership of them and became fierce defenders of these advancements. The cycle of interaction had been set in motion, and values began to affect material circumstances.

A fourth and very powerful explanation can be found in the enormous shift in the availability of resources generated as a consequence of fiscal and managerial autonomy and the temporary curbing of corruption. This was in spite of the fact that Bogotá's new autonomy did not include powers of taxation, because the capital district still operated within certain legally established boundaries. A report by the Bogotá Board of Finance stated:

> ... the transformation seen in finance over the course of the 1990s has been quite significant, so much so that the District has gone from being a perpetual fiscal basket case to having a solid fiscal outlook. (Fedesarrollo, 1997, p. 38)

Within 12 years (from 1986 through 1997) the capital's total budget went from 2.3 to 5 billion constant 1996 pesos, but the greatest increase came in 1996 (30%), a level that was sustained afterward. The share of the pie going to investment grew from 33% to 48% between 1992 and 1997. Budgets went from deficit spending to running surpluses.

One can deduce that there existed exogenous resource fluctuations (with respect to the local economy) of US$5 billion a year, which compounded the palliative effect of overseas remittances and which also had the ability to generate a revivifying multiplier effect on the local economy of the highest order. Of course a process such as this impacted and accelerated changes in residents' values, which is the subject of this account. Is this experience transferable? What can cities in this and other countries learn from Bogotá?

Bogotá has been the subject of intense international observation since the end of the 1990s. In 2002 the United Nations Development Program (UNDP) organized an event to spread the word about the city's successful experience. It has organized seminars and databases, and published the report *Bogotá: An Innovative Experience of Local Governance*, which was an important factor in the capital city's achievement of international recognition.

The foregoing lays out two kinds of problems. First, it remains to be seen whether the changes that took place in Bogotá's physical environment, and in the inner world of individual experiences, modified people's perceptions and attitudes in different areas of their axiological values—and in the event that they did, how so? That is, changes could have taken place in terms of deeper values—whether related to work, family, society, religion, trust, engagement in associational life, or tolerance, just to name a few.

The analysis of values and social capital in Bogotá, based on behaviors related to interpersonal and institutional trust, and civic participation in volunteer organizations, paints a complex picture of change (Sudarsky 2003, p. 224). Faith in institutions rose with regard to the military and the government, but diminished with regard to parties, unions, and Congress. Participation in volunteer organizations fell for the population as a whole, but rose among those with high levels of income and education, with age having little to do with it. The impact of technological, economic, and social changes that Robert Putnam found for the United States over the course of three or four decades (Putnam, 2000, p. 368), transpired in Bogotá in just six years.

The second problem, alluded to earlier, consists of how clearly the international community can reproduce certain aspects of Bogotá's experience. Perhaps the most attractive, immediate, and relatively easy of them to export is its public transit system, the over-ground "underground" train, TransMilenio, or *metrobus*.

What is not so clear is whether other cities can absorb the philosophy, the deeper self-image, the energy, and the obsessions of those who made what happened in Bogotá possible. This was really a thoroughgoing experiment in governance, as the UNDP has correctly identified it. It might be easier instead to search for a similar set of social conditions that call for such measures—when rates of new arrivals in a city have tapered off to the point where the majority of residents have now been born and raised there, where coverage of public services is near-universal, and where there exists political autonomy, among the most salient factors. But as for the actors who carry out the adoption of such policies, they will be harder to reproduce.

What Bogotá does teach, above all in the case of Latin America, is the lesson that *yes, you can*, which is no small lesson. Responsible administrations can in fact develop fiscal discipline. Corruption in the handling of public resources and duties can in fact be at least temporarily curbed. A sense of dignity and self-esteem can in fact be restored to the citizenry. Individuals can in fact be motivated to share a heightened sense of solidarity. Problems in areas such as traffic, transportation, public safety, and general services can in fact be solved. People's attitudes can in fact be changed. Values that have fallen into disuse or have become dysfunctional can in fact be tapped into and reignited.

If one were to write another article on what took place there, perhaps its title ought to be "Guided Acceleration in Cultural Change: Bogotá, 1995–2003," and open with the following quote from the UNDP:

> How is it that all this came about in a city that, up until 1992, was wallowing in a deep state of crisis in political, economic, and social terms? Bogotá as a city had seemed unworkable. Its growth was all helter-skelter, and the government had lost all control. Its social indicators lagged behind. Its public service agencies were teetering on the brink of bankruptcy. Its residents perceived corruption and *clientelism* to be the greatest evils plaguing their political system. [. . .] How could society summon the means to face down these challenges, seize opportunities, and turn them into positive results for its members? That is, how was the city made governable?

Much of the resulting report is an encouraging account of cultural change brought about by a couple of clear-eyed, visionary, driven, and incorruptible leaders in their own city. Visiting Bogotá in 2004 was like being in a European city, but with all the warmth and joy so typical of Latin America.

For work reasons, I returned there for three weeks in September 2010. Bogotá appeared to have fallen back into its old ways from the years before the Mockus-Peñalosa duo. The lesson I took away from my new visit was that change set in motion by culture is definitely possible, but its preservation requires a degree of continuity and institutionalization that had not been achieved by post-2003 administrations. Also, the geographic constituency of one city like Bogotá may not carry enough political weight or national influence.

Mockus ran for president in May 2010 as the Green Party candidate and lost to Santos (2010–2018), 22% to 69%. Peñalosa ran for mayor in October 2010 and lost to Petro, 25% to 32%, despite having won the support of former president Álvaro Uribe in addition to that of the Green Party. Disappointingly, Bogotá had gone *back to normal*.

Conclusion

The argument that all cultures change is based on the idea that although each culture has advantages and benefits for certain groups or in relation to certain objectives, each may also contain disadvantages and harms for other individuals or objectives. That tension becomes the engine of change. In *cultures of honor*, as we have seen, people can live with more pride and sense of community, but usually material well-being is lacking for large sections of the population due to the complications and difficulties of economic life, and individuality may also be stifled. In *cultures of achievement*, on the other hand, people generally live with more material satisfaction, but there is less interest in honoring traditions and customs, families tend to be dispersed, and there is not much appreciation for community life. *Cultures of joy* would require similar types of adjustments, depending on the side to which they tilt more strongly.

Change of values may take place as some groups in the *cultures of honor* set goals of improving the economic situation of their communities, which requires certain adjustments to some values, such as hard work, punctuality, innovation, risk appetite, discipline, thrift, frugality, entrepreneurship, competition, merit appreciation, and so on. By contrast, some groups of individuals in *cultures of achievement* can try to boost personal enjoyment, family connection, or community life, which may introduce certain adjustments to some values in order to reduce anxiety, excessive competitiveness, or the irrational depletion of natural resources.

9

Axiological Diagnosis

Axiological diagnosis refers to a methodology I developed in 2009 at the Cultural Change Institute (CCI) of the Fletcher School, Tufts University, aimed at measuring the *axiological* profile (i.e., the values structure) of a country in order to identify strengths and weaknesses (hence threats and opportunities) as a way to move some of the country's values and beliefs toward desirable ends, domestically chosen. In other words, it is a tool to put into action the concept of values as the building blocks of culture.

The basic idea is to use the CCI's typology of 25 values contrasting *progress-prone* versus *progress-resistant* attitudes (Table 9.1) in three subsets: (1) social values, focused on fairness and respect; (2) political values, linked to political rights, civil liberties, and freedom; and (3) economic values, related to sustainable prosperity.

The data are obtained through a closed-ended questionnaire applied to a national representative sample using conventional public opinion technique. The survey findings then are explored at depth through focus groups comprising selected agents of cultural change, following a set of guidelines for research.

As a way to relate the original CCI 25-factor typology to the questions from the 2000 World Values Survey (WVS) data set, a translation code was developed to clarify the CCI-WVS equivalences.[1] The survey was pilot-tested in Guatemala and administered in East Timor, Calabria, Italy, and Mexico (Basáñez, 2010).

The Theory

Because the CCI 25-factor typology was designed to contrast attitudes toward *progress*, it necessarily focuses only on the goals of cultures of *achievement*. In this sense it is partial; however, it measures cultural orientation toward hard work, punctuality, outcomes, and productivity, and hence allows an *axiological diagnosis*.

The main shortcoming of the CCI typology is theoretical, in that it assumes that the economy prevails over the political and social dimensions, and that *all*

TABLE 9.1

The 25-Values Typology

Factor	Progress-Prone Culture	Progress-Resistant Culture
WORLDVIEW		
1. Religion	Nurtures rationality, achievement; promotes material pursuits; focuses on this world; pragmatism	Nurtures irrationality; inhibits material pursuits; focuses on the other world; utopianism
2. Destiny	I can influence my destiny for the better.	Fatalism, resignation, sorcery
3. Time orientation	Future focus promotes planning, punctuality, deferred gratification	Present or past focus discourages planning, punctuality, saving
4. Wealth	Product of human creativity; expandable (positive sum)	What exists (zero-sum)
5. Knowledge	Practical, verifiable; facts matter, debate matters	Abstract, theoretical, cosmological, not verifiable
VALUES, VIRTUES		
6. Ethical code	Rigorous within realistic norms; feeds trust	Elastic, wide gap between utopian norms and behavior = mistrust
7. The lesser virtues	A job well done, tidiness, courtesy, punctuality matter	Lesser virtues unimportant; love, justice, courage matter
8. Education	Indispensable; promotes autonomy, heterodoxy, dissent, creativity	Less priority; promotes dependency, orthodoxy
ECONOMIC BEHAVIOR		
9. Work/achievement	Live to work: work leads to wealth	Work to live: work doesn't lead to wealth; work is for the poor
10. Frugality	The mother of investment and prosperity	A threat to equality
11. Entrepreneurship	Investment and creativity	Rent-seeking
12. Risk propensity	Moderate	Low; occasional adventures
13. Competition	Leads to excellence	Aggression; a threat to equality—and privilege
14. Innovation	Open; rapid adaptation	Suspicious; slow adaptation
15. Advancement	Merit, achievement	Family, patron, connections
SOCIAL BEHAVIOR		
16. Rule of law/ corruption	Reasonably law abiding; corruption is prosecuted	Money, connections matter; corruption is tolerated
17. Radius of identification and trust	Stronger identification with the broader society	Stronger identification with the narrow community
18. Family	The idea of "family" extends to the broader society	The family is a fortress against the broader society
19. Association (social capital)	Trust, identification breed cooperation, affiliation, participation	Mistrust breeds excessive individualism, anomie
20. The individual/ the group	Emphasizes the individual but not excessively	Emphasizes the collectivity

(continued)

TABLE 9.1

Continued

Factor	Progress-Prone Culture	Progress-Resistant Culture
21. Authority	Dispersed: checks and balances, consensus	Centralized: unfettered, often arbitrary
22. Role of elites	Responsibility to society	Power and rent-seeking; exploitative
23. Church-state relations	Secularized; wall between church and state	Religion plays major role in civic sphere
24. Gender relationships	If not a reality, equality at least not inconsistent with value system	Women subordinated to men in most dimensions of life
25. Fertility	The number of children should depend on the family's capacity to raise and educate them	Children are the gifts of God; they are an economic asset

Source: adapted from Lawrence E. Harrison, *The Central Liberal Truth* (New York: Oxford University Press, 2006), pp. 36–37.

countries would choose to move in the direction of *achievement*. Keeping in mind these conditions and limitations, the typology is indeed useful, because it may lead to material improvements in the three dimensions (political, economic, and social).

It is an error to assume that only countries dominated by illiteracy and poverty should try to induce change, or that highly developed countries have nothing to improve upon. A cursory review of statistics relating to suicide shows that these are problems that afflict more developed countries, and Confucian, Nordic, and former Soviet countries in particular. Suicides are individual behaviors, but may be reflective of problems that exist on a national level (Diamond, 1992, p. 203). Asking "how can value change help?" is part of this inquiry.

The analytical framework behind the 25-values typology goes as far back as 1980. It focuses on the same concerns of Hofstede, Schwartz, and Inglehart, all working on the search for the main drivers of behavior.[2] In 1985, Lawrence Harrison published his first book, *Underdevelopment Is a State of Mind* (Harrison, 1985), inspired by the cultural shock he experienced as an USAID officer working and living in Central American and the Caribbean for 13 years in two separate periods between 1962 and 1982. He became intimately familiar with the highly contrasting concepts of the individual, society, justice, law, government, family, time, religion, and many more, between Latin Americans and Anglo Americans.

From those observations, he hypothesized that *culture* explained why some countries develop more rapidly and equitably than others, and offered three fundamental worldviews (time orientation, rationality, and equality) that strongly influence three key values that explain *progressive* and *static* cultures: **radius of trust, ethical code**, and **work ethic** (see Figure 9.1).

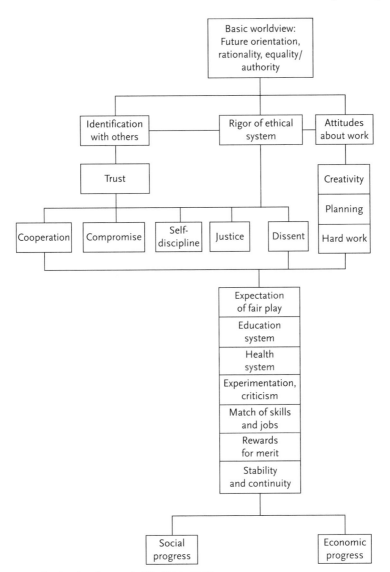

FIGURE 9.1 Harrison's values and attitudes systems

Lawrence Harrison, *Underdevelopment is a State of Mind: The Latin American Case,* Madison Books, 1985, p. 5. Reprinted with permission of Rowman & Littlefield.

At the Harvard 1990 Culture Matters Conference, participants developed the idea of contrasting elements of cultural values either as favorable or resistant to development (Grondona, 2000, pp. 44–55). To an original 20-values list, other conference participants contributed an additional five items. Together, these comprise the final CCI 25-values typology. Although the original formulation was not created according to a particular structure, four underlying axes later became apparent: worldview, social, economic, and political values.

The 25-Values Typology Questionnaire

The 25-values typology (Table 9.1) describes the two sides of the spectrum in a bipolar fashion. On the left side are progress-prone values (values favoring hard work over social interaction), and on the right side are progress-resistant (values favoring social interaction over hard work). The 25-values typology questionnaire developed 25 batteries of substantive questions (86) to specifically measure each of the 25 items on a 1 to 7 scale.

The batteries were not constructed as *direct questions*, but are meant to be asked in the *third person* in order to diminish *social desirability* effects. Also, the polarity of the questions is mixed in order to avoid identification of directionality by the respondents. There are also attitudinal (13) and socio-demographic (25) questions. The questionnaire was tested for three years (2005–2007) before the master questionnaire was released in 2008.

What are the key values in a particular culture to explain economic, political, and social behavior? Is hard work considered a driver of improved life circumstances? Is competition good or bad? Which is better in terms of political behavior: dissent or consent, friendship or truth? Which social behavior should we choose: trust or distrust of others? What motivates people more: social interaction or hard work? Which are the weak areas? How can strong areas move weak ones? The survey helps to answer these questions, but also identifies contradictions and paradoxes that call for further elaboration.

One way of diagnosing the axiology, namely, the values profile of a group, a community, or a country, is by combining local knowledgeable experts with foreign researchers who read and interpret the survey findings. In this way, situations, concepts, or relations that are natural and hence unnoticeable for the local party appear new and draw the attention of the foreign party. Proper diagnosis also requires an understanding of meanings and relations between ideas and values that normally are difficult for the foreign researcher to understand. To penetrate those obscure areas, the study moves into *focus group discussions* to clarify the way of thinking of the population under study.

The *focus group* discussions are typically conducted with the six groups that constitute the vehicles of value change identified by the CCI. Namely, (1) parents and health system personnel; (2) teachers and school administrators; (3) priests, pastors, clergy, and church administrators; (4) journalists and media administrators; (5) lawmakers, judges, and attorneys; and (6) business, political, and intellectual leaders. Those discussions are analyzed to reinforce the survey findings according to the CCI guidelines of research.

Once the survey findings and the focus group discussions are ready, it is necessary to move into the prescription stage. This phase calls for selecting the best possible combination of the six agents of change. In each case, the choice is dictated by the specific conditions under study, and on the outcome of the values survey and focus group discussions. The effect on values change of each of the six agents varies both in depth and length.

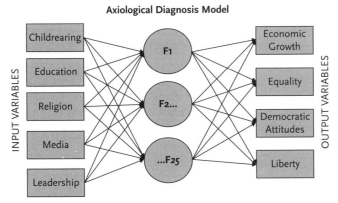

FIGURE 9.2 Axiological diagnosis model

Changing childrearing practices, for instance, will not be noticeable in a society's value profile until many years into the future, but those changes will be truly lasting. On the other end of the spectrum, electronic media can produce results quickly, but generally those effects evaporate rapidly. That is why a combination of all six agents is required to get both fast and lasting results.

The model behind the survey questionnaire is shown in Figure 9.2. The idea is to use the vehicles of values change (the *input variables*: childrearing, education, religion, media, law, and leadership) to modify key factors (F) and values identified with the questionnaire and the focus group discussions (*intermediate variables*), in order to achieve the desired outcomes (the *output variables*: economic growth, equality, democratic attitudes, liberty). The lower side of the figure underlines the need for a powerfully discriminatory questionnaire.

Testing and Validating the 25-Values Typology in Mexico

The questionnaire was applied in 2009 both in Timor Leste and Calabria, Italy, and in 2010 in Mexico. A pilot was also conducted in Guatemala in 2006 to test the questionnaire. The first step was getting a snapshot of the country by gathering basic census data relating to geography, demography, infrastructure, economy, employment, education, and health. Simultaneously, the public opinion survey was designed to be taken by 1,200 adults (18+ years old) randomly selected through statistical methods to conform to a representative sample of the national population in age, gender, income, education, region, and so on. The interviews were conducted face to face using the CCI 25-values typology questionnaire.

The full report also includes a cross-tabulation to explore each of the 125 questions broken down into 23 categories: gender, age, income, education, employment, region, town size, regional identity, pride of nationality, feelings of happiness, readership, TV viewing, political preference (right, center, left), trust in others, church attendance, civil status (married, single), number of children, household size, working hours, savings, socioeconomic level, and skin color. These 2,875 (23 x 125) items per country provide pieces of information that help in interpreting the survey findings.

The survey findings for Mexico are summarized in Figure 9.3, which shows each of the three dimensions (social, political, and economic) and the 25 values in order to get a snapshot of the *progress-prone* and *progress-resistant* attitudes of the country.

Once the weak-strong profile is clarified, local experts discuss what changes the population desires, and which of them may offer a good chance of success. After those preliminary goals are set, the local and foreign experts work together to select a combination of vehicles and strategies that could pave the way to progressive value change.

Another important consideration is that the initiative for the *axiological diagnosis* must be domestic. In other words, unless an interested group within a country, region, city, or community is convinced of the need and is committed to value change, the initiative has little chance of success.

Culture and values are always slowly evolving in response to changing conditions. Geography takes millennia to leave its imprint, and climate takes centuries. Historical forces or overhauling the legal system may require decades. But rapid changes can also happen, often as an outcome of crises such as wars or natural disasters. Such rapid changes can also, however, result from deliberate change generated by exceptional leaders and/or circumstances.

SUMMARY FINDINGS OF MEXICO SURVEY, 2010

1. Most Mexicans favor *progress* (51%) as defined by the CCI typology's progress-prone pole (Table 9.1), a minority (26%) hold resistant attitudes, and the rest (23%) have an intermediate position, ready to move toward one or other of the poles depending on market and government signals.
2. In terms of progress-prone attitudes, the social field is the strongest (65% progress-prone vs. 15% progress-resistant), the political is intermediate (48% vs. 27%) and the economic least favorable (39% vs. 36%).
3. The progress-prone are mostly in the social area (6 of 8 factors) and progress-resistance arises in the economic area (5 of 9). In politics there are 3 progress-resistant factors, but there are also 5 progress-prone.

Progress-Prone Factors

4. The social setting provides the greatest number of progress-prone factors of the entire spectrum of attitudes studied: daily virtues, importance of education, gender equality, solidarity, birth control, and code of ethics. But we identified some contradictions, in particular, the low appreciation of reading and the persistently low participation of women in senior

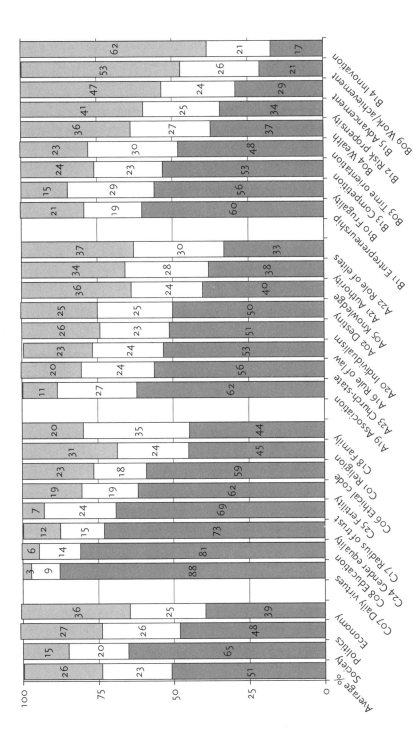

FIGURE 9.3 Summary of axiological diagnosis of Mexico

management and public companies (as opposed to increasing gender equality).

5. Despite three progress-resistant factors in the political area (responsibility of elites, accountability, and appetite for the truth), these may be balanced by five positive attitudes (high willingness to collaborate, respect for the separation of church and state, growing sense of respect for the law, individual responsibility, and control of own destiny).

6. In the economy, four progress-prone factors (entrepreneurial spirit, frugality, love of competition, and concern for the future) balance the four progress-resistant factors (low innovation, detachment from work, neglect of merit, and risk aversion).

Progress-Resistant Factors

7. Clearly, greater attention is required in four economic factors (low innovation, detachment from work, neglect of merit, and excessive fear of risk) that show the most progress-resistant attitudes to prosperity. Those who had positive attitudes may balance the resistance (between 17% and 34%).

8. In the political arena, there is no degree of progress-resistant factors as large as in the economic area, but attitudes toward the responsibility of elite accountability and appreciation for the truth are weak. Basically, equal percentages of Mexicans favor the progress-prone and progress-resistant attitudes in both these fields.

9. The relative progress-resistant factors of the social area are in the low trust in others and the high acceptance of eternal life.

Conclusion

Part IV has explored the ever-changing nature of culture, how this change happens, and if it is possible to lead the change toward desirable ends. It reviews the contributions of the six main agents of cultural change (family, school, religion, media, leadership, and the law), as well as the slow and fast processes of change. It briefly described how the improvements to society gained by higher education, higher income, urban dwelling, and the occupational transition from agriculture to industry and services, namely modernization, slowly lead to cultural change by generational replacement. To illustrate the process, it briefly mentioned the cases of Ireland, Spain, and Mexico. It also mentions how rapid change is possible, if rare, and cited the cases of the Japanese Meiji restoration, Turkey's Ataturk, Singapore under Lee Kwan You, and Bogotá under the *dupla* Mockus-Peñalosa. This review not only shows how cultural change is difficult to achieve, but also how it is even more difficult to sustain.

A question remains, whether cultural change can be conducted to desirable ends. If change is constantly occurring anyway, why not try to orient it in a certain direction? This chapter presents the methodology derived from the CCI

25-factors typology this author developed into an *Axiological Diagnosis*. It is a first step to determining a society's values profile, and may be followed by a process of selecting desirable ends, as well as the agents and strategies that may drive change. The exercise conducted in Mexico outlined here was also conducted in East Timor and Italy. The three cases show that cultural change is easier said than done, but that the possibility theoretically does exist. Fast cultural change requires either a strong, popular, and *respected* leader, or a deep and extended social mobilization to reach a successful end. External impositions simply cannot succeed.

Bottom line, it is up to the people and their local leaders to make it happen.

PART V

Concepts and Measures
of Development

In an increasingly performance-oriented society, metrics matter.
What we measure affects what we do. If we have the wrong metrics,
we will strive for the wrong things. In the quest to increase GDP, we
may end up with a society in which citizens are worse off.

—JOSEPH STIGLITZ, AMARTYA SEN, AND JUAN-PAUL FITOUSSI,
MISMEASURING OUR LIVES, P. XVII

10

The Objective and Subjective Development Indices

Current measures of development are not helping to set countries' incentives and priorities where they ought to be. The commission, created by former French president Nicolas Sarkozy at the beginning of 2008 and led by Joseph Stiglitz, Amartya Sen, and Juan-Paul Fitoussi, has covered the topic and explored alternatives extensively. But the problem is inherently attached to the method of measurement. All those metrics use *objective* data, while *subjective* data are barely used at all.

In other terms, *objective* metrics are generated from hard data (e.g., wealth, education level, life expectancy, pollution levels, etc.) from the old, simple, and limited GDP (gross domestic product) measure covered in the next section, to the new and complex *Global Competitiveness Report* of the World Economic Forum; while *subjective* metrics are derived from soft data. *Soft data* refer to answers from individual respondents collected through public opinion polls (nationally representative probabilistic surveys) covering a wide range of subjects.

Fields of specialization—*economics, politics, sociology* and many more—necessarily compartmentalize knowledge. But in the mind of the respondent, reality remains an integral whole and can only be captured by *subjective* indicators. Perceptions are fully intertwined and mutually influential; separating one from the other by fields is effectively impossible. *Culture* is the comprehensive integration of ideas, and that is the strength of a *subjective* index designed to capture the essence of culture. Some social scientists, accustomed to dealing mainly with hard data, may find it weak. It is not, as will be shown in the next chapter.

Measuring the Economy: Gross Domestic Product (GDP)

Today the majority of the world's countries report their GDP[1] statistics annually, which permits the keeping of a useful and more or less dependable historic record. Table 10.1 shows the 25 highest 2012 total GDPs of 181 nations with available data

TABLE 10.1

2012 Gross Domestic Product (GDP), in PPP terms (US$, trillions)*

—	European Union	$17.1	20%	15	Turkey	$1.4	1.6%
1	United States	$16.2	19%	16	Indonesia	$1.2	1.4%
2	China	$12.3	14%	17	Australia	$1.0	1.2%
3	India	$4.7	5.5%	18	Saudi Arabia	$0.88	1.0%
4	Japan	$4.5	5.2%	19	Poland	$0.85	1.0%
5	Germany	$3.4	3.9%	20	Iran (2009)	$0.83	1.0%
6	Russia	$3.4	3.9%	21	Netherlands	$0.72	0.8%
7	France	$2.4	2.8%	22	Thailand	$0.65	0.7%
8	United Kingdom	$2.4	2.7%	23	South Africa	$0.58	0.7%
9	Brazil	$2.3	2.7%	24	Egypt	$0.53	0.6%
10	Mexico	$2.0	2.3%	25	Colombia	$0.50	0.6%
11	Italy	$2.0	2.3%				
12	South Korea	$1.5	1.8%				
13	Canada	$1.5	1.7%		**Sum top 25:**	**$69.2**	80%
14	Spain	$1.5	1.7%		**World:**	**$86.1**	100%

* For full list and sources, see Appendix 4.

(see the full list, both ranked and alphabetical, in Appendix 4). Here we see that the combined GDP of those 181 nations amounts to $86.1 trillion (PPP[2])—25 countries provide 80% of the GDP and the remaining 156 countries provide 20%. This table shows that the GDP of the European Union ($17.1 trillion) exceeds that of the United States ($16.2 trillion), and also that China ($12.3 trillion), as a single country, has the second largest GDP in the world, earning two to three times more than India or Japan ($4.7 trillion and $4.5 trillion, respectively).

Measuring the GDP of a nation is undoubtedly useful—the G-20[3] list is basically derived from this one—but because it largely reflects the size of the population,[4] relying on this measure mainly shows overall economic power. To get a proper appreciation for a country's *development, per capita* GDP is an improvement—a better measurement—as Table 10.2 shows. A list of the richest 25 countries, with the highest *per capita* GDP, paints a very different picture from that created by the ranking of *total* GDPs.

The highest level of annual individual earnings (in terms of PPP) belongs to the citizens of Luxembourg ($88.3k) and the lowest to those of the Democratic Republic of Congo ($415). The worldwide average for annual individual earnings amounts to only $12.2k (see Appendix 5 for the full list both ranked and alphabetical). Additionally, this chart highlights that despite its economic clout, the United States is 8th in terms of per capita GDP, with average individual earnings of $51.7k, while China falls to 94th in the rankings, with a per capita GDP of $9,233. Fourteen European countries are included in the top 25, alongside four Asiatic nations or territories (Macao, Singapore, Hong Kong, and Japan) and three ex-colonies of Great Britain (United States, Canada, and Australia).

TABLE 10.2
The Top 25 Countries by 2012 per Capita GDP (US$, thousands)*

1	Luxembourg	$88.3	14	Netherlands	$43.1
2	Macao	$86.3	15	Sweden	$43.0
3	Qatar	$82.1	16	Canada	$42.5
4	Norway	$65.6	17	Denmark	$42.2
5	Singapore	$60.8	18	United Arab Emirates	$41.4
6	Switzerland	$53.3	19	Germany	$41.2
7	Brunei	$52.5	20	Belgium	$39.8
8	United States	$51.7	21	Finland	$38.3
9	Hong Kong	$51.1	22	Iceland	$37.6
10	Kuwait (2011)	$45.0	23	United Kingdom	$37.5
11	Australia	$44.6	24	France	$36.1
12	Ireland	$43.7	25	Japan	$35.2
13	Austria	$43.7	—	European Union	$33.6

* For full list and sources, see Appendix 5.

Although Qatar, Brunei, Kuwait, and the United Arab Emirates have superior per capita earnings to most other countries, these oil-producing countries do not, in fact, have greater levels of *development*. The price of petroleum, which first skyrocketed during the 1973 OPEC embargo, results in per capita GDPs so high that they create an exaggerated impression of national *development*. Such distortions are common not only to oil-producing nations; we see them also in those countries whose engines of development rely more on exports of a single natural resource of high value (e.g., diamonds, precious metals, cotton, etc.) than on the hard work of citizens.

Beyond the Economy: the *Human Development Index* (HDI)

In order to overcome distortions of this nature and move beyond measures of *economic strength*, the United Nations Development Program (UNDP) endeavored to create an index that would focus on the well-being of people more than on the states of markets and economies. The result of this initiative was the *Human Development Index*, whose creation and publication are indebted to both Sen and Pakistani economist Mahbub ul Haq.

Published annually since 1990, the HDI combines measurements of income with those of health and education, measured by life expectancy and level of education attained. In addition to identifying new ways of measuring international development, it has inspired groundbreaking indices that seek to measure things like gender inequality, income distribution, and poverty. Consequently, many countries use these metrics to create sub-national versions of the HDI.

As Table 10.3 shows, in the 2012 HDI (see the full list, both ranked and alphabetical, in Appendix 6), 16 of the 25 countries with the greatest human

TABLE 10.3
Top 25 Countries by Human Development (HDI, 2012)*

Rank	Country	Score	Rank	Country	Score
1	Norway	0.955	13	Hong Kong	0.906
2	Australia	0.938	13	Iceland	0.906
3	United States	0.937	15	Denmark	0.901
4	Netherlands	0.921	16	Israel	0.900
5	Germany	0.920	17	Belgium	0.897
6	New Zealand	0.919	18	Austria	0.895
7	Ireland	0.916	18	Singapore	0.895
7	Sweden	0.916	20	France	0.893
9	Switzerland	0.913	21	Finland	0.892
10	Japan	0.912	21	Slovenia	0.892
11	Canada	0.911	23	Spain	0.885
12	South Korea	0.909	24	Liechtenstein	0.883
			25	Italy	0.881

* For full list and sources, see Appendix 6.

development are European, with Norway in 1st place and the Netherlands in 4th; moreover, 4 countries are former British colonies (Australia in 2nd place; the United States in 3rd; New Zealand is 6th; and Canada is 11th). Three Asian countries appear in the top 25 (Japan, 10th; South Korea, 12th; Hong Kong, 13th). Israel—which geographically if not culturally belongs to the Middle East region—is positioned 16th. It is worth noting that none of the oil-producing countries on the previous list remains among the top 25 (Brunei is 30th; Qatar, 36th; United Arab Emirates, 41st; Kuwait, 54th; and Equatorial Guinea, 136th).

Toward a More Comprehensive Measure

A more complete measurement of development ought also to include *political rights* and *civil liberties* along the lines of Freedom House, the American organization established in 1941 in New York that has been dedicated to measuring democratic performance since 1972. Today, the organization generates comparative evaluations of civil liberties and political rights for 195 countries and 14 disputed territories (see the full list, both ranked and alphabetical, in Appendix 7). Table 10.4 shows the 50 countries that rank highest on political rights and civil liberties.

In the area of **political rights** they measure (1) electoral processes, (2) political participation and pluralism, and (3) functionality of government. On the topic of **civil liberties** they measure (1) freedom of expression and belief, (2) rights of free association and organization, (3) rule of law, and (4) individual rights and personal autonomy.

TABLE 10.4

Top 50 Countries on Political Rights and Civil Liberties (Freedom House, 2012)*

Rank	Country	Score	Rank	Country	Score
1	Finland	1.000	26	Switzerland	0.960
2	Iceland	1.000	27	Czech Republic	0.950
3	Luxembourg	1.000	28	Dominica	0.950
4	Norway	1.000	29	Estonia	0.950
5	San Marino	1.000	30	France	0.950
6	Sweden	1.000	31	Tuvalu	0.940
7	Barbados	0.990	32	Cyprus	0.930
8	Netherlands	0.990	33	Micronesia	0.930
9	Canada	0.980	34	Nauru	0.930
10	Denmark	0.980	35	Poland	0.930
11	Liechtenstein	0.980	36	St. Lucia	0.930
12	Australia	0.970	37	United States	0.930
13	Belgium	0.970	38	Palau	0.920
14	Ireland	0.970	39	Slovakia	0.920
15	Malta	0.970	40	Costa Rica	0.910
16	New Zealand	0.970	41	Kiribati	0.910
17	Portugal	0.970	42	Marshall Islands	0.910
18	United Kingdom	0.970	43	Slovenia	0.910
19	Uruguay	0.970	44	St. Kitts and Nevis	0.910
20	Andorra	0.960	45	Cape Verde	0.900
21	Austria	0.960	46	Lithuania	0.900
22	Bahamas	0.960	47	Mauritius	0.900
23	Chile	0.960	48	Grenada	0.890
24	Germany	0.960	49	St. Vincent and Gren.	0.890
25	Spain	0.960	50	Belize	0.880

* For full list and sources, see Appendix 7.

The highest rating a country can receive is 100, while 0 is the lowest. The average of all countries is used to calculate final classifications, which include ratings of *Free* (F), *Partially Free* (PF), and *Not Free* (NF).[5]

Twenty-five of 26 western European countries received the *Free* rating—the only exception being Turkey, which was classified as *Partially Free*. Of the 48 nations in sub-Saharan Africa, however, only 9 are listed as *Free* (Benin, Botswana, Cape Verde, Ghana, Mali, Mauritius, Namibia, São Tomé and Príncipe, and South Africa); among those in North Africa and the Middle East, only one country—Israel—received the same distinction.

The first four tables of this chapter measure the economic and political dimension, as well as education and health within the social dimension. Two other important factors of the **social** dimensions of *development* not accounted for in the measurements already reviewed are **income distribution**—a highly controversial topic in the United States—and **gender inequality**, a highly contro-versial one in the Muslim countries.

For many years, *income distribution* has been measured with the coefficient first developed by the Italian sociologist Corrado Gini[6] in 1912. According to this index, a value of 0 signifies perfect equality (*zero* concentration of wealth, or all people receiving the same income) and a value of 1 suggests the maximum level of inequality (one person holding all the wealth). On this scale, the country with the most equitable distribution of wealth in the world is Denmark, which has a coefficient of 0.248; the country with the most inequitable distribution is the Seychelles, which earned a mark of 0.658. The United States received a very poor coefficient of 0.408, ranking number 98. The top 50 countries are listed in Table 10.5 (see Appendix 8 for the full ranked and alphabetical list).

Another way of measuring *income distribution*, which is less exact but easier to understand, involves contrasting the average wealth of the richest 10% of the population with that of the poorest 10%. This metric measures the percentage of wealth in the hands of the top 10% as opposed to the bottom 10% (see Appendix 9 for the full ranked and alphabetical list). On this scale, Japan had the most equitable wealth distribution in the world in 1993, with a 4.5 to 1 ratio—which is to say that the richest 10% earned 4.5 times more than the poorest 10%.

Bolivia had the most inequitable distribution—157 to 1—and the global aver-age was 12 to 1. In the United States, the ratio was 15 to 1, meaning, in effect, that the poorest 10% of the United States population earned an average of $8,000 annually (or $24,000 for a family of three), whereas the average earnings of the richest 10% would amount to $120,000 per person per year (or $360,000 for a family of three). Contrasting the two metrics of Gini and ratios shows an incon-sistency that economists need to address. It is unlikely that Japan sank from #1 in 1993 to #72 in 2008, despite its economic crisis. Conversely, the United States shows more consistency, as it appeared as #72 in 1998 (measured by ratio) and appeared as #98 in 2000 (measured by Gini).

Income distribution produces quite a different ranking than that generated by economic and political data. Once the social dimension represented by this indica-tor is incorporated, those countries that remain on the egalitarian side of the spec-trum are generally in Europe, but also include nations of Confucian, Orthodox, and Islamic heritage; those on the less egalitarian end of the spectrum, however, are for the most part territories colonized by Spain, Portugal, and England—Australia and the United States among them. Of the 25 countries with the most inequitable income distribution, 11 are in Latin America and 12 are in sub-Saharan Africa.

Much like the dimension of *income inequality*, that of **gender inequality** also includes issues omitted from consideration by the indices we have so far exam-ined. Discrimination based on gender—as much as discrimination based on race, ethnicity, language, religion, wealth, sexual preference, or any other trait—harms the country where it is practiced. To be sure, all forms of discrimination are based on erroneous beliefs that often originate in long-active and generally unseen historical processes—beliefs that are simply assumed to be true. Perhaps

E 10.5

Coefficient for Income Distribution (Top 40 Countries and Bottom 20)*

Country Name	Gini	Year		Country Name	Gini	Year		Country Name	Gini	Year
Denmark	0.248	2011	21	European Union	0.307	2011	140	Swaziland	0.515	2010
Sweden	0.250	1999	22	Egypt	0.308	2008	141	Panama	0.519	2010
Norway	0.258	2000	23	Luxembourg	0.308	2000	142	Chile	0.521	2008
Slovak Rep.	0.260	2009	24	Tajikistan	0.308	2009	143	Paraguay	0.524	2010
Ukraine	0.264	2009	25	Armenia	0.309	2008	144	Lesotho	0.525	2003
Finland	0.269	2000	26	Iraq	0.309	2006	145	Suriname	0.529	1999
Belarus	0.272	2008	27	Netherlands	0.309	1999	146	Belize	0.531	1999
Malta	0.274	2008	28	Czech Rep.	0.310	2009	147	Zambia	0.546	2006
Serbia	0.278	2009	29	Hungary	0.312	2997	148	Brazil	0.547	2008
Afghanistan	0.278	2008	30	Slovenia	0.312	2004	149	Colombia	0.559	2010
Iceland	0.280	2006	31	South Korea	0.316	1998	150	Guatemala	0.559	2006
Bulgaria	0.282	2006	32	Timor-Leste	0.319	2007	151	Bolivia	0.563	2008
Germany	0.283	2000	33	Bangladesh	0.321	2010	152	Cent. African Rep.	0.563	2007
Cyprus	0.290	2005	34	Canada	0.326	2000	153	Honduras	0.570	2009
Kazakhstan	0.290	2009	35	France	0.327	1995	154	Angola	0.586	2000
Austria	0.292	2000	36	Nepal	0.328	2010	155	Haiti	0.592	2001
Ethiopia	0.298	2005	37	Belgium	0.330	2000	156	Botswana	0.610	1994
Montenegro	0.300	2008	38	Mali	0.330	2010	157	Micronesia	0.611	2000
Pakistan	0.300	2008	39	Moldova	0.330	2010	158	South Africa	0.631	2009
Romania	0.300	2008	40	Burundi	0.333	2005	159	Namibia	0.639	2004

* full list and sources, see Appendix 8.

the two most prevalent forms of discrimination in the world today are those based on gender and race.

In 1995, the UNDP's Report on Human Development introduced two measurements that highlight the plight of women (*Gender Development Index*, or GDI, and *Gender Empowerment Measure*, or GEM), and in 2010 these were merged into the *Gender Inequality Index* (GII), which is presented in Table 10.6. With the data generated by these measurements, it has become possible to verify that the more women participate in politics, the better a political system functions (Inglehart and Norris, 2003; Beltran, 2005).[7]

The transition from agriculture to manufacturing, which began at the outset of the 19th century, reinforced the social dominance of males, because heavy industrial work still required considerable physical strength. However, the transition to a postindustrial society—that is to say, a knowledge- and service-oriented society—has brought about greater gender equality in society as well as in the workplace. The women's liberation movements that began in some countries in the middle of the last century are only one expression of that transition. Most of today's advanced economies don't require muscular strength as much as intellectual strength, and women are demonstrating qualities that give them a relative advantage in the job market.

As measured by the GII (see Appendix 10 for the full ranked and alphabetical list), gender equality reaches the highest levels in Europe and the lowest in Africa, India, and in Islamic nations. Among the 25 countries with the highest

TABLE 10.6

Gender Equality Index (GII), 2013 (Top 40 and Bottom 20 Countries)*

Rank	Country	Value	Rank	Country	Value	Rank	Country Name	Val
1	Netherlands	0.045	21	Japan	0.131	128	Gambia	0.59
2	Sweden	0.055	22	Cyprus	0.134	129	Sudan	0.60
3	Switzerland	0.057	23	Greece	0.136	130	Kenya	0.60
3	Denmark	0.057	24	Poland	0.14	131	Burkina Faso	0.60
5	Norway	0.065	25	Israel	0.144	132	India	0.63
6	Germany	0.075	26	Luxembourg	0.149	132	Congo	0.63
6	Finland	0.075	27	South Korea	0.153	134	Papua New Guinea	0.63
8	Slovenia	0.08	28	Lithuania	0.157	135	Benin	0.63
9	France	0.083	29	Estonia	0.158	136	Zambia	0.62
10	Iceland	0.089	30	Macedonia	0.162	137	Cameroon	0.62
11	Italy	0.094	31	New Zealand	0.164	138	Côte d'Ivoire	0.63
12	Belgium	0.098	32	Slovakia	0.171	139	Mauritania	0.64
13	Singapore	0.101	33	Croatia	0.179	139	Sierra Leone	0.64
14	Austria	0.102	34	United Kingdom	0.205	141	Mali	0.64
15	Spain	0.103	35	China	0.213	142	Central Afr. Rep.	0.65
16	Portugal	0.114	36	Latvia	0.216	143	Liberia	0.65
17	Australia	0.115	36	Libya	0.216	144	Democratic Rep. of the Congo	0.68
18	Canada	0.119	38	Bulgaria	0.219	145	Saudi Arabia	0.68
19	Ireland	0.121	39	Malta	0.236	146	Niger	0.70
20	Czech Rep.	0.122	40	UAE	0.241	147	Afghanistan	0.71
						148	Yemen	0.74

* For full list and sources, see Appendix 10.

levels of gender equality, 20 are European, 2 are Asian (Singapore and Japan), and 2 are former British colonies (Australia and Canada); Israel, it should be noted, also makes the list. The United States, however, is not among the countries with the highest levels of gender equity; according to this measurement, it ranks 42.

The Objective Development Index (ODI)

HDI was a major, but still insufficient, advance in the measurement of *development*. Thus, a more comprehensive objective measurement ought to at least include data about political rights and civil liberties from the Freedom House index (FH), gender equality from the United Nations index (GII), and the level of income distribution (Gini index), which would still put it far from the optimal *dashboard* recommendations from the Sarkozy Commission.[8] ODI in particular misses a measure of sustainability due to the lack of consensus among experts. Table 10.7 aggregates those four indices to generate an *Objective Development Index* (ODI), in order to facilitate a more valid comparison among countries. Table 10.7 shows the ranking for 197 countries (see methodological details and the full ranked and alphabetical list in Appendix 11).

ctive Development Index (ODI)*

Rank	Country	Score	Rank	Country	Score	Rank	Country	Score
	Norway	1	67	Tunisia	0.557	133	Paraguay	0.376
	Sweden	0.992	68	Grenada	0.557	134	Nepal	0.374
	Denmark	0.98	69	Saint Kitts and Nevis	0.551	135	Tanzania	0.372
	Finland	0.958	70	Kazakhstan	0.55	136	Bolivia	0.37
	Netherlands	0.952	71	Bosnia and Herzegovina	0.549	137	Gabon	0.37
	Iceland	0.95	72	Turkey	0.543	138	Pakistan	0.368
	Germany	0.948	73	St. Vincent and the Grenadines	0.54	139	Benin	0.368
	Austria	0.919	74	Timor-Leste	0.538	140	Iran	0.365
	Switzerland	0.913	75	United Arab Emirates	0.537	141	Uzbekistan	0.359
	Canada	0.899	76	Palau	0.532	142	Cuba	0.355
	France	0.897	77	Antigua and Barbuda	0.524	143	Iraq	0.349
	Slovenia	0.896	78	Bahrain	0.522	144	South Africa	0.341
	Belgium	0.896	79	Malaysia	0.52	145	North Korea	0.34
	Australia	0.891	80	Lebanon	0.51	146	Solomon Islands	0.328
	San Marino	0.889	81	Peru	0.506	147	Botswana	0.327
	Luxembourg	0.889	82	Mexico	0.505	148	Cambodia	0.324
	Ireland	0.885	83	Brunei	0.503	149	Sao Tome and Principe	0.319
	Liechtenstein	0.884	84	Georgia	0.503	150	Togo	0.313
	Czech Republic	0.883	85	Thailand	0.499	151	Namibia	0.313
	Cyprus	0.875	86	Maldives	0.498	152	Myanmar	0.31
	Slovakia	0.874	87	Jamaica	0.496	153	Malawi	0.309
	Spain	0.872	88	Indonesia	0.494	154	Saudi Arabia	0.295
	Andorra	0.86	89	Azerbaijan	0.492	155	Syria	0.288
	Malta	0.854	90	Russia	0.483	156	Honduras	0.286
	South Korea	0.854	91	Belize	0.482	157	Burundi	0.284
	New Zealand	0.854	92	Tuvalu	0.481	158	Lesotho	0.282
	Monaco	0.849	93	Panama	0.48	159	Laos	0.274
	Italy	0.84	94	Nauru	0.478	160	Guatemala	0.265
	Japan	0.827	95	Algeria	0.477	161	Liberia	0.264
	Poland	0.822	96	Marshall Islands	0.472	162	Kenya	0.261
	Estonia	0.818	97	El Salvador	0.471	163	Sierra Leone	0.255
	United Kingdom	0.817	98	Philippines	0.466	164	Uganda	0.25
	Portugal	0.81	99	Oman	0.465	165	Ethiopia	0.237
	Greece	0.809	100	Kyrgyzstan	0.461	166	Burkina Faso	0.231
	Israel	0.783	101	Sri Lanka	0.46	167	Madagascar	0.221
	Hungary	0.782	102	Samoa	0.458	168	Papua New Guinea	0.22
	Croatia	0.779	103	Tajikistan	0.457	169	Djibouti	0.218
	Lithuania	0.778	104	Brazil	0.456	170	Niger	0.218
	Montenegro	0.777	105	Dominican Republic	0.454	171	Mauritania	0.211
	Bulgaria	0.776	106	Kiribati	0.454	172	Mozambique	0.209
	United States	0.776	107	India	0.447	173	Cameroon	0.209
	Serbia	0.764	108	Palestinian Territory	0.44	174	Afghanistan	0.207
	Latvia	0.739	109	Guyana	0.439	175	Nigeria	0.198
	Hong Kong	0.728	110	Tonga	0.437	176	Guinea-Bissau	0.198
	Romania	0.718	111	Ecuador	0.432	177	Côte d'Ivoire	0.192
	Singapore	0.65	112	Kosovo	0.43	178	Zambia	0.191
	Barbados	0.649	113	Suriname	0.427	179	Republic of Congo	0.191
	Ukraine	0.646	114	Jordan	0.427	180	Rwanda	0.188
	Albania	0.645	115	Ghana	0.423	181	Somalia	0.186
	Uruguay	0.639	116	Vietnam	0.421	182	Guinea	0.182
	Bahamas	0.637	117	Bangladesh	0.417	183	Mali	0.179
	Trinidad and Tobago	0.637	118	Vanuatu	0.416	184	Swaziland	0.173
	Mauritius	0.634	119	Egypt	0.409	185	Sudan	0.171
	Mongolia	0.633	120	Nicaragua	0.403	186	Eritrea	0.17
	Macedonia	0.618	121	Venezuela	0.402	187	South Sudan	0.157
	Chile	0.601	122	China	0.402	188	Yemen	0.155
	Moldova	0.599	123	Micronesia	0.399	189	Gambia	0.133
	Taiwan	0.599	124	Seychelles	0.397	190	Zimbabwe	0.123
	Libya	0.599	125	Cape Verde	0.397	191	Haiti	0.117
	Argentina	0.596	126	Qatar	0.392	192	Chad	0.112
	Saint Lucia	0.589	127	Senegal	0.391	193	Comoros	0.111
	Belarus	0.585	128	Fiji	0.391	194	Angola	0.09
	Costa Rica	0.581	129	Morocco	0.38	195	Democratic Rep. of the Congo	0.047
	Kuwait	0.576	130	Bhutan	0.379	196	Central African Rep.	0.038
	Dominica	0.563	131	Turkmenistan	0.378	197	Equatorial Guinea	0
	Armenia	0.56	132	Colombia	0.377			

The Nordic countries score the highest in the ODI rankings. **Norway**, which places 1st in HDI (which measures income, education, and health), is also in the top 5 of the other three indices (for gender equality, political rights/civil liberties, and income distribution). **Sweden** (2nd place overall) is 7th in HDI, 2nd in gender equality, 6th in rights-liberties, and 2nd in income distribution. **Denmark**, which is in 3rd place overall, is 15th in HDI, 3rd in gender equality, 10th in rights-liberties, and 1st in income distribution.

Table 10.7 highlights that, according to this index, the top five nations in the world are northern European countries. Of the former British colonies, **Canada** places highest (10th), followed by **Australia** (14th), and **New Zealand** (26th); the **United States** comes in a distant 41 overall—3rd in development, an unimpressive 42nd in gender equality, and a shocking 98th in distribution of wealth—trailing even its former parent country, the **United Kingdom**, whose overall score puts it in 28th place.

Nordic countries appear in the highest positions in most *objective* indices, with the sole exception of total GDP. The message of such measurements would seem to be, therefore, that it is *valuable* for a country to (1) attain a level of wealth that satisfies the material needs of the population; (2) create a series of institutional and social arrangements regarding food, hygiene, security, and health that increase life expectancy; (3) promote a high level of education among the general population, in accordance with the necessities of the country's economic structure and dominant industry; (4) foster a high level of respect for political rights and civil liberties that make life in the society easy and pleasant; (5) minimize social inequality (measured by disparities in wealth, assets, and opportunities) at all levels of the social pyramid and in specific geographic regions so that the society might preserve the dignity of human life; and, finally, (6) promote high levels of respect and tolerance for differences of race, gender, ethnicity, language, belief, sexual orientation, and other such traits, so that the most favorable circumstances for individual development and for the improvement of the collective well-being might be established.

The argument that it is essential to improve measurements of development is based on the assertion of the Sarkozy Commission that what we measure affects what we do. However, no one can be deluded that this will fundamentally change international relations, because at the end of the day *force* still prevails. Although there is a consensus that the UN's Human Development Index (HDI) is a better measure than GDP, the world's attention is not focused on Norway (first in HDI), but rather on the United States and China (first and second in GDP), and their ability to command the most powerful armies.

International bodies will most probably succeed in moving to measure development with a multidimensional approach such as ODI (which complements HDI's ranking of income, health, and education with measurements of gender equality, political rights and civil liberties, and income equality). Notwithstanding, the international order established by the Bretton Woods consensus is coming to an end, and it is currently not foreseeable whether a new international order—possibly based on an Asian hegemony—will give greater prominence to wisdom over force.

The *Subjective Development Index* (SDI)

This section presents a proposal for a *subjective* measurement of development based on the data gathered about individuals' perceptions through public opinion polls by the World Values Survey. It takes the two axes that produce Inglehart's *World Cultural Map* shown in Figure 2.4 in Chapter 2 (survival–self-expression and traditional–secular/rational), and combines them back into a single measure with a score for each country (methodological details in Appendix 12). Namely, it produces a ranking from the countries' scores on the *cultural map*, ranging from the highest, Sweden, to the lowest, Zimbabwe. In other words, this list is nothing but the numerical representation of the map.

As the discussion in Chapter 5 shows, the index could reflect cultures of *honor, achievement*, or *joy*, depending on the point in the *World Cultural Map* that is taken as reference. In this case I suggest taking the *achievement* option. The rationale behind it is that, as time passes, postindustrial countries show a propensity to move toward the upper-right corner of the *cultural map,* as shown in Figures 2.5 and 2.6 in Chapter 2.

One of the hypotheses behind the construction of this subjective index is that individuals use their cognitive abilities to internalize the outside world. The opinion surveys used in the World Values Survey explore a variety of subjects in hopes of apprehending the profound economic, political, and social values of individuals—values necessarily filtered through *shared systems of meanings, values, and beliefs*, which is to say, through cultures.

The *Subjective Development Index* (SDI) is the distance from each country's position to the greatest value on both the horizontal and vertical axes of the *cultural map*.[9] The top 10 countries on the SDI are in Europe, and 6 of those share a legacy of European Protestantism, while among the bottom 10 there are 6 Islamic (Pakistan, Jordan, Morocco, Iraq, Algeria, and Bangladesh), 3 African (Zimbabwe, Ghana, and Rwanda), and 1 Caribbean (Trinidad).

Comparing the Objective (ODI) and Subjective (SDI) Indices

When comparing the subjective and objective indices, a great resemblance to each other is found: 79% of their results correspond (correlation coefficient of $0.788; p < .001$ for Tables 10.7 and 10.8). But while the indices show similar results, they are not the same. More than half of the compared nations—50 of 96—maintain their relative rankings in both indices, changing positions by fewer than ten places. However, the rankings of 23 countries (one-quarter of the total) vary from index to index by anywhere from 20 to 54 places, as Table 10.9 shows.

TABLE 10.8
Subjective Development Index (SDI)**

Rank	Country	Score	Rank	Country	Score	Rank	Country	Scc
1	Sweden 5*	1	36	Cyprus 5*	0.345	71	Indonesia 5*	0.2
2	Norway 5*	0.9	37	Serbia 5*	0.341	72	Philippines 4*	0.2
3	Denmark 4*	0.833	38	Bosnia 4*	0.335	73	Mali 5*	0.2
4	Switzerland 5*	0.759	39	Portugal 4*	0.334	74	Zambia 5*	0.2
5	Andorra 5*	0.745	40	Hong Kong 5*	0.333	75	Venezuela 4*	0.2
6	Netherlands 5*	0.703	41	Brazil 5*	0.333	76	Russia 5*	0.2
7	Finland 5*	0.683	42	Vietnam 5*	0.326	77	Peru 4*	0.2
8	Iceland 4*	0.682	43	India 5*	0.325	78	Nigeria 4*	0.2
9	West Germany 5*	0.671	44	Bulgaria 5*	0.324	79	Georgia 3*	0.1
10	France 5*	0.657	45	Lithuania 4*	0.318	80	Colombia 5*	0.1
11	Australia 5*	0.648	46	Thailand 5*	0.317	81	Puerto Rico 4*	0.1
12	Belgium 4*	0.638	47	Malaysia 5*	0.314	82	Malta 4*	0.1
13	Austria 4*	0.63	48	Macedonia 4*	0.3	83	Iran 4*	0.1
14	Luxemburg 4*	0.625	49	Ukraine 5*	0.299	84	Azerbaijan 3*	0.1
15	Britain 5*	0.615	50	Estonia 4*	0.295	85	Burkina Faso 5*	0.1
16	New Zealand 5*	0.614	51	Taiwan 5*	0.292	86	El Salvador 4*	0.1
17	Czech Republic 4*	0.598	52	Dominican Republic 3*	0.291	87	Uganda 1*	0.1
18	East Germany 5*	0.588	53	Singapore 4*	0.29	88	Guatemala 4*	0.1
19	Greece 4*	0.586	54	Mexico 5*	0.281	89	Egypt 4*	0.1
20	Galicia 3*	0.57	55	Chile 5*	0.28	90	Tanzania 4*	0.1
21	Canada 5*	0.565	56	China 5*	0.277	91	Romania 5*	0.1
22	Slovenia 5*	0.55	57	Poland 5*	0.276	92	Bangladesh 4*	0.1
23	Japan 5*	0.538	58	Belarus 4*	0.269	93	Trinidad 5*	0.0
24	Italy 5*	0.511	59	Montenegro 4*	0.265	94	Rwanda 5*	0.0
25	Spain 5*	0.497	60	Ethiopia 5*	0.264	95	Algeria 4*	0.0
26	Israel 4*	0.494	61	Latvia 4*	0.251	96	Iraq 5*	0.0
27	Uruguay 5*	0.478	62	Kyrgyzstan 4*	0.239	97	Ghana 5*	0.0
28	Northern Ireland 4*	0.469	63	Hungary 4*	0.237	98	Morocco 5*	0.0
29	Croatia 4*	0.462	64	Turkey 5*	0.233	99	Jordan 4*	0.0
30	United States 5*	0.451	65	South Africa 5*	0.233	100	Pakistan 4*	0.0
31	Slovakia 4*	0.404	66	Armenia 3*	0.231	101	Zimbabwe 4*	0
32	Ireland 4*	0.397	67	Moldova 5*	0.231			
33	Moscow 2*	0.38	68	Saudi Arabia 4*	0.228			
34	Slovenia 2*	0.367	69	South Korea 5*	0.224			
35	Argentina 5*	0.361	70	Albania 4*	0.222			

* This number refers to the most recent WVS wave available for each country: 1 = c1980; 2 = c1990; 3 = c1995; 4 = c2000; 5 = c2005.

** For methodology and sources, see Appendix 12.

paring the Subjective Index (SDI) with the Objective Index (ODI)

Country	SDI	ODI	Country	SDI	ODI	Country	SDI	ODI
Sweden	1	2	Hong Kong	40	44	Venezuela	75	121
Norway	2	1	Brazil	41	104	Russia	76	90
Denmark	3	3	Vietnam	42	116	Peru	77	81
Switzerland	4	9	India	43	107	Nigeria	78	175
Andorra	5	23	Bulgaria	44	40	Georgia	79	84
Netherlands	6	5	Lithuania	45	38	Colombia	80	132
Finland	7	4	Thailand	46	85	Malta	82	24
Iceland	8	6	Malaysia	47	79	Iran	83	140
West Germany	9	7	Macedonia	48	55	Azerbaijan	84	89
France	10	11	Ukraine	49	48	Burkina Faso	85	166
Australia	11	14	Estonia	50	31	El Salvador	86	97
Belgium	12	13	Taiwan	51	58	Uganda	87	164
Austria	13	8	Dominican Republic	52	105	Guatemala	88	160
Luxembourg	14	16	Singapore	53	46	Egypt	89	119
United Kingdom	15	32	Mexico	54	82	Tanzania	90	135
New Zealand	16	26	Chile	55	56	Romania	91	45
Czech Republic	17	19	China	56	122	Bangladesh	92	117
East Germany	18	7	Poland	57	30	Trinidad & Tobago	93	52
Greece	19	34	Belarus	58	62	Rwanda	94	180
Canada	21	10	Montenegro	59	39	Algeria	95	95
Slovenia	22	12	Ethiopia	60	165	Iraq	96	143
Japan	23	29	Latvia	61	43	Ghana	97	115
Italy	24	28	Kyrgyzstan	62	100	Morocco	98	129
Spain	25	22	Hungary	63	36	Jordan	99	114
Israel	26	35	Turkey	64	72	Pakistan	100	138
Uruguay	27	50	South Africa	65	144	Zimbabwe	101	190
Croatia	29	37	Armenia	66	66			
United States	30	41	Moldova	67	57			
Slovakia	31	21	Saudi Arabia	68	154			
Ireland	32	17	South Korea	69	25			
Argentina	35	60	Albania	70	49			
Cyprus	36	20	Indonesia	71	88			
Serbia	37	42	Philippines	72	98			
nia and Herzegovina	38	71	Mali	73	183			
Portugal	39	33	Zambia	74	178			

The usefulness of the SDI very much lies in these differences, for the SDI includes the effect of culture, which is absent from objective measurements. This cultural effect, which is based on the axiological infrastructure stemming from a society's institutions, legal system, and religious roots, reveals the difference between the *subjective* perception of development by the individuals in a country and the *objective* measurements, which can come from a variety of indicators. Accordingly, in some countries people *feel* they live better than the indicators say, and in others the opposite is true. SDI, by definition, captures the mood of the nation.

Zimbabwe (101st), Philippines (72nd), Belarus (58th), Denmark (3rd), and Ukraine (49th) do not vary at all, while on the SDI Sweden (1st), Czech Republic (17th), and Luxembourg (14th), among others, make small gains. At the same time, Netherlands (6th), Norway (2nd), Chile (55th), and Germany (9th) fall slightly.

Of the countries that improve markedly on the SDI are, notably, Vietnam (42nd), Ethiopia (60th), Brazil (41st), India (43rd), and China (56th). On the other hand, the SDI demotes countries like Malta (82nd), Romania (91st), South Korea (69th), Trinidad and Tobago (93rd), and Poland (57th). I do not stop to analyze these variations now, but find it suggestive that 8 of 13 demoted countries (Romania, Poland, Hungary, Albania, Montenegro, Estonia, Latvia, and Azerbaijan) are former Soviet territories, while the remaining 5 are Islamic (Algeria and Jordan), African (Ghana) or small island (Malta and Trinidad & Tobago) nations. The most surprising case in this list is South Korea.

Does this suggest that cultural origin is, in the final analysis, destiny? Not really—because as we have observed, cultures are in the process of perpetual change: they continually face opportunities and critical junctures that trigger virtuous or vicious spirals. These spirals emerge through processes of decision-making utilized by individuals, families, corporations, and governments at all levels. Those opportunities result from new problems that arise unexpectedly each day. If the national leadership structure is synchronized in the right direction, the country will advance; if the decisions are misaligned, the country will retrogress.

Can a virtuous spiral extend itself indefinitely? Judging from centuries of world history, the answer is no. Virtuous spirals can, of course, bring individuals, families, firms, countries, or whole civilizations to the summit of success—and as they move toward the summit, the best of their abilities and values are put into play. But once significant success has been achieved and enjoyed for some time, a new and opposing spiral of arrogance is bound to begin, as generational replacement takes place. Individuals, families, firms, countries, or civilizations come to believe themselves special, selected, invincible—that they need no help from anyone, anywhere. It is with the rise of these beliefs that decline begins.

PART VI

The Driving Forces of Development

[. . .] it is finally ideas and their creation which for good and sometimes for evil are the fundamental driving force of the human condition.

—DOUGLASS NORTH, *UNDERSTANDING THE PROCESS OF ECONOMIC CHANGE*, P. 18

11

The Forces of Nature and Human Action

The debate over the drivers of development can historically be divided into two main schools of thought, emanating, fundamentally, from opposing worldviews represented in the works of the two deep thinkers of the 19th and 20th centuries: Karl Marx (1818–1883) and Max Weber (1864–1920). Is it changes in material conditions—*historical materialism*—that explain development as they settle, endure, and turn into *structures*? Or is it the *power of ideas*, the pursuit of ideals, referred to as Weber's *idealism*? These two eminent intellectuals, Marx and Weber, pursued this question from entirely incompatible philosophical positions.

Evidently they never debated each other directly. At the time of Marx's death in 1883, Weber was just 20 years old, but the latter ferociously criticized the ideas of the former, and the debates with Marx's followers were brutal. The same could be said of the later debates between the followers of each. But those debates have enriched the evolution of economic, political, and social thinking for the past 150 years.

Structural thinkers—particularly Adam Smith (1776) and Marx (1848), and more recently Lipset (1960), Rostow (1960), Diamond (1997), and others—have convincingly argued that it is the power of structures (geography, demography, economics, political systems, and the like) that drive development. The next section examines first the forces of nature (climate, geography, and demography), and then the forces of human action (economics, politics, and society).

Cultural theorists—descriptively Tocqueville (1835) and deeply Weber (1905), and in recent times Dealy (1977), Huntington (1993), Landes (1998), and others—have proposed that development is largely dependent upon the power of ideas. The following chapter (Chapter 12) is devoted to a brief discussion of the forces of culture.

Is the world moving thanks to a *push* from material conditions (Marx), or is it moving because of a *pull* from the power of ideas (Weber)? Are men being forced to action by the *circumstances* (Marx), or by the pursuit of *ideals* (Weber)? These discussions enlightened the academic and political debate, but offered no easy solution until an intellectual current emphasizing the *interaction* between culture and structure began to reveal itself in the form of *institutions*.

Antonio Gramsci (1891–1937) initiated the intermediary school of thought—**interactive explanations**—and Daniel Bell (1976), Geert Hofstede, (1980) Shalom Schwartz (1987), Ronald Inglehart (1990), Douglass North (2005), Daniel Yergin (1998), and Acemoglu and Robinson (2012), among others, have built upon it. They imply that structural forces are internalized by the individual or groups, reinterpreted in light of previous experiences, and returned to the outside world in the form of actions or decisions, immediate or delayed, as technological, intellectual, and/or institutional *innovations*. The last section of Chapter 12 addresses the interaction of structures and ideas.

The *Conditions* of Nature: Climate, Geography, and Demography

The deepest, most powerful, ultimate cause that has impacted and continues to impact the planet and its species over million of years is **climate**. It took climate variations of fewer than 5°C (9°F) to make us humans appear or disappear from the polar regions and/or the equator over hundreds of millennia and to populate the continents.

During the cooling periods, most of the Earth's surface was covered by ice and snow. During the warming periods, the tropical climate zones have stretched to the polar regions. With the relative climatic stabilization of the last 150 thousand years, as shown in Figure 11.1, *Homo sapiens* populated the planet as we know it today, driven by our hunter-gatherer instincts.

In this sense, climate is the driving force with the greatest explanatory power, except that its impact is so subtle and gradual as to be perceptible only across millennia. For the purposes of human metrics such as years or decades, then, climate gives the erroneous impression of acting as a constant. But that is wrong, because the effects of climate have historically affected individuals' values through generations. Colder climates taught discipline to primitive humans, while milder climates allowed less stressful living.

Climate and its mechanisms are highly complex processes, as evidenced by the Milankovitch cycles (Milankovitch, 1941[1969], p. 470) associated with planetary orbits around the Sun and the rotations of Earth on its axis. The planet cools and warms in combined cycles of 400,000, 100,000, 41,000, and 21,000 years. However, the scientific consensus today is that global warming for the last 100 years, as shown in Figure 11.2, is man-made. It threatens food production due to a decrease in crop yields, as well as an increase in extreme weather.

Another highly consequential effect of climate change is its impact on sea level. Many islands in the Pacific and Atlantic Oceans were accessible by land 20 millennia ago (Buchdahl, 1999, p. 49), when the sea level was 125 meters below its level today—more than the height of the Statue of Liberty (305 feet, or 93 meters). Sea levels today are the highest they have been in the last 120,000 years, and they will rise further as the climate continues warming. The rise threatens islands and coastal areas all over the world.

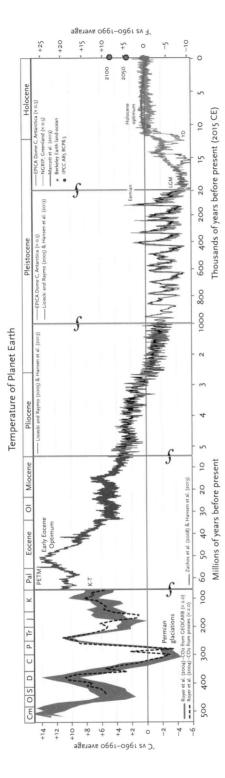

FIGURE 11.1   Earth temperature, 542 million years before the present

Image credit Glen Fergus. Obtained from Wikimedia Commons (http://commons.wikimedia.org/wiki/File:All_palaeotemps.png).

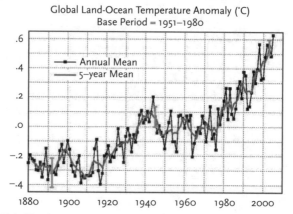

FIGURE 11.2 Global land-ocean temperature since 1880

Reprinted from James Hansen et al., 2006, "Global Temperature Change," PNAS, 103(39). Copyright (2006) National Academy of Sciences, U.S.A. Reprinted with permission.

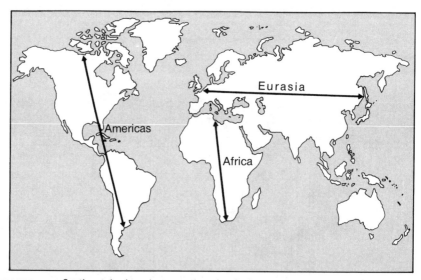

FIGURE 11.3 Continental axis and propagation of agriculture

Major Axes of the Continents, from Guns, Germs and Steel: The Fates of Human Societies by Jared Diamond. Copyright 1997 by Jared Diamond. Used by permission of W. W. Norton & Company, Inc.

Humans came across and adapted to new plants and animals, which in turn propagated themselves along the lengths of horizontal **geographic** axes, as shown in Figure 11.3. Due to the climatic similarity between regions of the same latitude, Eurasia was the landmass that saw the greatest propagation of flora and fauna. Africa and the Americas, with their large vertical axes, were not propitious for North–South propagation of plant and animal species, although the rich soils of Mesoamerica would grow potent maize, beans, and potatoes to sustain millions of inhabitants.

Geography and the environment interact by creating a great variety of habitats to which we have had to adapt ourselves: mountains, deserts, jungles, plains, islands, hills, and polar regions. Without a doubt, these each presented us with advantages and disadvantages, leaving their mark on our customs, conduct, traditions, myths, and, over the centuries, leading to our values and cultures. Climate, geography, and environment are interconnected systems that affect us all. Figure 11.4 shows the world's deep-sea currents. It illustrates, for example, the connection between and the reason behind the abundance of rainfall in Seattle and England, as well as hurricanes in the Atlantic and typhoons in the Pacific.

The effects of geography and environment are very profound and important for development, but as with climate, their impact is felt only over the course of centuries. For the purposes of measurement over years or decades, they appear to be constants. Nonetheless, when comparing some countries with others (islands vs. large landmasses, mountains vs. plains, coastal vs. landlocked regions, lands with or without natural resources, etc.), the residual impacts of these factors of development become more evident.

A population's size, growth rate, density, and make-up in terms of age, education, health, place of residence, and so on—that is, its **demography**—are elements with a great impact on development and which, at the same time, are affected by development. Population size has very deep roots in the past, linked to the abundance of food in the world's original regions for its four main crops (sorghum, wheat, rice, and corn), as shown in Figure 11.5.

It was not humans who developed the crops, but rather the crops that actually developed us. Humans were merely wandering—just passing by different regions of the planet—when in some regions they encountered a particularly nutritious and plentiful food supply. The availability of food encouraged groups to remain in those areas, and eventually allowed for demographic explosions. That is why Ethiopia, China, the Middle East, and Mesoamerica were among the first regions to send out mass migrations.

This can be seen if we look at population growth. The world's population remained below 268 million until the 10th century. But by the year 1820, it had quadrupled, to slightly over one billion. And in the fewer than 200 years since, it has grown sevenfold to reach 7 billion in 2011 (Maddison, 2007, p 376).

The size and speed of population growth has caused enormous changes in the wealth and poverty of nations, as well as their relative political power on the world stage. This is how the empires of antiquity (Babylonian, Egyptian, Greco-Roman, the Indus Valley, and Mesoamerican civilizations), as well as more recent ones (Arab, Ottoman, Portuguese, Spanish, Dutch, British, Soviet, and American) came into being.

As conditions in health and hygiene, education, urbanization, and life expectancy improved, countries became established as nations, with occasional disturbances such as widespread warfare, genocides, famines, or plagues. But what has perhaps weighed most heavily upon the course of development from the 18th century onward is scientific and technological advancement.

FIGURE 11.4 World deep-sea currents (Ocean Circulation Conveyor Belt)

NASA/JPL, http://www.jpl.nasa.gov/news/news.php?feature=2534.

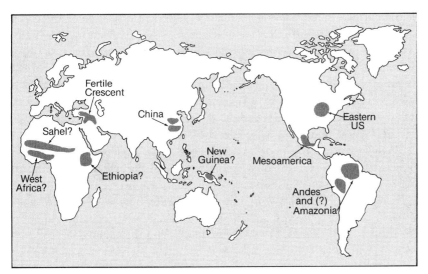

FIGURE 11.5 World's original agriculture zones

"A question mark indicates some uncertainty whether the rise of food production at that center was really uninfluenced by the spread of food production from other centers, or (in the case of New Guinea) what the earliest crops were." Centers of Origin of Food Production, from *Guns, Germs and Steel: The Fates of Human Societies* by Jared Diamond. Copyright 1997 by Jared Diamond. Used by permission of W. W. Norton & Company, Inc.

The *Conditions* of Human Action: Economics, Politics, and Society

Economic structures (agrarian, industrial, or service-based), **political structures** (imperial, feudal, colonial, democratic, dictatorial, capitalist, or communist), and **social structures** (egalitarian vs. unequal, rural vs. urban, working class vs. middle class) are also agents of change. Their impact may be measured in years, quarters, months, weeks, days, hours, or minutes by way of the distinct behaviors they unleash—from annual GDP growth to minute-by-minute stock exchange indexes.

One area of the social sciences that has received much attention due to its impact on development is the political and economic structures of powerful countries and their relations with and policies toward the rest of the world's countries. Of the six *ancient* empires, three arose in relative proximity to one another (Babylonia, Egypt, and Greece) and three umbrella clusters were remote from each other (China, Indus Valley, and Mesoamerica). Invariably, these empires were built on a combination of demography and technology—that is, when numerically large groups of humans managed to conquer and impose their rule onto other groups of humans, the latter were generally inferior in number and/or technological development.

EMPIRES AND COLONIES

Among the nine more recent empires of the last two millennia (Chinese, Roman, Arab, Ottoman, Portuguese, Spanish, French, Dutch, and British), the weight of demography was decisive for the first four; but for the last five, which were set up as colonial systems, the decisive factor was technology.

In the case of Holland and England, a new element began to have an important impact as well: institutional innovations—that is, the interaction between structure and culture. The appearance of legal and financial systems, which reduced uncertainty in property rights and trade, laid the foundations for the economic and political development that would bolster the power of both these countries—above all for England, from the industrial revolution forward.

England's originally poor agrarian colonies in what would become the United States, Canada, Australia, and New Zealand benefited from receiving the Protestant axiological foundation with its strong work ethic, in addition to the repertory of institutions that fostered enterprise and political equality. American independence and the United States' later territorial expansion in the 19th century enabled the country to experience sustained growth in its economy, without the responsibility and expense associated with maintaining world peace.

The American industrial boom was in its heyday at the beginning of the 20th century, while World War I was devastating for Europe. Within this framework, the Bolshevik Revolution of 1917 and the subsequent formation of a communist state came to define the bipolar world that would shape the 20th century: the United States of America versus the Union of Soviet Socialist Republics (USSR).

The worldwide Great Depression of the 1930s marked the beginning of a battle over the global economy, as represented by the two models of development seen in the United States and the Soviet Union. Between 1930 and 1950, the world seemed to be leaning toward the Soviet model (Yergin and Stanislaw, 1998, pp. xvi–xvii).

The end of World War II, the establishment of the United Nations, and the new world order represented by the Bretton Woods agreements (which created the World Bank and the International Monetary Fund), as well as the success of the Marshall Plan in Europe, energized the United States and international institutions to try a similar strategy in Latin America and Africa for a similar process of liberalization. It did not meet with the kind of success hoped for.

MODERNIZATION THEORY, *DEPENDENCY* SCHOOL, AND GLOBALIZATION

Back in the 1960s, one of the most influential currents of development was ***modernization theory***. It proceeded from the assumption that economic growth would bring development and consequently democracy. It basically postulated that economic prosperity was linked to a series of changes, including industrialization, urbanization, mass education, occupational specialization, bureaucratization, communications, and so on, which were, in turn, related to broader cultural, social, and political changes.

Once a society was engaged in a process of industrialization, a series of changes in other spheres followed (Lipset, 1960; Rostow, 1960). Rostow's theory of economic *take-off* suggested that sustained growth involved stages of development from traditional to modern. However, Rostow did not foresee the capacity of underdeveloped countries' elites to sequester the fruits of prosperity for their own benefit. Traditional societies were characterized by different economic activities, values, and political culture than were industrial and postindustrial societies.

Early modernization theories were criticized as economic determinism, linear, and ethnocentric, because they stressed the Western pattern as a model for arriving at modernity. Contemporary interpretations see the causal links to be reciprocal multifactorial changes that work together and are mutually reinforcing. In a way, modernization is conceived as a syndrome of economic, cultural, political, and social changes that are mutually supportive (Inglehart, 1990, 1997; Bell, 1973).

In the context of the Cold War, with much of the world ambivalent between communism and capitalism, and as a reaction against modernization, a line of thinking about economics in Latin America emerged known as the ***dependency school***. Now outdated, it basically held that the structure and international division of labor between commodity-exporting and industrialized countries was disadvantageous for the former and worked to the advantage of the latter. This debate dragged on until economic conditions brought about the collapse of communism, symbolized by the fall of the Berlin Wall in 1989.

The *dependency school* (Fernando Henrique Cardoso, Celso Furtado, and Andre Gunder Frank) was a reaction to early modernization theory. It originated in a debate over the problems of underdevelopment, particularly in Latin America. The dependency analysts argued that the region's integration into the world economy was central to its economic backwardness. Rather than being caused by *traditional* structures as modernization theorists suggested, underdeveloped countries were characterized by a series of core-periphery relationships at the international and national level, as they served as providers of raw materials at low prices fixed by the developed countries, which were advantageous for the importer and disadvantageous for the exporter country. These relationships worked to drain surplus capital from the region to the core.

Dependency views lost their appeal—not only around the world but also in Latin America, where they had gained influence during the 1960s and 1970s—when several authoritarian regimes like Argentina, Chile, and Brazil began democratic transitions.

The last decade of the 20th century and the first two decades of the 21st century have been dominated by an acceleration in the process of **globalization**, accompanied by the economic expansion of emerging countries led by the BRICs (Brazil, Russia, India, and particularly China) and the MISTs (Mexico, Indonesia, South Korea, and Turkey). Following the global economic crisis of 2008, mature industrialized societies in the West (particularly Europe and the United States) have been faced with dire situations, which are pulling at the seams of their social fabrics and putting their political systems to the test.

THREE MODELS OF DEVELOPMENT: THE UNITED STATES, THE SOVIET UNION, AND CHINA

In the last century the world has witnessed three models of development: the American, Soviet, and Chinese.[1] Each one was inspired by a completely different worldview. After years of operation, it is now clear that the incentives and variables were also totally different: economic incentives in the American model; political variables in the Soviet model; and social variables—demography—in the Chinese model. Each one, of course, showed strengths and weaknesses and different outcomes.

From the last quarter of the 19th century, the United States was a world economic engine and a magnet for immigration. No doubt, the American model *seemed* the best all around. After the American Great Depression of the 1930s, the world began to question the supremacy of the American model, and attention was directed to the Soviet model. Many countries and political parties fell into the policies propelled by Russia: England, Nordic, Latin American, and African countries, as well as China and later India. The collapse of the Berlin Wall in 1989 put the questioning to rest. However, the economic success enjoyed by China in the last three decades is again raising doubts about which is a better model.

The **American model**, established by the 1776 Declaration of Independence and the 1787 Constitution, has deep roots in Europe, starting from the time of European colonization by Rome. After the fall of the Roman Empire in 476 AD, Europe began slowly down the road toward its current make-up of nation-states. In reality this was not a process guided by the *pursuit* of ideals, as suggested by Weber. Rather, it was a process *driven* by circumstances, as Marx proposed. That is, what was done was what could be done, without much possibility of choosing between options. This is how, as Rome collapsed, monarchies and the feudal state—organized around agrarian labor and servitude—came to be.

It was more a matter of historical and geographic accident—due to its distance from Rome, the hub of the Empire—that a sort of proto-democratic and egalitarian legal system, which eventually inspired the American model, was planted and germinated in England. With the passing of centuries, this would lead to important differences between it and the rest of Europe. The Magna Carta of 1215, the civil war of 1642–1651, and the Glorious Revolution of 1688 ended in the consolidation of the nobles' rights over the power of the king in Parliament, which in turn opened the path to citizenship.

When, at the beginning of the 17th century, the English began migrating to the American colonies, they brought with them—as a result of these historical confrontations—the value they placed on their hard-won freedoms. Furthermore, the European Renaissance recovered the Greek and Roman notions of the ideal forms of government. This is what nurtured the authors—Jefferson in particular—of the United States' Declaration of Independence and Constitution.

The American model had a very strong axiological foundation—the deeply shared Protestant values of the 13 colonies—that included individualism, equal opportunity, open competition, and strong voting rights—for white male landowners, at least. That is, it was not based on some central ideal or theoretical model; instead, the country was built in an adversarial, dialectical manner, through the free and fierce competition of ideas and propositions. The Declaration of Independence of 1776 captures the axiological essence of the time in its second paragraph, where it states that

> . . . all men are created equal, endowed by their Creator with certain unalienable Rights, that among these are **Life**, **Liberty**, and the **Pursuit of Happiness**. [my emphasis]

There was a strong connection between American thinkers of this period and the ideas behind the French Revolution of 1789. Benjamin Franklin and Thomas Jefferson had served as the American ambassadors to France, and intellectual cross-pollination was abundant. The French equivalent—**liberty, equality, fraternity**—adopted from 1791 onward, reveals this connection. In this sense, the model could be attributed to both countries, but historically speaking, the United States came first.

Despite the overwhelming consensus surrounding George Washington during the first years of the new republic, conflict between the competing visions of John Adams and Thomas Jefferson began to take shape. While Adams was a firm believer in a centralized government, Jefferson deferred to individual states' rights. First came the Federalist and Democratic-Republican debates. Federalists then turned into *Whigs*, and later into Republicans, until the American political system finally developed the two current main political parties—Republican and Democratic—as an expression of the deep philosophical currents of society. But the debate was more about economics than about the political system. The same characteristics on display in terms of political values were also at work in the economy and the market: individualism, equal opportunity, open competition, and strong voting rights.

However, in this new postmaterialist stage, the traditional American model does not appear to be the most suitable and calls for improvement. The dysfunction is based on excessive consumption after the period of ascendency, already completed several decades ago, when the country achieved the highest levels of material and economic well-being in the world (Bell, 1976, p. 78).

Lenin (Vladimir Ilyich Ulyanov, 1870–1924) developed the Soviet model. He was inspired by Marx and built the model upon his ideas—the same ones that arose as a reaction against the early days of capitalism that Marx lived through (*the thesis*)—but intensively adapted them. Lenin discovered Marx in 1888 and became very active in political circles thereafter, which ended with his imprisonment in Siberia for three years in 1897. He was forced to live in and out of Russia, translating and updating Marxism, which gained him fame and respect in revolutionary circles.

When the 1917 Russian Revolution forced Tsar Nicholas II to abdicate, Lenin was in exile in Zurich. Returning to Russia was extremely difficult as it was in the middle of World War I, but the difficulties for train travel just added to the anticipation when his group finally arrived on April 16 in St. Petersburg. On the train trip, Lenin wrote his *April Theses*, mostly aimed at fellow Bolsheviks in Russia. Here he begins delineating the **Soviet model**, which was further detailed in his book published late that year, *The State and Revolution*.

Hypothetically, the Soviet model is ethically superior because it attempts to satisfy all peoples' needs. However, in practice, it showed deep limitations when confronted with human nature and perverse incentives. The proposition of constructing a strong state to uplift an egalitarian proletariat (*the antithesis*) was directly inspired by the Marxist conviction, although Lenin did not place the emphasis on the bourgeoisie, but on the proletariat. In summary, the use of *politics*—the strong proletarian state and class struggle—was to improve development. The American model was not conceived with the same degree of theoretical density seen in Lenin's Soviet model, or Mao's in China.

The **Chinese model** conceived by Mao and spelled out in his *Little Red Book* also derives from Marxist ideas, albeit tinged with the years of communist experience in the Soviet Union. Mao emphasized development in *society and culture* rather than politics. The decision to slow down demographic growth—the "one child policy"—would propel economic growth. But the idea of class struggle and exterminating the bourgeoisie was less emphasized. Despite the traumatic 150 years of China's initial encounters with the Western powers, the country began to recover rapidly after the end of World War II. Mao brought to his country the energy and commitment for change, battling severe drawbacks. That energy set the foundations of a political system that has been functional within its cultural framework.

After Mao's death in 1976 and the loosening of controls on land and the economy, the *Confucian* axiological infrastructure—appreciation for learning and hard work—that exists within the Chinese population, together with the extensive network of Chinese diaspora that exists all over the world, is making the recovery relatively rapid. China today shows the dynamism that the United States showed starting in 1880. Where this story will end is still an open question. The propagation of the Chinese model will be subject to the way China develops in the next decade or so.

In summary, in its attempts to achieve development in the 20th century, mankind experimented with the three paths described (American, Soviet, and Chinese), based on *intervening* in economic, political, or social variables, respectively. The American model is the most functional in terms of economic production, while the Soviet model ultimately showed itself not to be. For all of its supposed theoretical and ethical superiority, the Soviet system in practice revealed that, given a lack of incentive to compete and work hard, humans lose motivation and fall into a kind of *social despair*, thus rendering collective engagement all the more difficult. In other words, the Soviet model found its limitations when it applied the same political rationality to the economy. To some extent, the American model is finding its limitations in applying its economic rationality to politics, in addition to the unsustainability of growth for the current stage of capitalism. The Chinese model is still an open book, but it is showing remarkable results so far. How will their limitations manifest themselves?

12

The Power of Ideas

We now turn to the power of ideas. Hence, we leave Marx and enter the realm of Weber. How did ideas become powerful? How it is that humans began producing knowledge? And why? We share with the animal kingdom our survival instinct and two primordial impulses: eating and reproducing. Our zoological supremacy makes us the only species capable of making three unique contributions—life (in agriculture), beauty (in the arts), and knowledge (science)—as well as committing three horrific and shameful acts that no other species is capable of—ecocide, genocide, and suicide (Diamond, 1992, p. 137). We distinguish ourselves from most of the animal kingdom by our capacity for language, making tools, and self-consciousness. A number of other species (dolphins, primates, etc.) display considerable skill in the first two of these. But where we stand alone as a species is in our evolved consciousness, thinking, and knowledge. *Self-consciousness* is *the* distinctive mark of being human, and lies at the heart of cultures. This is why culture is a subtle, *weak*, but long-lasting force of development, as opposed to the *strong* but sometimes short-lived human forces.

Explosion of *Consciousness*

The discussion of the power of ideas evokes the evolution of philosophy, religion, and ethics. The German philosopher Karl Jasper (1883–1969), a close friend of Weber, called attention to the more or less simultaneous appearance of *intellectual revolutions* in China, India, the Middle East, and the West, sometime around the 8th century BC. Jaspers called this revolutionary occurrence the *Axial Age* to suggest its *pivotal* nature—its function as an axis around which a new world began to turn.[1]

In the 2000-year technological calm between the beginning of the *Iron Age* and the invention of gunpowder, there occurred the *Axial Age of Religion* and philosophy to which Jaspers refers. Beginning in the 8th century BC, humanity underwent a transcendental enlightenment: it was the age of the prophets of Israel, Isaiah, Jeremiah (655–586 BC), and Ezekiel (622–570 BC); of Zarathustra in Persia (?–583 BC); of Buddha in Nepal (563–483 BC); of Confucius in China (551–479 BC); and of Socrates (469–399 BC), Plato (428–348 BC), and Aristotle (384–322 BC) in Greece.

Three centuries later, Jesus appeared, and Muhammad entered six centuries later. It was not until the Protestant Reformation in the 16th century and the European Enlightenment in the 17th that the next great thought revolutions occurred—revolutions facilitated by the introduction of the printing press to Europe in 1440 AD. The final era—the *Technological Age*—began with the utilization of steam in 1769 (Bell, 1973[1999], p. xiii).

If, as Daniel Bell proposes, the last 200 years have been the *Axial Age of Technology*, it would mean that we are once again under the influence of *historic-materialism*—which is to say that *structural causes* are driving development. However, unlike the technology of the 18th and 19th centuries, which was predominately heuristic in nature (i.e., trial and error), today's technology is the product of an intense interaction between the social and physical worlds (i.e., of science and the market). In other words, we are really under the influence of the *interaction* of ideas and structural conditions. Moreover, sacred religious texts and works of great philosophers continue to exert a tremendous influence on modern individuals—an influence that is only amplified by means of electronic communication.

The interplay between the world of ideas and knowledge and the world of material concerns has been greatly intensified by technology; indeed, the appearance of new material circumstances (e.g., millions of vehicles by air, sea, and land) creates new problems (e.g., optimizing the movement of such vehicles), and in turn those problems force us to search for solutions that ultimately contribute to technological innovation (e.g., the Global Positioning System) and that are based on a combination of other technological advances (in this case, advances in satellite technology, cartography, wireless communication, and the like). The social and material impact of such innovation is enormous.

Intellectual Innovation: The Evolution of Knowledge and Science

How did our own inquisitiveness begin to pique our curiosity and appetite for reflection? Without a doubt, the environment provided primitive humans plenty of stimuli that were not easy to understand: the sun, the moon, rain, wind, lightning, nighttime, and death, just to name a few perplexing phenomena. And perhaps in that search for the meaning of life and death, for the explanation of nighttime and the vastness of the universe, philosophical and religious thoughts—that line of thinking which gives the power of ideas a leading role to play—began to take root.[2]

And so in this search there arose monotheisms, trinities, polytheisms, and atheisms—some closer to their ancestors and forebears; others, closer to the supernatural and metaphysical.

But the kingdoms of the gods of sun, moon, wind, lightning, and many other magical and metaphysical explanations and revelations began falling away before the advance of a naturalistic understanding as the fields of science and philosophy broadened. That is, the explanatory field left to religion grew ever smaller.

Following the philosophical and religious explosion that occurred in the half-millennium from the 8th to the 3rd centuries BC in India, Persia, Egypt, Greece, China, a relative intellectual calm set in—interrupted by the founding of Christianity in the 1st century AD and Islam in the 6th century—until the calm began to break again in the 14th century with the European Renaissance, followed in the 17th century by the Enlightenment.

Undoubtedly, material causes drove the slow advance of humankind from the *Stone Age* to the *Iron Age*. Until the 1st century, all of the ancient civilizations on Earth (Mesopotamian/Middle Eastern, Egyptian, Indian, Chinese, Greco-Roman, Mesoamerican) were at a relatively similar level of development, with a life expectancy of about 24 years (Maddison, 2006, p. 31).

Until the 14th century, China had more technological innovations and advances than Europe or the Islamic world. They had discovered or developed irrigation systems, sluiceways, cast iron, deep drilling, gunpowder, the compass, paper, porcelain, the printing press, and many more inventions (Diamond, 1997, p. 253).

Chinese knowledge in navigation, the cutting-edge technology of its day, was the most advanced there was, as was its shipbuilding. The establishment of a maritime route had begun as early as the 2nd century BC, and by the 12th century the Chinese had a standing navy. It is remarkable that over a 25-year period from 1405 onward, they made seven major voyages to Indonesia and India (Landes, 1998, p. 93).

Why didn't China discover America and conquer the world? This failure to explore was due to an internal policy decision supposedly founded on an interpretation of the *Analects of Confucius*: close the Celestial Empire off from the world of the barbarians. In 1500 the death penalty was decreed for anyone caught building ships with more than two masts. In 1525 the existing fleets were ordered destroyed. And in 1551 it was made a crime to sail the seas on a ship, even for the purpose of trade (Landes, 1998, p. 90). The indisputable success that China had achieved, and the resulting decision to isolate itself, explains the beginning of its *period of decadence*. It left the sea open to the West: first Portugal, then Spain, followed by Holland and England.

Trade overland between China and the West was centuries old. The Silk Road dates from the 3rd century BC, and benefited India, Persia, Arabia, Egypt, and Rome. Chinese innovations were so beneficial that they spread and were adopted throughout the ancient world.

The similarity in the level of development among different civilizations across Eurasia continued from the 1st century to the 14th. Per capita income in China in the 10th century was some 10% higher than in the West (Maddison, 2006, p. 44), but from the 16th century onward, Europe entered a frenzy of income growth previously unknown in world history. It took off with its technology, founded on ideas.

The second expansion of knowledge, from the 14th century onward, took place two millennia after the birth of philosophy and religion and set off the European Renaissance and the French Enlightenment, accelerated by the invention of the printing press. Among the most influential Western thinkers to emerge were Machiavelli, Copernicus, Luther, Galileo, Kepler, Descartes, Newton, Montesquieu, Adam Smith, Tocqueville, Marx, and Weber. Between them they would mold the histories of many countries.

Three types of **innovation** (intellectual, technological, and institutional) mutually reinforced each other. They all began showing the rising power of ideas, technology, and institutions: Machiavelli's justifications in *The Prince*; Luther's defiance of papal authority; Calvin's *salvation* through hard work; Hobbes's life in the state of nature as *solitary, poor, nasty, brutish, and short*; Descartes's *scientific method*; Locke's *empiricism*; Newton's laws of physics and *universal gravitation*; Montesquieu's *separation of powers*; and Voltaire's *freedoms* of religion, expression, and trade—to speak of only some of the theories of the great thinkers born prior to the 18th century.

Of those born during the 19th century, there were Tocqueville and his extraordinary description of *Democracy in America*; Darwin's *Origin of Species*; Marx's *historical materialism* and structure as the engine of development; Freud's *psychoanalysis*; Weber's evolution of ideas and cultural superstructure as the engine of history; Keynes's government interventionism in the economy; Gramsci's interaction of structure and superstructure (materialism and culture); and Hayek's governmental non-interference in the economy.

Relationships between *Conditions* and *Ideas*

The explosion of consciousness that became philosophical and religious systems, as well as the evolution of science and technology that at the end of the day has been coded into laws and institutions, are both deep sources of culture transmitted from one generation to the next by the six agents discussed in Chapter 7: families, teachers, churches, media, leaders, and the law. These six agents are not only *carriers*, but also *modifiers* of culture. It is within them that the absorption and reinterpretation of culture occurs—that is, within them the *interaction of* conditions and ideas takes place.

IMPACT OF CONDITIONS ON IDEAS

Table 12.1 simulates the modernization process by using data from countries at different stages of the development process, as measured by the WVS: income level, urbanization, and occupational and educational indicators. The assumption is that those countries which today show high levels of development for these four indicators started out in the lower ranges for each of these some seven or

TABLE 12.1

Axiological Change by Different Conditions, WVS 2010 (% Agree)

	Respect for Parents[a]	Appreciation for Hard Work[b]
GDP Per Capita[c]		
High ($15,000 or more)	68	46
Medium ($3,000–14,999)	85	63
Low ($2,999 or less)	89	78
Urban Population[d]		
High (75% or more)	60	38
Medium (50%–74%)	78	62
Low (49% or less)	86	67
Population Employed in Services (%)[e]		
High (66% or more)	62	37
Medium (34%–65%)	82	63
Low (33% or less)	93	78
Literacy Rates (%)[f]		
High (96.6% or more)	72	54
Medium (85%–96.5%)	87	55
Low (84% or less)	96	67
Age Group		
Up to 34 years old	72	56
35–54 years old	72	55
55 years or older	79	57
Cultural Zone		
Africa	93	74
Islam	86	61
South Asia	89	56
Latin America	96	35
Orthodox	85	76
Confucian	73	62
Catholic Europe	74	54
Protestant Europe	51	28
Protestant English	62	51

[a] Regardless of the qualities and faults of one's parents, one must always love and respect them. Source: World Values Survey.

[b] Percentage who mention hard work as a quality that children should learn at home. Source: World Values Survey.

[c] World Bank data GDP Per Capita from 2007, or closest year, in PPP terms (Current International $).

[d] Urban population as percentage of total population, from World Bank (2007 or closest available data).

[e] World Bank data from 2007 or closest year.

[f] World Bank data from 2007 or closest year.

eight decades ago—that is, the structural change unleashed by the modernization process effectively set off a change in values and culture.

The four items used to measure the modernization process (level of economic development, level of urbanization, percentage of population employed in the tertiary sector, and literacy rate) consistently point to a decrease in *respect for parents* and *work ethic*, as these four indicators increase. It is also important to point out two additional factors. First, the axiological starting point varies greatly depending on the cultural zone to which a country belongs. And second, axiological change is *not* a product of age.

In low-income countries, 89% of the population say that one should always love and respect one's parents, whereas in high-income countries only 68% agree with this statement. The contrast for the other variables is similar: for urbanization it is 86% versus 60%; for type of employment, 93% versus 62%; and for literacy rate, 90% versus 72%. One's age, however, has almost no effect on respect for parents, while one's cultural zone has a very strong impact, which ranges from around 90% among African, Islamic, South Asian, Latin American, and Orthodox countries, to just 51% in Protestant Europe or 62% among Protestant English.

It could be said that a weakening in respect for parents is not a good sign. The historical root of the tradition of unconditional respect for parents is certainly understandable. In a primitive group, where conflicts could easily turn to violence, tolerating challengers for authority in the home would be overly risky. This is less the case with postindustrial societies. It is also possible that human relationships are increasingly based on equity and genuine respect, rather than on reverential fear. It is equally true for friendships, marriages, parenthood, or any other relationship. Why should children love and respect parents who do not show respect for their children? Should a husband or wife love and respect a spouse who shows no signs of love and respect for the other?

Hard work appears to be out of fashion in the postindustrial world, and the low appreciation is particularly surprising and counterintuitive among Protestants. The degree of decline is consistent and strongly related to three of the four modernization indicators shown in Table 12.1. In low-income countries, 78% of the population say that children should be taught to work hard, while in high-income countries only 46% say so. When looking at urbanization the contrast is similar: 67% versus 38%. And when looking at tertiary sector employment, it is even stronger (78% vs. 37%), although for literacy it is not as strong (67% vs. 54%). When looking at age, the variation disappears (57% vs. 56%). When looking at cultural zones, the impact ranges from less than 35% in Latin America and Protestant Europe to 76% among Orthodox, 74% African, 61% Islamic, and 56% South Asian countries. This pattern of behavior seems to suggest that in modern societies *smart* work is more highly valued than *hard* work.[3]

IMPACT OF IDEAS ON CONDITIONS

There are two ways in which ideas can alter conditions: through technology and through institutions. Technology, being the application of knowledge to practical ends, materializes as the construction and use of tools. Today the repertory of tools we use can be numbered in the hundreds of thousands. Notwithstanding, a short list of barely three dozen of the most profoundly transformative technological innovations in history ranges from the most primitive instruments, such as axes, spears, and the mastery of fire, dating back a couple million years, to the GPS, developed in the last few years.

The great technological inventions and discoveries in *general use* predominantly fall into five major categories: food production, energy, transportation, communications, and war. In the area of **food production**, six stand out: the ax, spear, bow and arrow, agriculture, vessels, and the plow. In **energy**, four: fire, steam, oil, and electricity. In **transportation**, eight: the domestication of animals, navigation, the wheel, cart, railroad, automobile, aviation, and containers. In **communications**, nine: writing, printing, the radio, telephone, film, television, the computer, the Internet, and GPS. And in **war**, four: the sword, armor, firearms, and nuclear power (clearly not of general use). The first 15 major innovations on this list arose over the course of two million years, while the last 16 have all come about since the 14th century (Appendix 13).

Of course, many improvements and combinations have been left off this list. The number can also be expanded if one modifies the concept. For example, one could include not only tools in general use, but those used for scientific study and research: the microscope, telescope, X-rays, and so on (Fallows, 2013). In any case, the purpose of this overview is not to produce an exhaustive list, but rather to underline some of the most powerful technological innovations in the social, political, and economic development of nations.

Additionally, useful innovations last a very long time. One could say that our *food production* technology remains dependent on agriculture and raising livestock, basically developed around 10,000 years ago. Our oil and electrical *energy* technologies were developed during the second half of the 19th century. Our *transportation* in the form of automobiles and airplanes was developed during the first half of the 20th century. Our *communications* have become ever more concentrated on platforms and systems built upon the development of the Internet, coming out of the last quarter of the 20th century. And finally, *wars* are increasingly fought with sophisticated technologies such as aircraft, ships, and costly *intelligent* weapons developed around the use of nuclear power, discovered in the mid-20th century.

A convincing analysis of technology's social impact is Daniel Bell's book *The Coming of Post-Industrial Society,* published in 1973. His approach and terminology spread rapidly among scholars, and his book is required reading for those seeking to understand development. But if his concept was sound in 1973, his prologue to the 1999 edition is even more so.

In 1999 Bell developed the idea of the *axial age of technology* (Bell, 1999, p. xiii) as the foundation of industrial society, achieved upon mastering the use of energy (steam, electricity, oil, and gas), vertically integrating corporations, and introducing mass production. But the key change that explains the advent of postindustrial society is in the new relationship between science and technology, in the *codification of theoretical knowledge.* The greatest technological advances of the 20th century, he wrote, derived from the scientific revolutions in physics and biology.

Bell proposed a *technological ladder* that defines development: (1) based on agricultural and extractive resources; (2) light manufacturing (textiles, shoes, etc.); (3) heavy industry (ships, cars, engineering); (4) high technology (instrumentation, optics, microelectronics, computing, telecommunications); (5) the future: biotechnology, materials science, space stations, and satellites (1999, p. lxxiii).

It is the cumulative effect of key values—and their influence on humans' ability to take advantage of opportunities—that present countries with critical forks in the road, from which they must choose which path to follow.

Today, the theories of economist Douglass North regarding the importance of institutions to the economic, political, and social development of nations are perhaps the most sophisticated—and the clearest. North, it should be noted, is also perhaps the most clearly *interactionist* theorist working today. In his book *Understanding the Process of Economic Change,* North says

> . . . one can argue that the Christian religious framework of the Middle Ages provided a hospitable filter for learning that led to the adaptations congenial to economic growth; or alternatively that the specific geographic / economic / institutional context of the medieval western world provided the unique experiences responsible for the resultant adaptations. In fact it was *a combination of the two sets of experiences* that produced the adaptations in the belief structure that were conducive to economic growth and political/ civil freedoms. [my emphasis] (North, 2005, p. 136)

While North is primarily concerned with trying to understand the process of economic change, his work has ultimately covered extensive territory and succeeds in illuminating larger truths about the process of development. In his conception, economic change comes from three sources: demographic change; accumulated knowledge; and economic, political, and social institutional development (2005, p. 101). These ideas clearly reinforce his position as an *interactionist*: demographic change signifies the power of structures; accumulated knowledge suggests the power of ideas and culture; and institutional development is the result of their interaction. Although North does not consider technological innovation, this is clearly a parallel to institutional innovation, which is his focus.

But North goes farther, saying that he considers cultures and institutions two sides of the same coin: "Belief systems therefore are the internal representation and institutions the external manifestation of that representation" (2005, p. 49). It is here where Acemoglu and Robinson (2012) fall short in their first three chapters and miss North's point about the equivalence of culture and institutions.

North goes on to highlight the close link between the world of ideas and beliefs and the world of institutions when, speaking of Europe, he states

> Where did the belief system come from? [. . .] Its origins are in the way religious beliefs (and reaction to those beliefs) evolved in medieval-early modern

Europe and the way those beliefs in turn were heavily influenced by the unique experiences that characterized that part of the world. (2005, p. 101)

Although North scarcely notes the importance of religions and legal systems to the shaping of belief systems, his work yields support to the cultural hyper clusters of *achievement* and *honor*:

> The contrasting achievement characteristic of economies geared to dealing with the *physical environment* and those constructed to deal with the *human environment* raise fundamental questions about the basic divergent patterns that have evolved to result in *economic growth* on the one hand and *stagnation* on the other. [my emphasis] (2005, p. 101)

North arrives at the world of ideas through the finished expressions of cultures. He sees the forest, but not the trees. In the biological analogy, he sees the organism (the culture), but doesn't pay attention to the genes (the values). In the musical analogy, he listens to the symphony (the culture), but he doesn't pay attention to individual notes (the values)—thus his assertion quoted at the opening of Part III of this text. For those who have come to study cultures through observation and examination of cultural values (i.e., *axiology*), it is precisely in such values that the basic building blocks are found. Just as a few genes produce many forms of life, or a few notes many symphonies; in the case of culture, a handful of values spinning on three key axes produce the seven thousand micro cultures associated with the world's languages. These micro cultures keep on aggregating until they collapse into the three *hyper clusters* by the action of religions and legal systems—the cultures of *achievement*, focused on managing the *physical environment* (the economy, production, work); the cultures of *honor*, focused on managing the *human environment* (social interactions, friends, family); and, in between the two, the cultures of *joy*.

Given the parallel but opposing nature of these cultural *hyper clusters*, it is clear that what is positive in one is negative in the other: in cultures of *achievement*, the reward is the procurement of material satisfaction, but that frequently requires the postponement of emotional satisfaction. In cultures of *honor*, however, individuals are privileged to enjoy relationships with family and friends, but material satisfaction must often be deferred.

INTERACTION BETWEEN CONDITIONS AND IDEAS

A schematic summary of Part VI, devoted to the driving forces of development, is provided in Table 12.2, which consists of the 15 drivers of development discussed thus far, highlighting that development is truly a multifactorial outcome. Also, from the table it is possible to think about potential combinations of factors that allow for larger contributions. For instance, *schools* (factor 9) can have an impact on factors 8 and 11. Similarly, *leadership* (factor 13) can influence or even steer changes in conditions for factors 5, 6, and 7.

TABLE 12.2
Fifteen Drivers of Development

1. Material and structural conditions (Marx)	2. Culture and ideas (Weber)
1.1. Natural conditions	**2.1. Cultural agents**
1. Climate	8. Families
2. Geography	9. Schools
3. Environment	10. Religion
4. Demography	11. Media
	12. Law
1.2. Human conditions	13. Leadership
5. Political	
6. Economic	**2.2. Intellectual innovation**
7. Social	14. Social sciences
	15. Natural sciences

An attempt to quantify the relative contributions of structural conditions and ideas on development was created by my colleague Matteo Marini over the course of two summers at the Fletcher School. It was based on the *Subjective Development Index* (SDI) that I developed in 2009 from the World Values Survey data and presented in Chapter 10. In the first part of his essay, Marini tests Tocqueville's statement that: ". . . even the most favorable geographic locations and the best laws cannot maintain a constitution in despite of mores." He based his analysis on the conceptual model shown in Figure 12.1, which makes clear its *interactive* relevance.

In the top portion he lists the two structural *forces,* which he labels *resource endowment* and *political institutions,* corresponding to driving force 6 and 5 of Table 12.2. The effects of these two structural drivers on *agency* are mediated by a set of social values specific to the cultural group to which individuals belong. This set of values (social mentality) is the byproduct of the circular interaction existing between the results in terms of national prosperity and governance and the feedback loops that they generate, year after year. The cultural agents mentioned in items 8 to 13 of Table 12.2 are responsible for the elaboration and transmission of such social values, located at the core of Figure 12.1.

Applying this conceptual framework produces the results summarized in Table 12.3, using regression analysis for the impact of beliefs and attitudes on economic growth. Basically, the regression analysis demonstrates that cultural factors (SDI) are the second best predictor of GDP per capita, along with resource endowment (physical capital) and political institutions (democracy) (Marini, 2013, p. 209). Making the total impact of Beta coefficients equal 100, 42% is the contribution of resource endowment, 38% that of cultural factors, and 20% the contribution of the institutional ones. In conclusion, economic development has a multifactorial

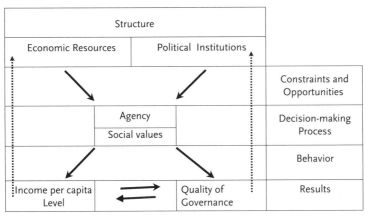

FIGURE 12.1 Marini's conceptual interaction model: Structure and agency

Reprinted from Matteo Marini, 2013, "The Traditions of Modernity," *The Journal of Socio-Economics, 47*, p. 206, with permission from Elsevier.

explanation, in which resource endowment, cultural, and institutional factors play a role. Note that in order to avoid the problem of reverse causality, the cultural factor SDI has entered the solution of the model with a lagged period $(t{-}1)$. In other words, cultural factors are statistically significant, although expressed by respondents five years earlier than economic and political conditions.

This is not to say that cultural factors must be necessarily preconditions of economic growth. As we have stated in the previous pages, structural changes may induce cultural ones as well.

Marini's analysis finds that shifts toward more achievement-oriented cultural values will actually tend to cause increases in GDP per capita. Specifically, he writes, "Since the average GDP per capita of the country sample is $16,130, the percent increase in GDP per capita would be expected to range from a minimum of 0.9% [. . .] in the case of 'entrepreneurship' to a maximum of 1.9% [. . .] in the case of 'education'. These figures are impressive, considering that they are determined by a 1% shift of population in only one specific cultural factor" (Marini, 2013, p. 214). This would mean an annual increase in per capita income of between US$115 and US$323.

Conclusion and Guidelines for Future Research

As we have seen, cultural change is a process that begins slowly, and begins with the individual. When conditions are favorable to structural change, it accelerates and spreads almost virally, resulting in the modification of the technological and/or institutional environment, which may in turn become a new structural condition that will force the cycle to begin anew.

TABLE 12.3
Marini's Impact of Culture

Independent Variables	Beta Coefficients	Standardized Beta
Physical capital	4.33*** (0.859)	0.39***
Human capital	10.93 (9.301)	0.09
Democratic institutions	0.64*** (0.206)	0.19***
Subjective Development Index (SDI) t–1	8.31*** (2.027)	0.35***
Dummy 3th wave	−0.51 (3.507)	
Dummy 4th wave	0.61 (3.347)	
Dummy 5th wave	2.19 (3.374)	
Intercept	−26.53*** (8.671)	
Observations	108	
$R2$	0.72	

Determinants of GDP per capita country levels—OLS regressions—pooled cross sections.
Dependent variable: GDP per capita at purchasing power parity; constant prices 2005.
Coefficients are statistically different from zero if marked by (***) at 1% level, (**) at 5% level, and (*) at 10% level.

In sum, cultures are not static—they are constantly changing. When structural conditions change, so do our perceptions of the world at large, along with the values associated with those perceptions. Thus, new currents of ideas and the accumulation of knowledge bring about technological and institutional innovations, which in turn change structural conditions.

A macro-review of the history of human life on our planet reveals that during some periods development was driven by *material conditions and structures*, while in other periods it has been driven by *ideas and culture*.

Much has happened to us as a species in the 2.5 million years of evolution since the Stone Age as *Homo habilis* and *Homo erectus*. That past determined our hunter-gatherer behavior, before we emigrated out of northeast Africa, the point of departure. How did we populate the planet before the flourishing of civilizations? Evidently, we walked, because that was the available *technology* for migration.

But even more interesting, the peopling of the earth was linked to the ongoing search for propitious hunting grounds, gathering sites, and dwellings. That is, a group of humans would slowly collect in an area and, as the group grew larger, younger families would begin peeling off in search of new territories until they reached the far corners of the world, like a low-intensity viral epidemic. Up to that point, *conditions* were the driving force.

Ideas entered the scene at a very preliminary stage, as each group faced the need to explain everyday *mysteries* (the sun, the moon, rain, night, etc.) and the elders passed down these ideas through oral tradition to new generations, as well as rules for proper behavior, all of which was shared in their own language. These were the rudimentary elements of the deep understanding of culture: as *a shared system of meanings, values, and beliefs*.

But the dispersion and nomadic mobility of these groups, as well as the absence of any means of written records, impeded a massive cultural expansion. Mankind would have to await the establishment of permanent settlements brought about by the discovery of agriculture over the past 10,000 years, which gave *environmental conditions* the upper hand once again.

Agriculture signified a *technological revolution* that brought with it not only stability, but also population growth. Those situated in fertile regions experienced the most growth: Mesopotamia, the Nile River Valley, China, India, and Mesoamerica. As groups grew in size, the rules governing the behavior of group members grew, likewise becoming more complex. Now *geography* played the most influential role in the rise of political systems. Great irrigated plains such as those in China and Egypt required the regulation of water for agriculture; complex, centralized systems of power developed in response.

The accumulation of power in the hands of imperial and pharaonic dynasties allowed these agricultural lands to expand, not to mention some of the great public works projects of antiquity, such as the Egyptian pyramids and, two thousand years later, the Great Wall of China. But the enormous accumulation of centralized power had its drawbacks. China of the 12th century, with its great wealth and technological brilliance, could easily have discovered America. Why didn't it? Because the Emperor forbade navigation.

Up until then, **demography, geography**, and **technology**—that is, *material conditions*—had been the drivers of the ascent of mankind. Beginning in the 8th century BC, philosophies and religions—that is, **culture**—began to influence the course of history.

Unlike China and Egypt, which occupied large landmasses, the rise of Greco-Roman and later European civilization took place in a region geographically more like a jigsaw puzzle, one occupied by many tribes with different languages. Of necessity, many city-states and petty kingdoms arose, which were bound to resolve their differences through constant armed conflict.

Buttressed by *demographic* growth and the consolidation of *strong political systems* with sizable armies, through expansion and conquest, the city-states of the Mediterranean began to give way to Hellenistic civilization, the Greek Empire, the Roman Republic, and the Roman Empire.

Of particular significance would be the Christian penetration of the Roman Empire—a **cultural** factor—and the substitution of Roman polytheism by Trinitarian Christian monotheism in the year 380 AD. The fall of the Western Roman Empire in the year 476 AD ushered in the period known as the Middle Ages in Europe, which would last for a thousand years.

The feudal state—*material conditions* of the economy—arose in Europe beginning in the 9th century, followed later by nation-states, which were profoundly influenced by the power of the Vatican and the Catholic Church—a *cultural* force. Of particular relevance were the Crusades against the Muslims to regain access to Jerusalem beginning in the year 1095, as well as the establishment of the Inquisition in the 12th century to combat heresy, which was reinforced by the start of the Spanish Inquisition in 1480.

While Europe was struggling through the Dark Ages, beginning in the 7th century the Islamic caliphates flourished, both in trade and in knowledge, and expanded rapidly from the Arabian Peninsula until their political system stretched from India to Spain. Beginning in 1299, political power shifted to the Ottoman Empire for the next six centuries, until it was dissolved in 1923 with the creation of Turkey. A combination of both **culture** *and* **conditions** was decisive here.

But beginning with Portuguese naval expeditions in 1424, and in particular with the Spanish discovery of the Americas in 1492, European territorial expansion and economic growth took off.

Over the two millennia that transpired between the birth of philosophies and religions around the 8th century BC and about the end of the European Middle Ages in the 14th century, there were neither revolutionary technological innovations (such as agriculture or steam power), nor catastrophic impacts in geographic, demographic, or climatic terms, except for *the plague* that decimated Europe between 1348 and 1350. In other words, *material conditions* remained at a level of gradual and low-intensity change for these 20 centuries.

Meanwhile, the wars of religion and beliefs—between Europe and the Arab world, and, in the heart of Europe, between the Reformation and Counter-Reformation movements—dominated the historical scene. That is, **culture**—values and beliefs expressed through religions and the judicial and political institutions of nation-states—constituted the arena where the battle for development and geopolitics was fought.

Beginning in the 16th century, the shadow of these cultural rearrangements, coupled with chance, would cast itself over territories new and old, allowing for a better understanding of the world as it is today. Latin America would be occupied by the Iberian empires of Spain and Portugal, which would transmit their language, religion, laws, and the Counter-Reformation from the old world to the new. Portugal and Holland would dominate the South Sea Islands between China and Australia. England would do so with India, North America, and parts of Africa, the Caribbean, and the South Pacific. France would establish her *dominions*, in the shadow of England, across the globe: North America, the Caribbean, India, Africa, and Southeast Asia.

The part played by Jews, who served as guardians and involuntary vessels of knowledge during these centuries, deserves mention. The teaching of reading and writing was to spread first and foremost with them. They flourished in Portugal and Spain equally as much in the field of navigational science, until their expulsion by the Catholic monarchs in 1492 led them to seek refuge primarily in Holland, England, Turkey, and North Africa.

The advanced commercial and financial laws and *institutions* of Holland and England, combined with the knowledge that Jewish immigrants brought with them, and the ebullience of Protestantism, soon were made manifest in Holland's naval and commercial expansion from 1585 onward (Landes, 1999,

p. 140). Shortly thereafter, England began its own naval expansion centered on trade with India (Landes, 1999, p. 152).

England had the good fortune to be considered by the Roman Empire as a far-off land of very little interest. England's location allowed it to take in the positive effects of democratic institutions from the Roman Republic, while largely skipping out on the negative effects of the Roman Empire and its codes, which came to dominate the rest of Continental Europe.

The English cultural combination of oral legal procedure and respect for individual rights and liberties—won beginning with the Magna Carta of 1215, the Civil War of 1642–1651, and the Glorious Revolution of 1688—laid the foundation for the industrial revolution unleashed by the steam engine. The English king had been forced by his nation's feudal lords to proclaim their rights and liberties, and was obliged to respect them. Those *accidents* of history laid an excellent foundation for the innovation, flexibility, and legal predictability that would light the fuse of the industrial revolution. The **interaction** of cultural conditions (law, science, political ideas, and religion) and material circumstances (demography, trade, and political structures) would unleash in England a period of growth and development as yet unknown to the rest of the world.

The original Weberian Protestant motivation has been left in the past, in the wake of rising secularism. The rationale for constant effort and delayed gratification lost traction in the face of mass consumption and instant gratification in the second half of the 20th century. This is the iron law of marketing. This was the beginning of the end.

Conclusion

This is a book that traces the link from values to cultures and from cultures to development. Values are the building blocks of cultures. Cultures encapsulate the *values* that make economic, social, and political life either easier or more difficult—namely, development. But the definition of development is not *only* material progress.

The book begins with the culture shocks that I experienced in England and later in Japan, which created the cognitive dissonance that fired my interest in the topic. My initial response to reduce such dissonance was the proposition of the three value axes model (hard work as prize or punishment, trust or distrust, and autonomy or obedience) based on the three key dimensions (economic, social, and political, respectively). This model received its preliminary empirical validation 20 years later, at the University of Michigan, with the second wave of the World Values Survey (WVS). My personal intellectual journey ends, in a sense, in this book—facilitated, enriched, and consolidated by the seminar I began teaching at the Fletcher School of Tufts University in 2008.

The concept of culture proposed by this book—a *shared system of meanings*—sets the tone by identifying its essential elements—*languages, identities,* and *norms.* These, in turn, allow us to winnow down from about 7,000 *micro* cultures (by language), to 200 *mezzo* cultures (by nationalities), to 8 *macro* cultures (by main religions), to three *hyper* cultures (by legal systems): *honor, achievement,* and *joy.* Also, I outline the historical path by which cultures have evolved: from *honor* (from the primitive tribes) all the way up to *achievement* (beginning with the industrial revolution), to *joy* (by the end of World War II), which is currently pursued by a few postmaterialist countries, and paradoxically enjoyed since long ago by the elites around the world and most colonial Catholic countries and some Buddhist countries.

The book also reviews the importance of the six agents of cultural transmission and change (family, school, religion, media, leadership, and the law). It further argues in favor of reviewing and questioning the definition and measurement of *development,* and the outcomes associated with it, through the metrics that have been used to define it: from the *basic dichotomies* to the discredited idea of *progress* to the United Nations' *Universal Declaration of Human Rights.* It notes how the world for millennia took population growth derived from rich agriculture—and hence army strength—as the metric of success. Starting with the age of discovery and colonization, it was the control, possession, and trade of valuable goods (gold, silver, spices, cotton, wool, etc.) that defined it. Later, as the industrial revolution began, abundant production and trade leading to **wealth** of both individuals and countries was taken as the symbol of *progress.*

Each explanation for countries' wealth or poverty (resources, geography, climate, demographics, technology, trade, politics, culture, institutions, etc.) has been elaborated with seriousness, depth, and an abundance of data by very earnest academics, and all without a doubt have added to the answer. Current research is heading ever more in the direction of quantifying the contribution of each of the possible factors to the final result.

The question of why some countries are rich and others poor is nothing new. Adam Smith posed it in 1776 (*The Wealth of Nations*), David Landes took it up again in 1998 (*The Wealth and Poverty of Nations*), the World Bank in 2006 (*Where Is the Wealth of Nations?*) and Acemoglu and Robinson in 2012 (*Why Nations Fail*). Smith locates the answer in structural causes (the division of labor) and Landes discovers it in culture, while Acemoglu and Robinson reject both of these, instead deciphering it as their interaction: through institutions.

Among humans, and as a characteristic we share with the species of the animal kingdom, the strong impose themselves upon the weak. This is neither new nor strange and, accordingly, exploitation by the strong is not a sufficient explanation for why some countries are rich and others poor. The United States and the Soviet Union, of course, took advantage of their strengths and extracted wealth from countries in their respective spheres of influence in the past half century. But so did the British, Dutch, French, Spanish, and Portuguese empires with their colonies a few centuries prior; and so on going back to the Arab caliphates, all the way to Rome and Greece, to say nothing of Egypt and Babylon, or the Mayans, Aztecs, and Incas.

The inclination toward domination, exploitation, and conflict is certainly present in our species, but it is not all that makes us what we are, nor is it a sufficient explanation for why some countries are rich and others poor. The other essential and possibly distinctive human trait is that, besides being hyper-conflictive, we are also hyper-cooperative. And it is quite possibly precisely this trait that has brought us to the higher states of evolution and dominion over nature that we have achieved (Pinker, 2011, pp. 56, 661).

However, despite advances and retrogressions of **wealth** observed throughout the course of history, no real systematic metric was available until after the American Great Depression of 1930. The current measure of economic performance—GDP—began in 1934. It still serves to define which are the most influential countries of the world (apart from the UN Security Council) as represented in the *Group of 7* (G-7) or the *Group of 20* (G-20). It took half a century for the United Nations Development Program (UNDP) to construct the *Human Development Index* (HDI), presented in 1990, which blends education and health with GDP per capita. As good as the HDI has been, it is not enough. It leaves out essential metrics on political performance, income, gender equality, and sustainability. As the Sarkozy Commission suggested in 2008, *if we have the wrong metrics, we will strive for the wrong things.*

In order to associate values and cultures with a more comprehensive concept of development, the book proposes an *Objective Development Index* (ODI). It combines HDI with the gender equality index (GII, also developed by UNDP), plus the index of political performance constructed by Freedom House, as well as the Gini coefficient to measure income and wealth distribution. The most notable gap of ODI is a measure of sustainability, which will have to wait for a more stable and widely scientifically accepted index to become available.

ODI dramatically changes the position of the United States from number 3 in HDI (after Norway and Australia) to number 41. Although ODI is closely associated with HDI (they show a correlation coefficient of .89), by incorporating the three additional measures, the US ranking declines markedly. HDI measures factors where the United States has been striving (bottom line material achievement through income and education), but it omits gender and income equality plus political performance measures. In that sense, Sarkozy's intuition was right, as France shows up in ODI as number 11, up from 20 in HDI.

The book tackles the question of what drives development by reviewing the debates over the past 150 years, particularly between Marx's and Weber's ideas and followers: Is it material conditions or ideas that are the main drivers of development? What are the impacts of climate, geography, environment, demography, and migration on development? Can the strong forces of nature be measured? The most powerful agent of change in the world, as measured over millions of years, is climate—so much so that over the past 540 million years there have been five mass extinctions of species due to the effects of either catastrophic events such as the impact of an asteroid that brought about the extinction of the dinosaurs, dating back 65 million years, or slow cycles of global warming and cooling (Finlayson, 2009, p. 3). After climate, the next most powerful agent of change is geography, as measured over the millennia. Continental drift and the shape of the continents influenced the propagation of diverse plant and animal species, as well as the pattern for the peopling of the planet over the last 100 millennia (Diamond, 1992, p. 45).

The physical environment (jungle or desert, plains or mountains, tropics, or polar regions) also exercises influence over the course of change by indirect effect on human behavior over centuries, which in turn affects the environment. Shortening the scale to decades, demography is another factor underlying change, due simply to the effects of growth, decline, aging, or migration on a population. This is how the great empires and civilizations of antiquity arose (the Babylonians, Persians, Assyrians, Egyptians, the Indus Valley civilization, the Chinese, Greeks, Romans, Aztecs, Mayans, and Incas), which in turn gave rise to the most populous and economically powerful countries of today. Demographic strength sooner or later translates into economic strength, and likewise into political strength.

After reviewing the strong forces of nature and human action, one would have to conclude that Marx was in some sense right: material conditions drive development. However, these *material conditions* (or historical mate-rialism) explain merely one-third of relevant change. What about the other two-thirds?

A second third comes from Max Weber's response that belief systems—that is, culture and ideas—are the engine of change. He pieced together the contribu-tions of philosophy and religion beginning in the 8th century BC and the arts and sciences beginning in 15th century Europe: the Renaissance, Protestant Reformation, Enlightenment, and French encyclopedists. Alexis de Tocqueville also noted the power of ideas and culture. Communism and capitalism in the 20th century were strains of thought that unleashed clearly powerful social movements affecting global development. With today's instant, globalized communications, change driven by culture and ideas has sped up—witness the Arab Spring and other recent, viral social movements facilitated by social media—although the durability and direction of such changes are still uncertain. The origin and direction of development are grounded in thought processes. In this sense, Weber was also right. Assuming again that culture explains another third of relevant change, there is still one third missing.

This long-standing dilemma about the causes of development is deep from a theoretical point of view. The contradiction (raised as *thesis* and *antithesis*) between Marx and Weber and their followers caused the ambivalence between capitalism and communism in the twentieth century, as well as its corollary, the Cold War. This contradiction between material forces (Marx) and ideas (Weber) as drivers of development finally has been revealed as a false contradiction. In fact, both are true, but a third driver is missing: the interaction *between* the two, as Gramsci sensed in 1928 and North further developed in 2005, with his recog-nition of institutions as the embodiment of culture.

Neither North nor Gramsci paid particular attention to the contradiction between the Marxist and Weberian schools of thought—Gramsci because he was almost a contemporary of Weber, and North because his field is limited to eco-nomics and he focuses on *institutions*, while I place the emphasis on *institutional innovation*. However, in practice the principles and ideas of both represent a *syn-thesis* that resolves the contradiction between Marx and Weber. This does not mean that the impact of material conditions or the impact of ideas disappears. Not at all. What it means is that in addition to the two, there must be added the impact of their interaction. *Innovation* is the mother, while *technology and insti-tutions* are the children.

The origin of this idea comes from the world of biology. In that discipline, the effect of both genetics and the environment in the development of organisms was well established. But it wasn't until the second half of the twentieth century that the effect of a third factor was discovered: gene-environment interaction. As I delved into the contradiction between Marx and Weber, I began to think that something similar happens in the social sciences; the interaction of cir-cumstances and ideas as an additional impetus to change. This is especially true because innovation leaves its footprints in the form of intellectual, technological, and institutional change.

The **interaction** between material conditions (Marx) and ideas (Weber) translates into *innovation*—either institutional, technological, or intellectual. Namely, innovation emerges from the tension between material and structural conditions on the one side, with ideas and culture on the other side. Depending on their academic field, analysts place greater emphasis on material and structural conditions, or on culture and ideas, or on institutions, underestimating the contributions of the other fields.

But the interaction between *ideas* and *conditions* does not end with those actions and decisions undertaken by individuals or groups. Repeated over time, these actions and decisions shape intellectual currents and patterns of behavior—currents and patterns that can be ephemeral in nature, like fashion, or, on the other hand, long lasting to the point that they bring about new *structures*.

Humans as individuals synthesize and internalize the outside world and our past by way of values and beliefs that we receive from our families, schooling, peers, churches, media, the law, and our business, intellectual, and political leaders. Such axiological scaffolding, which we all receive, prepares us for the day-to-day decision-making and problem-solving we face as individuals.

Individual problem-solving and decision-making employ and take great advantage of intellectual and technological innovation. For *collective* problems, however, that is not enough. They demand political solutions that eventually turn into public policies. Public policies over time may evolve into law and **institutional innovations**.

It is precisely in innovation that the interaction between *mind and matter* materializes: between *material and structural conditions* on the one side, with culture and ideas or *superstructure* on the other side. Technology, ideas, and institutions are direct evidence of human *intention* forged in the collision of opposing forces: demand and supply for technology, or liberal and conservative thinking for institutions. In North's words, institutions are *ideas' creations* (North, 2005, p. 18).

In summary, the central message of this book is that the three primary cultures—honor, achievement, and joy—give frame, structure, and meaning to the dominant motivations (political, economic, or social, respectively) in each of the countries of the world. Understanding the essence, origin, evolution, meaning, and consequences of each of these three cultures is the first step in giving them the respect they deserve, and thereby improving the chances of communication and understanding among individuals and countries as a whole.

This main message is buttressed by five supporting arguments:

1. Three basic values—in their many possible combinations—explain all cultures;
2. All cultures are worthy of respect;
3. Cultures are always changing;
4. It is essential to improve the measurement of development, and the Objective Development Index is a significant improvement over existing metrics;

5. The previously unsolvable dilemma of the opposing explanations of development—matter over ideas or ideas over matter—is resolved through the concept of *innovation* (either intellectual, technological, or institutional).

Further Research

What is, then, the as yet nonexistent model that can best respond to today's circumstances? Should it be a combination of the productive dynamism of the *achievement-oriented cultures*, such as the United States, Germany, and China, with the passion and joie de vivre cultures, such as France, Italy, and Spain? What about the respect for tradition, natural resources, and the environment of some *honor* cultures that would increase world sustainability, along the lines of Albania, Gabon, or Mauritius?[1]

It is not easy to find examples in real life of a country that comes close to an ideal model of a fluid and flexible labor market, highly productive, combined with ample social well-being and widely available healthcare and education, complemented with respect and care for traditions, nature, and the environment. Japanese society is one example of a culture that combines key aspects of both *achievement* and *honor* cultures—but not those of *joy*.

In other words, how do we marry the competitiveness and labor market flexibility of the United States with the social safety net, health, and education programs enjoyed by the Nordic and most European countries? The question is, how many countries need to dismantle their rigid and overly protectionist labor laws, and how many others need to expand their health coverage and spending on education, without getting ourselves lost in utopian thinking?

Deep changes today must come from desires and aspirations, as well as initiatives and actions shared among the citizens, which translate into clear electoral mandates for their leaders. In societies as complex and diverse as those of today, it is hard to imagine replicating changes such as those brought about in Japan (1868), or Turkey (1923), or Singapore (1959), but it is not impossible, as the Bogotá case (2003) shows.

Can migrant populations serve as an example of cultural change and blending? Minorities from cultures of achievement (Jews or Confucians, for example) who establish themselves in another cultural context clearly have an advantage, as much for the values that they carry as for the sense of solidarity arising from their minority status. But in these cases, there is not a cultural shift—but rather a reinforcement and intensification of their original axiological repertoire of achievement-oriented values.

Minorities from cultures of *joy* and *honor* migrating to countries with cultures of *achievement* illustrate the axiological combination to which I refer: the Indians in England, the Turks in Germany, the Algerians in France, the Italians or Hispanics in the United States. Those who triumph in the host society must absorb and practice the most functional *values of achievement* while stripping themselves of the least functional aspects of their original cultures, while keeping their *core values*; ultimately, in order to maintain the nucleus of the culture of joy or honor, they are forced to find a balanced way to combine multiple sets of values.

As a way of ending, I share a last anecdote based on my life journey from the *culture of honor* of the almost rural town of 25,000 inhabitants where I was born, to the *culture of achievement* I came to admire in my graduate student days in England, encapsulated in my *idealization* of work, trust, and autonomy-dissent where I live in the Boston area today.

When my family and I moved to the United States in 1995, I brought with me a lot of complaints about Mexico and Latin culture—in which I included Italy, Spain, and Argentina. I blamed our never-ending socializing, long daily breakfasts, lunches, and dinners, the lack of discipline for working hours, and unpunctuality filled with family and friends' interruptions, for our inability to achieve prosperity and efficiency. Our culture was a *social garden*, but a *work desert*. I felt relieved by working in the United States, where nobody dares to interrupt your *sacred* time, not even after working hours.

That feeling was great for the first couple of years, until I began missing a little bit the spontaneity and human warmth of friendship and social interaction. Our children began developing a bicultural skill—they could switch not only from one language to the other, but from one culture to the other, without much apparent difficulty. The rewarding and intense working experience that had fulfilled me so greatly entered a phase of decreasing returns, in which I began increasingly to reconcile with the Latin *carefree joy*. I began feeling that the culture of achievement might really be the polar opposite of what I had run away from. I started to suspect that I had unwittingly arrived at a *work garden*, but a *social desert*. I hence began a new and still unfinished search for a balance combining the best of both worlds. The outcome of that *pursuit of ideal joy* will have to wait for the ending of this chapter of my life.

APPENDIX 1

Methodological Note for Tables 4.1–4.6

Population (thousands): Total population in country.
Source: World Bank World Development Indicators, 2011 or latest available data

Population Density: Number of people per square kilometer.
Source: World Bank World Development Indicators, 2010 or latest available data
Gross Domestic Product, GDP (billions of $): GDP in current international dollars ($), PPP.
Source: World Bank World Development Indicators, 2012 or latest available data

GDP per Capita (dollars): In current international dollars ($), PPP.
Source: World Bank World Development Indicators, 2012 or latest available data

Agriculture (% of GDP): Value added by agriculture calculated as a % of GDP.
Source: World Bank World Development Indicators, latest available data

Industry (% of GDP): Value added by industry as a % of GDP.
Source: World Bank World Development Indicators, latest available data

Services (% of GDP): Value added by services as a % of GDP.
Source: World Bank World Development Indicators, latest available data

Gini Index: A measure of income inequality that can technically range from 0 to 100, with the *smallest value* equaling the *least unequal* country. The highest value is 66 (Seychelles) and lowest 25 (Denmark) in this data set.
Source: World Bank World Development Indicators, latest available data and supplemented by data from CIA Factbook and Wikipedia where data are missing

Literacy rate: Percentage of adults (15 years and older) who are literate.
Source: World Bank World Development Indicators and CIA Factbook, latest available data

Gender Inequality Index (GII): Indicators used are maternal mortality ratio, adolescent fertility rate, share of national parliament seats held by women, secondary/higher educational levels, and women's participation in the work force, and so on. *The smaller the GII, the lower inequality*; in this data set the data range from 0.045 (the Netherlands) to 0.747 (Yemen). In the *ranking*, the higher the number, the higher the gender inequality.

Source: UN Development Programme, 2012 (Human Development Reports)

Human Development Index (HDI): Indicators used are life expectancy at birth, mean years of schooling, expected years of schooling and GNI per capita (US dollar, PPP). *The higher the score, the higher level of development*. The score ranges from 0.955 (Norway) to 0.304 (Niger). In the *ranking*, the higher the number, the lower level of development.

Source: UN Development Programme, 2012 (Human Development Reports)

Freedom House Freedom Score: Constructed by summing the components of the Civil Liberties and Political Rights score (electoral processes, political pluralism and participation, functioning of government, freedom of expression and belief, associational and organizational rights, rule of law, and personal autonomy and individual rights). *The lower the number, the less free a country is*; the data set range from a score of 100 to 2.

Source: Freedom in the World Sub-scores (Civil Liberties and Political Rights), 2013

Colonial Power: Primary colonial power—France, Great Britain, Portugal, Spain, Germany, Belgium, Italy.

Source: Wikipedia

Legal Tradition: Based on legal system—common, civil, or Islamic.

Source: Legal Systems of the World, Wikipedia

Religion Data (% of population): Percentage of population, depending on region; the data are divided by the major religious denominations. For dominant religions they are divided into subgroups, such as Catholics/Protestants (Christians) and Shiites/Sunnis (Muslim).

Source: CIA Factbook, The Association of Religion Data Archives (ARDA)

Objective Development Index: Composite score calculated from countries' ranked and standardized scores on Human Development Index, Gini Index, Gender Inequality Index, and Freedom House Civil and Political freedoms score. *The higher the score, the more "developed" a country is.*

Subjective Development Index: Calculated using the World Values Survey score on the Traditional–Secular/Rational, and Survival–Self-Expression indices. Each country's score is calculated by measuring the distance to the countries with the highest score in each index (Japan and Sweden). *The higher the score, the more "developed" a country is.*

Corruption Index: The Corruption Perceptions Index is produced annually by Transparency International, drawing on data from independent institutions specializing in governance and business climate analysis. The higher the score, the more corrupt a country is perceived to be. The global average was calculated by averaging the scores of each region.

APPENDIX 2

Methodological Note for Tables 5.1–5.5

Standardized Subculture Scores

In order to explore which values stand out in each cultural cluster (*honor, achievement*, and *joy*, further distinguishing between European and Latin American Catholics), we transformed the variables into a comparable scale. This is necessary since the questions of the World Values Survey have different base scales, and a simple mean comparison would not be very informative.

Instead, we standardized all variables at the world level, that is, we standardized each variable (question) over the entire sample. Subsequently, we calculated the mean, standard deviation, minimum, and maximum for the four subcultures. This procedure allowed us to see how observations vary for each variable within a cultural subgroup, as compared to the world baseline (which will have a mean of 0 and standard deviation of 1). For example, say that variable *A* in subgroup *X* has a mean of 2 and a standard deviation of 1.5. Comparing that to the world variable with a mean of 0 and a standard deviation of 1, we can tell that the values and variability of subgroup *X* are much different from the world. Below is a step-by-step account for the calculation of the cultural scores.

The data set we used was an integrated European and World Value Survey stata data file containing all the waves available for all countries (*EVS_WVS_LF_dataset_1981_2008_v2011_06_11_INTERNAL.dta*).

First, we limited our analysis to Waves 5 (WVS 2005–2007) and 6 (EVS 2008–2010), as we are interested in exploring the current values that distinguish each subculture. Including older waves could distort the sample by adding in a time factor, as we know that many countries' values have changed over time. The total number of observations for the last two waves is 150,778.

Second, the countries were split into four cultural groups: *honor, achievement*, and *joy*, further distinguishing between European and Latin American Catholics. We included a separate category for European Catholic since those countries are generally more socially conservative than countries normally

Honor	Achievement	Joy (European Catholic)
Albania	Australia	Andorra
Azerbaijan	Canada	Austria
Armenia	China	Belgium
Bosnia and Herzegovina	Taiwan	Croatia
Bulgaria	Denmark	Czech Republic
Belarus	Finland	France
Georgia	Hong Kong	Hungary
Greece	Iceland	Italy
Indonesia	Japan	Lithuania
Iran	South Korea	Luxembourg
Iraq	Netherlands	Malta
Jordan	New Zealand	Poland
Malaysia	Norway	Portugal
Moldova	Sweden	Slovakia
Montenegro	Switzerland	Slovenia
Morocco	United Kingdom	Spain
Romania	United States	Ireland
Russia	West Germany	
Serbia	East Germany	**Joy (Latin America)**
Turkey	Northern Ireland	
Ukraine	Trinidad and Tobago	Argentina
Macedonia	Vietnam	Brazil
Egypt	Estonia	Chile
Kosovo	Latvia	Colombia
Cyprus		Guatemala
Northern Cyprus		Mexico
Ethiopia		Peru
Ghana		Uruguay
India		
Mali		
Rwanda		
South Africa		
Thailand		
Burkina Faso		
Zambia		
OBS: 69,754	**OBS: 39,225**	**OBS: 30,212**

clustering in the *achievement* category, but more progressive (economically and socially) than countries in the *joy* cluster. As such, we expected European Catholic countries to "moderate" *achievement* and *joy* values in opposite directions.

For several countries, we were initially unclear as to how to categorize them because their values border different cultural categories. For example, Estonia is a post-communist country, but is today a member of the European Union and is much more closely aligned to *achievement* countries in its economic, social, and political development. In order to determine in which category the countries were to be placed we looked at their religious, legal, and political setup.

Third, in Stata we standardized all variables in the dataset (using *zval*), and then calculated the mean, standard deviation, minimum, and maximum for each of the four subcultures (using *Collapse*) out of the standardized world variables.

Finally, for each subculture we ranked the variables by their mean (from largest/positive to smallest/negative) and looked at which variables stood out in each subculture as compared to the world.

Alphabetical Standardized Scores for the Countries of the World Values Survey Map

#	Nation & wave*	Trad Rat values	Surv Self values	2013HD2**	HD2***z-score
	Albania 4	0.07	-1.14	1.99	0.497
1	Algeria 4	-1.48	-0.74	2.78	0.260
2	Andorra 5	0.80	1.62	1.86	0.536
3	Argentina 5	-0.66	0.38	0.84	0.841
4	Armenia 3	0.55	-1.31	2.64	0.302
5	Australia 5	0.21	1.75	1.40	0.674
6	Austria 4	0.25	1.43	1.12	0.757
7	Azerbaijan 3	-0.14	-1.38	2.08	0.470
8	Bangladesh 4	-1.21	-0.93	2.70	0.284
9	Belarus 4	0.89	-1.23	2.90	0.225
10	Belgium 4	0.50	1.13	1.07	0.772
11	Bosnia 4	0.34	-0.65	1.77	0.563
12	Brazil 5	-0.98	0.61	0.93	0.814
13	Britain 5	0.06	1.68	1.18	0.740
14	Bulgaria 5	1.13	-1.01	2.92	0.219
15	BurkinaFas 5	-1.32	-0.49	2.37	0.383
16	Canada 5	-0.26	1.91	1.39	0.677
17	Chile 5	-0.87	0.00	1.43	0.665
18	China 5	0.80	-1.16	2.74	0.272
19	Colombia 5	-1.87	0.60	1.83	0.545
20	Croatia 4	0.08	0.31	0.55	0.928
21	Cyprus 5	-0.56	0.13	0.99	0.796
22	Czech 4	1.23	0.38	1.63	0.605
23	Denmark 4	1.16	1.87	2.47	0.353
24	Domin. Rep 3	-1.05	0.33	1.28	0.710

#	Nation & wave**	Trad Rat values	Surv Self values	2013HD2*	HD2**z-score
51	Latvia 4	0.72	-1.27	2.77	0.263
52	Lithuania 4	0.98	-1.00	2.76	0.266
53	Luxemburg 4	0.42	1.13	0.99	0.796
54	Macedonia 4	0.12	-0.72	1.62	0.608
55	Malaysia 5	-0.73	0.09	1.20	0.734
56	Mali 5	-1.25	-0.08	1.89	0.527
57	Malta 99	-1.53	-0.03	2.12	0.458
58	Mexico 5	-1.47	1.03	1.72	0.578
59	Moldova 5	0.47	-1.28	2.53	0.335
60	Montenegro 4	0.86	-1.24	2.88	0.231
61	Morocco 5	-1.32	-1.04	2.92	0.219
62	Moscow 2	1.44	-0.79	3.01	0.192
63	N. Ireland 4	-0.33	0.84	0.39	0.976
64	N. Zealand 5	0.00	1.86	1.30	0.704
65	Neth'lands 5	0.71	1.39	1.54	0.632
66	Nigeria 4	-1.53	0.28	1.81	0.551
67	Norway 5	1.39	2.17	3.00	0.195
68	Pakistan 4	-1.42	-1.25	3.23	0.126
69	Peru 4	-1.36	0.03	1.89	0.527
70	Philippines 4	-1.21	-0.11	1.88	0.530
71	Poland 5	-0.78	-0.14	1.48	0.650
72	Portugal 4	-0.90	0.49	0.97	0.802
73	Puerto Rico 4	-2.07	1.12	2.41	0.371
74	Romania 5	-0.39	-1.55	2.50	0.344
75	Russia 5	0.49	-1.42	2.69	0.287

#	Country					#	Country				
25	E Germany 5	1.46	0.26	1.98	0.500	76	Rwanda 5	-1.57	-0.62	2.75	0.269
26	Egypt 4	-1.61	-0.46	2.63	0.305	77	S Africa 5	-1.09	-0.10	1.75	0.569
27	El Salvador 4	-2.06	0.53	2.09	0.467	78	S Korea 5	0.61	-1.37	2.76	0.266
28	Estonia 4	1.27	-1.19	3.24	0.123	79	Saudi Arab. 4	-1.31	0.15	1.72	0.578
29	Ethiopia 5	-0.65	-0.36	1.57	0.623	80	Serbia 5	0.35	-0.62	1.75	0.569
30	Finland 5	0.82	1.12	1.38	0.680	81	Singapore	-0.54	-0.28	1.38	0.680
31	France 5	0.63	1.13	1.20	0.734	82	Slovakia 4	0.67	-0.43	1.88	0.530
32	Galicia 3	-0.04	1.34	0.74	0.871	83	Slovenia 2	0.64	-0.62	2.04	0.482
33	Georgia 3	-0.04	-1.31	2.05	0.479	84	Slovenia 5	0.73	0.36	1.15	0.749
34	Ghana 5	-1.94	-0.29	2.79	0.257	85	Spain 5	0.09	0.54	0.33	0.994
35	Greece 4	0.77	0.55	1.00	0.793	86	Sweden 5**	1.86	2.35	3.65	0.000
36	Guatemala 4	-1.70	-0.17	2.43	0.365	87	Switzerland 5	0.74	1.90	2.08	0.470
37	Hong Kong 5	1.20	-0.98	2.96	0.207	88	Taiwan 5	1.16	-1.18	3.12	0.159
38	Hungary 4	0.40	-1.22	2.40	0.374	89	Tanzania 4	-1.84	-0.15	2.55	0.329
39	Iceland 4	0.44	1.63	1.51	0.641	90	Thailand 5	-0.64	0.01	1.19	0.737
40	India 5	-0.36	-0.21	1.13	0.754	91	Trinidad 5	-1.83	-0.26	2.65	0.299
41	Indonesia 5	-0.47	-0.80	1.83	0.545	92	Turkey 5	-0.89	-0.33	1.78	0.560
42	Iran 4	-1.22	-0.45	2.23	0.425	93	Uganda 1	-1.42	-0.50	2.48	0.350
43	Iraq 5	-0.40	-1.68	2.64	0.302	94	Ukraine 5	0.30	-0.83	1.91	0.521
44	Ireland 4	-0.91	1.18	1.31	0.701	95	Uruguay 5	-0.37	0.99	0.58	0.919
45	Israel 4	0.26	0.36	0.68	0.889	96	USA 5	-0.81	1.76	1.79	0.557
46	Italy 5	0.13	0.60	0.31	1.000	97	Venezuela 4	-1.60	0.43	1.73	0.575
47	Japan 5	1.96	-0.05	2.79	0.257	98	Vietnam 5	-0.30	-0.26	1.12	0.757
48	Jordan 4	-1.61	-1.05	3.22	0.129	99	W Germany 5	1.31	0.74	1.49	0.647
49	Kyrgyz 4	-0.15	-0.91	1.62	0.608	100	Zambia 5	-0.77	-0.62	1.95	0.509
50						101	Zimbabwe 4	-1.50	-1.36	3.42	0.069

* Survey year: 1 = 1980; 2 = 1990; 3 = 1995; 4 = 2000; 5 = 2005.

** HD2 (Hypothenus distance to the center) = SQRT(((highest-lowest)-country)^2)+SQRT(((highest-lowest)-country)^2).

*** Standardized = (max score "0" to "x") * (N-min) / (max − min).

**** Hypothenus distance to Sweden/Japan (HD1) = SQRT(((B$49-B2)^2)+((C$87-C2)^2)).

APPENDIX 4

Total GDP (Gross Domestic Product), 2012, Purchasing Power Parity in Current International US Dollars

		(Billions)
	World	86,119
	European Union	17,108
1	United States	16,245
2	China	12,269
3	India	4,716
4	Japan	4,487
5	Germany	3,378
6	Russia	3,373
7	France	2,372
8	United Kingdom	2,368
9	Brazil	2,327
10	Mexico	2,022
11	Italy	2,018
12	South Korea	1,540
13	Canada	1,484
14	Spain	1,481
15	Turkey	1,358
16	Indonesia	1,204
17	Australia	1,012
18	Saudi Arabia	883
19	Poland	854
20	Iran (2009)	832
21	Netherlands	723
22	Thailand	645
23	South Africa	576
24	Egypt	534
25	Colombia	498
26	Malaysia	495
27	Pakistan	491
28	Argentina (2006)	469

(continued)

		(Billions)
29	Nigeria	450
30	Belgium	443
31	Switzerland	426
32	Philippines	420
33	Sweden	409
34	Venezuela	397
35	Chile	391
36	United Arab Emirates	381
37	Austria	370
38	Hong Kong	366
39	Romania	363
40	Vietnam	336
41	Ukraine	333
42	Norway	329
43	Algeria	325
44	Singapore	323
45	Peru	323
46	Bangladesh	286
47	Greece	286
48	Czech Republic	281
49	Portugal	267
50	Israel	252
51	Denmark	236
52	Kazakhstan	230
53	Hungary	218
54	Finland	207
55	Ireland	201
56	Morocco	173
57	Qatar	168
58	Ecuador	149
59	Belarus	145
60	New Zealand	143
61	Kuwait (2011)	141
62	Slovakia	136
63	Iraq	136
64	Angola	125
65	Sri Lanka	125
66	Syria	120
67	Bulgaria	117
68	Uzbekistan	105
69	Libya (2009)	105
70	Tunisia	104
71	Dominican Republic	103
72	Ethiopia	102
73	Azerbaijan	94

		(Billions)
74	Croatia	90
75	Serbia	85
76	Sudan	80
77	Oman (2011)	78
78	Guatemala	76
79	Kenya	75
80	Tanzania	73
81	Lithuania	73
82	Lebanon	64
83	Panama	62
84	Costa Rica	61
85	Yemen	58
86	Slovenia	57
87	Bolivia	55
88	Turkmenistan	54
89	Uruguay	54
90	Ghana	51
91	Cameroon	50
92	Uganda	48
93	Macao	48
94	Luxembourg	47
95	Afghanistan	47
96	Latvia	44
97	El Salvador	44
98	Paraguay	40
99	Nepal	40
100	Côte d'Ivoire	40
101	Jordan	38
102	Cambodia	37
103	Bosnia and Herzegovina	36
104	Trinidad and Tobago	36
105	Honduras	33
106	Bahrain	32
107	Botswana	32
108	Estonia	32
109	Albania	30
110	Democratic Republic of Congo	27
111	Cyprus	27
112	Chad	27
113	Georgia	26
114	Senegal	26
115	Gabon	26
116	Mozambique	25
117	Armenia	25
118	Macedonia	25

(continued)

		(Billions)
119	Burkina Faso	25
120	Nicaragua	24
121	Zambia	24
122	Equatorial Guinea	22
123	Brunei	22
124	Madagascar	22
125	Papua New Guinea	20
126	Mauritius	19
127	Laos	19
128	Republic of Congo	19
129	Jamaica (2005)	19
130	Mali	18
131	Tajikistan	18
132	Namibia	17
133	Benin	16
134	Rwanda	15
135	Mongolia	15
136	Kyrgyzstan	13
137	Niger	13
138	Haiti	12
139	Malta	12
140	Guinea	12
141	Iceland	12
142	Malawi	12
143	Moldova	12
144	Bahamas	12
145	Mauritania	9.7
146	Montenegro	8.9
147	Sierra Leone	8.0
148	Barbados	7.5
149	Togo	6.9
150	Swaziland	6.4
151	Burundi	5.4
152	Bhutan	4.9
153	Central African Republic	4.9
154	Suriname	4.7
155	Fiji	4.3
156	Lesotho	4.0
157	Eritrea	3.4
158	Gambia	3.4
159	Maldives	3.0
160	Guyana	2.7
161	Liberia	2.7
162	Belize	2.6
163	Cape Verde	2.4

		(Billions)
164	Seychelles	2.3
165	Saint Lucia	2.1
166	Timor-Leste	2.0
167	Guinea-Bissau	1.8
168	Antigua and Barbuda	1.7
169	Djibouti (2007)	1.7
170	Solomon Islands	1.7
171	Grenada	1.2
172	Saint Vincent and Grenadines	1.2
173	Vanuatu	1.1
174	Saint Kitts and Nevis	1.0
175	Comoros	0.9
176	Dominica	0.9
177	Samoa	0.8
178	Tonga	0.5
179	Micronesia	0.4
180	Palau	0.4
181	Kiribati	0.3
182	São Tome and Principe	0.3

* Data is for 2011.

** Data is for the following years (latest available): Iran 2009, Argentina 2006, Libya 2009, Jamaica 2005, Barbados 2009, Djibouti 2007.

Countries in Alphabetical Order

Afghanistan 47; Albania 30; Algeria 325; Angola 125; Antigua and Barbuda 1.7; Argentina (2006) 469; Armenia 25; Australia 1,012; Austria 370; Azerbaijan 94; Bahamas 12; Bahrain 32; Bangladesh 286; Barbados 7.5; Belarus 145; Belgium 443; Belize 2.6; Benin 16; Bhutan 4.9; Bolivia 55; Bosnia and Herzegovina 36; Botswana 32; Brazil 2,327; Brunei 22; Bulgaria 117; Burkina Faso 25; Burundi 5.4; Cambodia 37; Cameroon 50; Canada 1,484; Cape Verde 2.4; Central African Republic 4.9; Chad 27; Chile 391; China 12,269; Colombia 498; Comoros 0.9; Costa Rica 61; Côte d'Ivoire 40; Croatia 90; Cyprus 27; Czech Republic 281; Democratic Republic of Congo 27; Denmark 236; Djibouti (2007) 1.7; Dominica 0.9; Dominican Republic 103; Ecuador 149; Egypt 534; El Salvador 44; Equatorial Guinea 22; Eritrea 3.4; Estonia 32; Ethiopia 102; European Union 17,108; Fiji 4.3; Finland 207; France 2,372; Gabon 26; Gambia 3.4; Georgia 26; Germany 3,378; Ghana 51; Greece 286; Grenada 1.2; Guatemala 76; Guinea-Bissau 1.8; Guinea 12; Guyana 2.7; Haiti 12; Honduras 33; Hong Kong 366; Hungary 218; Iceland 12; India 4,716; Indonesia 1,204; Iran (2009) 832; Iraq 136; Ireland 201; Israel 252; Italy 2,018; Jamaica (2005) 19; Japan 4,487; Jordan 38; Kazakhstan 230; Kenya 75; Kiribati 0.3; Kuwait (2011) 141; Kyrgyzstan 13; Laos 19; Latvia 44; Lebanon 64; Lesotho 4.0; Liberia 2.7; Libya (2009) 105; Lithuania 73; Luxembourg 47; Macao 48; Macedonia 25; Madagascar 22; Malawi 12; Malaysia 495; Maldives 3.0; Mali 18; Malta 12; Mauritania 9.7; Mauritius 19; Mexico 2,022; Micronesia 0.4; Moldova 12; Mongolia 15; Montenegro 8.9; Morocco 173; Mozambique 25; Namibia 17; Nepal 40; Netherlands 723; New Zealand 143; Nicaragua 24; Niger 13; Nigeria 450; Norway 329; Oman (2011) 78; Pakistan 491; Palau 0.4; Panama 62; Papua New Guinea 20; Paraguay 40; Peru 323; Philippines 420; Poland 854; Portugal 267; Qatar 168; Republic of Congo 19; Romania 363; Russia 3,373; Rwanda 15; Saint Kitts and Nevis, 1.0; Saint Lucia, 2.1; Samoa, 0.8; São Tome and Principe, 0.3; Saudi Arabia 883; Senegal 26; Serbia 85; Seychelles 2.3; Sierra Leone 8.0; Singapore 323; Slovakia 136; Slovenia 57; Solomon Islands 1.7; South Africa 576; South Korea 1,540; Spain 1,481; Sri Lanka 125; Saint Vincent and Grenadines, 1.2; Sudan 80; Suriname 4.7; Swaziland 6.4; Sweden 409; Switzerland 426; Syria 120; Tajikistan 18; Tanzania 73; Thailand 645; Timor-Leste 2.0; Togo 6.9; Tonga 0.5; Trinidad and Tobago 36; Tunisia 104; Turkey 1,358; Turkmenistan 54; United Arab Emirates 381; Uganda 48; Ukraine 333; United Kingdom 2,368; United States 16,245; Uruguay 54; Uzbekistan 105; Vanuatu 1.1; Venezuela 397; Vietnam 336; World 86,119; Yemen 58; Zambia 24.

Source: 2012 World Bank Data or latest available: http://data.worldbank.org/indicator/NY.GDP.MKTP.PP.CD.

APPENDIX 5

GDP (Gross Domestic Product) per Capita, 2012 (Purchasing Power Parity), Current International US Dollars

1	Luxembourg	88,286
2	Macao	86,341
3	Qatar	82,106
4	Norway	65,640
5	Singapore	60,800
6	Switzerland	53,281
7	Brunei	52,482
8	United States	51,749
9	Hong Kong	51,103
10	Kuwait (2011)	44,988
11	Australia	44,598
12	Ireland	43,683
13	Austria	43,661
14	Netherlands	43,105
15	Sweden	43,021
16	Canada	42,533
17	Denmark	42,173
18	United Arab Emirates	41,397
19	Germany	41,245
20	Belgium	39,751
21	Finland	38,271
22	Iceland	37,636
23	United Kingdom	37,456
---	Euro area	36,115
24	France	36,104
25	Japan	35,178
---	European Union	33,609

(continued)

275

26	Italy	33,134
27	New Zealand	32,219
28	Spain	32,043
29	Israel	31,869
30	Saudi Arabia	31,214
31	Bahamas	31,116
32	South Korea	30,801
33	Cyprus	30,768
34	Equatorial Guinea	29,742
35	Malta	29,030
36	Slovenia	27,474
37	Seychelles	26,729
38	Czech Republic	26,698
39	Trinidad and Tobago	26,550
40	Barbados (2009)	26,488
41	Oman (2011)	25,806
42	Portugal	25,389
43	Greece	25,331
44	Slovakia	25,175
45	Bahrain	24,590
46	Lithuania	24,374
47	Estonia	23,631
48	Russia	23,501
49	Chile	22,363
50	Poland	22,162
51	Hungary	21,959
52	Latvia	21,905
53	Croatia	20,964
54	Antigua and Barbuda	19,640
55	Palau	18,722
56	Saint Kitts and Nevis	18,384
57	Turkey	18,348
58	Libya (2009)	17,534
59	Romania	17,004
60	Malaysia	16,919
61	Mexico	16,734
62	Panama	16,346
63	Botswana	16,105
64	Bulgaria	16,044
65	Uruguay	15,776
66	Gabon	15,765
67	Belarus	15,327
68	Mauritius	14,902
69	Lebanon	14,373
70	Montenegro	14,358
71	Kazakhstan	13,667

72	Venezuela	13,267
73	Costa Rica	12,733
74	Dominica	12,426
---	World	12,222
75	Argentina (2006)	12,016
76	Macedonia	11,834
77	Serbia	11,801
78	Brazil	11,716
79	Saint Lucia	11,427
80	Iran (2009)	11,310
81	South Africa	11,255
82	Saint Vincent and Grenadines	11,047
83	Grenada	10,928
84	Peru	10,765
85	Colombia	10,436
86	Turkmenistan	10,411
87	Azerbaijan	10,125
88	Dominican Republic	10,038
89	Thailand	9,660
90	Ecuador	9,637
91	Tunisia	9,636
92	Albania	9,403
93	Bosnia and Herzegovina	9,392
94	China	9,083
95	Maldives	8,925
96	Suriname	8,722
97	Algeria	8,447
98	Armenia	8,417
99	Belize	7,937
100	Namibia	7,442
101	Ukraine	7,298
102	Jamaica (2005)	7,083
103	El Salvador	6,991
104	Egypt	6,614
105	Bhutan	6,591
106	Sri Lanka	6,146
107	Paraguay	6,038
108	Jordan	6,037
109	Angola	6,006
110	Georgia	5,806
111	Mongolia	5,374
112	Syria	5,347
113	Morocco	5,220
114	Bolivia	5,196
115	Swaziland	5,161
116	Guatemala	5,019

(continued)

117	Tonga	4,881
118	Fiji	4,877
119	Indonesia	4,876
120	Cape Verde	4,846
121	Vanuatu	4,531
122	Samoa	4,493
123	Republic of Congo	4,354
124	Philippines	4,339
125	Iraq	4,177
126	Honduras	4,174
127	Nicaragua	4,006
128	India	3,813
129	Vietnam	3,787
130	Micronesia	3,726
131	Uzbekistan	3,533
132	Moldova	3,368
133	Guyana	3,344
134	Solomon Islands	3,076
135	Laos	2,879
136	Papua New Guinea	2,851
137	Pakistan	2,741
138	Nigeria	2,666
139	Kiribati	2,618
140	Mauritania	2,561
141	Cambodia	2,454
142	Yemen	2,448
143	Kyrgyzstan	2,370
144	Cameroon	2,312
145	Tajikistan	2,192
146	Djibouti (2007)	2,170
147	Sudan	2,162
148	Chad	2,135
149	Ghana	2,014
150	Côte d'Ivoire	2,006
151	Lesotho	1,931
152	Gambia	1,917
153	Senegal	1,908
154	Bangladesh	1,851
155	São Tome and Principe	1,822
156	Kenya	1,737
157	Zambia	1,684
158	Timor-Leste	1,660
159	Tanzania	1,575
160	Afghanistan	1,561
161	Benin	1,557
162	Burkina Faso	1,488

163	Nepal	1,457
164	Sierra Leone	1,337
165	Rwanda	1,332
166	Uganda	1,330
167	Comoros	1,210
168	Haiti	1,208
169	Mali	1,195
170	Ethiopia	1,109
171	Guinea-Bissau	1,101
172	Central African Republic	1,077
173	Guinea	1,051
174	Togo	1,034
175	Mozambique	1,007
176	Madagascar	962
177	Niger	769
178	Malawi	753
179	Liberia	639
180	Eritrea	557
181	Burundi	551
182	Democratic Republic of Congo	415

Countries in Alphabetical Order

Afghanistan 1,561; Albania 9,403; Algeria 8,447; Angola 6,006; Antigua and Barbuda 19,640; Argentina (2006) 12,016; Armenia 8,417; Australia 44,598; Austria 43,661; Azerbaijan 10,125; Bahamas 31,116; Bahrain 24,590; Bangladesh 1,851; Barbados 26,488; Belarus 15,327; Belgium 39,751; Belize 7,937; Benin 1,557; Bhutan 6,591; Bolivia 5,196; Bosnia and Herzegovina 9,392 Botswana 16,105; Brazil 11,716; Brunei 52,482; Bulgaria 16,044; Burkina Faso 1,488; Burundi 551; Cabo Verde 4,846; Cambodia 2,454; Cameroon 2,312; Canada 42,533; Central African Republic 1,077; Chad 2,135; Chile 22,363; China 9,083; Colombia 10,436; Comoros 1,210; Costa Rica 12,733; Côte d'Ivoire 2,006; Croatia 20,964; Cyprus 30,768; Czech Republic 26,698; Democratic Republic of Congo 415; Denmark 42,173; Djibouti (2007) 2,170; Dominica 12,426; Dominican Republic 10,038; Ecuador 9,637; Egypt 6,614; El Salvador 6,991; Equatorial Guinea 29,742; Eritrea 557; Estonia 23,631; Ethiopia 1,109; Euro area 36,115; European Union 33,609; Fiji 4,877; Finland 38,271; France 36,104; Gabon 15,765; Gambia 1,917; Georgia 5,806; Germany 41,245; Ghana 2,014; Greece 25,331; Grenada 10,928; Guatemala 5,019; Guinea 1,051; Guinea-Bissau 1,101; Guyana 3,344; Haiti 1,208; Honduras 4,174; Hong Kong 51,103; Hungary 21,959; Iceland 37,636; India 3,813; Indonesia 4,876; Iran (2009) 11,310; Iraq 4,177; Ireland 43,683; Israel 31,869; Italy 33,134; Jamaica (2005) 7,083; Japan 35,178; Jordan 6,037; Kazakhstan 13,667; Kenya 1,737; Kiribati 2,618; Kuwait (2011) 44,988; Kyrgyzstan 2,370; Laos 2,879; Latvia 21,905; Lebanon 14,373; Lesotho 1,931; Liberia 639; Libya (2009) 17,534; Lithuania 24,374; Luxembourg 88,286; Macao 86,341; Macedonia 11,834; Madagascar 962; Malawi 753; Malaysia 16,919; Maldives 8,925; Mali 1,195; Malta 29,030; Mauritania 2,561; Mauritius 14,902; Mexico 16,734; Micronesia 3,726; Moldova 3,368; Mongolia 5,374; Montenegro 14,358; Morocco 5,220; Mozambique 1,007; Namibia 7,442; Nepal 1,457; Netherlands 43,105; New Zealand 32,219; Nicaragua 4,006; Niger 769; Nigeria 2,666; Norway 65,640; Oman (2011) 25,806; Pakistan 2,741; Palau 18,722; Panama 16,346; Papua New Guinea 2,851; Paraguay 6,038; Peru 10,765; Philippines 4,339; Poland 22,162; Portugal 25,389; Qatar 82,106; Republic of Congo 4,354; Romania 17,004; Russia 23,501; Rwanda 1,332; Saint Kitts and Nevis 18,384; Saint Lucia 11,427; Saint Vincent and the Grenadines 11,047; Samoa 4,493; São Tome and Principe 1,822; Saudi Arabia 31,214; Senegal 1,908; Serbia 11,801; Seychelles 26,729; Sierra Leone 1,337; Singapore 60,800; Slovakia 25,175; Slovenia 27,474; Solomon Islands 3,076; South Africa 11,255; South Korea 30,801; Spain 32,043; Sri Lanka 6,146; Sudan 2,162; Suriname 8,722; Swaziland 5,161; Sweden 43,021; Switzerland 53,281; Syria 5,347; Tajikistan 2,192; Tanzania 1,575; Thailand 9,660; Timor-Leste 1,660; Togo 1,034; Tonga 4,881; Trinidad and Tobago 26,550; Tunisia 9,636; Turkey 18,348; Turkmenistan 10,411; Uganda 1,330; Ukraine 7,298; United Arab Emirates 41,397; United Kingdom 37,456; United States 51,749; Uruguay 15,776; Uzbekistan 3,533; Vanuatu 4,531; Venezuela 13,267; Vietnam 3,787; World 12,222; Yemen 2,448; Zambia 1,684

Source: World Bank Data: http://data.worldbank.org/indicator/NY.GDP.PCAP.PP.CD.

APPENDIX 6

Human Development Index (HDI), UNDP, 2012

HDI Rank	Country	Value
1	Norway	0.955
2	Australia	0.938
3	United States	0.937
4	Netherlands	0.921
5	Germany	0.920
6	New Zealand	0.919
7	Ireland	0.916
7	Sweden	0.916
9	Switzerland	0.913
10	Japan	0.912
11	Canada	0.911
12	South Korea	0.909
13	Hong Kong	0.906
13	Iceland	0.906
15	Denmark	0.901
16	Israel	0.900
17	Belgium	0.897
18	Austria	0.895
18	Singapore	0.895
20	France	0.893
21	Finland	0.892
21	Slovenia	0.892
23	Spain	0.885
24	Liechtenstein	0.883
25	Italy	0.881
26	Luxembourg	0.875
26	United Kingdom	0.875
28	Czech Republic	0.873
29	Greece	0.860

(continued)

HDI Rank	Country	Value
30	Brunei Darussalam	0.855
31	Cyprus	0.848
32	Malta	0.847
33	Andorra	0.846
33	Estonia	0.846
35	Slovakia	0.840
36	Qatar	0.834
37	Hungary	0.831
38	Barbados	0.825
39	Poland	0.821
40	Chile	0.819
41	Lithuania	0.818
41	United Arab Emirates	0.818
43	Portugal	0.816
44	Latvia	0.814
45	Argentina	0.811
46	Seychelles	0.806
47	Croatia	0.805
48	Bahrain	0.796
49	Bahamas	0.794
50	Belarus	0.793
51	Uruguay	0.792
52	Montenegro	0.791
52	Palau	0.791
54	Kuwait	0.790
55	Russia	0.788
56	Romania	0.786
57	Bulgaria	0.782
57	Saudi Arabia	0.782
59	Cuba	0.780
59	Panama	0.780
61	Mexico	0.775
62	Costa Rica	0.773
63	Grenada	0.770
64	Libya	0.769
64	Malaysia	0.769
64	Serbia	0.769
67	Antigua and Barbuda	0.760
67	Trinidad and Tobago	0.760
69	Kazakhstan	0.754
70	Albania	0.749
71	Venezuela	0.748
72	Dominica	0.745
72	Georgia	0.745
72	Lebanon	0.745

HDI Rank	Country	Value
72	Saint Kitts and Nevis	0.745
76	Iran	0.742
77	Peru	0.741
78	Macedonia	0.740
78	Ukraine	0.740
80	Mauritius	0.737
81	Bosnia and Herzegovina	0.735
82	Azerbaijan	0.734
83	Saint Vincent and Grenadines	0.733
84	Oman	0.731
85	Brazil	0.730
85	Jamaica	0.730
87	Armenia	0.729
88	Saint Lucia	0.725
89	Ecuador	0.724
90	Turkey	0.722
91	Colombia	0.719
92	Sri Lanka	0.715
93	Algeria	0.713
94	Tunisia	0.712
95	Tonga	0.710
96	Belize	0.702
96	Dominican Republic	0.702
96	Fiji	0.702
96	Samoa	0.702
100	Jordan	0.700
101	China	0.699
102	Turkmenistan	0.698
103	Thailand	0.690
104	Maldives	0.688
105	Suriname	0.684
106	Gabon	0.683
107	El Salvador	0.680
108	Bolivia	0.675
108	Mongolia	0.675
110	Occupied Palestinian Territories	0.670
111	Paraguay	0.669
112	Egypt	0.662
113	Moldova	0.660
114	Philippines	0.654
114	Uzbekistan	0.654
116	Syria	0.648
117	Micronesia	0.645
118	Guyana	0.636
119	Botswana	0.634

(continued)

HDI Rank	Country	Value
120	Honduras	0.632
121	Indonesia	0.629
121	Kiribati	0.629
121	South Africa	0.629
124	Vanuatu	0.626
125	Kyrgyzstan	0.622
125	Tajikistan	0.622
127	Vietnam	0.617
128	Namibia	0.608
129	Nicaragua	0.599
130	Morocco	0.591
131	Iraq	0.590
132	Cape Verde	0.586
133	Guatemala	0.581
134	Timor-Leste	0.576
135	Ghana	0.558
136	Equatorial Guinea	0.554
136	India	0.554
138	Cambodia	0.543
138	Laos	0.543
140	Bhutan	0.538
141	Swaziland	0.536
142	Congo	0.534
143	Solomon Islands	0.530
144	São Tome and Principe	0.525
145	Kenya	0.519
146	Bangladesh	0.515
146	Pakistan	0.515
148	Angola	0.508
149	Myanmar	0.498
150	Cameroon	0.495
151	Madagascar	0.483
152	Tanzania	0.476
153	Nigeria	0.471
154	Senegal	0.470
155	Mauritania	0.467
156	Papua New Guinea	0.466
157	Nepal	0.463
158	Lesotho	0.461
159	Togo	0.459
160	Yemen	0.458
161	Haiti	0.456
161	Uganda	0.456
163	Zambia	0.448
164	Djibouti	0.445

HDI Rank	Country	Value
165	Gambia	0.439
166	Benin	0.436
167	Rwanda	0.434
168	Côte d'Ivoire	0.432
169	Comoros	0.429
170	Malawi	0.418
171	Sudan	0.414
172	Zimbabwe	0.397
173	Ethiopia	0.396
174	Liberia	0.388
175	Afghanistan	0.374
176	Guinea-Bissau	0.364
177	Sierra Leone	0.359
178	Burundi	0.355
178	Guinea	0.355
180	Central African Republic	0.352
181	Eritrea	0.351
182	Mali	0.344
183	Burkina Faso	0.343
184	Chad	0.340
185	Mozambique	0.327
186	Congo (Democratic Republic)	0.304
186	Niger	0.304

Countries in Alphabetical Order

Afghanistan 0.374; Albania 0.749; Algeria 0.713; Andorra 0.846; Angola 0.508; Antigua and Barbuda 0.76; Argentina 0.811; Armenia 0.729; Australia 0.938; Austria 0.895; Azerbaijan 0.734; Bahamas 0.794; Bahrain 0.796; Bangladesh 0.515; Barbados 0.825; Belarus 0.793; Belgium 0.897; Belize 0.702; Benin 0.436; Bhutan 0.538; Bolivia 0.675; Bosnia and Herzegovina 0.735; Botswana 0.634; Brazil 0.73; Brunei Darussalam 0.855; Bulgaria 0.782; Burkina Faso 0.343; Burundi 0.355; Cambodia 0.543; Cameroon 0.495; Canada 0.911; Cape Verde 0.586; Central Afr. Rep. 0.352; Chad 0.34; Chile 0.819; China 0.699; Colombia 0.719; Comoros 0.429; Congo 0.534; Congo (Dem. Rep.) 0.304; Costa Rica 0.773; Côte d'Ivoire 0.432; Croatia 0.805; Cuba 0.78; Cyprus 0.848; Czech Republic 0.873; Denmark 0.901; Djibouti 0.445; Dominica 0.745; Dominican Rep. 0.702; Ecuador 0.724; Egypt 0.662; El Salvador 0.68; Equatorial Guinea 0.554; Eritrea 0.351; Estonia 0.846; Ethiopia 0.396; Fiji 0.702; Finland 0.892; France 0.893; Gabon 0.683; Gambia 0.439; Georgia 0.745; Germany 0.92; Ghana 0.558; Greece 0.86; Grenada 0.77; Guatemala 0.581; Guinea 0.355; Guinea-Bissau 0.364; Guyana 0.636; Haiti 0.456; Honduras 0.632; Hong Kong 0.906; Hungary 0.831; Iceland 0.906; India 0.554; Indonesia 0.629; Iran 0.742; Iraq 0.59; Ireland 0.916; Israel 0.9; Italy 0.881; Jamaica 0.73; Japan 0.912; Jordan 0.7; Kazakhstan 0.754; Kenya 0.519; Kiribati 0.629; Kuwait 0.79; Kyrgyzstan 0.622; Laos 0.543; Latvia 0.814; Lebanon 0.745; Lesotho 0.461; Liberia 0.388; Libya 0.769; Liechtenstein 0.883; Lithuania 0.818; Luxembourg 0.875; Macedonia 0.74; Madagascar 0.483; Malawi 0.418; Malaysia 0.769; Maldives 0.688; Mali 0.344; Malta 0.847; Mauritania 0.467; Mauritius 0.737; Mexico 0.775; Micronesia 0.645; Moldova 0.66; Mongolia 0.675; Montenegro 0.791; Morocco 0.591; Mozambique 0.327; Myanmar 0.498; Namibia 0.608; Nepal 0.463; Netherlands 0.921; New Zealand 0.919; Nicaragua 0.599; Niger 0.304; Nigeria 0.471; Norway 0.955; Occupied Palestinian Territories 0.67; Oman 0.731; Pakistan 0.515; Palau 0.791; Panama 0.78; Papua New Guinea 0.466; Paraguay 0.669; Peru 0.741; Philippines 0.654; Poland 0.821; Portugal 0.816; Qatar 0.834; Romania 0.786; Russia 0.788; Rwanda 0.434; Saint Kitts and Nevis 0.745; Saint Lucia 0.725; Saint Vincent and Grenadines 0.733; Samoa 0.702; São Tome and Principe 0.525; Saudi Arabia 0.782; Senegal 0.47; Serbia 0.769; Seychelles 0.806; Sierra Leone 0.359; Singapore 0.895; Slovakia 0.84; Slovenia 0.892; Solomon Islands 0.53; South Africa 0.629; South Korea 0.909; Spain 0.885; Sri Lanka 0.715; Sudan 0.414; Suriname 0.684; Swaziland 0.536; Sweden 0.916; Switzerland 0.913; Syria 0.648; Tajikistan 0.622; Tanzania 0.476; Thailand 0.69; Timor-Leste 0.576; Togo 0.459; Tonga 0.71; Trinidad and Tobago 0.76; Tunisia 0.712; Turkey 0.722; Turkmenistan 0.698; United Arab Emirates 0.818; Uganda 0.456; Ukraine 0.74; United Kingdom 0.875; United States 0.937; Uruguay 0.792; Uzbekistan 0.654; Vanuatu 0.626; Venezuela 0.748; Vietnam 0.617; Yemen 0.458; Zambia 0.448; Zimbabwe 0.397

Source: UNDP, HDR: https://data.undp.org/dataset/Table-2-Human-Development-Index-trends/efc4-gjvq.

APPENDIX 7

Political Rights and Civil Liberties in the World, 2013 (Freedom House Index)

Rank	Country	Score
1	Finland	1.000
2	Iceland	1.000
3	Luxembourg	1.000
4	Norway	1.000
5	San Marino	1.000
6	Sweden	1.000
7	Barbados	0.990
8	Netherlands	0.990
9	Canada	0.980
10	Denmark	0.980
11	Liechtenstein	0.980
12	Australia	0.970
13	Belgium	0.970
14	Ireland	0.970
15	Malta	0.970
16	New Zealand	0.970
17	Portugal	0.970
18	United Kingdom	0.970
19	Uruguay	0.970
20	Andorra	0.960
21	Austria	0.960
22	Bahamas	0.960
23	Chile	0.960
24	Germany	0.960
25	Spain	0.960
26	Switzerland	0.960
27	Czech Republic	0.950
28	Dominica	0.950

(continued)

Rank	Country	Score
29	Estonia	0.950
30	France	0.950
31	Tuvalu	0.940
32	Cyprus	0.930
33	Micronesia	0.930
34	Nauru	0.930
35	Poland	0.930
36	Saint Lucia	0.930
37	United States	0.930
38	Palau	0.920
39	Slovakia	0.920
40	Costa Rica	0.910
41	Kiribati	0.910
42	Marshall Islands	0.910
43	Slovenia	0.910
44	Saint Kitts and Nevis	0.910
45	Cape Verde	0.900
46	Lithuania	0.900
47	Mauritius	0.900
48	Grenada	0.890
49	Saint Vincent and Grenadines	0.890
50	Belize	0.880
51	Hungary	0.880
52	Italy	0.880
53	Japan	0.880
54	Taiwan	0.880
55	Monaco	0.870
56	Croatia	0.860
57	Mongolia	0.860
58	South Korea	0.860
59	Ghana	0.840
60	Latvia	0.840
61	Greece	0.830
62	Benin	0.820
63	Panama	0.820
64	Brazil	0.810
65	Bulgaria	0.810
66	Israel	0.810
67	Romania	0.810
68	Samoa	0.810
69	Sao Tome and Prin.	0.810
70	South Africa	0.810
71	Trinidad and Tobago	0.810
72	Antigua and Barbuda	0.800

Rank	Country	Score
73	Argentina	0.800
74	Vanuatu	0.790
75	Serbia	0.780
76	El Salvador	0.770
77	Suriname	0.770
78	India	0.760
79	Namibia	0.760
80	Dominican Republic	0.750
81	Senegal	0.750
82	Botswana	0.740
83	Jamaica	0.730
84	Tonga	0.730
85	Lesotho	0.720
86	Montenegro	0.720
87	Guyana	0.710
88	Peru	0.710
89	Sierra Leone	0.700
90	Bolivia	0.690
91	Seychelles	0.670
92	Tanzania	0.660
93	Indonesia	0.650
94	Mexico	0.650
95	Moldova	0.650
96	Solomon Islands	0.650
97	Macedonia	0.640
98	Albania	0.630
99	East Timor	0.630
100	Philippines	0.630
101	Bosnia and Herzegovina	0.620
102	Paraguay	0.620
103	Zambia	0.620
104	Colombia	0.610
105	Turkey	0.610
106	Ecuador	0.600
107	Georgia	0.600
108	Liberia	0.600
109	Malawi	0.600
110	Mozambique	0.590
111	Papua New Guinea	0.590
112	Tunisia	0.580
113	Guatemala	0.570
114	Ukraine	0.570
115	Bangladesh	0.560
116	Niger	0.560

(continued)

Rank	Country	Score
117	Comoros	0.550
118	Kenya	0.550
119	Burkina Faso	0.530
120	Thailand	0.530
121	Singapore	0.520
122	Honduras	0.510
123	Nicaragua	0.510
124	Lebanon	0.490
125	Malaysia	0.480
126	Bhutan	0.470
127	Nepal	0.470
128	Maldives	0.460
129	Nigeria	0.460
130	Haiti	0.430
131	Kosovo	0.430
132	Libya	0.430
133	Morocco	0.430
134	Sri Lanka	0.430
135	Togo	0.430
136	Armenia	0.420
137	Pakistan	0.420
138	Kuwait	0.410
139	Kyrgyzstan	0.410
140	Uganda	0.400
141	Guinea	0.390
142	Venezuela	0.390
143	Egypt	0.380
144	Fiji	0.370
145	Algeria	0.350
146	Central Afr. Rep.	0.350
147	Madagascar	0.350
148	Burundi	0.340
149	Côte d'Ivoire	0.340
150	Gabon	0.340
151	Jordan	0.340
152	Mauritania	0.340
153	South Sudan	0.310
154	Angola	0.300
155	Guinea-Bissau	0.300
156	Brunei	0.290
157	Burma	0.290
158	Cambodia	0.290
159	Congo, Republic of	0.290
160	Djibouti	0.290

Rank	Country	Score
161	Afghanistan	0.260
162	Kazakhstan	0.260
163	Russia	0.260
164	Iraq	0.250
165	Mali	0.250
166	Qatar	0.250
167	Yemen	0.250
168	Zimbabwe	0.250
169	Rwanda	0.240
170	Tajikistan	0.240
171	Azerbaijan	0.230
172	Cameroon	0.230
173	The Gambia	0.230
174	Oman	0.230
175	Chad	0.210
176	Swaziland	0.210
177	Bahrain	0.200
178	Congo (Dem. Rep.)	0.200
179	United Arab Emirates	0.190
180	Vietnam	0.190
181	China	0.180
182	Ethiopia	0.180
183	Iran	0.160
184	Belarus	0.140
185	Cuba	0.110
186	Laos	0.110
187	Sudan	0.110
188	Equatorial Guinea	0.080
189	Saudi Arabia	0.080
190	Syria	0.070
191	Turkmenistan	0.070
192	Uzbekistan	0.040
193	Eritrea	0.030
194	North Korea	0.030
195	Somalia	0.020

Countries in Alphabetical Order

Albania 0.630; Andorra 0.960; Antigua and Barbuda 0.800; Argentina 0.800; Australia 0.970; Austria 0.960; Bahamas 0.960; Bangladesh 0.560; Barbados 0.990; Belgium 0.970; Belize 0.880; Benin 0.820; Bhutan 0.470; Bolivia 0.690; Bosnia and Herzegovina 0.620; Botswana 0.740; Brazil 0.810; Bulgaria 0.810; Burkina Faso 0.530; Canada 0.980; Cape Verde 0.900; Chile 0.960; Colombia 0.610; Comoros 0.550; Costa Rica 0.910; Croatia 0.860; Cyprus 0.930; Czech Republic 0.950; Denmark 0.980; Dominca 0.950; Dominican Republic 0.750; East Timor 0.630; Ecuador 0.600; El Salvador 0.770; Estonia 0.950; Finland 1.000; France 0.950; Georgia 0.600; Germany 0.960; Ghana 0.840; Greece 0.830; Grenada 0.890; Guatemala 0.570; Guyana 0.710; Haiti 0.430; Honduras 0.510; Hungary 0.880; Iceland 1.000; India 0.760; Indonesia 0.650; Ireland 0.970; Israel 0.810; Italy 0.880; Jamaica 0.730; Japan 0.880; Kenya 0.550; Kiribati 0.910; Kosovo 0.430; Latvia 0.840; Lebanon 0.490; Lesotho 0.720; Liberia 0.600; Libya 0.430; Liechtenstein 0.980; Lithuania 0.900; Luxembourg 1.000; Macedonia 0.640; Malawi 0.600; Malaysia 0.480; Maldives 0.460; Malta 0.970; Marshall Islands 0.910; Mauritius 0.900; Mexico 0.650; Micronesia 0.930; Moldova 0.650; Monaco 0.870; Mongolia 0.860; Montenegro 0.720; Morocco 0.430; Mozambique 0.590; Namibia 0.760; Nauru 0.930; Nepal 0.470; Netherlands 0.990; New Zealand 0.970; Nicaragua 0.510; Niger 0.560; Nigeria 0.460; Norway 1.000; Palau 0.920; Panama 0.820; Papua New Guinea 0.590; Paraguay 0.620; Peru 0.710; Philippines 0.630; Poland 0.930; Portugal 0.970; Romania 0.810; Samoa 0.810; San Marino 1.000; Sao Tome and Principe 0.810; Senegal 0.750; Serbia 0.780; Seychelles 0.670; Sierra Leone 0.700; Singapore 0.520; Slovakia 0.920; Slovenia 0.910; Solomon Islands 0.650; South Africa 0.810; South Korea 0.860; Spain 0.960; Sri Lanka 0.430; Saint Kitts and Nevis 0.910; Saint Lucia 0.930; Saint Vincent and Grenadines 0.890; Suriname 0.770; Sweden 1.000; Switzerland 0.960; Taiwan 0.880; Tanzania 0.660; Thailand 0.530; Tonga 0.730; Trinidad and Tobago 0.810; Tunisia 0.580; Turkey 0.610; Tuvalu 0.940; Ukraine 0.570; United Arab Emirates 0.190; United Kingdom 0.970; United States 0.930; Uruguay 0.970; Vanuatu 0.790; Zambia 0.620

Source: http://www.freedomhouse.org/report/freedom-world-aggregate-and-subcategory-scores.

Freedom House Index Components

POLITICAL RIGHTS

A. Electoral Process

1. Is the head of government or other chief national authority elected through free and fair elections?
2. Are the national legislative representatives elected through free and fair elections?
3. Are the electoral laws and framework fair?

B. Political Pluralism and Participation

1. Do the people have the right to organize in different political parties or other competitive political groupings of their choice, and is the system open to the rise and fall of these competing parties or groupings?
2. Is there a significant opposition vote and a realistic possibility for the opposition to increase its support or gain power through elections?
3. Are the people's political choices free from domination by the military, foreign powers, totalitarian parties, religious hierarchies, economic oligarchies, or any other powerful group?

   4. Do cultural, ethnic, religious, or other minority groups have full political rights and electoral opportunities?

C. Functioning of Government

   1. Do the freely elected head of government and national legislative representatives determine the policies of the government?
   2. Is the government free from pervasive corruption?
   3. Is the government accountable to the electorate between elections, and does it operate with openness and transparency?

Additional Discretionary Political Rights Questions

   1. For traditional monarchies that have no parties or electoral process, does the system provide for genuine, meaningful consultation with the people, encourage public discussion of policy choices, and allow the right to petition the ruler?
   2. Is the government or occupying power deliberately changing the ethnic composition of a country or territory so as to destroy a culture or tip the political balance in favor of another group?

CIVIL LIBERTIES

D. Freedom of Expression and Belief

   1. Are there free and independent media and other forms of cultural expression? (Note: In cases where the media are state-controlled but offer pluralistic points of view, the survey gives the system credit.)
   2. Are religious institutions and communities free to practice their faith and express themselves in public and private?
   3. Is there academic freedom, and is the educational system free of extensive political indoctrination?
   4. Is there open and free private discussion?

E. Associational and Organizational Rights

   1. Is there freedom of assembly, demonstration, and open public discussion?
   2. Is there freedom for nongovernmental organizations? (Note: This includes civic organizations, interest groups, foundations, etc.)
   3. Are there free trade unions and peasant organizations or equivalents, and is there effective collective bargaining? Are there free professional and other private organizations?

F. Rule of Law

   1. Is there an independent judiciary?

2. Does the rule of law prevail in civil and criminal matters? Are police under direct civilian control?

3. Is there protection from political terror, unjustified imprisonment, exile, or torture, whether by groups that support or oppose the system? Is there freedom from war and insurgencies?

4. Do laws, policies, and practices guarantee equal treatment of various segments of the population?

G. Personal Autonomy and Individual Rights

1. Do citizens enjoy freedom of travel or choice of residence, employment, or institution of higher education?

2. Do citizens have the right to own property and establish private businesses? Is private business activity unduly influenced by government officials, the security forces, political parties/organizations, or organized crime?

3. Are there personal social freedoms, including gender equality, choice of marriage partners, and size of family?

4. Is there equality of opportunity and the absence of economic exploitation?

APPENDIX 8

Income Distribution Ranking, Gini Coefficient (World Bank, Unless Noted)

	Country	Gini	Year
1	Denmark	0.248	2011
2	Sweden	0.250	1999
3	Norway	0.258	2000
4	Slovak Republic	0.260	2009
5	Ukraine	0.264	2009
6	Finland	0.269	2000
7	Belarus	0.272	2008
8	Malta	0.274	2008
9	Serbia	0.278	2009
10	Afghanistan	0.278	2008
11	Iceland	0.280	2006
12	Bulgaria	0.282	2006
13	Germany	0.283	2000
14	Cyprus	0.290	2005
15	Kazakhstan	0.290	2009
16	Austria	0.292	2000
17	Ethiopia	0.298	2005
18	Montenegro	0.300	2008
19	Pakistan	0.300	2008
20	Romania	0.300	2008
21	European Union	0.307	2011
22	Egypt, Arab Republic	0.308	2008
23	Luxembourg	0.308	2000
24	Tajikistan	0.308	2009
25	Armenia	0.309	2008
26	Iraq	0.309	2006
27	Netherlands	0.309	1999
28	Czech Republic	0.310	2009

(continued)

	Country	Gini	Year
29	Hungary	0.312	2997
30	Slovenia	0.312	2004
31	South Korea	0.316	1998
32	Timor-Leste	0.319	2007
33	Bangladesh	0.321	2010
34	Canada	0.326	2000
35	France	0.327	1995
36	Nepal	0.328	2010
37	Belgium	0.330	2000
38	Mali*	0.330	2010
39	Moldova	0.330	2010
40	Burundi	0.333	2005
41	India	0.334	2005
42	Azerbaijan	0.337	2008
43	Croatia	0.337	2008
44	Switzerland	0.337	2008
45	Indonesia	0.340	2005
46	Poland	0.341	2009
47	Greece	0.343	2000
48	Ireland	0.343	2000
49	Togo	0.344	2006
50	Albania	0.345	2008
51	Niger	0.346	2008
52	Spain	0.347	2000
53	Australia	0.352	1994
54	Algeria	0.353	1995
55	Sudan	0.353	2008
56	Guinea-Bissau	0.355	2002
57	Jordan	0.355	2010
58	West Bank and Gaza	0.355	2009
59	Vietnam	0.356	2008
60	Syrian Arab Rep	0.358	2004
61	Estonia	0.360	2004
62	Italy	0.360	2000
63	United Kingdom	0.360	1999
64	Bosnia and Herzegovina	0.362	2007
65	Kyrgyz Republic	0.362	2009
66	New Zealand*	0.362	1997
67	Mongolia	0.365	2008
68	Latvia	0.366	2008
69	Laos	0.367	2008
70	Uzbekistan	0.367	2003
71	Maldives	0.374	2004
72	Japan	0.376	2008
73	Lithuania	0.376	2008

	Country	Gini	Year
74	Tanzania	0.376	2006
75	Yemen, Republic	0.377	2005
76	Cambodia	0.379	2008
77	Bhutan	0.381	2006
78	Liberia	0.382	2007
79	Iran	0.383	2005
80	Portugal	0.385	1997
81	Benin	0.386	2003
82	Cameroon	0.389	2007
83	Malawi	0.390	2004
84	Mauritius	0.390	2006
85	Turkey	0.390	2008
86	Israel	0.392	2001
87	Senegal	0.392	2005
88	Guinea	0.394	2007
89	Burkina Faso	0.398	2008
90	Chad	0.398	2003
91	Thailand	0.400	2009
92	Russia	0.401	2008
93	Sri Lanka	0.403	2006
94	Trinidad and Tobago	0.403	1992
95	Mauritania	0.405	2008
96	Nicaragua	0.405	2005
97	Turkmenistan	0.408	1998
98	United States	0.408	2000
99	Morocco	0.409	2007
100	Qatar	0.411	2006
101	Georgia	0.413	2008
102	Tunisia	0.414	2005
103	Côte d'Ivoire	0.415	2008
104	Gabon	0.415	2005
105	Sierra Leone	0.425	2003
106	Saint Lucia	0.426	1995
107	Fiji	0.428	2009
108	Ghana	0.428	2006
109	Philippines	0.430	2009
110	Macedonia	0.432	2009
111	Hong Kong	0.434	1996
112	Madagascar	0.441	2010
113	Uganda	0.443	2009
114	Congo, Democratic Republic	0.444	2006
115	Argentina	0.445	2010
116	Guyana	0.445	1998
117	Venezuela*	0.448	2006
118	Uruguay	0.453	2010

(continued)

	Country	Gini	Year
119	Jamaica	0.455	2004
120	South Sudan	0.455	2009
121	Mozambique*	0.457	2008
122	Malaysia	0.462	2009
123	Dominican Republic	0.472	2010
124	Congo, Republic	0.473	2005
125	Singapore	0.473	2011
126	Gambia, The	0.475	2003
127	Kenya	0.477	2005
128	China	0.480	2009
129	Peru	0.481	2010
130	El Salvador	0.483	2009
131	Mexico	0.483	2008
132	Nigeria	0.488	2010
133	Ecuador	0.493	2010
134	Zimbabwe	0.501	1995
135	Cape Verde	0.505	2001
136	Costa Rica	0.507	2009
137	São Tome and Principe	0.508	2001
138	Rwanda	0.508	2011
139	Papua New Guinea	0.509	1996
140	Swaziland	0.515	2010
141	Panama	0.519	2010
142	Chile	0.521	2008
143	Paraguay	0.524	2010
144	Lesotho	0.525	2003
145	Suriname	0.529	1999
146	Belize	0.531	1999
147	Zambia	0.546	2006
148	Brazil	0.547	2008
149	Colombia	0.559	2010
150	Guatemala	0.559	2006
151	Bolivia	0.563	2008
152	Central African Republic	0.563	2007
153	Honduras	0.570	2009
154	Angola	0.586	2000
155	Haiti	0.592	2001
156	Botswana	0.610	1994
157	Micronesia	0.611	2000
158	South Africa	0.631	2009
159	Namibia	0.639	2004

Note: 0 = zero inequality; 1 = 1 person holds all income.

Countries in Alphabetical Order

Afghanistan 0.278; Albania 0.345; Algeria 0.353; Angola 0.586; Argentina 0.445; Armenia 0.309; Australia 0.352; Austria 0.292; Azerbaijan 0.337; Bangladesh 0.321; Belarus 0.272; Belgium 0.330; Belize 0.531; Benin 0.386; Bhutan 0.381; Bolivia 0.563; Bosnia and Herzegovina 0.362; Botswana 0.610; Brazil 0.547; Bulgaria 0.282; Burkina Faso 0.398; Burundi 0.333; Cambodia 0.379; Cameroon 0.389; Canada 0.326; Cape Verde 0.505; Central African Republic 0.563; Chad 0.398; Chile 0.521; China 0.480; Colombia 0.559; Comoros 0.643; Congo, Democratic Republic 0.444; Congo, Republic 0.473; Costa Rica 0.507; Côte d'Ivoire 0.415; Croatia 0.337; Cyprus 0.290; Czech Republic 0.310; Denmark 0.248; Dominican Republic 0.472; Ecuador 0.493; Egypt, Arab Republic 0.308; El Salvador 0.483; Estonia 0.360; Ethiopia 0.298; European Union 0.307; Fiji 0.428; Finland 0.269; France 0.327; Gabon 0.415; Gambia, The 0.475; Georgia 0.413; Germany 0.283; Ghana 0.428; Greece 0.343; Guatemala 0.559; Guinea 0.394; Guinea-Bissau 0.355; Guyana 0.445; Haiti 0.592; Honduras 0.570; Hong Kong 0.434; Hungary 0.312; Iceland 0.280; India 0.334; Indonesia 0.340; Iran,0.383; Iraq 0.309; Ireland 0.343; Israel 0.392; Italy 0.360; Jamaica 0.455; Japan 0.376; Jordan 0.355; Kazakhstan 0.290; Keny 0.477; Kyrgyz Republic 0.362; Laos 0.367; Latvia 0.366; Lesotho 0.525; Liberia 0.382; Lithuania 0.376; Luxembourg 0.308; Macedonia 0.432; Madagascar 0.441; Malawi 0.390; Malaysia 0.462; Maldives 0.374; Mali* 0.330; Malta 0.274; Mauritania 0.405; Mauritius 0.390; Mexico 0.483; Micronesia 0.611; Moldova 0.330; Mongolia 0.365; Montenegro 0.300; Morocco 0.409; Mozambique* 0.457; Namibia 0.639; Nepal 0.328; Netherlands 0.309; New Zealand* 0.362; Nicaragua 0.405; Niger 0.346; Nigeria 0.488; Norway 0.258; Pakistan 0.300; Panama 0.519; Papua New Guinea 0.509; Paraguay 0.524; Peru 0.481; Philippines 0.430; Poland 0.341; Portugal 0.385; Qatar 0.411; Romania 0.300; Russia 0.401; Rwanda 0.508; Sao Tome and Principe 0.508; Senegal 0.392; Serbia 0.278; Seychelles 0.658; Sierra Leone 0.425; Singapore 0.473; Slovak Republic 0.260; Slovenia 0.312; South Africa 0.631; South Korea 0.316; South Sudan 0.455; Spain 0.347; Sri Lanka 0.403; Saint Lucia 0.426; Sudan 0.353; Suriname 0.529; Swaziland 0.515; Sweden 0.250; Switzerland 0.337; Syrian Arab Republic 0.358; Tajikistan 0.308; Tanzania 0.376; Thailand 0.400; Timor-Leste 0.319; Togo 0.344; Trinidad and Tobago 0.403; Tunisia 0.414; Turkey 0.390; Turkmenistan 0.408; Uganda 0.443; Ukraine 0.264; United Kingdom 0.360; United States 0.408; Uruguay 0.453; Uzbekistan 0.367; Venezuela* 0.448; Vietnam 0.356; West Bank and Gaza 0.355; Yemen, Republic 0.377; Zambia 0.546; Zimbabwe 0.501.

Source: All data are from the World Bank, except starred entries (*), which are from the CIA World Factbook.

APPENDIX 9

Ratio Index of Income Distribution (Richest 10% Average versus Poorest 10% Average)

	Country	R/P 10%	Year
1	Japan	4.5	1993
2	Czech Republic	5.2	1996
3	Bosnia and Herzegovina	5.5	2001
4	Hungary	5.6	2002
5	Finland	5.7	2000
6	Slovenia	5.9	1998
7	Norway	6	2000
8	Taiwan (ROC)	6.1	2002 est.
9	Sweden	6.2	2000
10	Kyrgyzstan	6.4	2003
11	Ethiopia	6.5	2000
12	Pakistan	6.6	2002
13	Slovakia	6.7	1996
14	Austria	6.8	2004
15	Luxembourg	6.8	2000
16	Belarus	6.9	2002
17	Germany	6.9	2000
18	Albania	7.2	2004
19	Croatia	7.2	2003 est.
20	Romania	7.4	2003
21	Bangladesh	7.5	2000 est.
22	Ukraine	7.6	2006
23	Tajikistan	7.8	2003
24	Indonesia	7.9	2002
25	Egypt	8	2000
26	Kazakhstan	8	2004 est.
27	Mongolia	8.2	2002
28	Belgium	8.3	2000

(continued)

	Country	R/P 10%	Year
29	France	8.3	2004
30	Moldova	8.3	2003
31	Laos	8.4	2002
32	India	8.6	2004
33	South Korea	8.6	2005 est.
34	Yemen	8.6	2003
35	Poland	8.7	2002
36	Bulgaria	8.8	2005
37	Switzerland	8.9	2000
38	Netherlands	9.2	1999
39	Portugal	9.2	1995 est.
40	Tanzania	9.3	2000
41	Benin	9.4	2003
42	Ireland	9.4	2000
43	Azerbaijan	9.5	2001
44	Canada	9.5	2000
45	Algeria	9.6	1995
46	Vietnam	10	2004
47	Spain	10.2	2000
48	Lithuania	10.3	2003
49	Greece	10.4	2000 est.
50	Uzbekistan	10.6	2003
51	Estonia	11	2003
52	Malawi	11	2004
53	Jordan	11.3	2003
54	Burkina Faso	11.5	2003
55	Latvia	11.6	2003
56	Myanmar	11.6	1998
57	Italy	11.7	2000
58	Israel	11.8	2005
59	Mauritania	11.8	2000
60	Morocco	11.9	1999
61	Cambodia	12	2004
62	Denmark	12	2000 est.
63	Turkmenistan	12.2	1998
64	Macedonia	12.3	2003
65	Senegal	12.4	2001
66	Thailand	12.4	2002
67	Mali	12.6	2001
68	Australia	12.7	1994
69	Russia	12.8	2002
70	United Kingdom	13.6	1999
71	Ghana	13.7	1999
72	Tunisia	13.7	2000
73	United States	15	2007 est.

	Country	R/P 10%	Year
74	Georgia	15.2	2003
75	Cameroon	15.4	2001
76	Nicaragua	15.4	2001
77	Philippines	15.5	2003
78	Nepal	15.6	2004
79	Uganda	16.4	2002
80	Iran	16.9	1998
81	Côte d'Ivoire	17	2002
82	Jamaica	17	2004
83	Turkey	17.1	2003
84	Singapore	17.3	1998
85	Ecuador	17.5	2006
86	Nigeria	17.5	2003
87	Uruguay	17.9	2003
88	Rwanda	18.2	2000
89	Kenya	18.6	2000
90	Mozambique	18.8	2002
91	Burundi	19.3	1998
92	Madagascar	19.3	2001
93	The Gambia	20.6	1998
94	Guinea	21.6	2006
95	China (PRC)	21.8	2004
96	Papua New Guinea	23.8	1996
97	Mexico	24.6	2004
98	Swaziland	25.4	2001
99	Armenia	25.8	2004
100	Guyana	26	1999
101	Malaysia	28	2003 est.
102	Dominican Republic	29.4	2005
103	Peru	31.5	2003
104	South Africa	31.9	2000
105	Chile	32.1	2003
106	Argentina	35	2007
107	Honduras	35.2	2003
108	Sri Lanka	36.1	2003/04
109	Brazil	37.1	2007
110	Costa Rica	37.4	2003
111	Niger	44.3	1995
112	Guatemala	48.2	2002
113	Lesotho	48.2	2002 est.
114	Venezuela	50.3	2003
115	El Salvador	55.4	2002
116	Colombia	56.3	2008
117	Panama	61.4	2003
118	Paraguay	65.9	2003

(continued)

	Country	R/P 10%	Year
119	Central African Republic	68.1	1993
120	Haiti	68.1	2001
121	Guinea-Bissau	84.8	1991
122	Sierra Leone	87.2	1989
123	Namibia	129	2003
124	Bolivia	157	2002
	World	**12**	**2002 est.**

Countries in Alphabetical Order

Albania 7.2; Algeria 9.6; Argentina 35; Armenia 25.8; Australia 12.7; Austria 6.8; Azerbaijan 9.5; Bangladesh 7.5; Belarus 6.9; Belgium 8.3; Benin 9.4; Bolivia 157.3; Bosnia and Herzegovina 5.5; Brazil 37.1; Bulgaria 8.8; Burkina Faso 11.5; Burundi 19.3; Cambodia 12; Cameroon 15.4; Canada 9.5; Central African Republic 68.1; Chile 32.1; China (PRC) 21.8; Colombia 56.3; Costa Rica 37.4; Côte d'Ivoire 17; Croatia 7.2; Czech Republic 5.2; Denmark 12; Dominican Republic 29.4; Ecuador 17.5; Egypt 8; El Salvador 55.4; Estonia 11; Ethiopia 6.5; Finland 5.7; France 8.3; The Gambia 20.6; Georgia 15.2; Germany 6.9; Ghana 13.7; Greece 10.4; Guatemala 48.2; Guine 21.6; Guinea-Bissau 84.8; Guyana 26; Haiti 68.1; Honduras 35.2; Hungary 5.6; India 8.6; Indonesia 7.9; Iran 16.9; Ireland 9.4; Israel 11.8; Italy 11.7; Jamaica 17; Japan 4.5; Jordan 11.3; Kazakhstan 8; Kenya 18.6; South Korea 8.6; Kyrgyzstan 6.4; Laos 8.4; Latvia 11.6; Lesotho 48.2; Lithuania 10.3; Luxembourg 6.8; Macedonia 12.3; Madagascar 19.3; Malawi 11; Malaysia 28; Mali 12.6; Mauritania 11.8; Mexico 24.6; Moldova 8.3; Mongolia 8.2; Morocco 11.9; Mozambique 18.8; Myanmar 11.6; Namibia 129; Nepal 15.6; Netherlands 9.2; Nicaragua 15.4; Niger 44.3; Nigeria 17.5; Norway 6; Pakistan 6.6; Panama 61.4; Papua New Guinea 23.8; Paraguay 65.9; Peru 31.5; Philippines 15.5; Poland 8.7; Portugal 9.2; Romania 7.4; Russia 12.8; Rwanda 18.2; Senegal 12.4; Sierra Leone 87.2; Singapore 17.3; Slovakia 6.7; Slovenia 5.9; South Africa 31.9; Spain 10.2; Sri Lanka 36.1; Swaziland 25.4; Sweden 6.2; Switzerland 8.9; Taiwan (ROC) 6.1; Tajikistan 7.8; Tanzania 9.3; Thailand 12.4; Tunisia 13.7; Turkey 17.1; Turkmenistan 12.2; Uganda 16.4; Ukraine 7.6; United Kingdom 13.6; United States 15; Uruguay 17.9; Uzbekistan 10.6; Venezuela 50.3; Vietnam 10; Yemen 8.6; World 12.

* Data show the ratio of the household income or consumption share of the richest group to that of the poorest. Household income or consumption by percentage share (%), The World Factbook, CIA, updated on January 24, 2008.

Note: To calculate the value given in the table for this appendix, the highest 10% value was divided by the lowest 10% value.

APPENDIX 10

Gender Inequality Index (GII, Human Development Program, 2012 Data)

Rank 2012	Country	Value 2012
1	Netherlands	0.045
2	Sweden	0.055
3	Switzerland	0.057
3	Denmark	0.057
5	Norway	0.065
6	Germany	0.075
6	Finland	0.075
8	Slovenia	0.080
9	France	0.083
10	Iceland	0.089
11	Italy	0.094
12	Belgium	0.098
13	Singapore	0.101
14	Austria	0.102
15	Spain	0.103
16	Portugal	0.114
17	Australia	0.115
18	Canada	0.119
19	Ireland	0.121
20	Czech Republic	0.122
21	Japan	0.131
22	Cyprus	0.134
23	Greece	0.136
24	Poland	0.140
25	Israel	0.144
26	Luxembourg	0.149
27	South Korea	0.153
28	Lithuania	0.157

(continued)

Rank 2012	Country	Value 2012
29	Estonia	0.158
30	Macedonia	0.162
31	New Zealand	0.164
32	Slovakia	0.171
33	Croatia	0.179
34	United Kingdom	0.205
35	China	0.213
36	Latvia	0.216
36	Libya	0.216
38	Bulgaria	0.219
39	Malta	0.236
40	United Arab Emirates	0.241
41	Albania	0.251
42	United States	0.256
42	Hungary	0.256
42	Malaysia	0.256
45	Bahrain	0.258
46	Tunisia	0.261
47	Kuwait	0.274
48	Vietnam	0.299
49	Moldova	0.303
50	Trinidad and Tobago	0.311
51	Russia	0.312
51	Kazakhstan	0.312
53	Bahamas	0.316
54	Azerbaijan	0.323
55	Romania	0.327
56	Mongolia	0.328
57	Ukraine	0.338
57	Tajikistan	0.338
59	Oman	0.340
59	Armenia	0.340
61	Barbados	0.343
62	Costa Rica	0.346
63	Cuba	0.356
64	Maldives	0.357
64	Kyrgyzstan	0.357
66	Chile	0.360
66	Thailand	0.360
68	Turkey	0.366
69	Uruguay	0.367
70	Mauritius	0.377
71	Argentina	0.380
72	Mexico	0.382
73	Peru	0.387

Rank 2012	Country	Value 2012
74	Algeria	0.391
75	Sri Lanka	0.402
76	Rwanda	0.414
77	Philippines	0.418
78	Lebanon	0.433
79	Belize	0.435
80	Myanmar	0.437
81	Georgia	0.438
82	El Salvador	0.441
83	Ecuador	0.442
84	Morocco	0.444
85	Brazil	0.447
86	Namibia	0.455
87	Jamaica	0.458
88	Colombia	0.459
89	Nicaragua	0.461
90	Tonga	0.462
90	South Africa	0.462
92	Bhutan	0.464
93	Venezuela	0.466
94	Suriname	0.467
95	Paraguay	0.472
96	Cambodia	0.473
97	Bolivia	0.474
98	Burundi	0.476
99	Jordan	0.482
100	Honduras	0.483
100	Laos	0.483
102	Botswana	0.485
102	Nepal	0.485
104	Guyana	0.490
105	Gabon	0.492
106	Indonesia	0.494
107	Iran	0.496
108	Panama	0.503
109	Dominican Republic	0.508
110	Uganda	0.517
111	Bangladesh	0.518
112	Swaziland	0.525
113	Lesotho	0.534
114	Guatemala	0.539
115	Senegal	0.540
116	Zimbabwe	0.544
117	Qatar	0.546
118	Syria	0.551

(continued)

Rank 2012	Country	Value 2012
119	Tanzania	0.556
120	Iraq	0.557
121	Ghana	0.565
122	Togo	0.566
123	Pakistan	0.567
124	Malawi	0.573
125	Mozambique	0.582
126	Egypt	0.590
127	Haiti	0.592
128	Gambia	0.594
129	Sudan	0.604
130	Kenya	0.608
131	Burkina Faso	0.609
132	India	0.610
132	Congo	0.610
134	Papua New Guinea	0.617
135	Benin	0.618
136	Zambia	0.623
137	Cameroon	0.628
138	Côte d'Ivoire	0.632
139	Mauritania	0.643
139	Sierra Leone	0.643
141	Mali	0.649
142	Central African Republic	0.654
143	Liberia	0.658
144	Congo (Democratic Republic)	0.681
145	Saudi Arabia	0.682
146	Niger	0.707
147	Afghanistan	0.712
148	Yemen	0.747

Source: UNDP, HDR: https://data.undp.org/dataset/
Table-4-Gender-Inequality-Index/pq34-nwq7.

Countries in Alphabetical Order

Afghanistan 0.712; Albania 0.251; Algeria 0.391; Argentina 0.380; Armenia 0.340; Australia 0.115; Austria 0.102; Azerbaijan 0.323; Bahamas 0.316; Bahrain 0.258; Bangladesh 0.518; Barbados 0.343; Belgium 0.098; Belize 0.435; Benin 0.618; Bhutan 0.464; Bolivia 0.474; Botswana 0.485; Brazil 0.447; Bulgaria0.219; Burkina Faso 0.609; Burundi 0.476; Cambodia 0.473; Cameroon 0.628; Canada 0.119; Central African Republic 0.654; Chile 0.360; China 0.213; Colombia 0.459; Congo 0.610; Congo (Democratic Republic) 0.681; Costa Rica 0.346; Côte d'Ivoire 0.632; Croatia 0.179; Cuba 0.356; Cyprus 0.134; Czech Republic 0.122; Denmark 0.057; Dominican Republic 0.508; Ecuador 0.442; Egypt 0.590; El Salvador 0.441; Estonia 0.158; Finland 0.075; France 0.083; Gabon 0.492; Gambia 0.594; Georgia 0.438; Germany 0.075; Ghana 0.565; Greece 0.136; Guatemala 0.539; Guyana 0.490; Haiti 0.592; Honduras 0.483; Hungary 0.256; Iceland 0.089; India 0.610; Indonesia 0.494; Iran 0.496; Iraq 0.557; Ireland 0.121; Israel 0.144; Italy 0.094; Jamaica 0.458; Japan 0.131; Jordan 0.482; Kazakhstan 0.312; Kenya 0.608; Kuwait 0.274; Kyrgyzstan 0.357; Laos 0.483; Latvia 0.216; Lebanon 0.433; Lesotho 0.534; Liberia 0.658; Libya 0.216; Lithuania 0.157; Luxembourg 0.149; Macedonia 0.162; Malawi 0.573; Malaysia 0.256; Maldives 0.357; Mali 0.649; Malta 0.236; Mauritania 0.643; Mauritius 0.377; Mexico 0.382; Moldova 0.303; Mongolia 0.328; Morocco 0.444; Mozambique 0.582; Myanmar 0.437; Namibia 0.455; Nepal 0.485; Netherlands 0.045; New Zealand 0.164; Nicaragua 0.461; Niger 0.707; Norway 0.065; Oman 0.340; Pakistan 0.567; Panama 0.503; Papua New Guinea 0.617; Paraguay 0.472; Peru 0.387; Philippines 0.418; Poland 0.140; Portugal 0.114; Qatar 0.546; Romania 0.327; Russia 0.312; Rwanda 0.414; Saudi Arabia 0.682; Senegal 0.540; Sierra Leone 0.643; Singapore 0.101; Slovakia 0.171; Slovenia 0.080; South Africa 0.462; South Korea 0.153; Spain 0.103; Sri Lanka 0.402; Sudan 0.604; Suriname 0.467; Swaziland 0.525; Sweden 0.055; Switzerland 0.057; Syria 0.551; Tajikistan 0.338; Tanzania 0.556; Thailand 0.360; Togo 0.566; Tonga 0.462; Trinidad and Tobago 0.311; Tunisia 0.261; Turkey 0.366; United Arab Emirates 0.241; Uganda 0.517; Ukraine 0.338; United Kingdom 0.205; United States 0.256; Uruguay 0.367; Venezuela 0.466; Vietnam 0.299; Yemen 0.747; Zambia 0.623; Zimbabwe 0.544

APPENDIX 11

Objective Development Index (ODI)

Rank ODI	Country	Score ODI*	Rank HDI	HDI* 2012	Rank GII	GII*/** 2012	Rank FH	FH 2012	Rank Gini	Gini */**
1	Norway	1.000	1	1.000	5	0.971	4	1.000	3	0.976
2	Sweden	0.992	7	0.940	2	0.986	6	1.000	2	0.995
3	Denmark	0.980	15	0.917	3	0.983	10	0.980	1	1.000
4	Finland	0.958	21	0.904	6	0.956	1	1.000	6	0.949
5	Netherlands	0.952	4	0.947	1	1.000	8	0.990	27	0.851
6	Iceland	0.950	13	0.925	10	0.936	2	1.000	11	0.922
7	Germany	0.948	5	0.946	6	0.956	24	0.960	13	0.915
8	Austria	0.919	18	0.908	14	0.919	21	0.960	16	0.893
9	Switzerland	0.913	9	0.935	3	0.982	26	0.960	44	0.783
10	Canada	0.899	11	0.932	18	0.895	9	0.980	34	0.810
11	France	0.897	20	0.905	9	0.946	30	0.950	35	0.807
12	Slovenia	0.896	21	0.902	8	0.949	43	0.910	30	0.844
13	Belgium	0.896	17	0.910	12	0.924	13	0.970	37	0.800
14	Australia	0.891	2	0.974	17	0.900	12	0.970	53	0.746
15	San Marino	0.889	22	0.887	19	0.881	5	1.000	39	0.814
16	Luxembourg	0.889	26	0.877	26	0.851	3	1.000	23	0.854
17	Ireland	0.885	7	0.940	19	0.892	14	0.970	48	0.768
18	Liechtenstein	0.884	24	0.889	19	0.881	11	0.980	39	0.814
19	Czech Republic	0.883	28	0.873	20	0.890	27	0.950	28	0.849
20	Cyprus	0.875	31	0.835	22	0.872	32	0.930	14	0.898
21	Slovakia	0.874	35	0.824	32	0.820	39	0.920	4	0.971
22	Spain	0.872	23	0.892	15	0.917	25	0.960	52	0.759
23	Andorra	0.860	33	0.833	19	0.881	20	0.960	39	0.814
24	Malta	0.854	32	0.834	39	0.728	15	0.970	8	0.937
25	South Korea	0.854	12	0.928	27	0.845	58	0.860	31	0.834
26	New Zealand	0.854	6	0.944	31	0.830	16	0.970	66	0.722

27	Monaco	0.849	22	0.887	19	0.881	55	0.870	39	0.814
28	Italy	0.840	25	0.885	11	0.930	52	0.880	62	0.727
29	Japan	0.827	10	0.933	21	0.876	53	0.880	72	0.688
30	Poland	0.822	39	0.795	24	0.865	35	0.930	46	0.773
31	Estonia	0.818	33	0.832	29	0.839	29	0.950	61	0.727
32	United Kingdom	0.817	26	0.877	34	0.772	18	0.970	63	0.727
33	Portugal	0.810	43	0.787	16	0.901	17	0.970	80	0.666
34	Greece	0.809	29	0.853	23	0.870	61	0.830	47	0.768
35	Israel	0.783	16	0.916	25	0.858	66	0.810	86	0.649
36	Hungary	0.782	37	0.809	42	0.699	51	0.880	29	0.844
37	Croatia	0.779	47	0.769	33	0.809	56	0.860	43	0.783
38	Lithuania	0.778	41	0.789	28	0.840	46	0.900	73	0.688
39	Montenegro	0.777	52	0.748	22	0.872	86	0.720	18	0.873
40	Bulgaria	0.776	57	0.734	38	0.752	65	0.810	12	0.917
41	United States	0.776	3	0.972	42	0.699	37	0.930	98	0.610
42	Serbia	0.764	64	0.714	38	0.752	75	0.780	9	0.927
43	Latvia	0.739	44	0.783	36	0.756	60	0.840	68	0.712
44	Hong Kong	0.728	13	0.925	13	0.920	91	0.663	111	0.546
45	Romania	0.718	56	0.740	55	0.598	67	0.810	20	0.873
46	Singapore	0.650	18	0.907	13	0.920	121	0.520	125	0.451
47	Barbados	0.649	38	0.800	61	0.575	7	0.990	126	0.430
48	Ukraine	0.646	78	0.670	57	0.582	114	0.570	5	0.961
49	Albania	0.645	70	0.683	41	0.706	98	0.630	50	0.763
50	Uruguay	0.639	51	0.749	69	0.541	19	0.970	118	0.500
51	Bahamas	0.637	49	0.752	53	0.614	22	0.960	126	0.430
52	Trinidad and Tobago	0.637	67	0.701	50	0.621	71	0.810	94	0.622
53	Mauritius	0.634	80	0.665	70	0.527	47	0.900	84	0.654

(continued)

Rank ODI	Country	Score ODI*	Rank HDI	HDI* 2012	Rank GII	GII*/** 2012	Rank FH	FH 2012	Rank Gini	Gini*/**
54	Mongolia	0.633	108	0.570	56	0.596	57	0.860	67	0.715
55	Macedonia	0.618	78	0.669	30	0.833	97	0.640	110	0.551
56	Chile	0.601	40	0.791	66	0.551	23	0.960	142	0.334
57	Moldova	0.599	113	0.547	49	0.632	95	0.650	39	0.800
58	Taiwan	0.599	103	0.544	69	0.555	54	0.880	80	0.651
59	Libya	0.599	64	0.714	36	0.755	132	0.430	12	0.730
60	Argentina	0.596	45	0.779	71	0.522	73	0.800	115	0.520
61	Saint Lucia	0.589	88	0.646	83	0.455	36	0.930	106	0.566
62	Belarus	0.585	50	0.751	38	0.752	184	0.140	7	0.941
63	Costa Rica	0.581	62	0.719	62	0.571	40	0.910	136	0.368
64	Kuwait	0.576	54	0.747	47	0.673	138	0.410	58	0.726
65	Dominica	0.563	72	0.676	83	0.455	28	0.950	126	0.430
66	Armenia	0.560	87	0.652	59	0.580	136	0.420	25	0.851
67	Tunisia	0.557	94	0.626	46	0.692	112	0.580	102	0.595
68	Grenada	0.557	63	0.716	83	0.455	48	0.890	126	0.430
69	Saint Kitts and Nevis	0.551	72	0.678	83	0.455	44	0.910	126	0.430
70	Kazakhstan	0.550	69	0.691	51	0.620	162	0.260	15	0.898
71	Bosnia and Herzegovina	0.549	81	0.662	83	0.462	101	0.620	64	0.722
72	Turkey	0.543	90	0.642	68	0.542	105	0.610	85	0.654
73	Saint Vincent and the Grenadines	0.539	83	0.659	83	0.455	49	0.890	126	0.430
74	Timor-Leste	0.538	134	0.418	69	0.555	99	0.630	32	0.827
75	United Arab Emirates	0.537	41	0.789	40	0.721	179	0.190	58	0.726
76	Palau	0.532	52	0.747	90	0.406	38	0.920	132	0.338
77	Antigua and Barbuda	0.524	67	0.700	83	0.455	72	0.800	126	0.430
78	Bahrain	0.522	48	0.755	45	0.696	177	0.200	58	0.726
79	Malaysia	0.520	64	0.714	42	0.699	125	0.480	122	0.478

80	Lebanon	0.510	72	0.677	78	0.447	124	0.490	58	0.726
81	Peru	0.506	77	0.671	73	0.512	88	0.710	129	0.432
82	Mexico	0.505	61	0.723	72	0.520	94	0.650	131	0.427
83	Brunei	0.503	30	0.846	42	0.699	156	0.290	122	0.478
84	Georgia	0.503	72	0.676	81	0.439	107	0.600	101	0.598
85	Thailand	0.499	103	0.592	66	0.551	120	0.530	91	0.629
86	Maldives	0.498	104	0.590	64	0.555	128	0.460	71	0.693
87	Jamaica	0.496	85	0.655	87	0.412	83	0.730	119	0.495
88	Indonesia	0.494	121	0.498	106	0.360	93	0.650	45	0.776
89	Azerbaijan	0.492	82	0.660	54	0.604	171	0.230	42	0.783
90	Russia	0.483	55	0.743	51	0.620	163	0.260	92	0.627
91	Belize	0.482	96	0.611	79	0.444	50	0.880	146	0.310
92	Tuvalu	0.481	106	0.557	90	0.406	31	0.940	132	0.338
93	Panama	0.480	59	0.732	108	0.347	63	0.820	141	0.339
94	Nauru	0.478	106	0.557	90	0.406	34	0.930	132	0.338
95	Algeria	0.477	93	0.628	74	0.507	145	0.350	54	0.744
96	Marshall Islands	0.472	106	0.557	90	0.406	42	0.910	132	0.338
97	El Salvador	0.471	107	0.578	82	0.436	76	0.770	130	0.427
98	Philippines	0.466	114	0.538	77	0.468	100	0.630	109	0.556
99	Oman	0.465	84	0.656	59	0.579	174	0.230	58	0.726
100	Kyrgyzstan	0.461	125	0.489	64	0.556	139	0.410	65	0.722
101	Sri Lanka	0.460	92	0.631	75	0.490	134	0.430	93	0.622
102	Samoa	0.458	96	0.612	90	0.406	68	0.810	132	0.338
103	Tajikistan	0.457	125	0.488	57	0.583	170	0.240	24	0.854
104	Brazil	0.456	85	0.654	85	0.427	64	0.810	148	0.271
105	Dominican Republic	0.454	96	0.611	109	0.340	80	0.750	123	0.454
106	Kiribati	0.454	121	0.499	90	0.406	41	0.910	132	0.338

(continued)

Rank ODI	Country	Score ODI*	Rank HDI	HDI* 2012	Rank GII	GII*/** 2012	Rank FH	FH 2012	Rank Gini	Gini */**
107	India	0.447	136	0.384	132	0.195	78	0.760	41	0.790
108	Occupied Palestinian Territory	0.440	110	0.561	83	0.462	162	0.346	58	0.739
109	Guyana	0.439	118	0.509	104	0.366	87	0.710	116	0.520
110	Tonga	0.437	95	0.624	90	0.406	84	0.730	132	0.338
111	Ecuador	0.432	89	0.645	83	0.434	106	0.600	133	0.402
112	Kosovo	0.430	112	0.550	126	0.223	131	0.430	6	0.870
113	Suriname	0.427	105	0.583	94	0.399	77	0.770	145	0.315
114	Jordan	0.427	100	0.609	99	0.377	151	0.340	57	0.739
115	Ghana	0.423	135	0.391	121	0.259	59	0.840	108	0.561
116	Vietnam	0.421	127	0.481	48	0.638	180	0.190	59	0.737
117	Bangladesh	0.417	146	0.325	111	0.325	115	0.560	33	0.822
118	Vanuatu	0.416	124	0.495	90	0.406	74	0.790	132	0.338
119	Egypt	0.409	112	0.550	126	0.223	143	0.380	22	0.854
120	Nicaragua	0.403	129	0.453	89	0.407	123	0.510	96	0.617
121	Venezuela	0.402	71	0.682	93	0.399	142	0.390	117	0.512
122	China	0.402	101	0.607	35	0.761	181	0.180	128	0.434
123	Micronesia	0.399	117	0.523	90	0.406	33	0.930	157	0.115
124	Seychelles	0.397	46	0.770	70	0.527	91	0.670	161	0.000
125	Cape Verde	0.397	132	0.433	121	0.259	45	0.900	135	0.373
126	Qatar	0.392	36	0.813	117	0.286	166	0.250	100	0.602
127	Senegal	0.391	154	0.255	115	0.294	81	0.750	87	0.649
128	Fiji	0.391	96	0.611	90	0.406	144	0.370	107	0.561
129	Morocco	0.380	130	0.441	84	0.431	133	0.430	99	0.607
130	Bhutan	0.379	140	0.359	92	0.403	126	0.470	77	0.677
131	Turkmenistan	0.378	102	0.604	51	0.620	191	0.070	97	0.610
132	Colombia	0.377	91	0.638	88	0.410	104	0.610	149	0.241

133	Paraguay	0.376	111	0.560	95	0.391	102	0.620	143	0.327
134	Nepal	0.374	157	0.244	102	0.372	127	0.470	36	0.805
135	Tanzania	0.372	152	0.264	119	0.272	92	0.660	74	0.688
136	Bolivia	0.370	108	0.569	97	0.388	90	0.690	151	0.232
137	Gabon	0.370	106	0.582	105	0.364	150	0.340	104	0.593
138	Pakistan	0.368	146	0.324	123	0.255	137	0.420	19	0.873
139	Benin	0.368	166	0.203	135	0.184	62	0.820	81	0.663
140	Iran	0.365	76	0.672	107	0.358	183	0.160	79	0.671
141	Uzbekistan	0.359	114	0.538	64	0.556	192	0.040	70	0.710
142	Cuba	0.355	59	0.730	63	0.557	185	0.110	126	0.430
143	Iraq	0.349	131	0.438	120	0.271	164	0.250	26	0.851
144	South Africa	0.341	121	0.500	90	0.406	70	0.810	158	0.066
145	North Korea	0.340	103	0.544	69	0.555	194	0.030	80	0.651
146	Solomon Islands	0.328	143	0.347	90	0.406	96	0.650	132	0.338
147	Botswana	0.327	119	0.507	102	0.372	82	0.740	156	0.117
148	Cambodia	0.324	138	0.366	96	0.390	158	0.290	76	0.680
149	São Tome and Principe	0.319	144	0.339	132	0.195	69	0.810	137	0.366
150	Togo	0.313	159	0.238	122	0.257	135	0.430	49	0.766
151	Namibia	0.313	128	0.467	86	0.416	79	0.760	159	0.046
152	Myanmar	0.310	149	0.298	80	0.441	157	0.290	80	0.651
153	Malawi	0.309	170	0.175	124	0.248	109	0.600	83	0.654
154	Saudi Arabia	0.295	57	0.735	145	0.093	189	0.080	58	0.726
155	Syria	0.288	116	0.528	118	0.279	190	0.070	60	0.732
156	Honduras	0.286	120	0.503	100	0.376	122	0.510	153	0.215
157	Burundi	0.284	178	0.078	98	0.386	148	0.340	40	0.793
158	Lesotho	0.282	158	0.241	113	0.304	85	0.720	144	0.324
159	Laos	0.274	138	0.368	100	0.375	186	0.110	69	0.710

(continued)

Rank ODI	Country	Score ODI*	Rank HDI	HDI* 2012	Rank GII	GII*/** 2012	Rank FH	FH 2012	Rank Gini	Gini */**
160	Guatemala	0.265	133	0.426	114	0.296	113	0.570	150	0.241
161	Liberia	0.264	174	0.129	143	0.127	108	0.600	78	0.673
162	Kenya	0.261	145	0.330	130	0.198	118	0.550	127	0.441
163	Sierra Leone	0.255	177	0.084	139	0.148	89	0.700	105	0.568
164	Uganda	0.250	161	0.233	110	0.328	140	0.400	113	0.524
165	Ethiopia	0.237	173	0.141	123	0.243	182	0.180	17	0.878
166	Burkina Faso	0.231	183	0.060	131	0.196	119	0.530	89	0.634
167	Madagascar	0.221	151	0.275	125	0.234	147	0.350	112	0.529
168	Papua New Guinea	0.220	156	0.248	134	0.185	111	0.590	139	0.363
169	Djibouti	0.218	164	0.216	123	0.243	160	0.290	16	0.630
170	Niger	0.218	186	0.000	146	0.057	116	0.560	51	0.761
171	Mauritania	0.211	155	0.250	139	0.149	152	0.340	95	0.617
172	Mozambique	0.209	185	0.035	125	0.234	110	0.590	121	0.490
173	Cameroon	0.209	150	0.294	137	0.169	172	0.230	82	0.656
174	Afghanistan	0.207	175	0.108	147	0.050	161	0.260	10	0.926
175	Nigeria	0.198	153	0.257	133	0.183	129	0.460	132	0.415
176	Guinea-Bissau	0.198	176	0.091	133	0.183	155	0.300	56	0.739
177	Côte d'Ivoire	0.192	168	0.196	138	0.164	149	0.340	103	0.593
178	Zambia	0.191	163	0.221	136	0.177	103	0.620	147	0.273

179	Republic of Congo	0.191	142	0.353	132	0.195	159	0.290	124	0.451
180	Rwanda	0.188	167	0.199	76	0.474	169	0.240	138	0.365
181	Somalia	0.186	173	0.141	123	0.243	195	0.020	6	0.870
182	Guinea	0.182	178	0.078	139	0.148	141	0.390	88	0.644
183	Mali	0.179	182	0.062	141	0.140	165	0.250	38	0.800
184	Swaziland	0.173	141	0.356	112	0.316	176	0.210	140	0.349
185	Sudan	0.171	171	0.168	129	0.204	187	0.110	55	0.744
186	Eritrea	0.170	181	0.071	123	0.243	193	0.030	17	0.878
187	South Sudan	0.157	171	0.168	129	0.204	153	0.310	120	0.495
188	Yemen	0.155	160	0.237	148	0.000	167	0.250	75	0.685
189	Gambia	0.133	165	0.207	128	0.218	173	0.230	126	0.446
190	Zimbabwe	0.123	172	0.143	116	0.290	168	0.250	134	0.383
191	Haiti	0.117	161	0.233	127	0.221	130	0.430	155	0.161
192	Chad	0.112	184	0.054	142	0.132	175	0.210	90	0.634
193	Comoros	0.111	169	0.192	124	0.248	117	0.550	160	0.037
194	Angola	0.090	148	0.314	137	0.169	154	0.300	154	0.176
195	Democratic Republic of Congo	0.047	186	0.000	144	0.094	178	0.200	114	0.522
196	Central African Republic	0.038	180	0.073	142	0.132	146	0.350	152	0.232
197	Equatorial Guinea	0.000	136	0.384	131	0.179	188	0.080	37	0.020

* Standardized/** Inverted

Countries in Alphabetical Order

Afghanistan 0.207; Albania 0.645; Algeria 0.477; Andorra 0.860; Angola 0.090; Antigua and Barbuda 0.524; Argentina 0.596; Armenia 0.560; Australia 0.891; Austria 0.919; Azerbaijan 0.492; Bahamas 0.637; Bahrain 0.522; Bangladesh 0.417; Barbados 0.649; Belarus 0.585; Belgium 0.896; Belize 0.482; Benin 0.368; Bhutan 0.379; Bolivia 0.370; Bosnia and Herzegovina 0.549; Botswana 0.327; Brazil 0.456; Brunei 0.503; Bulgaria 0.776; Burkina Faso 0.231; Burundi 0.284; Cambodia 0.324; Cameroon 0.209; Canada 0.899; Cape Verde 0.397; Central African Republic 0.038; Chad 0.112; Chile 0.601; China 0.402; Colombia 0.377; Comoros 0.111; Costa Rica 0.581; Côte d'Ivoire 0.192; Croatia 0.779; Cuba 0.355; Cyprus 0.875; Czech Republic 0.883; Democratic Republic of Congo 0.047; Denmark 0.980; Djibouti 0.218; Dominica 0.563; Dominican Republic 0.454; Ecuador 0.432; Egypt 0.409; El Salvador 0.471; Equatorial Guinea 0.000; Eritrea 0.170; Estonia 0.818; Ethiopia 0.237; Fiji 0.391; Finland 0.958; France 0.897; Gabon 0.370; Gambia 0.133; Georgia 0.503; Germany 0.948; Ghana 0.423; Greece 0.809; Grenada 0.557; Guatemala 0.265; Guinea 0.182; Guinea-Bissau 0.198; Guyana 0.439; Haiti 0.117; Honduras 0.286; Hong Kong 0.728; Hungary 0.782; Iceland 0.950; India 0.447; Indonesia 0.494; Iran 0.365; Iraq 0.349; Ireland 0.885; Israel 0.783; Italy 0.840; Jamaica 0.496; Japan 0.827; Jordan 0.427; Kazakhstan 0.550; Kenya 0.261; Kiribati 0.454; Kosovo 0.430; Kuwait 0.576; Kyrgyzstan 0.461; Laos 0.274; Latvia 0.739; Lebanon 0.510; Lesotho 0.282; Liberia 0.264; Libya 0.599; Liechtenstein 0.884; Lithuania 0.778; Luxembourg 0.889; Macedonia 0.618; Madagascar 0.221; Malawi 0.309; Malaysia 0.520; Maldives 0.498; Mali 0.179; Malta 0.854; Marshall Islands 0.472; Mauritania 0.211; Mauritius 0.634; Mexico 0.505; Micronesia 0.399; Moldova 0.599; Monaco 0.849; Mongolia 0.633; Montenegro 0.777; Morocco 0.380; Mozambique 0.209; Myanmar 0.310; Namibia 0.313; Nauru 0.478; Nepal 0.374; Netherlands 0.952; New Zealand 0.854; Nicaragua 0.403; Niger 0.218; Nigeria 0.198; North Korea 0.340; Norway 1.000; Occupied Palestinian Territory 0.440; Oman 0.465; Pakistan 0.368; Palau 0.532; Panama 0.480; Papua New Guinea 0.220; Paraguay 0.376; Peru 0.506; Philippines 0.466; Poland 0.822; Portugal 0.810; Qatar 0.392; Republic of Congo 0.191; Romania 0.718; Russia 0.483; Rwanda 0.188; Saint Kitts and Nevis 0.551; Saint Lucia 0.589; Saint Vincent and the Grenadines 0.539; Samoa 0.458; San Marino 0.889; São Tome and Principe 0.319; Saudi Arabia 0.295; Senegal 0.391; Serbia 0.764; Seychelles 0.397; Sierra Leone 0.255; Singapore 0.650; Slovakia 0.874; Slovenia 0.896; Solomon Islands 0.328; Somalia 0.186; South Africa 0.341; South Korea 0.854; South Sudan 0.157; Spain 0.872; Sri Lanka 0.460; Sudan 0.171; Suriname 0.427; Swaziland 0.173; Sweden 0.992; Switzerland 0.913; Syria 0.288; Taiwan 0.599; Tajikistan 0.457; Tanzania 0.372; Thailand 0.499; Timor-Leste 0.538; Togo 0.313; Tonga 0.437; Trinidad and Tobago 0.637; Tunisia 0.557; Turkey 0.543; Turkmenistan 0.378; Tuvalu 0.481; Uganda 0.250; Ukraine 0.646; United Arab Emirates 0.537; United Kingdom 0.817; United States 0.776; Uruguay 0.639; Uzbekistan 0.359; Vanuatu 0.416; Venezuela 0.402; Vietnam 0.421; Yemen 0.155; Zambia 0.191; Zimbabwe 0.123

Methodology

In order to expand the calculations for the Objective Development Index (ODI) to include all the countries in the data set, we used regional values and the values of the regional countries most similar to the missing country value. We used this technique, though imperfect, as expanding the index provides valuable insight into a country's welfare and development position in the world. Furthermore, it allows us to explore how a country's global position changes in a multidimensional index as compared to a singular measures such as GDP per capita, or the Human Development Index.

The ODI is a composite score based on a country's HDI, GII, Freedom House's measurement on civil and political rights, and Gini index. As this information is not available for all countries, we chose to input missing values based on the following process:

- If possible, we used the missing GII/HDI/FH/Gini value of the *most similar country* to the missing country in the country's given region: Africa (Central, East, Horn, North, and West), Asia, Middle East and North Africa, Oceania, Orthodox, Western, Caribbean, Latin America, and Central-South Asia.Ø Similarity was measured by the country that scored most similarly to a country on five different factors: population, GDP/capita, Gini index, literacy, and HDI. These categories were chosen as they are important elements and outcomes of a country's development, and of which two measures are part of the ODI calculation. For example, Angola was assigned the GII of Cameroon, as Cameroon was the Central African country most similar to Angola on three dimensions; population size, literacy levels, and HDI.
- However, if there was not one singular country that stood out as most similar in the region, we used the regional average for the missing country value. If there were five different countries that were most similar to the country with the missing value along the five dimensions, the regional average was used. For example, Nigeria was most similar to Ghana (population), Mauritania (GDPpc), Gambia (Gini), Liberia (literacy) and Senegal (HDI), so the regional GII average for West Africa was used.
- In addition, if there were not sufficient regional data available (average or country), the average of neighbors was used, or an average of the limited existing data (too limited to be conceptualized as the regional average). For example, there were no GII values for the countries in the Horn of Africa, so the average of neighboring "triad" was used instead: Kenya, Sudan, and Uganda.

In order to fill in the data for all missing country values, for some countries we had to input data for either one or two categories. Most commonly, the GII and Gini index were missing.

See the following tables to explore which values were used for what countries.

- Oceania: For GII all countries have the value of Tonga. For Gini all countries have the average of Fiji and Micronesia.

Country	Region	Population	GDP/Capita	Gini	Literacy	HDI	INPUT
Hong Kong	Asia	Singapore	Singapore	Philippines	Thailand/China	South Korea	Singapore
Myanmar	Asia	South Korea	N/A	N/A	Vietnam/Indonesia/Malaysia	Cambodia	RA*
North Korea	Asia	Sri Lanka	N/A	N/A	Japan	N/A	RA*
Taiwan	Asia	N/A	N/A	N/A	N/A	N/A	RA*
Timor-Leste	Asia	N/A	N/A	N/A	N/A	N/A	RA*

Country	Region	Population	GDP/Capita	Gini	Literacy	HDI	INPUT
Brunei	CSA	Turkmenistan	Malaysia	N/A	Malaysia	N/A	Malaysia
Turkmenistan	CSA	Kyrgyzstan	Kazakhstan	Uzbekistan	Kazakhstan	Uzbekistan	Kazakhstan
Uzbekistan	CSA	Malaysia	Pakistan	Kyrgyzstan	Kyrgyzstan	Tajikistan	Kyrgyzstan

Country	Region	Population	GDP/Capita	Gini	Literacy	HDI	INPUT
Angola	Africa (Central)	Cameroon	Rep. of Congo	CAR	Cameroon	Cameroon	Cameroon
Chad	Africa (Central)	CAR	STP	Cameroon	CAR	DRC	CAR
Equatorial Guinea	Africa (Central)	STP	Gabon	Angola	STP	Rep. of Congo	RA*
São Tome & Principe	Africa (Central)	Eq. Guinea	Cameroon	Rep. of Congo	Gabon	Rep. of Congo	Rep. of Congo
Comoros	Africa (East)	Mauritius	Rwanda	Seychelles	Malawi	Malawi	Malawi
Madagascar	Africa (East)	Mozambique	Mozambique	Uganda	Burundi	Tanzania	Mozambique
Seychelles	Africa (East)	Comoros	Mauritius	Comoros	Mauritius	Mauritius	Mauritius
Djibouti	Africa (Horn)	Eritrea	Ethiopia	Somalia	Eritrea	Ethiopia	Ethiopia/Eritrea
Eritrea	Africa (Horn)	Somalia	Ethiopia	N/A	Djibouti	Ethiopia	Ethiopia
Ethiopia	Africa (Horn)	Somalia	Eritrea	Somalia	Djibouti	Ethiopia	Somalia
Somalia	Africa (Horn)	Eritrea	N/A	Ethiopia	Ethiopia	N/A	Ethiopia
South Sudan	Africa (North)	Sudan	Sudan	Sudan	Sudan	Sudan	Sudan
Cape Verde	Africa (West)	Guinea-Bissau	Mauritania	Nigeria	Ghana	Ghana	Ghana
Guinea	Africa (West)	Benin	Mali	Senegal	Sierra Leone	Sierra Leone	Sierra Leone
Guinea-Bissau	Africa (West)	Gambia	Burkina Faso	Niger	Cote d'Ivoire	Sierra Leone	RA*
Nigeria	Africa (West)	Ghana	Mauritania	Gambia	Liberia	Senegal	RA*

Country	Region	Population	GDP/Capita	Gini	Literacy	HDI	INPUT
Antigua & Barbuda	Caribbean	N/A	N/A	N/A	N/A	N/A	RA*
Bahamas	Caribbean	Belize	Barbados	N/A	Grenada	Cuba	RA*
Barbados	Caribbean	Bahamas	T & T	N/A	Cuba	Bahamas	Bahamas
Cuba	Caribbean	Haiti	DR	N/A	Barbados	Grenada	RA*
Dominica	Caribbean	Bermuda	St. V & G	N/A	Suriname	St. Kitts & Nevis	RA*
Grenada	Caribbean	Aruba	Turks & Caicos	N/A	St. V & G	T & T	RA*
St. Kitts & Nevis	Caribbean	Cayman Islands	Puerto Rico	N/A	Bermuda	Dominica	RA*
St. Lucia	Caribbean	Curacao	Turks & Caicos	Guyana	DR	Jamaica	RA*
St. V & G	Caribbean	Aruba	St. Lucia	N/A	Grenada	N/A	RA*

Country	Region	Population	GDP/Capita	Gini	Literacy	HDI	INPUT
Bahrain	MENA	Kosovo	Saudi Arabia	N/A	Turkey	Kuwait	RA*
Bosnia & Herz.	MENA	N/A	N/A	N/A	N/A	N/A	RA*
Kosovo	MENA	Qatar	Egypt	Egypt	Bahrain	N/A	Egypt
Kuwait	MENA	Oman	UAE	N/A	Jordan	Bahrain	RA*
Lebanon	MENA	Albania	Libya	N/A	UAE	Algeria	RA*
Palestine	MENA	N/A	N/A	N/A	N/A	N/A	RA*
Oman	MENA	Albania	Saudi Arabia	N/A	Saudi Arabia	Azerbaijan	RA*
Saudi Arabia	MENA	Yemen	Bahrain	N/A	Oman	Kuwait	RA*
UAE	MENA	Libya	Kuwait	N/A	Lebanon	Qatar	RA*

Country	Region	Population	GDP/Capita	Gini	Literacy	HDI	INPUT
Belarus	Orthodox	Bulgaria	Bulgaria	Serbia	Ukraine/Georgia/Armenia	Montenegro	Bulgaria
Montenegro	Orthodox	Cyprus	Bulgaria	Romania	Serbia/Bulgaria/Cyprus	Russia	Cyprus
Serbia	Orthodox	Bulgaria	Macedonia	Belarus	Bulgaria/Romania/Cyprus	Bulgaria	Bulgaria

Country	Region	Population	GDP/Capita	Gini	Literacy	HDI	INPUT
Andorra	Western	N/A	N/A	N/A	N/A	N/A	RA*
Lichtenstein	Western	Monaco	N/A	N/A	Luxembourg	N/A	RA*
Monaco	Western	Lichtenstein	N/A	N/A	Switzerland	N/A	RA*
San Marino	Western	Monaco	N/A	N/A	Israel	N/A	RA*

* Data is for 2011.
** Data is for the following years (latest available): Iran 2009, Argentina 2006, Libya 2009, Jamaica 2005, Barbados 2009, Djibouti 2007.

APPENDIX 12

Subjective Development Index (SDI) Methodology

The Subjective Development Index (SDI) derives from Inglehart's *World Cultural Map* (Figure 2.4 in Chapter 2). It combines the map's two axes (survival–self-expression and traditional–secular/rational) into a single line in such a way that a unique value for each country is generated, enabling a world ranking. In other words, it turns the cultural map into an index. The WVS cultural map dynamics from the last 30 years (Figure 2.5 in Chapter 2) show that countries move toward the upper-right corner of the map, at least for most of the countries on the top right side.

Starting from this observation, SDI is the calculation of the distance of each country in the world cultural map to the highest position closer to the upper-right corner of the map. Sweden was the highest score in the survival–self expression axis in the 5th wave (2.35) and Japan was the highest in the traditional–secular/rational axis (1.96). Hence, a hypothetical country score of 2.35 and 1.96 is taken as the highest point of reference.

To measure the distance between an actual country and the maximum hypothetical score, the hypotenuse formula ($a^2 + b^2 = c^2$) from the Pythagorean theorem is used:

> In any right-angled triangle, the area of the square whose side is the hypotenuse c (the side opposite the right angle) is equal to the sum of the areas of the squares whose sides are the two legs a and b (the two sides that meet at a right angle).

The graphic representation is shown in Figure A12.1.

In the *World Cultural Map* the scores for the "two legs" a and b of any country are always known: they are the distances in the axes scores to the hypothetical maximum. But the score c, or *linear combination* of the two axes for the *new* index, is unknown.

In order to find the c score, or *linear combination*, the hypotenuse formula can also be expressed as $c = \sqrt{a^2 + b^2}$ (where $\sqrt{}$ stands for square root).

Applying the formula to find the *linear combination* distance between Sweden, the closest country to the hypothetical maximum, the procedure is as follows: the *a* score is the difference between the hypothetical maximum in the survival–self-expression axis (2.35) and the actual Sweden scores on the same axis (2.35). In this case the distance *a* is 0. The *b* score is the difference between the hypothetical maximum on the traditional–secular/rational axis (1.96) and the actual Sweden score on the same axis (1.86). In this case the distance *b* is 0.10. In summary, $a = 0 + b = 0.10$. Applying the formula: $0^2 + 0.10^2 = 0 + 0.01 = 0.01$. Hence, the square root of $0.01 = 0.10$.

At the other end of the spectrum, Zimbabwe is the most distant country from the hypothetical maximum. The procedure is the same: the *a* score or difference between the hypothetical maximum in the survival–self-expression axis (2.35) and the actual Zimbabwe scores on the same axis (-1.36) is 3.71. The *b* score or difference between the hypothetical maximum on the traditional–secular/rational axis (1.96) and the actual Zimbabwe score on the same axis (-1.50) is 3.46. In summary, $a = 3.71 + b = 3.46$. Applying the formula: $3.71^2 + 3.46^2 = 13.76 + 11.97 = 25.74$. Hence, the square root of $25.74 = 5.07$.

Another expression of the same formula is:

$$\text{Distance (country}_i \text{ highest score)} = \sqrt{((\text{SURVSELF highest score} - \text{SURVSELF country}_i)^2 + (\text{TRADRAT highest score} - \text{TRADRAT country}_i)^2)} \text{ where } i = 1 \dots n.$$

The *index* is the measurement of the distance from each country to the greatest value on both the horizontal axis of the cultural map and on the vertical axis. These distances range from 0.10 (that of Sweden) to 5.07 (that of Zimbabwe). The scores for all the countries are shown in Table A12.1.

The index's benefits lies in its ability to (1) classify countries in a way that allows us to compare their positions in a ranking order; and (2) to perform further statistical analysis by producing a continuum value. In order to make the scale comparable with other international indices, it is inverted and standardized so that the higher the value, the better the ranking in the index. The calculations' results are shown in Table A12.2 and the index in Table A12.3.

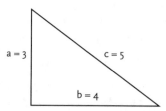

FIGURE A12.1 Pythagorean theorem and the hypotenuse formula

TABLE A12.1

World Cultural Map Scores: Score Values for the *World Values Survey Map*'s Axes

Nation and Wave	Trad Rat Values	Surv Self Values	HD1[1]
Albania 4[2]	0.07	-1.14	3.97
Algeria 4	-1.48	-0.74	4.62
Andorra 5	0.8	1.62	1.37
Argentina 5	-0.66	0.38	3.28
Armenia 3	0.55	-1.31	3.92
Australia 5	0.21	1.75	1.85
Austria 4	0.25	1.43	1.94
Azerbaijan 3	-0.14	-1.38	4.28
Bangladesh 4	-1.21	-0.93	4.56
Belarus 4	0.89	-1.23	3.74
Belgium 4	0.5	1.13	1.90
Bosnia 4	0.34	-0.65	3.41
Brazil 5	-0.98	0.61	3.42
Britain 5	0.06	1.68	2.01
Bulgaria 5	1.13	-1.01	3.46
Burkina Faso 5	-1.32	-0.49	4.34
Canada 5	-0.26	1.91	2.26
Chile 5	-0.87	0	3.68
China 5	0.8	-1.16	3.70
Colombia 5	-1.87	0.6	4.21
Croatia 4	0.08	0.31	2.77
Cyprus 5	-0.56	0.13	3.36
Czech 4	1.23	0.38	2.10
Denmark 4	1.16	1.87	0.93
Dominican Republic 3	-1.05	0.33	3.62
East Germany 5	1.46	0.26	2.15
Egypt 4	-1.61	-0.46	4.54
El Salvador 4	-2.06	0.53	4.41
Estonia 4	1.27	-1.19	3.61
Ethiopia 5	-0.65	-0.36	3.76
Finland 5	0.82	1.12	1.68
France 5	0.63	1.13	1.80
Galicia 3	-0.04	1.34	2.24
Georgia 3	-0.04	-1.31	4.17
Ghana 5	-1.94	-0.29	4.71
Greece 4	0.77	0.55	2.16
Guatemala 4	-1.7	-0.17	4.44
Hong Kong 5	1.2	-0.98	3.42
Hungary 4	0.4	-1.22	3.90
Iceland 4	0.44	1.63	1.68
India 5	-0.36	-0.21	3.45
Indonesia 5	-0.47	-0.8	3.98
Iran 4	-1.22	-0.45	4.24

(continued)

TABLE A12.1

Continued

Nation and Wave	Trad Rat Values	Surv Self Values	HD1[1]
Iraq 5	-0.4	-1.68	4.67
Ireland 4	-0.91	1.18	3.10
Israel 4	0.26	0.36	2.62
Italy 5	0.13	0.6	2.53
Japan 5	1.96	-0.05	2.40
Jordan 4	-1.61	-1.05	4.93
Kyrgyz 4	-0.15	-0.91	3.88
Latvia 4	0.72	-1.27	3.83
Lithuania 4	0.98	-1	3.49
Luxemburg 4	0.42	1.13	1.96
Macedonia 4	0.12	-0.72	3.58
Malaysia 5	-0.73	0.09	3.51
Mali 5	-1.25	-0.08	4.03
Malta 4	-1.53	-0.03	4.22
Mexico 5	-1.47	1.03	3.68
Moldova 5	0.47	-1.28	3.92
Montenegro 4	0.86	-1.24	3.75
Morocco 5	-1.32	-1.04	4.72
Moscow 2	1.44	-0.79	3.18
Northern Ireland 4	-0.33	0.84	2.74
New Zealand 5	0	1.86	2.02
Netherlands 5	0.71	1.39	1.58
Nigeria 4	-1.53	0.28	4.06
Norway 5	1.39	2.17	0.60
Pakistan 4	-1.42	-1.25	4.94
Peru 4	-1.36	0.03	4.05
Philippines 4	-1.21	-0.11	4.01
Poland 5	-0.78	-0.14	3.70
Portugal 4	-0.9	0.49	3.41
Puerto Rico 4	-2.07	1.12	4.21
Romania 5	-0.39	-1.55	4.55
Russia 5	0.49	-1.42	4.05
Rwanda 5	-1.57	-0.62	4.61
South Africa 5	-1.09	-0.1	3.91
South Korea 5	0.61	-1.37	3.96
Saudi Arabia 4	-1.31	0.15	3.94
Serbia 5	0.35	-0.62	3.38
Singapore 4	-0.54	-0.28	3.63
Slovakia 4	0.67	-0.43	3.06
Slovenia 2	0.64	-0.62	3.25
Slovenia 5	0.73	0.36	2.34
Spain 5	0.09	0.54	2.60
Sweden 5	1.86	2.35	0.10

TABLE A12.1

Continued

Nation and Wave	Trad Rat Values	Surv Self Values	HD1[1]
Switzerland 5	0.74	1.9	1.30
Taiwan 5	1.16	-1.18	3.62
Tanzania 4	-1.84	-0.15	4.55
Thailand 5	-0.64	0.01	3.50
Trinidad 5	-1.83	-0.26	4.60
Turkey 5	-0.89	-0.33	3.91
Uganda 1	-1.42	-0.5	4.42
Ukraine 5	0.3	-0.83	3.59
Uruguay 5	-0.37	0.99	2.70
United States 5	-0.81	1.76	2.83
Venezuela 4	-1.6	0.43	4.04
Vietnam 5	-0.3	-0.26	3.45
West Germany 5	1.31	0.74	1.74
Zambia 5	-0.77	-0.62	4.03
Zimbabwe 4	-1.5	-1.36	5.07

[1] Hypothenus distance (HD1) = SQRT(((B$49-B2)^2)+((C$87-C2)^2)).

[2] Survey year: 1 = 1980; 2 = 1990; 3 = 1995; 4 = 2000; 5 = 2005.

TABLE A12.2

Hypotenuse Distance (HD) or Linear Combination Scores

Standardized Values for the World Values Survey Map's Countries

	Nation and Wave**	Trad Rat Values	Surv Self Values	HD*	Standard Score
1	Sweden 5	1.86	2.35	0.10	1.000
2	Norway 5	1.39	2.17	0.60	0.900
3	Denmark 4	1.16	1.87	0.93	0.833
4	Switzerland 5	0.74	1.9	1.30	0.759
5	Andorra 5	0.8	1.62	1.37	0.745
6	Netherlands 5	0.71	1.39	1.58	0.703
7	Finland 5	0.82	1.12	1.68	0.683
8	Iceland 4	0.44	1.63	1.68	0.682
9	West Germany 5	1.31	0.74	1.74	0.671
10	France 5	0.63	1.13	1.80	0.657
11	Australia 5	0.21	1.75	1.85	0.648
12	Belgium 4	0.5	1.13	1.90	0.638
13	Austria 4	0.25	1.43	1.94	0.630
14	Luxemburg 4	0.42	1.13	1.96	0.625
15	Britain 5	0.06	1.68	2.01	0.615
16	New Zealand 5	0	1.86	2.02	0.614
17	Czech 4	1.23	0.38	2.10	0.598
18	East Germany 5	1.46	0.26	2.15	0.588
19	Greece 4	0.77	0.55	2.16	0.586
20	Galicia 3	-0.04	1.34	2.24	0.570
21	Canada 5	-0.26	1.91	2.26	0.565
22	Slovenia 5	0.73	0.36	2.34	0.550
23	Japan 5	1.96	-0.05	2.40	0.538
24	Italy 5	0.13	0.6	2.53	0.511

	Nation and Wave	Trad Rat Values	Surv Self Values	HD*	Standard Score
52	Dominican Republic 3	-1.05	0.33	3.62	0.291
53	Singapore 4	-0.54	-0.28	3.63	0.290
54	Mexico 5	-1.47	1.03	3.68	0.281
55	Chile 5	-0.87	0	3.68	0.280
56	China 5	0.8	-1.16	3.7	0.277
57	Poland 5	-0.78	-0.14	3.7	0.276
58	Belarus 4	0.89	-1.23	3.74	0.269
59	Montenegro 4	0.86	-1.24	3.75	0.265
60	Ethiopia 5	-0.65	-0.36	3.76	0.264
61	Latvia 4	0.72	-1.27	3.83	0.251
62	Kyrgyz 4	-0.15	-0.91	3.88	0.239
63	Hungary 4	0.4	-1.22	3.9	0.237
64	Turkey 5	-0.89	-0.33	3.91	0.233
65	South Africa 5	-1.09	-0.1	3.91	0.233
66	Armenia 3	0.55	-1.31	3.92	0.231
67	Moldova 5	0.47	-1.28	3.92	0.231
68	Saudi Arabia 4	-1.31	0.15	3.94	0.228
69	South Korea 5	0.61	-1.37	3.96	0.224
70	Albania 4	0.07	-1.14	3.97	0.222
71	Indonesia 5	-0.47	-0.8	3.98	0.220
72	Philippines 4	-1.21	-0.11	4.01	0.213
73	Mali 5	-1.25	-0.08	4.03	0.211
74	Zambia 5	-0.77	-0.62	4.03	0.209
75	Venezuela 4	-1.6	0.43	4.04	0.207

#	Country				
25	Spain 5	0.09	0.54	2.60	0.497
26	Israel 4	0.26	0.36	2.62	0.494
27	Uruguay 5	-0.37	0.99	2.70	0.478
28	N. Ireland 4	-0.33	0.84	2.74	0.469
29	Croatia 4	0.08	0.31	2.77	0.462
30	United States 5	-0.81	1.76	2.83	0.451
31	Slovakia 4	0.67	-0.43	3.06	0.404
32	Ireland 4	-0.91	1.18	3.10	0.397
33	Moscow 2	1.44	-0.79	3.18	0.380
34	Slovenia 2	0.64	-0.62	3.25	0.367
35	Argentina 5	-0.66	0.38	3.28	0.361
36	Cyprus 5	-0.56	0.13	3.36	0.345
37	Serbia 5	0.35	-0.62	3.38	0.341
38	Bosnia 4	0.34	-0.65	3.41	0.335
39	Portugal 4	-0.9	0.49	3.41	0.334
40	Hong Kong 5	1.2	-0.98	3.42	0.333
41	Brazil 5	-0.98	0.61	3.42	0.333
42	Vietnam 5	-0.3	-0.26	3.45	0.326
43	India 5	-0.36	-0.21	3.45	0.325
44	Bulgaria 5	1.13	-1.01	3.46	0.324
45	Lithuania 4	0.98	-1	3.49	0.318
46	Thailand 5	-0.64	0.01	3.50	0.317
47	Malaysia 5	-0.73	0.09	3.51	0.314
48	Macedonia 4	0.12	-0.72	3.58	0.300
49	Ukraine 5	0.3	-0.83	3.59	0.299
50	Estonia 4	1.27	-1.19	3.61	0.295
51	Taiwan 5	1.16	-1.18	3.62	0.292

#	Country				
76	Russia 5	0.49	-1.42	4.05	0.206
77	Peru 4	-1.36	0.03	4.05	0.206
78	Nigeria 4	-1.53	0.28	4.06	0.204
79	Georgia 3	-0.04	-1.31	4.17	0.181
80	Colombia 5	-1.87	0.6	4.21	0.173
81	Puerto Rico 4	-2.07	1.12	4.21	0.173
82	Malta 4	-1.53	-0.03	4.22	0.171
83	Iran 4	-1.22	-0.45	4.24	0.168
84	Azerbaijan 3	-0.14	-1.38	4.28	0.159
85	BurkinaFas 5	-1.32	-0.49	4.34	0.148
86	El Salvador 4	-2.06	0.53	4.41	0.133
87	Uganda 1	-1.42	-0.5	4.42	0.131
88	Guatemala 4	-1.7	-0.17	4.44	0.127
89	Egypt 4	-1.61	-0.46	4.54	0.107
90	Tanzania 4	-1.84	-0.15	4.55	0.105
91	Romania 5	-0.39	-1.55	4.55	0.105
92	Bangladesh 4	-1.21	-0.93	4.56	0.103
93	Trinidad 5	-1.83	-0.26	4.6	0.095
94	Rwanda 5	-1.57	-0.62	4.61	0.092
95	Algeria 4	-1.48	-0.74	4.62	0.090
96	Iraq 5	-0.4	-1.68	4.67	0.081
97	Ghana 5	-1.94	-0.29	4.71	0.073
98	Morocco 5	-1.32	-1.04	4.72	0.072
99	Jordan 4	-1.61	-1.05	4.93	0.029
100	Pakistan 4	-1.42	-1.25	4.94	0.027
101	Zimbabwe 4	-1.5	-1.36	5.07	0.000

* Hypothenus distance (HD) = SQRT((B$49-B2)^2)+((C$87-C2)^2)).

** Survey year: 1 = 1980; 2 = 1990; 3 = 1995; 4 = 2000; 5 = 2005.

*** Standarized = (Maximum score on a desired scale from "0" to "x") * (N-minimum)/(max − min).

TABLE A12.3

The *Subjective Development Index* (SDI), Country Scores and Ranking

1	Sweden 5*	1.000
2	Norway 5*	0.900
3	Denmark 4*	0.833
4	Switzerland 5*	0.759
5	Andorra 5*	0.745
6	Netherlands 5*	0.703
7	Finland 5*	0.683
8	Iceland 4*	0.682
9	West Germany 5*	0.671
10	France 5*	0.657
11	Australia 5*	0.648
12	Belgium 4*	0.638
13	Austria 4*	0.630
14	Luxemburg 4*	0.625
15	Britain 5*	0.615
16	New Zealand 5*	0.614
17	Czech 4*	0.598
18	East Germany 5*	0.588
19	Greece 4*	0.586
20	Galicia 3*	0.570
21	Canada 5*	0.565
22	Slovenia 5*	0.550
23	Japan 5*	0.538
24	Italy 5*	0.511
25	Spain 5*	0.497
26	Israel 4*	0.494
27	Uruguay 5*	0.478
28	Northern Ireland 4*	0.469
29	Croatia 4*	0.462
30	United States 5*	0.451
31	Slovakia 4*	0.404
32	Ireland 4*	0.397
33	Moscow 2*	0.380
34	Slovenia 2*	0.367
35	Argentina 5*	0.361
36	Cyprus 5*	0.345
37	Serbia 5*	0.341
38	Bosnia 4*	0.335
39	Portugal 4*	0.334
40	Hong Kong 5*	0.333
41	Brazil 5*	0.333
42	Vietnam 5*	0.326
43	India 5*	0.325
44	Bulgaria 5*	0.324

ABLE A12.3
Continued

45	Lithuania 4*	0.318
46	Thailand 5*	0.317
47	Malaysia 5*	0.314
48	Macedonia 4*	0.300
49	Ukraine 5*	0.299
50	Estonia 4*	0.295
51	Taiwan 5*	0.292
52	Dominican Republic 3*	0.291
53	Singapore 4*	0.290
54	Mexico 5*	0.281
55	Chile 5*	0.280
56	China 5*	0.277
57	Poland 5*	0.276
58	Belarus 4*	0.269
59	Montenegro 4*	0.265
60	Ethiopia 5*	0.264
61	Latvia 4*	0.251
62	Kyrgyz 4*	0.239
63	Hungary 4*	0.237
64	Turkey 5*	0.233
65	South Africa 5*	0.233
66	Armenia 3*	0.231
67	Moldova 5*	0.231
68	Saudi Arab. 4*	0.228
69	South Korea 5*	0.224
70	Albania 4*	0.222
71	Indonesia 5*	0.220
72	Philippines 4*	0.213
73	Mali 5*	0.211
74	Zambia 5*	0.209
75	Venezuela 4*	0.207
76	Russia 5*	0.206
77	Peru 4*	0.206
78	Nigeria 4*	0.204
79	Georgia 3*	0.181
80	Colombia 5*	0.173
81	Puerto Rico 4*	0.173
82	Malta 4*	0.171
83	Iran 4*	0.168
84	Azerbaijan 3*	0.159
85	Burkina Faso 5*	0.148
86	El Salvador 4*	0.133
87	Uganda 1*	0.131
88	Guatemala 4*	0.127

(continued)

ABLE A12.3
Continued

89	Egypt 4*	0.107
90	Tanzania 4*	0.105
91	Romania 5*	0.105
92	Bangladesh 4*	0.103
93	Trinidad 5*	0.095
94	Rwanda 5*	0.092
95	Algeria 4*	0.090
96	Iraq 5*	0.081
97	Ghana 5*	0.073
98	Morocco 5*	0.072
99	Jordan 4*	0.029
100	Pakistan 4*	0.027
101	Zimbabwe 4*	0.0

* This number refers to the most recent survey available for each country.

APPENDIX 13

Selected World-Changing Technological Innovations

Areas

1. **Food (6)**: axe/spear/bow and arrow/agriculture/pottery/plough
2. **Energy (4)**: fire domestication/steam engine/oil/electricity
3. **Transportation (8)**: animal domestication/wheel/sea shipping/horse wagon/railroad/automobile/air flying/cargo container
4. **Communications (10)**: writing/printing press/mail system/radio broadcasting/telephone/cinema/TV/personal computer/Internet/GPS
5. **War (4)**: sword/armor/firearms/atomic energy

Chronology (m = millions of years / k = thousands of years)

Axe (2.6 m)[1] / spear/fire domestication (1.7 m)[2] / bow and arrow/pottery/sea shipping/agriculture (8k BC)[3] / animal domestication/plough/wheel (3.5k BC)[4] / writing (3k BC)[5] / sword/armor/horse wagon/fire arms/printing press (1440) / steam engine (1769) / railroad (1811) / mail system (1840) / oil (1850) / telephone (1876) / electricity (1880) / automobile (1885) / cinema (1896) / air flying (1853–1908) / radio broadcasting (1909) / atomic energy (1945) / TV (1936–1948) / cargo container (1970) / personal computer (1976) / Internet (1992) / GPS (1996).

50 Greatest Breakthroughs since the Wheel (Source: James Fallows, The Atlantic, November 2013.)

1. **The printing press**, 1430s
2. **Electricity**, late 19th century

3. **Penicillin**, 1928
4. **Semiconductor electronics**, mid-20th century
5. **Optical lenses**, 13th century
6. **Paper**, 2nd century
7. **The internal combustion engine**, late 19th century
8. **Vaccination**, 1796
9. **The Internet**, 1960s
10. **The steam engine**, 1712
11. **Nitrogen fixation**, 1918
12. **Sanitation systems**, mid-19th century
13. **Refrigeration**, 1850s
14. **Gunpowder**, 10th century
15. **The airplane**, 1903
16. **The personal computer**, 1970s
17. **The compass**, 12th century
18. **The automobile**, late 19th century
19. **Industrial steelmaking**, 1850s
20. **The pill**, 1960
21. **Nuclear fission**, 1939
22. **The green revolution**, mid-20th century
23. **The sextant**, 1757
24. **The telephone**, 1876
25. **Alphabetization**, first millennium BC
26. **The telegraph**, 1837
27. **The mechanized clock**, 15th century
28. **Radio**, 1906
29. **Photography**, early 19th century
30. **The moldboard plow**, 18th century
31. **Archimedes' screw**, 3rd century BC
32. **The cotton gin**, 1793
33. **Pasteurization**, 1863
34. **The Gregorian calendar**, 1582
35. **Oil refining**, mid-19th century
36. **The steam turbine**, 1884
37. **Cement**, 1st millennium BC
38. **Scientific plant breeding**, 1920s
39. **Oil drilling**, 1859
40. **The sailboat**, 4th millennium BC
41. **Rocketry**, 1926
42. **Paper money**, 11th century
43. **The abacus**, 3rd millennium BC
44. **Air-conditioning**, 1902
45. **Television**, early 20th century
46. **Anesthesia**, 1846
47. **The nail**, 2nd millennium BC

48. **The lever**, 3rd millennium BC
49. **The assembly line**, 1913
50. **The combine harvester**, 1930s

THE ATLANTIC PANEL OF EXPERTS

Michelle Alexopoulos Professor of economics, University of Toronto

Leslie Berlin Historian of business and technology, Stanford; author, *The Man Behind the Microchip: Robert Noyce and the Invention of Silicon Valley*

John Doerr General partner, Kleiner Perkins Caufield & Byers

George Dyson Historian of technology; author, *Turing's Cathedral and Darwin Among the Machines*

Walter Isaacson President and CEO, the Aspen Institute; author, *Steve Jobs, Einstein: His Life and Universe*, and *Benjamin Franklin: An American Life*

Joi Ito Director, MIT Media Lab

Alexis Madrigal Senior editor, *The Atlantic*; author, *Powering the Dream: The History and Promise of Green Technology*

Charles C. Mann Journalist; author, *1491: New Revelations of the Americas Before Columbus* and *1493: Uncovering the New World Columbus Created*

Joel Mokyr Professor of economics and history, Northwestern University

Linda Sanford Senior vice president for enterprise transformation, IBM

Astro Teller Captain of moonshots, Google[x]; cofounder, Cerebellum Capital and BodyMedia

Padmasree Warrior Chief technology and strategy officer, Cisco Systems

Source: James Fallows, *The Atlantic*, November 2013.

NOTES

Introduction

1. Contrasting total economic output in GDP terms vs. GDP per capita vs. democracy measures. See Tables 10.1, 10.2, and 10.4 in Chapter 10.

2. I took the terms *honor* and *achievement* from Nisbett and Dove (1996) and McClelland (1961), respectively. *Joy* is my own.

3. The World Values Survey (WVS) is today one of the largest publicly available global data banks of information garnered through representative national surveys for sociological research. The two other key data sets on values reviewed in Chapter 1 are the ones gathered by Geert Hofstede and Shalom Schwartz. The Pew Research Center, ISSP (International Social Survey Program), and the Gallup World Poll are also collecting valuable cross-cultural data, in addition to the several regional *barometers*. The World Values Survey has been conducted six times between 1980 and 2014, and it offers a unique opportunity to track changes in human values. This survey project arose from the Eurobarometer, which in 1980 expanded to include 14 countries on six continents. In order to monitor shifts in values, the series was replicated in 1990 in 43 countries, coordinated by Ronald Inglehart until 2013. It was replicated again in 1995, 2000, 2005, and 2010, and involves around 100 countries. Its data and details are publicly available at www.worldvaluessurvey.org. Throughout this book, I use the 2004 World Values Survey sourcebook (except when noted), because a full 2010–2015 version is not yet available.

4. White Anglo Saxon Protestant.

5. "Impurity" in this sense indicating a chauvinistic and religious sentiment arising from the Catholic inquisition against "heresy" from either fellow Catholics or "infidels" (non-Catholics, be they Jews, Muslims, or others).

6. Although I use it extensively in this research, not everybody is pleased with the WVS. A first set of criticisms comes from those colleagues (anthropologists, psychologists, ethnologists) who reject surveys in general as a useful social research method (Kagan, 2012, p. 95; Mayone Stycos, 1981, p. 450). This position is understandable because these scholars' focus is very specific (either an individual or a tribe) and the need for in-depth understanding is clear. Surveys are good for panoramic pictures, but they are not good for detail. A second group of general objections, although accepting of survey research, does not find it useful to study values simply by asking questions about them. Some suggest it is best to keep a record of behavior or emotions (Csikszentmihalyi, 1990). A third set of objections are not concerned with the two previously mentioned, but rather argue that there are methodological problems with the WVS and/or with the theoretical framework developed by Inglehart (Haller, 2002; Lakatos, 2012; Abramson, 2011).

7. The former Soviet law is today almost extinct.

8. Jerry Kagan's ideas (2009, chapter 3) and our frequent conversations are behind many of my propositions.

9. See lists of values in Chapter 8 at the introduction to *process of change*.

10. The ideas presented in this book crystallized during my seminar *Values, Cultures and Development* at the Fletcher School, Tufts University (which I continued after its original professor, Lawrence E. Harrison, retired) and build upon the concepts reviewed from the perspective of social psychology (Smith and Bond, 1994, p. 35) and crosscultural studies (Minkov, 2013, part 1).

11. Culture: "The customary beliefs, social forms, and material traits of a racial, religious, or social group; also, the characteristic features of everyday existence (as diversions or a way of life) shared by people in a place or time *<popular culture> <southern culture>*; or the set of shared attitudes, values, goals, and practices that characterizes an institution or organization <a *corporate culture* focused on the bottom line>; or the set of values, conventions, or social practices associated with a particular field, activity, or societal characteristic <studying the effect of computers on *print culture*> <changing the *culture of materialism* will take time." 2014, *Merriam-Webster Dictionary* online.

12. Credit for its ratification was due in no small part to general outrage at the atrocities of World War II, as well as to the work of US First Lady Eleanor Roosevelt, who drew on her experiences during the Great Depression and her participation in the UN Human Rights Commission to push for its approval.

13. For example, gender equality among Islamic nations.

Chapter 1

1. Schumpeter (1942), Banfield (1958), McClelland (1961), Almond and Verba (1963), Myrdal (1968), Rangel (1977), Harrison (1985), Landes (1998).

2. A pioneering and relatively complete analysis of values, balancing theoretical and philosophical concerns together with empirical evidence, is the one presented in Rokeach's book *The Nature of Human Values* (1973). His line of thinking is very much behind Schwartz's work. Georgas, Vijver, and Berry (2004) make a thorough review and validation of the topic, concluding that psychological variables (values) show systematic relationships with cluster membership of countries (cultures). Another thorough analysis of countries' cultures is the one presented by the British polyglot Richard Lewis (1996[2012]). From a non-academic setting, using his powerful intuition and rich travel experience, he also finds three cultures—linear active, multi-active, and reactive. To simplify, Hofstede is very useful for business, Inglehart for politics and political scientists, Schwartz for social psychology, and Lewis for the traveler. My research is useful for current and aspiring leaders, as well as for those who study leadership, because it focuses on understanding the rationality of human groups as citizens.

3. New York, Albany, Utica, Ontario, Buffalo, Detroit, Niagara Falls, Montreal, Quebec, Boston, Hartford, Philadelphia, Pittsburgh, Cincinnati, Nashville, Memphis, New Orleans, Norfolk, and Washington, DC, were among their main stops.

4. Mores: "The fixed morally binding customs of a particular group." *Merriam-Webster Dictionary*.

5. Or perhaps more accurately, as Schwartz would term it, a *non-autonomic* country, to avoid Hofstede's *individualism*, mentioned in a later chapter.

6. Traditions/norms are equivalent at the individual level to the rationale of cultures of *honor*; goals are to cultures of *achievement*; and emotions are the individual rationale for cultures of *joy*.

7. These can be found in the introduction to Chapter 8, in the section on processes of change.

8. In his study of capitalism, Weber was following the ideas and findings of his good friend and colleague Sombart (1915).

Chapter 2

1. Axiology: "The study of the nature, types, and criteria of values and of value judgments especially in ethics." *Merriam-Webster Dictionary.*

2. A series of public opinion surveys conducted at least twice a year since 1973 on behalf of the European Commission.

3. In the World Values Survey conference in Budapest in 2004, Hans-Dieter Klingemann made a tribute to Inglehart in honor of his seventieth birthday. He highlighted the intellectual journey made possible by Inglehart's contributions to the study of world cultures, characterizing it as a voyage from *Point land* (dimension zero) to *Line land* (the first dimension), then to *Flat land* (the second dimension)—and ending with the hope of one day arriving at *Space land* (the third dimension), hinted at by our Swedish colleague, Thorleif Pettersson, in that meeting. Klingemann recalled the way in which the proposal of materialism–postmaterialism had *rescued* sociopolitical theory, previously confined to dimension zero, and which in 1971 Inglehart had singlehandedly carried to the first dimension. The proposal of the *World Culture Map* in 1997 carried it further into the second dimension.

Chapter 4

1. The spread of human populations has been calculated at a pace of 60 kilometers per generation, estimated at about 20 years for earlier humans. The pace of the spread is based on the time elapsed that it took to cover the 15,500 kilometers from Ethiopia to Lake Mungo in Australia (Finlayson, 2009, p. 16).

2. Libya in 1951; Tunisian and Morocco in 1956; Ghana in 1957; the rest during the 1960s, except for those which remained under Portuguese rule until 1975 (Angola, Cape Verde, Mozambique, Guinea-Bissau, and São Tomé and Principe); and Zimbabwe, which was not recognized until 1980.

3. The Gini index of income distribution goes from 0 to 1. A value of 0 means perfect equality (zero concentration of wealth, or all people receiving the same income) and a value of 1 suggests the maximum level of inequality (one person holding all the wealth).

4. The SERF Index (Fukuda-Parr et al., 2015) is an excellent response to the challenge, measuring Amartya Sen's expansion of freedoms concept. They take six universal rights (food, health, education, housing, work, and social security) and through careful statistical analysis and data gathering show their interconnection, as well as the relevance of gender equality to improving development.

5. India is home to the world's third-largest Muslim population, yet its 177 million Muslims are only 15% the size of its Hindu population. China's mere 2% Muslim population still adds up to 23 million people.

6. Theologian, jurist, philosopher, and mystic of Persian descent, referred to by some historians as the single most influential Muslim after the Prophet Muhammad.

7. AD years of 325, 381, 431, 451, 553, 680 and 787, until the formal Schism of 1054.

8. (1) being a well-situated chain of islands; (2) with a favorable ratio of agricultural to forested land; and (3) being of a large enough yet manageable size.

9. (1) the royal family; (2) its isolation from the West; and (3) stability.

10. (1) forestry; (2) demography (near-zero population growth); and (3) institutional (the Meiji Restoration).

11. Europe changed from a single political unit, as it had been during the Roman Empire, to a collection of more than 5,000 baronies in the 15th century. As trade, the spread of knowledge, and war technology increased, the number shrank down to about 500 baronies by the 17th century, to 200 by the early 19th century, and was further consolidated into fewer than 30 nations by 1953 (Pinker, 2011, p. 74). With the rise of the European Economic Community, the last 50 years have witnessed a dramatic acceleration of the integration process back to one unit.

Chapter 5

1. It is important to be cautious about this item, because the Western and the Islamic meaning may refer to two different concepts. Apparently, what in the West is referred to *homosexuality* corresponds rather to *transgender* in Islam. The initiation of sexual life among young men is apparently widespread, socially accepted, and shows no effect in their adult life. A more nuanced question will need to be designed to capture the real meaning of this subject.

Chapter 6

1. Puerto Rico is not really an independent nation, despite its contradictory name in Spanish as *Independent Associated State*.

Chapter 7

1. Families with 3 or more children add another 6.8% and one-child families represent a 12.1% of 78.8 million family households in 2010.

2. Catholicism emphasized for many years the interpretation of the biblical expulsion of Adam and Eve from the Garden of Eden as a punishment for eating the fruit from the tree of knowledge. Hence, knowledge, learning, and studying had to be evil. How much of that attitude still prevails among many poor Catholic groups in the *world*?

3. The short poem by Robert Fulghum, "All I Really Need To Know I Learned in Kindergarten," may summarize the spirit of these pedagogues.

4. For a brief and insightful account of the US educational system, the 2010 American documentary *Waiting for Superman* by director Davis Guggenheim is a good source.

5. The European Crusades of the Middle Ages, the Northern Ireland conflict in the 20th century, and the religious wars that divided India and Pakistan are but a few examples.

6. The *Fairness Doctrine* was a policy of the US Federal Communications Commission (FCC) that required broadcasters to present controversial issues of public

importance in an honest, equitable, and balanced manner. The FCC formally removed in 2011 the language that implemented it.

7. Japan established the Tokyo Electric Light Company (TELC, now TEPCO: Tokyo Electric Power Company) in 1887, whereas in the United States, Thomas A. Edison opened the first commercial power plant just five years earlier.

8. The former Soviet system law is practically inexistent today.

9. In Chile, the emergency number for the police (Carabineros) is actually 133.

10. The percentage of cases that are solved in the process, with no need to reach the judge.

Chapter 8

1. Admitted by government, although the news reported higher figures.

2. When I was invited to visit Colombia to observe the changes in Bogotá, the capital, it brought to mind a very old personal anecdote. It must have been in 1960 when the president of Mexico visited the small town where I was born. My father was a congressman and invited me to accompany him on their field trip. I did not let the opportunity pass me by. For the first time I heard an enthusiastic group of federal government executives say that "now big changes are finally on their way, as their predecessors had not known what they were doing." I was impressed by these statements, which I wholeheartedly believed. I was 13 years old. I became less and less convinced of this the more I heard it repeated by every new team each time there was a change of administration. Thirty-four years later, I had become very skeptical about big changes. When I heard about sea changes in public attitudes in Bogotá, the first image that popped into my mind was of those federal government members in 1960.

Chapter 9

1. An empirical testing of the CCI's 25 values' correlation with progress was contrasted with the World Values questions; the findings indicated that 11 items received strong confirmation; 3 moderate; 2 were ultimately deemed unimportant; and for 9 there were no comparable data (Inglehart: 2004).

2. The scholars participated in the Moscow Symposium, *Culture, Cultural Change, and Economic Development,* in May 2010, jointly sponsored by the Russian State University Higher School of Economics and the Cultural Change Institute, Fletcher School, Tufts University.

Chapter 10

1. GDP is the market value of all officially recognized final goods and services produced within a country in a year. It is a measure that has been used since 1934.

2. Purchasing power parity (PPP) is an adjustment to the relative value of different currencies for international comparisons. An example is the *Economist's* Big Mac Index, which compares the prices of a Big Mac burger in McDonald's restaurants around the world.

3. The Group of Twenty (G-20) was originally a group of finance ministers and central bank governors from 20 major economies who began meeting in 1999. Since 2008 heads of government began meeting periodically.

4. Both metrics—GDP and population size—hold a correlation coefficient of .51.

5. The methodology used in constructing this rating system is available online at www.freedomhouse.org.

6. The Gini coefficient measures how a country's wealth and income are distributed.

7. Recent research suggests an interesting relationship between women and tools. Prior to the Bronze Age, when the hoe was the main agricultural tool, women's role was more important. However, the introduction of the plow around 6000 BC radically changed both agriculture and the role of women, because this new tool demanded the significant physical strength of males (Alesina, 2013b).

8. Attempts at solving the problems of evaluating natural capital are the UNU-IHDP, *Inclusive Wealth Report 2012*, and the WAVES partnership (Wealth Accounting and the Valuation of Ecosystem Services) at www.wavespartnership.org/en.

9. The calculations that result in Table 10.8 (SDI) are presented in Appendix 12.

Chapter 11

1. For an outstanding review of ancient models of development—China, India, Ottoman and Greco-Roman—see Fukuyama (2011).

Chapter 12

1. If we think of the evolution of our species in those terms, it is possible to identify at least five axial ages: *Stone, Bronze, Iron, Religions,* and *Technology.* These periods are all defined by modifications to the preexisting material conditions. The *Stone Age* is estimated to have lasted 2.5 million years, and to have ended around the 4th millennium BC, when the smelting of alloys brought about the *Bronze Age.* This period, which lasted roughly 2000 years, was not characterized solely by developments in metallurgy, but also by the invention of writing, which accelerated the transmission and accumulation of knowledge. The next great leap forward was the *Iron Age*, beginning in India and the Middle East around 1300 BC and lasting until the appearance of gunpowder and firearms in approximately AD 700.

2. Millions of years of evolution left us very useful equipment in the form of "six universal emotions: anger, sadness, happiness, fear, disgust, and surprise" (Herz, 2012, p. 29). Fear, happiness, and sadness must have been behind the search for explanations, just as anger, surprise, and disgust must have moved us to take action.

3. Table 12.1 measures axiological change, using two key values that shape culture: respect for parents and work ethic. The data comes from the World Values Survey (WVS). One limitation in terms of measuring changes in values is that the data for this survey only goes back 30 years, whereas the structural impact of the modernization process must have been at work for at least 5 to 8 decades.

It is difficult to find the pattern of changes in values over the years by looking at individual countries. There are too many specific variables that could be responsible for such changes. One way of solving such a limitation is to aggregate the data for several countries. In this analysis we used data from the 81 countries included in the World Values Surveys from 1995 and 2000. Given the diverse set of countries included, it is possible to replicate the modernization process. That is, we look at the values for pre-modern countries (high illiteracy, low urbanization, few people employed in the service sector, low per capita income) as compared to intermediate and postmodern countries (low illiteracy, high urbanization, many people employed in the service sector, high per capita income).

Conclusion

1. These three *honor* countries are listed among the top 20 countries of the 2013 *Environmental Impact Mitigation Index* of the World Energy Council, where the United States is listed as number 86. This type of care and concern, though, is present in many of the Native American Nations.

Appendix 13

1. Semaw, S., Rogers, M. J., Quade J., Renne, P. R., Butler, R. F., Domínguez-Rodrigo, M., Stout, D., Hart, W. S., Pickering, T., Simpson, S. W. (2003), "2.6-Million-Year-Old Stone Tools and Associated Bones from OGS-6 and OGS-7, Gona, Afar, Ethiopia." *Journal of Human Evolution*, 45, 169–177.

2. James, Steven R. (February 1989), "Hominid Use of Fire in the Lower and Middle Pleistocene: A Review of the Evidence," *Current Anthropology* (University of Chicago Press), 30(1), 1–26.

3. Diamond, Jared (1992), *The Third Chimpanzee: The Evolution and Future of the Human Animal*, Harper Perennial, 2006, p. 182.

4. Anthony, David A. (2007), *The Horse, the Wheel, and Language: How Bronze-Age Riders from the Eurasian Steppes Shaped The Modern World*. Princeton, NJ: Princeton University Press, p. 67.

5. Diamond, Jared (1997), *Guns, Germs and Steel: the Fates of Human Societies*. Norton, 2005, p. 218.

BIBLIOGRAPHY

Acemoglu, Daron, and Robinson, James A. (2012). *Why Nations Fail: The Origins of Power, Prosperity and Poverty*. New York: Crown Business.

Acemoglu, Daron, Johnson, S., and Robinson, J. (2005). "Institutions as Fundamental Cause of Long-Run Growth." In P. Aqhion and S. Durlaut (Eds.), *Handbook of Economic Growth*, 1A, 385–472. Boston: Elsevier.

Adams, Michael. (2003). *Fire and Ice: United States, Canada and the Myth of Converging Values*. Toronto: Penguin Canada.

Alduncin, Enrique. (1986). *Los Valores de los Mexicanos: Entre la Tradición y la Modernidad*. México City: Banamex.

Alduncin, Enrique. (1991). *Los Valores de los Mexicanos: México en Tiempos de Cambio*. México City: Banamex.

Alduncin, Enrique. (1993). *Los Valores de los Mexicanos: En Busca de una Esencia*, México City: Banamex.

Alduncin, Enrique, ed. (2004). *Los Valores de los Mexicanos: Cambio y Permanencia*. México City: Banamex.

Alesina, A., and Giuliano, P. (2013a). "Family Ties." National Bureau of Economic Research. : Cambridge, MA, Working Paper 18966.

Alesina, A., Giuliano, P., and Nunn, N. (2013b). "On the Origins of Gender Roles: Women and the Plough." *The Quarterly Journal of Economics*, 128(2), 469–530.

Almond, Gabriel, and Verba, Sidney. (1963). *The Civic Culture: Political Attitudes and Democracy in Five Nations*. Princeton, NJ: Princeton University Press.

Alwin, Duane. (1986). "Religion and Parental Child-Rearing Orientations: Evidence of a Catholic-Protestant Convergence." *American Journal of Sociology*, 92, 412–440.

Apter, David E. (1965). *The Politics of Modernization*. Chicago: University of Chicago Press.

Arias, Oscar. (2011). "Culture Matters: The Real Obstacles to Latin America Development." *Foreign Affairs*, January/February, 90(1), 2–6.

Banfield, Edward C. (1958). *The Moral Basis of a Backward Society*. New York: Free Press.

Barrett, David B., Kurian, G. T., and Johnson, T. M. (2001). *World Christian Encyclopedia*. Oxford: Oxford University Press.

Basáñez, Miguel. (1986). "Tradiciones Combativas y Contemplativas: México Mañana." *Revista Mexicana de Ciencias Políticas*. México: UNAM, No. 125, July–September, 1986.

Basáñez, Miguel. (1993). *Protestant and Catholic Ethics: An Empirical Comparison*. Presentation at the World Values Survey Conference, El Paular, Spain, September 27, 1993.

Basáñez, Miguel. (2006). "The Camel and the Needle." In L. Harrison L. and P. Berger (Eds.), *Developing Cultures: Case Studies*. New York: Routledge.

Basáñez, Miguel. (2010). "Axiological Diagnosis: Measuring Cultural Capital and Change." *Culture, Cultural Change, and Economic Development Symposium,* State University Higher School of Economics, Moscow, Russia, May 2010.

Basáñez, Miguel, Inglehart, R., and Nevitte, N. (2007). "North American Convergence—Revisited." *Norteamérica, Revista Académica,* July–December, 2(2), 21–61.

Basáñez, Miguel, and Reyes Heroles, Federico. (2003). "Actualización del Nacionalismo Mexicano." In Rafael Fernández de Castro (Ed.), *En la Frontera del Imperio.* México: Ariel.

Bell, Daniel. (1973 [1999]). *The Coming of Post-Industrial Society.* New York: Basic Books.

Bell, Daniel. (1976 [2013]). *The Cultural Contradictions of Capitalism.* New York: Basic Books.

Bellah, Robert N., et al. (1985). *Habits of the Heart: Individualism and Commitment in American Life.* New York: Harpers.

Beltrán, Tatiana. (2005). *Gender Equality and Democracy: A Comparative Perspective.* PhD dissertation, University of Michigan.

Berger, Peter. (1969). *A Rumor of Angels: Modern Society and the Rediscovery of the Supernatural.* Garden City, NY: Anchor Books.

Berger, Peter. (1979). *The Heretical Imperative: Contemporary Possibilities of Religious Affirmation.* Garden City, NY: Anchor Books.

Berger, Peter, and Huntington, S., Eds. (2002). *Many Globalizations: Cultural Diversity in the Contemporary World.* New York: Oxford University Press.

Berger, Peter, and Zijderveld, Anton. (2009). *In Praise of Doubt: How to Have Convictions Without Becoming a Fanatic.* New York: HarperOne.

Blum, Ulrich, and Dudley, Leonard. (2001). "Religion and Economic Growth: Was Weber Right?" *Journal of Evolutionary Economics, 11,* 207–230.

Boyd, Robert, and Richerson, Peter J. (2005). *The Origin and Evolution of Cultures.* New York: Oxford University Press.

Braudel, Fernand. (1995). *The Mediterranean and the Mediterranean World at the Age of Philip II.* 2 vols. Berkeley: University of California Press.

Bronowski, Jacob. (1973[2011]). *The Ascent of Man.* London: BBC Books.

Brooks, David. (2011). "The Spirit of Enterprise." *New York Times,* December 1, 2011, http://www.nytimes.com/2011/12/02/opinion/brooks-the-spirit-of-enterprise. html?_r=0.

Buchdahl, J. (1999). *Atmosphere, Climate and Environment.* Manchester, UK: Manchester Metropolitan University.

Calderisi, Robert. (2007). *The Trouble with Africa.* New York: Palgrave Macmillan.

Camp, Roderic A. (1980). *Mexico's Leaders, Their Education and Recruitment.* Tucson: University of Arizona Press.

Camp, Roderic A. (1984). *The Making of a Government: The Socialization of Political Leaders in Post-Revolutionary Mexico.* Tucson: University of Arizona Press.

Camp, Roderic A. (1985). *Intellectuals and the State in Twentieth-Century Mexico.* Austin: University of Texas Press.

Camp, Roderic A. (1989). *Entrepreneurs and Politics in Twentieth-Century Mexico.* New York: Oxford University Press.

Camp, Roderic A. (1992). *Generals in the Palacio, the Military in Modern Mexico.* New York: Oxford University Press.

Camp, Roderic A. (1993). *Who's Who in Mexico Today.* Boulder, CO: Westview Press.

Camp, Roderic A. (1997). *Crossing Swords, Politics and Religion in Mexico.* New York: Oxford University Press.

Camp, Roderic A., Ed. (2001). *Citizen Views of Democracy in Latin America.* Pittsburgh: University of Pittsburgh Press.

Camp, Roderic A. (2002). *Mexico's Mandarins, Crafting a Power Elite for the 21st Century.* Berkeley: University of California Press.

Camp, Roderic A. (2005). *Mexico's Military on the Democratic Stage.* Washington, DC: Center for Strategic & International Studies/Praeger.

Camp, Roderic A. (2007). *Politics in Mexico: The Democratic Consolidation.* New York: Oxford University Press.

Camp, Roderic A. (2010). *The Metamorphosis of Leadership in a Democratic Mexico.* New York: Oxford University Press.

Camp, Roderic A. (2011). *Mexico: What Everyone Needs to Know.* New York: Oxford University Press.

Camp, Roderic A. (2011). *Mexican Political Biographies, 1939–2009,* 4th ed. Austin: University of Texas Press.

Camp, Roderic A. (2012). *Oxford Handbook of Mexican Politics.* New York: Oxford University Press.

Camp, Roderic A. (2013). *Politics in Mexico: Democratic Consolidation or Decline?* New York: Oxford University Press.

Campbell, Joseph. (1959[1991]). *The Masks of Gods: Primitive Mythology.* New York: Penguin Compass.

Campbell, Joseph. (1962[1991]). *The Masks of Gods: Oriental Mythology.* New York: Penguin Compass.

Campbell, Joseph. (1964[1991]]). *The Masks of Gods: Occidental Mythology.* New York: Penguin Compass.

Cantera Carlomagno, Marcos. (2008). *Las Venas Tapadas de América Latina.* Montevideo, Uruguay: Linardi y Risso.

Cantoni, Davide. (2009). "The Economic Effects of the Protestant Reformation: Testing the Weber Hypothesis in the German Lands." Cambridge, MA: Harvard University Job Market Paper, http://www.people.fas.harvard.edu/~cantoni/cantoni_jmp_2_7_1.pdf.

Cardoso, Fernando Henrique, and Faletto, Enzo. (1979). *Dependency and Development in Latin America.* Berkeley: University of California Press.

Cercas, Javier. (2009[2011]). *The Anatomy of a Moment.* New York: Bloomsbury.

Cipolla, Carlo M., Ed. (1970). *The Economic Decline of Empires.* London: Methuen.

Clark, Colin. (1940). *Conditions of Economic Progress.* London: Macmillan.

Cohen, Patricia. (2010). "'Culture of Poverty' Makes a Comeback." *New York Times,* October 18, p. A1.

Cunningham, Lawrence, and Reich, John. (2002). *Culture and Values: A Survey of the Humanities,* Vol. 1, 5th ed. New York: Thomson Learning.

Dalton, Russell J. (1996). *Citizen Politics: Public Opinion and Political Parties in Industrial Democracies.* Chatham, NJ: Chatham House.

DANE—DAPD. (2003). *Encuesta de Calidad de Vida*. Alcaldía Mayor de Bogotá.

Dávila, Julio D. (2004). "La Transformación de Bogotá." In Fernando Cepeda (Ed.), *Fortalezas de Colombia*. Bogotá: Editorial Planeta Colombiana para el Banco Interamericano de Desarrollo y Colección Ariel, Ciencia Política.

Dawes, Robyn M. (1988). *Rational Choice in an Uncertain World*. New York: Harcourt Brace Jovanovich.

Dawkins, Richard. (1976). *The Selfish Gene*. Oxford: Oxford University Press, 2006.

De Waal, Frans. (1982[2007]). *Chimpanzee Politics: Power and Sex among Apes*. Baltimore, MD: Johns Hopkins University Press.

Dealy, Glen. (1977). *The Public Man: An Interpretation of Latin American and Other Catholic Countries*. Amherst: University of Massachusetts Press.

Dealy, Glen. (1992). *The Latin Americans: Spirit and Ethos*. Boulder, CO: Westview Press.

Dennett, Daniel C. (1995). *Darwin's Dangerous Idea: Evolutions and the Meanings of Life*. New York: Simon & Schuster.

Dennett, Daniel C. (2006). *Breaking the Spell: Religion as a Natural Phenomenon*. New York: Penguin Group.

Deutsch, Karl W. (1974). "Theories of Imperialism and Neocolonialism." In Steven J. Rosen and James R. Kurth (Eds.), *Testing Theories of Economic Imperialism*. Lexington, MA: Lexington Books.

Diamond, Jared. (1992). *The Third Chimpanzee: The Evolution and Future of the Human Animal*. New York: Harper.

Diamond, Jared. (1997). *Guns, Germs, and Steel: The Fates of Human Societies*. : New York: W. W. Norton.

Diamond, Jared. (2005). *Collapse: How Societies Choose to Fail or Succeed*. New York: Penguin.

Diamond, Jared. (2012). "Romney Hasn't Done His Homework." *New York Times*, August 2, p. A19.

Diamond, Jared, and Robinson, James A., Eds. (2010). *Natural Experiments of History*. Cambridge, MA: Harvard University Press.

Diaz Guerrero, Rogelio. (1994[2008]). *Psicología del Mexicano: Descubrimiento de la Etnopsicología*. México: Trillas.

Diener, Ed, and Suh, Eunkook M., Eds. (2000). *Culture and Subjective Well-being*. Cambridge, MA: MIT Press.

Duverger, Christian. (2012). *Crónica de la Eternidad*. México: Taurus.

Easterly, William. (2006). *The White Man's Burden*. New York: Penguin.

Easterly, William. (2013). *The Tyranny of Experts: Economists, Dictators, and the Forgotten Rights of the Poor*. New York: Basic Books.

Ebel, Roland H., Taras, Raymond, and Cochrane, James D. (1991). *Political Culture and Foreign Policy in Latin America: Case Studies from the Circum-Caribbean*. Albany: State University of New York Press.

Engels, Friedrich. (1884[2010]). *The Origin of the Family, Private Property and the State*. New York: Penguin Classics.

Esmer, Yilmaz, and Pettersson, Thorleif R., Eds. (2007). *Measuring and Mapping Cultures: 25 Years of Comparative Value Surveys*. Dordrecht: Brill.

Fallows, James. (2013). "The 50 Greatest Breakthroughs since the Wheel." *The Atlantic*, November.

Fedesarrollo. (1997). *Memorias 95/97*. Secretaría de Hacienda de Bogotá, Alcaldía Mayor de Bogotá.

Ferguson, Niall. (2011). *Civilization: The West and the Rest*. New York: Penguin Press.

Finlayson, Clive. (2009). *The Humans Who Went Extinct*. Oxford: Oxford University Press.

Fisher, D. H. (1989). *Albion's Seed: Four British Falkways en América*. Oxford: Oxford University Press.

Fisher, Glen. (1997). *Mindsets: The Role of Culture and Perception in International Relations*. Boston: Intercultural Press.

Fiske, Alan Page. (1991). *The Structures of Social Life*. New York: Free Press.

Fiske, Alan Page. (1992). "The Four Elementary Form of Sociality: Framework for a Unified Theory of Social Relations." *Psychological Review*,99(4), 689–723.

Foa, Roberto, A. Nemirovskaya, and E. Mostovova. (2013). "Internal Empires I: Social Institutions of the Frontier." SSRN: Higher School of Economics Research Paper No. WP BRP 09/SOC/2012.

Fontaine, Poortinga, and Delbeke, Schwartz. (2008). "Structural Equivalence of the Values Domain across Cultures." *Journal of Cross-Cultural Psychology*, 39(4), 345–365.

Fromm, Eric. (1965). *Escape from Freedom*. New York: Avon.

Fukuda-Parr, Sakiko, Lawson-Remer, Terra, and Randolph, Susan. (2015). *Fulfilling Social and Economic Rights*. Oxford: Oxford University Press.

Fukuyama, Francis. (1992). *The End of History and the Last Man*. New York: Free Press.

Fukuyama, Francis. (1995). *Trust: Human Nature and the Reconstitution of Social Order*. New York: Free Press.

Fukuyama, Francis. (2011). *The Origins of Political Order: From Prehuman Times to the French Revolution*. New York: Farrar, Straus and Giroux.

Fukuyama, Francis. (2014). *Political Order and Political Decay: From the Industrial Revolution to the Globalization of Democracy*. New York: Farrar, Straus and Giroux.

Galeano, Eduardo. (1971[2010]). *Las Venas Abiertas de América Latina*. México: Siglo XXI.

García Hamilton, José Ignacio. (1990). *Los Orígenes de La cultura latina Autoritaria (e Improductiva)*. Buenos Aires: Calbino y Asociados.

Geert Hofstede, Gert Jan Hofstede & Michael Minkov, "Cultures and Organizations: Software of the Mind," Revised and Expanded Third Edition, McGraw-Hill New York 2010.

Georgas, James, van de Vijver, Fons J. R., and Berry, John W. (2004). "The Ecocultural Framework, Ecosocial Indices, and Psychological Variables in Cross-Cultural Research." *Journal of Cross-Cultural Psychology*, 35(1), 74–96.

Germani, Gino. (1969). *Sociología de la modernización; estudios teóricos, metodológicos y aplicados a América Latina*. Buenos Aires: Paidos.

Giddens, Anthony. (1984[1986]). *The Constitution of Society: Outline of the Theory of Structuration*. Berkeley: University of California Press.

González Casanova, Pablo. (1965). *La Democracia en México*. México: Era.

Grondona, Mariano. (2000). "A Cultural Typology of Economic Development." In L. Harrison and S. Huntington (Eds.), *Culture Matters: How Values Shape Human Progress*. New York: Basic Books.

Grossman, Henryk. (1934[2006]). "The Beginnings of Capitalism and the New Mass Morality." *Journal of Classical Sociology*, 6(2), 201–213.

Hammerich, Kai, and Lewis, Richard D. (2013). *Fish Can't See Water: How National Culture Can Make or Break Your Corporate Strategy.* Chichester, UK: John Wiley & Sons.

Hansen, James, et al. (2006). "Global Temperature Change." *PNAS, 103*(39), 14288–14293.

Harrison, Lawrence E. (1985[2000]). *Underdevelopment Is a State of Mind: The Latin American Case.* Lanham, MD: Madison Books.

Harrison, Lawrence E. (1992). *Who Prospers: How Cultural Values Shape Economic and Political Success.* New York: Basic Books.

Harrison, Lawrence E. (1997). *The Pan-American Dream: Do Latin America's Cultural Values Discourage True Partnership with the US and Canada?* Boulder, CO: Westview Press.

Harrison, Lawrence E. (2006). *The Central Liberal Truth.* Oxford: Oxford University Press.

Harrison, Lawrence E. (2013). *Jews, Confucians, and Protestants.* Lanham, MD: Rowman & Littlefield.

Harrison, L., and Berger, P., Eds. (2006). *Developing Cultures: Case Studies.* New York: Routledge.

Harrison, L., and Huntington, S., Eds. (2000). *Culture Matters.* New York: Basic Books.

Harrison, L., and Kagan, J., Eds. (2006). *Developing Cultures: Essays on Cultural Change.* New York: Routledge.

Hart, Samuel L. (1971). "Axiology: Theory of Values." *Philosophy and Phenomenological Research, 32*(1), 29–41.

Hartz, Louis. (1964). *The Founding of New Societies.* New York: Harcourt Brace.

Hernández, Pedro F. (2003). *Los Valores de los Mexicanos: Retratos de los Mexicanos.* México: Banamex.

Herrnstein, Richard J., and Murray, Charles. (1994). *The Bell Curve: Intelligence and Class Structure in American Life.* New York: Free Press.

Herz, Rachel. (2012). *That's Disgusting: Unraveling the Mysteries of Repulsion.* New York: W. W. Norton.

Hofstede, Geert. (1980[1984]). *Culture's Consequences: International Differences in Work-Related Values.* Thousand Oaks, CA: Sage.

Hofstede, Geert. (2001). *Culture's Consequences (Second Edition): Comparing Values, Behaviors, Institutions and Organizations Across Nations.* Thousand Oaks, CA: Sage.

Hofstede, Geert. (2011). "Dimensionalizing Cultures: The Hofstede Model in Context." *Online Readings in Psychology and Culture, 2*(1), http://dx.doi.org/10.9707/2307-0919.1014.

Hofstede, Geert, and Hofstede, Gert Jan. (2005). *Cultures and Organizations: Software of the Mind.* New York: McGraw Hill.

Hoodbhoy, Pervez. (2002). "Islamic Failure." *Prospect Magazine,* Issue 71, February.

Huntington, Samuel P. (1993). "The Clash of Civilizations?" *Foreign Affairs,* Summer, 72(3), 22–49.

Huntington, Samuel P. (1996). *The Clash of Civilizations and the Remaking of World Order.* New York: Simon & Schuster.

Huntington. Samuel P. (2004). *Who Are We? The Challenges to America's National Identity.* New York: Simon & Schuster.

Hurtado, Osvaldo. (2008). "Culture and Development in Latin America." Cultural Change Conference, The Fletcher School, Tufts University, October.

IDCT. (2002). *Bogotá: Una Decisión Bien Tomada.* Alcaldía Mayor de Bogotá: Asesoría Región y Competitividad/Instituto Distrital de Cultura y Turismo.

INEGI. (1998). Estadísticas Históricas de México, Vol. 1. México.

Inglehart, Ronald. (1971). "The Silent Revolution in Europe: Intergenerational Chance in Post-Industrial Societies." *American Political Science Review*, 65(4), 991–1017.

Inglehart, Ronald. (1977). *The Silent Revolution: Changing Values and Political Styles among Western Publics*. Princeton, NJ: Princeton University Press.

Inglehart, Ronald. (1990). *Culture Shift in Advanced Industrial Society*. Princeton, NJ: Princeton University Press.

Inglehart, Ronald. (1997). *Modernization and Postmodernization: Cultural, Economic and Political Change in 43 Societies*. Princeton, NJ: Princeton University Press.

Inglehart, Ronald. (2004). "Testing the Progress Typology." *Culture Matters Conference*, The Fletcher School, Tufts University, March 27–28.

Inglehart, R., and Baker, Wayne E. (2000). "Modernization, Cultural Change, and the Persistence of Traditional Values." *American Sociological Review*, 65(1), 19–51.

Inglehart, R., Basáñez, M., and Nevitte, N. (1994). *Convergencia en Norteamérica: Comercio, Política y Cultura*. México: Siglo XXI.

Inglehart, R., Basáñez, M., et al. (2004). *Human Beliefs and Values*. México: Siglo XXI.

Inglehart, R., Basáñez, M. et al. (2010). *Changing Human Beliefs and Values: 1981–2007*. México: Siglo XXI.

Inglehart, R., and Carballo, Marita. (1997). "Does Latin America Exists? (And Is There a Confucian Culture?) A Global Analysis of Cross Cultural Differences." *PS: Political Science and Politics*, 30(1), 34–47.

Inglehart, R., Nevitte, N., and Basáñez, M. (1996). *North American Trajectory: Trade, Politics and Values*. New York: Aldine de Gruyter.

Inglehart, R., and Norris, Pippa. (2003). *Rising Tide: Gender Equality and Cultural Change around the World*. New York: Cambridge University Press.

Inglehart, R., and Welzel, C. (2005). *Modernization, Cultural Change, and Democracy*. Cambridge: Cambridge University Press.

Inoguchi, T., Basáñez, M., et al. (2005). *Values and Life Styles in Asia*. México: Siglo XXI.

Inoguchi, T., and Fujii, S. (2013). *The Quality of Life in Asia: A Comparison of Quality of Life in Asia*. Dordrecht: Springer.

Jacobs, Wilbur R. (1974). "Pre-Columbian Indian Demography." *William & Mary Quarterly*, 31, 123–132.

Johnson, Steven. (2001[2004]). *Emergence: The Connected Lives of Ants, Brains, Cities and Software*. New York: Scribner.

Judt, Tony. (2010). *Ill Fares the Land*. New York: Penguin Books.

Kaase, Max, and Newton, Kenneth. (1995). *Beliefs in Government*. Oxford: Oxford University Press.

Kagan, Jerome. (1962[1983]). *Birth to Maturity: A Study in Psychological Development*. New Haven, CT: Yale University Press.

Kagan, Jerome. (1984[1994]). *The Nature of the Child*. New York: Basic Books.

Kagan, Jerome. (1998). *Three Seductive Ideas*. Cambridge, MA: Harvard University Press.

Kagan, Jerome. (2002). *Surprise, Uncertainty and Mental Structure*. Cambridge, MA: Harvard University Press.

Kagan, Jerome. (2009). *The Three Cultures: Natural Sciences, Social Sciences and the Humanities in the 21st Century*. New York: Cambridge University Press.

Kagan, Jerome. (2010a). *The Temperamental Thread: How Genes, Culture, Time and Luck Make Us Who We Are*. New York: Dana Press.

Kagan, Jerome. (2010b). *The Role of the Family in the Acquisition of Values*. Paper delivered at the Higher School of Economics, Moscow Symposium, May 2010 (unpublished).

Kagan, Jerome. (2012). *Psychology's Ghosts: The Crisis in the Profession and the Way Back*. New Haven, CT: Yale University Press.

Kagan, Jerome. (2013). *The Human Spark: The Science of Human Development*. New York: Basic Books.

Kagan, Jerome, and Snidman, Nancy. (2004). *The Long Shadow of Temperament*. Cambridge, MA: Harvard University Press.

Kagan, Sharon L., & Lowenstein, Amy E. (2006). "Cultural Values and Parenting Education." In L. Harrison and J. Kagan (Eds.), *Developing Cultures: Essays on Cultural Change*. New York: Routledge.

Kahneman, Daniel. (2011). *Thinking, Fast and Slow*. New York: Farrar Straus and Giroux.

Kaiser, Stephen. (1991). "Introduction to the Japanese Writing System." In *Kodansha's Compact Kanji Guide*. Tokyo: Kondansha International.

Kaku, Michio. (2011). *Physics of the Future: How Science Will Shape Human Destiny and Our Daily Lives by the Year 2100*. New York: Doubleday.

Kim, Sung Ho. (Fall 2012 edition). "Max Weber." *The Stanford Encyclopedia of Philosophy*, Edward N. Zalta (Ed.), http://plato.stanford.edu/archives/fall2012/entries/weber/.

Kissinger, Henry. (1994). *Diplomacy*. New York: Simon & Schuster.

Kissinger, Henry. (2014). *World Order*. New York: Penguin Press.

Klitgaard, Robert. (1990). *Tropical Gangsters*. New York: Basic Books.

Knott, David, Muers, S., and Aldridge, S. (2008). *Achieving Culture Change: A Policy Framework*. London: Cabinet Office, Discussion Paper.

Kojetin, B. A. (1988). "Separating the Seekers from the Doubters." Paper presented at annual meeting of the Society for the Scientific Study of Religion, Chicago, October.

La Porta, Rafael, López de Silanes, F., and Shleifer, A. (2008). "The Economic Consequences of Legal Origins." *Journal of Economic Literature*, 46(2), 285–332.

Lakatos, Zoltán. (2012). "Alternatives to Inglehart's Values Construct." Working paper, presented at the *International Sociological Association* Conference, Sydney, Australia, July.

Lamm, Richard D. (2006). "Public Policy and Culture." In L. E. Harrison and J. Kagan (Eds.), *Developing Cultures: Essays on Cultural Change*. New York: Routledge.

Landes, David S. (1998[1999]). *The Wealth and Poverty of Nations: Why Some Are So Rich and Some So Poor*. New York: W. W. Norton.

Laveaga, Gerardo. (2006). *El Sueño de Inocencio*. México: Planeta.

Layard, Richard. (2005). *Happiness: Lessons from a New Science*. New York: Penguin.

Lenski, Gerhard. (1963). *The Religious Factor: A Sociological Study of Religion's Impact on Politics, Economic and Family Life*. New York: Anchor Books.

Lessig, Lawrence. (2011). *Republic, Lost: How Money Corrupt Congress—and a Plan to Stop it*. New York: Hachette Book Group.

Lewis, Oscar. (1961[1982]). *Los Hijos de Sánchez*. México: Grijalbo.

Lewis, Richard D. (1996[2012]). *When Cultures Collide: Leading across Cultures*. London: Nicholas Brealey.

Lickona, Thomas. (2006). "Character Education: Restoring Virtue to the Mission of Schools." In L. Harrison and J. Kagan (Eds.), *Developing Cultures: Essays on Cultural Change*. New York: Routledge.

Linz, Juan. (1978). *The Breakdown of Democratic Regimes: Crisis, Breakdown and Reequilibration.* Baltimore, MD: John Hopkins University Press.

Lipset, Seymour Martin. (1960). *Political Man.* Garden City, NY: Doubleday.

Lipset, Seymour Martin. (1963). *The First New Nation: The United States in Historical and Comparative Perspective,* New York: Basic Books.

Lipset, Seymour Martin. (1990). *Continental Divide: The Values and Institutions of the United States and Canada.* Toronto and Washington, DC: C. D. Howe Institutes and National Planning Association.

Maddison, Angus. (2006). *The World Economy.* Paris: OECD.

Maddison, Angus. (2007). *Contours of the World Economy, 1–2030 AD.* Oxford: Oxford University Press.

Marini, Matteo B. (2013). "The Traditions of Modernity." *Journal of Socio-Economics, 47,* 205–217.

Markus, Hazel R., and Conner, A. (2013). *Clash!: 8 Cultural Conflicts That Make Us Who We Are.* New York: Penguin.

Mattei, Ugo. (2003). "A Theory of Imperial Law: A Study on U.S. Hegemony and the Latin Resistance." *Global Jurist Frontiers, 3*(2), http://www.repository.law.indiana.edu/ijgls/vol10/iss1/14.

McClelland, David C. (1961[1967]). *The Achieving Society.* New York: Free Press.

Meadows, Donella, et al. (1972). *The Limits to Growth.* New York: Universe Books.

Meyer, Erin. (2014). *The Culture Map: Breaking Through the Invisible Boundaries of Global Business.* New York: Public Affairs.

Milbrath, Lester, and Goel, M. (1977). *Political Participation.* Chicago: Rand McNally.

Milankovitch, Milutin. ([Belgrade, 1941]1969). *Canon of Insolation and the Ice Age Problem.* Jerusalem: IPST Press.

Minkov, Michael. (2010). *Cultural Differences in a Globalizing World.* Bingley, UK: Emerald Group.

Minkov, Michael. (2013). *Cross-Cultural Analysis: The Science and Art of Comparing the World's Modern Societies and Their Cultures.* Thousand Oaks, CA: Sage.

Moisi, Dominique. (2010). *The Geopolitics of Emotion: How Cultures of Fear, Humiliation, and Hope are Reshaping the World.* New York: Anchor Books.

Moreno, Alejandro. (2005). *Nuestros Valores: Los Mexicanos en México y en EEUU al Inicio del Siglo XXI.* México: Banamex.

Morris, Ian. (2010). *Why the West Rules—for Now: The Pattern of History, and What They Reveal About the Future.* New York: Farrar, Straus and Giroux.

Morrison, Terri, and Conaway, Wayne A. (1995[2006]). *Kiss, Bow, or Shake Hands.* Avon, MA: Adams Media.

Morse, Richard M. (1982). *El espejo de Próspero: Un Estudio de la Dialéctica del Nuevo Mundo.* México: Siglo XXI.

Murray, Charles. (2012). *Coming Apart: The State of White America 1960–2010.* New York: Crown Forum.

Myrdal, Gunnar. (1968). *Asian Drama: An Inquiry into the Poverty of Nations.* New York: Pantheon.

Nair, Kusum. (1961). *Blosoms in the Dust: The Human Element in Indian Development.* London: Gerald Duckworth.

Neumayer, Eric. (2003). "Socioeconomic Factors and Suicide Rates at Large-Unit Aggregate Levels." *Urban Studies, 40,*(13), 2769–2776.

Nevitte, Neil. (1996). *Decline of Deference: Canadian Value Change in Cross National Perspective.* Peterborough: Broadview Press.

Nisbett, Richard E. (2003). *The Geography of Thought: How Asians and Westerners Think Differently . . . and Why.* New York: Free Press.

Nisbett, Richard E. (2009). *Intelligence and How to Get it: How Schools and Cultures Count.* New York: W. W. Norton.

Nisbett, Richard E., and Cohen, Dove. (1996). *Culture of Honor: The Psychology of Violence in the South.* Boulder, CO: Westview Press.

North, Douglass C. (2005). *Understanding the Process of Economic Change.* Princeton, NJ: Princeton University Press.

OECD. (2011). *How's Life: Measuring Well-being.* Paris: OECD Publishing.

Oppenheimer, Stephen. (2003). *Out of Eden: the Peopling of the World.* London: Robinson.

Parás, Pablo. (2013). *The Power of Perceptions: How Social Capital is being impacted by Crime and Corruption in Mexico.* PhD dissertation, University of Connecticut.

Parenti, Michael. (1965). "Political Values and Religious Cultures: Jews, Catholics and Protestants." Paper presented at the Annual Meeting of the Society for the Scientific Study of Religion, New York, October 29, and published in the *Journal for the Scientific Study of Religion,* Autumn 1967, 6(2), 259–269.

Pastor, Robert. (2006). "A North American Community." *Norteamérica,* June, 1(1), 209–219.

Piketty, Thomas. (2014). *Capital in the Twenty-First Century.* Cambridge, MA: Harvard University Press.

Pinker, Steven. (2011). *The Better Angels of Our Nature: Why Violence Has Declined.* New York: Penguin.

Porter, Michael E., and Kramer, Mark R. (2011). "Creating Shared Value." *Harvard Business Review,* 89(1/2), 62–77.

Prior, Markus. (2007). *Post-Broadcast Democracy: How Media Choice Increases Inequality in Political Involvement and Polarizes Elections.* Cambridge: Cambridge University Press.

Pezeworski, Adam, et al., Eds. (2000[2008]). *Democracy and Development: Political Institutions and Well-Being in the World, 1950–1990.* New York: Cambridge University Press.

Putnam, Robert. (1993). *Making Democracy Work: Civic Traditions in Modern Italy.* Princeton, NJ: Princeton University Press.

Putnam, Robert. (2000). *Bowling Alone: The Collapse and Revival of American Community.* New York: Simon and Schuster.

Putnam, Robert. (2010). *American Grace: How Religion Divides and Unites Us.* New York: Simon and Schuster.

Pizano, Lariza. (2003). *Bogotá y el Cambio: Percepciones sobre la Ciudad y la Ciudadanía.* Universidad Nacional de Colombia (IEPRI) y Universidad de los Andes (CESO).

Randall, Laura, Ed. (2006). *Changing Structure of Mexico.* London: Routledge.

Rangel, Carlos. (1977). *The Latin American: Their Love-Hate Relationship with the US.* New York and London: Harcourt Brace Jovanovich.

Rao, Vijayendra, and Walton, Michael, Eds. (2004). *Culture and Public Action*. Stanford, CA: Stanford University Press.

Reimers, F., and Villegas, E. (2006). "Educating Democratic Citizens in Latin America." In L. Harrison and J. Kagan (Eds.), *Developing Cultures: Essays on Cultural Change*. New York: Routledge.

Reinert, Erik S. (2008). *How Rich Countries Got Rich . . . and Why Poor Countries Stay Poor*. New York: Public Affairs.

Richerson, Peter J., and Boyd, Robert. (2005). *Not by Genes Alone: How Culture Transformed Human Evolution*. Chicago: University of Chicago Press.

Rideout, Victoria J., Foehr, Ulla G., and Roberts, Donald F. (2010). *Generation M2: Media in the Lives of 8- to 18-Year Olds*. The Henry J. Kaiser Family Foundation, https://kaiserfamilyfoundation.files.wordpress.com/2013/04/8010.pdf.

Ridley, Matt. (1999[2006]). *Genome: The Autobiography of a Species in 23 Chapters*. New York: Harper.

Riesman, David. (1950). *The Lonely Crowd*. New Haven, CT: Yale University Press.

Rokeach, M. (1973). *The Nature of Human Values*. New York: Free Press.

Rostow, Walt W. (1960). *The Stages of Economic Growth*. Cambridge: Cambridge University Press.

Ryerson, W. N. (2009). "The Effectiveness of Entertainment Mass Media in Changing Behavior." *Population Media Center*, http://www.populationmedia.org/wp-content/uploads/2008/02/effectiveness-of-entertainment-education-112706.pdf.

Sachs, Jeffrey D. (2005). *The End of Poverty*. New York: Penguin.

Sachs, Jeffrey D. (2013). "Restoring Virtue Ethics in the Quest for Happiness." In Helliwell, Layard, and Sachs, *World Happiness Report 2013*, http://unsdsn.org/wp-content/uploads/2014/02/WorldHappinessReport2013_online.pdf.

Sanchez, Octavio. (2010). "Culture and Legal Dogmatism in an Era of Immaterial Wealth: The Case of Latin America." Paper delivered at the Higher School of Economics, Moscow Symposium, May 2010 (unpublished).

Schonfeld, Reese. (2006). "The Global Battle for Cultural Domination." in L. Harrison and J. Kagan (Eds.), *Developing Cultures: Essays on Cultural Change*. New York: Routledge.

Schumpeter, Joseph A. (1942[2008]). *Capitalism, Socialism and Democracy*. New York: Harper Perennial.

Schwanitz, Dietrich. (2006). *Cultura: Todo lo que Hay que Saber*. Madrid: Taurus.

Schwartz, S. H., and Bilsky, W. (1987). "Toward a Universal Psychological Structure of Human Values." *Journal of Personality and Social Psychology, 53*, 550–562.

Schwartz, S. H., and Bilsky, W. (1990). "Toward a Theory of the Universal Content and Structure of Values: Extensions and Cross Cultural Replications." *Journal of Personality and Social Psychology, 58*, 878–891.

Schwartz, S. H., Cieciuch, J., Vecchione, M., Davidov, E., Fischer, R., Beierlein, C., Ramos, A., Verkasalo, M., Lönnqvist, J.-E., Demirutku, K., Dirilen-Gumus, O., and Konty, M. (2012). "Refining the Theory of Basic Individual Values." *Journal of Personality and Social Psychology, 103*, 663–688.

Schwartz, Shalom H. (1992). "Universals in the Content and Structure of Values: Theory and Empirical Tests in 20 Countries." In M. Zanna (Ed.), *Advances in Experimental Social Psychology* (Vol. 25, pp. 1–65). New York: Academic Press.

Schwartz, Shalom H. (1994a). "Beyond Individualism-Collectivism: New Cultural Dimensions of Values." In U. Kim, H. C. Triandis, C. Kagitcibasi, S.-C. Choi, and G. Yoon (Eds.), *Individualism and Collectivism: Theory, Method, and Application.* Thousand Oaks, CA: Sage.

Schwartz, Shalom H. (1994b). "Are There Universal Aspects in the Structure and Contents of Human Values?" *Journal of Social Issues, 50*(4), 19–45.

Schwartz, Shalom H. (2006). "A Theory of Cultural Value Orientations: Explication and Applications." *Comparative Sociology, 5*(2), 137–182.

Schwartz, Shalom H. (2008). "Cultural Value Orientations: Nature and Implications of National Differences." *Psychology Journal of the Higher School of Economics, 5*(2), 37–67. English translation available at http://blogs.helsinki.fi/valuesandmorality/files/2009/09/Schwartz-Monograph-Cultural-Value-Orientations.pdf.

Schwartz, Shalom H. (2012). "Values and Religion in Adolescent Development: Cross-National and Comparative Evidence." In Gisela Trommsdorf et al. (Eds.), *Values, Religion, and Culture in Adolescent Development.* Cambridge: Cambridge University Press.

Sen, Amartya. (1984[1999]). *Resources, Values and Development.* New Delhi: Oxford India Paperbacks.

Sen, Amartya. (1999). *Development as Freedom.* New York: Anchor Books.

Sen, Amartya. (2006). "How Does Culture Matter?" In V. Rao and M. Walton (Eds.), *Culture and Public Action.* Stanford, CA: Stanford University Press.

Shultz, Richard H. (2013). *The Marines Take Anbar: The Four-Year Fight Against Al Qaeda.* Annapolis, MD: Naval Institute Press.

Sidanius, Jim, and Pratto, Felicia. (1999). *Social Dominance: An Intergroup Theory of Social Hierarchy and Oppression.* New York: Cambridge University Press.

Silvert, Kalman. (1967). *Churches and States: The Religious Institution and Modernization.* New York: American Universities Field Staff.

Small, Mario Luis, Harding, D., and Lamont, M. (2010). "Reconsidering Culture and Poverty." *The Annals of the American Academy of Political and Social Science, USA*: Sage, 627, 6–27.

Smith, Adam. (1767[2010]). *The Theory of Moral Sentiments.* New York: General Books.

Smith, Adam. (1776[2003]). *The Wealth of Nations.* New York: Bantam Classics.

Smith, Joel. (2005). "Fire and Ice (Book Review)." *American Review of Canadian Studies, 35*(1), 157–160.

Smith, Michael E. (2005). "City Size in Late Post-Classic Mesoamerica." *Journal of Urban History, 31*(4), 403–434.

Smith, Peter B., and Bond, Michael H. (1994). *Social Psychology across Cultures.* Boston: Allyn and Bacon.

Sokoloff, K. L., and Engerman, S. L. (2000). "History Lessons: Institutions, Factors Endowments, and Paths of Development in the New World." *Journal of Economic Perspectives, 14*(3), 217–232.

Sombart, Werner. (1915). *The Jews and Modern Capitalism.* New York: E. P. Dutton.

Sommers, Marc, and Uvin, Peter. (2011). "Youth in Rwanda and Burundi: Contrasting Visions." *US Institute of Peace*, Special Report 293, October.

Stein, Andrew J. (1992). "Religion and Mass Politics in Central America." Paper presented at the New England Council of Latin American Studies, Boston University, October 24.

Steele, Liza G., and Lynch, Scott M. (2012). "The Pursuit of Happiness in China: Individualism, Collectivism, and Subjective Well-Being During China's Economic and Social Transformation," Social Indicators Research. Princeton, NJ: Springer.

Stiglitz, Joseph E., Sen, Amartya, and Fitoussi, Jean-Paul. (2010). *Mis-measuring Our Lives: Why GDP Doesn't Add Up.* New York: New Press.

Sudarsky, John. (2003). *Densidad y Articulación de la Sociedad Civil de Bogotá: Localida-des y Sectores 1997–2001*, Alcaldía Mayor de Bogotá.

Sudarsky, John. (2004). "Aprendiendo a Construir Ciudadanía." In Fernando Cepeda (Ed.), *Fortalezas de Colombia*. Bogotá: Editorial Planeta Colombiana para el Banco Interameri-cano de Desarrollo y Colección Ariel, Ciencia Política.

Taleb, Nassim N. (2012). *Antifragile: Things That Gain from Disorder.* New York: Random House.

Thaler, Richard H., and Sunstein, Cass R. (2008[2009]). *Nudge: Improving Decision about Health, Wealth, and Happiness.* New York: Penguin.

The Economist, August 20, 2011. "The Flight from Marriage."

Time. (1928). "China: Heaven, Observe," February 6.

Tignor, Robert, et al. (2002[2008]). *Worlds Together, Worlds Apart: A History of the World.* New York: W. W. Norton.

Tocqueville, Alexis de. (1835[1988]). *Democracy in America.* New York: Harper Perennial.

Triandis, Harry C. (1996). "The Psychological Measurement of Cultural Syndromes." *American Psychologist*, April, 51(4), 407–415.

Trommsdorf, Gisela, and Chen, Xinyin, Eds. (2012). *Values, Religion and Culture in Adolescent Development.* Cambridge: Cambridge University Press.

Turner, Frederick J. (1920). *The Frontier in American History.* Mineola, NY: Dover.

Turner, Frederick. (1993). "Studying Political Culture in the 1990's: New Tools, New Concepts, New Implications." Paper presented at the Conference Comparative Approaches Toward Latin America: Issues and Methods, Quito, Ecuador, July 29.

UNDP. (2004). *Bogotá: Una Experiencia Innovadora de Gobernabilidad Local*, Bogotá, March.

US Census Bureau. (2012). *Statistical Abstract of the US.* Washington, DC.

USAID, Democracy International, and Cultural Change Institute. (2010). *Timor-Leste Values Study*: Final Report.

UNU-IHDP and UNEP. (2012). *Inclusive Wealth Report.* United Nations University-International Human Dimensions Programme on Global Environmental Change.

Veliz, Claudio. (1980). *The Centralist Tradition of Latin America.* Princeton, NJ: Princeton University Press.

Verba, Sidney, Nie, Norman, and Kim, Jae-on. (1978). *Participation and Political Equality.* Cambridge and New York: Cambridge University Press.

Waldman, Katy. (2013). "Young People in Japan Have Given Up on Sex." *Slate, Washington Post.*

Weber, Max. (1905[2002]). *The Protestant Ethic and the Spirit of Capitalism and Other Writings*, translated by P. Baehr and G. Wells. New York: Penguin Books.

Weber, Max. (1905[2011]). *The Protestant Ethic and the Spirit of Capitalism*. New York and Oxford: Oxford University Press.

Weber, Max. (1917[2013]). *The Religions of India*. New Delhi: Munshiram Manoharlal.

Weber, Max. (1917[1967]). *The Ancient Judaism*. New York: Free Press.

Weber, Max. (1917[1968]). *The Religion of China: Confucianism and Taoism*. New York: Free Press.

Weber, Max. (1922[1993]). *The Sociology of Religion*. Boston: Beacon Press.

Weber, Max. (1978). *Selections in Translation*, edited by W. G. Runciman. Cambridge: Cambridge University Press.

Welch, Michael R., and David C. Leege. (1991). "Dual Reference Groups and Political Orientations: An Examination of Evangelically Oriented Catholics." *American Journal of Political Science*, 35(1).

Whyte, William. (1956). *The Organization Man*. New York: Simon and Schuster.

Wiarda, Howard J. (1992). *Politics and Social Change in Latin America: Still a Distinct Tradition?* Boulder, CO: Westview Press.

Wilkinson, Richard, and Pickett, Kate. (2010). *The Spirit Level: Why Greater Equality Makes Society Stronger*. New York: Bloomsbury Press.

Woodward, Collin. (2011). *American Nations: A History of the Eleven Rival Regional Cultures of North America*. New York: Viking Penguin.

World Bank. (2006). *Where Is the Wealth of Nations: Measuring Capital for the 21st Century*. Washington, DC: World Bank.

Wyer, Robert S., Chiu, Chi-yue, and Hong, Ying-yi, Eds. (2009). *Understanding Culture: Theory, Research and Application*. New York: Taylor and Francis Group.

Yergin, Daniel, and Stanislaw, Joseph. (1998). *The Commanding Heights: The Battle for the World Economy*. New York: Touchstone.

Yinger, J. Milton. (1957). *Religion, Society and the Individual: An Introduction to the Sociology of Religion*. New York: Macmillan.

Yinger, J. Milton. (1961[1969]). *Sociology Looks at Religion*. London: Macmillan.

Yinger, J. Milton. (1970). *The Scientific Study of Religion*. New York: Macmillan.

Zaid, Gabriel. (1985). "Escenarios sobre el fin del PRI." *Vuelta* 103, junio.

INDEX

Acemoglu, Daron, 24, 226, 244, 253
achievement cultures: Asian & Confucian
   countries, 90–96, 94*t*, 108–9, 160*t*, 259–60,
   402*nn*8–10; change in, 195; cultural
   development in, 72–74, 72*f*, 76–78, 78*t*;
   empirical profiles of, 115–19, 116*t*, 117*t*,
   118*t*, 126–27, 139*f*, 261–63; family in, 159;
   GDP increases in, 247; gender attitudes/
   equality in, 118–19, 118*t*, 123; historical
   transition of cultures and, 18–19;
   homosexuality acceptance in, 121, 123,
   402*n*1; overview, 25–26; punctuality &
   efficiency in, 122–24, 127*t*; religion/belief
   in God in, 18, 115, 117, 118*t*; tradition and
   authority in, 117*t*, 118; Western countries
   & their offshoots, 96–100, 99*t*, 108–9,
   110*t*, 259–60, 402*n*11; WVS analysis, 129,
   153, 154
Adams, John, 235
Afghanistan: family in, 153; FHI rank/
   score, 291*t*; GDP of, 87, 271*t*, 278*t*; gender
   attitudes/equality in, 88, 366*t*; HDI rank/
   value, 88, 285*t*; income in, 87, 353*t*; literacy
   in, 88; ODI & SDI ranks/scores, 88, 376*t*;
   overview, 85*t*; population of, 88
Africa: *See also Specific countries*;
   authority (respect for) in, 136; Central
   Africa overview, 82*t*; colonies in, 84;
   development in, 79–81, 80*f*; East Africa
   overview, 82*t*; feeling of freedom in, 146;
   gender attitudes/equality in, 135, 268;
   homosexuality acceptance in, 151; honor
   cultures, 79–84, 80*f*, 82*t*, 108–9, 110*t*,
   120, 259–60, 401*nn*1–4; Horn of Africa
   overview, 82*t*; income equality opinions
   in, 149; income in, 214; individualism vs.
   collectivism in, 49*t*; joy cultures in, 126;
   law in, 84; liberalization in, 232; masculine
   vs. feminine culture in, 50*t*; national pride
   in, 141; North Africa overview, 82*t*; power
   distance in, 46*t*; religion/belief in God in,
   84, 120, 139; Southern Africa overview,
   82*t*; state-oriented culture in, 78; tradition
   and authority in, 53, 55*f*; trust in, 143;
   uncertainty avoidance in, 47*t*; West Africa
   overview, 82*t*; work in, 241*t*, 242
age, axiological change by, 241*t*

age-based opinions on: competition, 151;
   feeling of freedom, 146; happiness, 131;
   homosexuality acceptance, 151; income
   equality, 149; national pride, 141; parental
   respect, 132; religion/belief in God, 139,
   141; right to a job, 135; trust, 143
agriculture, cultural development from,
   71–72, 229, 231*f*, 249
Albania: competition beliefs in, 149, 150*t*;
   feeling of freedom in, 147*t*; FHI rank/
   score, 88, 289*t*; GDP of, 87, 271*t*, 277*t*;
   gender attitudes/equality in, 88, 134*t*, 364*t*;
   happiness in, 129, 130*t*; HDI rank/value,
   282*t*; homosexuality acceptance in, 152*t*;
   income equality beliefs in, 148*t*; income
   in, 354*t*, 359*t*; joy & friendship rank, 128*t*;
   life satisfaction in, 145*t*; national pride in,
   142*t*; ODI & SDI ranks/scores, 88, 277*t*,
   371*t*, 393*t*; overview, 85*t*; parental respect
   in, 133*t*; religion/belief in God in, 138*t*,
   140*t*; tradition and authority in, 121*t*, 127*t*,
   137*t*; trust in, 144*t*; WVS scores, 266*t*, 387*t*
Alexopoulos, Michelle, 397
Algeria: competition beliefs in, 150*t*; feeling
   of freedom in, 147*t*; FHI rank/score, 290*t*;
   GDP of, 81, 87, 270*t*, 277*t*; gender attitudes/
   equality in, 83, 134*t*, 135, 365*t*; happiness
   in, 130*t*; HDI rank/value, 84, 283*t*;
   homosexuality acceptance in, 152*t*; income
   equality beliefs in, 148*t*, 149; income in,
   354*t*, 360*t*; joy & friendship rank, 128*t*;
   life satisfaction in, 145*t*, 146; national
   pride in, 142*t*; ODI & SDI ranks/scores,
   84, 373*t*, 394*t*; overview, 82*t*, 85*t*; parental
   respect in, 133*t*; population of, 81; religion/
   belief in God in, 138*t*, 140*t*; tradition and
   authority in, 55*f*, 121*t*, 127*t*, 137*t*; trust in,
   143, 144*t*; WVS scores, 266*t*, 387*t*
Andorra: FHI rank/score, 287*t*; HDI rank/value,
   282*t*; joy & friendship rank, 128*t*; ODI & SDI
   ranks/scores, 277*t*, 370*t*, 392*t*; punctuality &
   efficiency in, 127*t*; tradition and authority in,
   121*t*; WVS scores, 266*t*, 387*t*, 390*t*
Angola: FHI rank/score, 290*t*; GDP of, 83,
   270*t*, 277*t*; HDI rank/value, 284*t*; income
   in, 356*t*; ODI & SDI ranks/scores, 84, 377*t*;
   overview, 82*t*

363

Tanzania: competition beliefs in, 150*t*, 151; feeling of freedom in, 147*t*; FHI rank/score, 289*t*; GDP of, 271*t*, 278*t*; gender attitudes/equality in, 134*t*, 366*t*; happiness in, 130*t*, 131; HDI rank/value, 284*t*; homosexuality acceptance in, 152*t*; income equality beliefs in, 148*t*; income in, 355*t*, 360*t*; joy & friendship rank, 128*t*; life satisfaction in, 145*t*, 146; national pride in, 142*t*; ODI & SDI ranks/scores, 375*t*, 394*t*; overview, 82*t*; parental respect in, 133*t*; religion/belief in God in, 138*t*, 140*t*; tradition and authority in, 55*f*, 57*t*, 121*t*, 127*t*, 137*t*; trust in, 144*t*; WVS scores, 267*t*, 389*t*

technology/innovations: colonialism and, 72; innovation, 238–40, 404*n*2; inventions by category, 243; types of innovation, 240; world changing, 395–97

Teller, Astro, 397

Thailand: FHI rank/score, 290*t*; GDP of, 95, 269*t*, 277*t*; gender attitudes/equality in, 364*t*; HDI rank/value, 283*t*; income in, 355*t*, 360*t*; individualism vs. collectivism in, 49*t*; joy & friendship rank, 128*t*; masculine vs. feminine culture in, 50*t*; ODI & SDI ranks/scores, 277*t*, 373*t*, 393*t*; overview, 94*t*; power distance in, 46*t*; punctuality & efficiency in, 127*t*; tradition and authority in, 121*t*; uncertainty avoidance in, 47*t*; on *World Cultural Map*, 65*f*; WVS scores, 267*t*, 389*t*, 391*t*

Timor/Timor-Leste: FHI rank/score, 289*t*; GDP of, 273*t*, 278*t*; HDI rank/value, 284*t*; income in, 354*t*; ODI & SDI ranks/scores, 372*t*; on trust & autonomy map, 14*f*; 25-values typology in, 201

Tobago. *See* Trinidad & Tobago

Tocqueville, Alexis de, 31–34, 33*t*, 62, 225, 240, 246, 400*nn*3–5

Togo: FHI rank/score, 290*t*; GDP of, 272*t*, 279*t*; gender attitudes/equality in, 366*t*; HDI rank/value, 284*t*; income in, 354*t*; ODI & SDI ranks/scores, 375*t*; overview, 82*t*

Tonga: FHI rank/score, 289*t*; GDP of, 273*t*, 278*t*; gender attitudes/equality in, 365*t*; HDI rank/value, 283*t*; ODI & SDI ranks/scores, 374*t*

transportation inventions, 243, 395

Trinidad & Tobago: FHI rank/score, 288*t*; GDP of, 105, 271*t*, 276*t*; gender attitudes/equality in, 106, 364*t*; HDI rank/value, 282*t*; income in, 106, 355*t*; joy & friendship rank, 128*t*; literacy in, 106; ODI & SDI ranks/scores, 106, 371*t*, 394*t*; overview,

104*t*; population, 105; tradition and authority in, 121*t*, 127*t*; WVS scores, 267*t*, 389*t*

trust, 5– 6, 6, 10–11, 14*f*, 143, 144*t*, 399*n*4

Tunisia: Arab Spring in, 168; FHI rank/score, 88, 289*t*; GDP of, 270*t*, 277*t*; gender attitudes/equality in, 83, 364*t*; HDI rank/value, 84, 283*t*; income in, 88, 355*t*, 360*t*; ODI & SDI ranks/scores, 84, 88, 372*t*; overview, 82*t*, 85*t*; population of, 81

Turkey: competition beliefs in, 150*t*; economic expansion of, 233; feeling of freedom in, 147*t*; FHI rank/score, 88, 289*t*; GDP of, 87, 269*t*, 276*t*; gender attitudes/equality in, 134*t*, 364*t*; happiness in, 130*t*, 131; HDI rank/value, 283*t*; homosexuality acceptance in, 151, 152*t*; income equality beliefs in, 148*t*, 149; income in, 355*t*, 361*t*; individualism vs. collectivism in, 49*t*; joy & friendship rank, 128*t*; leadership in, 170–71; life satisfaction in, 145*t*, 146; masculine vs. feminine culture in, 50*t*; national pride in, 142*t*; ODI & SDI ranks/scores, 277*t*, 372*t*, 393*t*; overview, 85*t*; parental respect in, 132, 133*t*; power distance in, 46*t*; religion/belief in God in, 138*t*, 140*t*; tradition and authority in, 55*f*, 56*f*, 57*t*, 121*t*, 127*t*, 137*t*; on trust & autonomy map, 14*f*; trust in, 144*t*; uncertainty avoidance in, 47*t*; on *World Cultural Map*, 65*f*; WVS scores, 267*t*, 389*t*

Turkmenistan: FHI rank/score, 88, 291*t*; GDP of, 271*t*, 277*t*; HDI rank/value, 283*t*; income in, 88, 355*t*, 360*t*; literacy in, 88; ODI & SDI ranks/scores, 374*t*; overview, 85*t*; population of, 87

Turks & Caicos, 104*t*, 105

Tuvalu, 288*t*, 373*t*

25-values typology, 197*t*–98*t*, 200–4, 201*f*, 203*f*

Uganda: competition beliefs in, 150*t*; feeling of freedom in, 147*t*; FHI rank/score, 290*t*; GDP of, 271*t*, 279*t*; gender attitudes/equality in, 134*t*, 135, 365*t*; happiness in, 130*t*; HDI rank/value, 284*t*; homosexuality acceptance in, 152*t*; income equality beliefs in, 148*t*, 149; income in, 355*t*, 361*t*; joy & friendship rank, 128*t*; life satisfaction in, 145*t*, 146; national pride in, 141, 142*t*; ODI & SDI ranks/scores, 277*t*, 376*t*, 393*t*; overview, 82*t*; parental respect in, 132, 133*t*; population of, 81; religion/belief in God in, 138*t*, 140*t*; tradition and authority in, 55*f*, 121*t*, 127*t*, 137*t*; on trust & autonomy map, 14*f*; trust in, 144*t*; on *World Cultural Map*, 65*f*; WVS scores, 267*t*, 389*t*